Advance Praise for

UPROOTING RACISM

Uprooting Racism continues to be a powerful and wonderful book,
a major contribution to our understanding of racism as white people.
It answers many of the questions whites have thought about but were
afraid to discuss. Not only does Kivel address tough issues related to
whiteness and racism, creating greater understanding of the complexities
of these issues, but he also identifies specific ways that whites can be
allies for change — all done with honesty, forthrightness, respect,
and from the heart. For any white person who is sincere about
working for social justice, here's the source.

— Judith H. Katz, Ed. D., author of *White Awareness:*
Handbook for Anti-Racism Training; and *The Inclusion Breakthrough:*
Unleashing the Real Power of Diversity

Paul Kivel writes with clarity and depth in a style that is adequately
complex for understandings of racism in our time. He uses his writing
power to illuminate all the systems, inner and outer, which lead to inequitable
distribution of power, respect, money, safety, security, and opportunity
in the world. Kivel's work inspires workers for social justice
in many sectors of the U.S. today. His bibliography
alone is worth the price of the book.

— Peggy McIntosh, founder and co-director, National SEED Project
on Inclusive Curriculum, author *White Privilege:*
Unpacking the Invisible Knapsack

...a courageous, accessible and practical guide for those who
are interested in ending racism. With great wisdom and compassion,
Paul asks each of us to take responsibility for our part in maintaining a system
that is catastrophic for all. I appreciate that he does so without blaming or
shaming, and that he gives clear and useful tools for ending oppression.
As an African-American, I am delighted to have a book to recommend
to white (as well as other) folks interested in creating a world
wherein racism is obsolete. Read this book!

— Akaya Windwood, consultant on diversity and organizations

Uprooting Racism is a fact-filled resource for teachers and parents to use in educating ourselves and our young people about the history and the hidden costs of racism in our communities. Kivel presents simple, meaningful actions we can all take to build a more just and healthy society.

— Jackie Shonerd, parent and Coordinator for Conflict Resolution Programs, Oakland, (CA) Unified School District

As a woman of color actively engaged in social justice movements for over 25 years, I have often longed for a book like *Uprooting Racism* to help white people understand the institutional, systematic, and persistent character of racism in our world. Paul Kivel has written a handbook for all of us to be able to have a language to critically examine racism in our lives, and to take action against racism in our personal lives and in our work for peace and justice.

— Luz Guerra, activist consultant/writer

This expanded volume is even more comprehensive, heart-felt and easy to use. The book helps people take responsibility for re-making our institutions while avoiding the guilt and blame trap. An updated and very useful bibliography and in-depth index make this revised edition even more essential as a resource and guide. It is a must for anyone who wants to create settings in which respectful, fair and trusting relations are the norm.

— Margo Adair, author of *Meditations on Everything Under the Sun* and founder of Tools for Change

...the 'how-to manual' for whites to work with people of color to create an inclusive, just world in the 21st century. *Uprooting Racism* succinctly describes how intricately racism is tied to all institutions and our daily lives. The new edition also tackles current issues including immigration policy, voting rights, and a brief history of our relationship with Arab-Americans. It should be in the toolbox of anyone who is working for an anti-racist society.

— Maggie Potapchuk, Senior Program Associate, Network of Alliances, Bridging Race and Ethnicity (NABRE), a program of the Joint Center for Political and Economic Studies

Those of us who commit to the life-long journey of being anti-racist whites need lots of help. The revised edition of *Uprooting Racism* offers a clear vision of the journey's destination, an invaluable and accessible map and a set of tools for the steps we must take to get there. ...I recommend it highly and plan to use it in my own work.

— Louise Derman-Sparks, co-director, of the Early Childhood Equity Alliance. Author of *Teaching/Learning Anti-Racism: A Developmental Approach*

UPROOTING
RACISM

HOW WHITE PEOPLE CAN
WORK FOR RACIAL JUSTICE

Paul Kivel

NEW SOCIETY PUBLISHERS

Cataloguing in Publication Data:
A catalog record for this publication is available from the National Library of Canada.

Cover design by Diane McIntosh.

Printed in Canada by Friesens. Second Printing September, 2003.

New Society Publishers acknowledges the support of the Government of Canada through the Book Publishing Industry Development Program (BPIDP) for our publishing activities, and the assistance of the Province of British Columbia through the British Columbia Arts Council.

BRITISH
COLUMBIA
ARTS COUNCIL
Supported by the Province of British Columbia

Paperback ISBN: 0-86571-459-2

Inquiries regarding requests to reprint all or part of *Uprooting Racism: How White People Can Work for Racial Justice* should be addressed to New Society Publishers at the address below.

To order directly from the publishers, please add $4.50 shipping to the price of the first copy, and $1.00 for each additional copy (plus GST in Canada). Send check or money order to:

New Society Publishers
P.O. Box 189, Gabriola Island, BC V0R 1X0, Canada
1-800-567-6772

New Society Publishers' mission is to publish books that contribute in fundamental ways to building an ecologically sustainable and just society, and to do so with the least possible impact on the environment, in a manner that models this vision. We are committed to doing this not just through education, but through action. We are acting on our commitment to the world's remaining ancient forests by phasing out our paper supply from ancient forests worldwide. This book is one step towards ending global deforestation and climate change. It is printed on acid-free paper that is **100% old growth forest-free** (100% post-consumer recycled), processed chlorine free, and printed with vegetable based, low VOC inks. For further information, or to browse our full list of books and purchase securely, visit our website at: www.newsociety.com

NEW SOCIETY PUBLISHERS   www.newsociety.com

Contents

Part III Being Allies

Part IV The Effects of History

Part V Fighting Institutional Racism

PART VI   DEMOCRATIC, ANTI-RACIST MULTICULTURALISM

CONCLUSION

Lists, Diagrams, and Exercises

Acknowledgments

W<small>E HAVE A LONG AND DISTINGUISHED HISTORY</small> on this continent of white people who have fought against racism and racial violence. This history begins in the days of Antonio de Montesinos and Bartolomé de Las Casas, Spanish priests who documented and protested against the atrocities that Columbus and other early conquistadores committed against the Native Americans in the West Indies. It continues today with white people fighting against hate crimes, police brutality, housing and job discrimination, and the recent attacks against immigrants and poor people of color. These efforts by white people have been inspired by the constant, unrelenting fight by people of color for survival, for justice, and for an end to the political, economic, and cultural exploitation they have experienced in this country.

My deepest gratitude goes to the multitudes of people of color who have challenged racism in small and large ways over the centuries, and who have demonstrated by their lives that the lies of racism are untrue and inhumane and violate the integrity of each person who colludes with injustice.

I am also proud to be Jewish and to be able to contribute to the historic struggle of Jewish people to survive waves of anti-Semitism and create our lives anew in the framework of freedom and justice that Judaism provides. I want to acknowledge my Jewish foreparents and the many Jews who are still on the frontlines of the battle for racial justice because they understand the connections between anti-Semitism and racism.

There are many people who have inspired my work and writing, most of whom I have never met. I have read their words, heard their songs, witnessed their actions, and hope to be true to their vision.

I want to acknowledge specifically those who I have learned from and who have supported my work in the last few years. They are Bill Aal, Margot Adair, Martin Cano, Jim Coates, Hari Dillon, Steve Falk, Isoke Femi, Margot Gibney, Sonia Jackson, Francie Kendall, David Landes, Lee Mun-Wah, Nell Myhand, Namane Mohlabane, Daphne Muse, Ayana Morse, Kiran Rana, John Tucker, Akaya Windwood, Shirley Yee, and my mother, Betty Jean Kivel.

I also thank my wonderful "Jews schmooze" group: Alina Evers, Chaya Gusfield, Julie Nesnansky, Adee Horn, Ariel Luckey, Aurora Levins-Morales, Ilana Schatz, Richard Shapiro, and Penny Rosenwasser.

Several people reviewed early drafts of the book and gave me support and feedback. Special thank yous to Robert Allen, Kostas Bagakis, Allan Creighton, Victor Lewis, Yeshi Neumann, Barry Shapiro, and Hugh Vasquez.

It has been my great pleasure and challenge over the years to work with Heru-Nefera Amen, Victor Lewis, and Allan Creighton at the Oakland Men's Project and Nell Myhand,

Hugh Vasquez, and Shirley Yee at the Todos Institute. I have learned much from their passion for justice, their gentle caring, and their fierce dedication to freedom.

My partner, Micki, has been a loving support, insightful editor, wonderful co-parent, and shares my vision of a just world.

My appreciation also goes to the staff at New Society Publishers who, despite going through substantial internal change during the production of the first edition, provided strong and consistent support to this project from their initial enthusiasm for the book, through the final editing and production. My thanks to Barbara Hirshkowitz and T. L. Hill at New Society Publishers and to Chel Avery for her copyediting, and Margie Politzer for her cover design. My special thanks to Martin Kelley who guided it through the entire process with skill and dedication. Chris Plant has been the guiding light for the revised edition. Audrey McClellan has provided excellent editing, and the cover design is by Diane McIntosh.

To my family
Micki, my love
Ariel, Shandra, and Ryan,
my inspiration

and to all those
fighting for justice

Preface

BEFORE I WROTE THIS BOOK I accumulated a long list of reasons why it was an important project. Racism is pervasive, its effects devastating, the need to fight against it urgent. People of color are being blamed for our social problems and attacked on all fronts. Recent immigrants, African-American women on welfare, youth of color, and affirmative action programs are just some of the current targets of white anger. It seems like gains we made in civil rights and social justice in the 1960s and 1970s are being rolled back in the 1980s and 1990s.

I could also see the huge impact racism had on my relationships with other people, on what my children learned in school, on how we dealt with economic issues at the state and federal level, and on what sports and music I paid attention to. Racism is everywhere, influencing us at every turn. There is no shortage of immediate reasons why writing a book like this one is a project that needed to be done.

In the workshops my co-workers and I were facilitating, participants were eager to talk about these issues and anxious to become involved. Somehow, few of them were able to translate their understanding of the issues and their commitment to ending racism into concrete community action. When they asked me for resources there were no guides for critical thinking and social action I could point them to. What was available about racism or white people was theoretical — interesting but not practical.

With all this in mind, I sat down to write this book. I suddenly accumulated a long list of reasons why I couldn't do it. I wasn't qualified. The subject was too big. The issue was too important. How could I add anything new? The connections between racism, anti-Semitism, gender, and economic issues were too complex. People of color have addressed all the issues much more powerfully than I could. I would make mistakes. I would leave important pieces out. People of color would be angry at me. Other white people would call me racist. Jews would say I didn't write enough about anti-Semitism. Gentiles would say I wrote too much. People would expect me to have all the answers. The entire task felt formidable, scary, fraught with problems, and I felt ill-equipped to carry it out successfully.

I procrastinated. I hoped someone else would do it. "There must be someone else who knows more, or writes better, or knows how to say it the right way." "There's certainly someone who could do it without making mistakes or looking foolish." These thoughts went through my mind as I waited for someone else to step forward.

Then one day I recognized these feelings. They were the same feelings that white people experience in our workshops — the same "reasons" they give for not doing more to stop racism. I knew that if I let these feelings stop me from taking the risk of writing this book I would be succumbing to the paralysis that often keeps white people from taking action against racial injustice. When confronting the reality of racism we become sad, angry, overwhelmed, confused, numb, lonely, tired, bored, anxious, and passive. When faced with the need to intervene, speak up, or take action against racism, we become tentative and uncertain, filled with questions and concerns, waiting for someone more qualified to step up.

There is no one who can take our place or do our part. I realized it was crucial for me to write what I could; that was my responsibility. Yes, it's scary. Yes, I will make mistakes. I don't know all the answers; I won't be able to cover everything; some people might not like what I write. But a book like this needs to be written, and I'm in a position to write it.

Many white people have stood up against racism. They used their feelings to guide them to action, not to stop their involvement. I needed to call on their examples of risk taking, moral integrity, and strategic action to realize that what I do makes a difference.

I'm sure you will experience many feelings as you read this book. Let them guide you, but don't let them stop you. It is easy to become overwhelmed by our feelings, by how much there is to do, and by how confusing and risky it seems. We need to concentrate on what it is we can do, how we can make a difference.

Whenever I become overwhelmed thinking about how much there is to do, I remind myself of a saying by Rabbi Tarfon. I hope it will guide you as well.

It is not upon you to finish the work.
Neither are you free to desist from it.

Introduction to the Revised Edition

WHEN I WROTE UPROOTING RACISM SEVEN YEARS AGO, I wanted to address the institutional and organizational structures that maintain and perpetuate racism. These are still strongly entrenched in our society. My hope was that if we, as white people, could better understand the injustice on which our lives and our society are based and could see the collaborative role that we play in maintaining racism, we would be more motivated to combat it, and more effective at doing so.

I also wanted my book to address the daily indignities and attacks that people of color continue to experience. Last week, for example, three of the African-American women who live in the apartment next door to us described how they have been harassed by a white resident in the apartment on the other side of them. This person not only drops trash and dog shit onto their driveway and parking spots, but also calls them "niggers" when they complain. When they call the police, the officers don't take down all the details of the situation, minimize the incident, and discourage them from pursuing the matter.

Last night I was at a board meeting for a local organization with which I volunteer. One of the white members, referring to the newest group of board members, most of whom are people of color, started out a sentence with "When we brought these people on board … " When a board member who was a person of color objected to being called one of "these people" the white board member replied, "You know I didn't mean it like that."

Today one of the two African-American women who are checkout clerks at my local grocery store (the other 15 or so checkout staff are white) told me about an incident that happened the day before. A customer had mistaken her for the other African-American staff person. When the woman politely reminded the customer that she was not the other clerk, the customer replied, "Well it's an easy mistake to make. You know how all African Americans look alike." The woman I was talking to had barely been able to restrain herself from making an aggressive comeback to this customer's remarks and was still visibly upset as she recounted the incident to me. I looked down the aisle at the other African-American checker and noticed immediately that she bore no physical resemblance to the woman I was talking with.

Every day I hear a new story, read a new report, witness the devastating impact of racism on our community. I don't ask for these stories, but I listen carefully when I hear them. I don't take them personally or try to defend white people. I know that these stories are not about me and that sometimes the white people involved have no conscious intention of hurting a person of color. These stories are about the everyday discrimination and disrespect towards people of color that racism produces and that people of color have to live with. What should I do when I hear these stories?

Sometimes listening is enough, especially if I am listening without offering excuses, defenses, explanations, or minimizations. Often more is called for. I try to think of how I can respond to these incidents. I am sympathetic to the store clerk and affirm that she's justified in being upset. I call up the board member and talk about the comment he made. I volunteer to be part of a group that confronts our racist neighbor. My actions never feel like enough, but I have learned that they do make a difference.

Since I wrote Uprooting Racism, I have become even more acutely aware of how interdependent our lives are and how dependent I am on the low-paid work of people of color in the United States and in other countries. I look at the label on my jeans, shirts, or underwear; I track the work that produced my computer, TV, or microwave; I learn more about who grows, picks, cans, packs, and prepares the food I eat; I notice who cleans the public buildings and classrooms I use. Often it is people of color in poorly paid, low-status jobs who allow me to enjoy the benefits of inexpensive clothes, low-priced electronic equipment, cheap food, and clean and well-maintained public spaces.

Just walking down the street to the park makes me aware of this interconnection and dependency. I meet people like Renee, who maintains the flowers and trees in the park down the block from us. Now in his 50s, he emigrated here from the Philippines many years ago and has raised his children in this country. Or people like Dereje, an immigrant from Ethiopia who is on the city's mosquito abatement team. When the owners of the apartments next to the park call the city to complain about the mosquitoes, Dereje comes out and mixes the chemicals into the pond to control the bugs.

My daily life is interwoven with the lives of hundreds, if not thousands, of people of color. Yet so much of their lives and work and culture is ridiculed, exploited, or rendered invisible by our society that often I don't see them, I don't make the connections. My ignorance and subsequent inaction contribute to their exploitation, discrimination, and scapegoating. I become a partner in racism, a collaborator in injustice.

In the last few years I had been hopeful that we were making some inroads in recognizing and addressing racism. However, watching the response to the September 11, 2001, World Trade Center and Pentagon bombings, I fear we have suffered a major setback. There has been an alarming increase in hate crimes against Arab Americans, against Muslims, and even against those who are mistaken for members of these two groups, such as Sikhs, whose men traditionally wear turbans. For example, in Arizona soon after the bombing, Balbir Singh Sodhi, a Sikh, was killed by a white man who said as he was arrested, "I'm a patriot, I'm a damn American all the way." Adel Karas, an Egyptian Christian grocer, was killed at the market he owned. Waqar Hasan, a Pakistani Muslim, was found shot dead at his store in a section of Dallas. On October 7 two men stabbed Swaran Kaur Bhullar, shouting at her, "This is what you get for what you've done to us." The list goes on: an attack on a Moroccan gas-station attendant in Illinois; an attempt to run over a Pakistani woman in a parking lot in Huntington, New York; the arrest of an armed man who was dumping gasoline in the parking lot of a Seattle mosque.

Not only Arab Americans suffer from anti-Arab discrimination and misplaced patriotism. Besides "mistaken" hate crimes, African Americans, Latino/as, and Asian

Americans are threatened by racial profiling on our streets and at our borders. And all of us face attacks on our civil liberties, increased police and military surveillance, and the further shifting of resources from education, health, and other social programs to defense, security, and prisons.

On the other hand, in this time of increased fear I have been heartened by the number of white people (as well as many non-Arab people of color) who have stood in solidarity with Arab Americans and with Muslims. They have challenged stereotypes and misinformation and confronted scapegoating and harassment. They have acted as allies in the best tradition of white people. I hope that my book will continue to support that tradition of social responsibility.

I know that many white people find it hard to read about racism. I have been told stories of how students, required to read this book, would read a section and then throw the book across the room because they were so upset at what I was saying and what it meant for their lives. But then they would go across the room, pick up the book, and read another section. That is what it takes to confront racism. We need to keep going back and picking up the task no matter how uncomfortable, sad, angry, discouraged, or frustrated we become in the process. Being an ally is like that. We keep learning, doing our best, leaving something out, making mistakes, doing it better next time.

Now, more than ever, we as white people need to put our shoulders to the task of working with people of color to uproot racism. As I discuss in more detail in the book, it is inadequate to say "I am not prejudiced," and morally evasive to say "I treat everyone the same." In a world in which racism continues to be one of the bedrocks of our organizations and institutions, in which most people of color, every single day, are confronted with the repercussions of racial discrimination, harassment, and exploitation, we must ask ourselves "What do I stand for? Who do I stand with? Do I stand for racial justice, the end of discrimination and racial violence, and a society truly based on equal opportunity? Do I stand with people of color and white allies in the struggle to uproot racism?"

These are the questions I challenge you with as you begin to read this book.

What do you stand for?
Who do you stand with?
What are you going to do about it?

I hope this book helps you to be clearer and more effective in answering these questions.

Paul Kivel
March 2002

A note to readers outside the United States

Many of the examples used in the book are from the United States, where I live and about which I have more access to information. Many reports, studies, and accounts of racism in other white majority societies show similar patterns of racism against people of color in such countries as Great Britain, Canada, France, Germany, Australia, and New Zealand. For example, the Parekh Report, "The Future of Multi-ethnic Britain," documents extensive institutional and cultural racism throughout Great Britain. If you live in a white majority country, talk to people of color, investigate the studies and reports, and don't let yourself be complacent or indifferent simply because the situation is not exactly the same as that which I describe in the United States.

Introduction: "Only Justice Can Put Out the Fire"[1]

THIS IS A BOOK ABOUT RACISM FOR WHITE PEOPLE. It is not another book about how bad racism is, filled with facts and figures about inequality and injustice. In this book I want to talk to you personally about what racism means to those of us who are white, and how we can make a difference in the struggle for racial justice.

There is fire raging across the United States — usually a series of brush fires erupting whenever conditions are right, sometimes a firestorm, always a smoldering cauldron. Whether it is major urban uprisings, intellectual debates, or everyday conflicts in our neighborhoods and schools, racism is burning us all. Some of us have third-degree burns or have died from its effects; many others live in the charred wreckage. Most of us suffer first- and second-degree burns at some time in our lives. We all live with fear in the glow of the fire's menacing and distorted light.

As white people we do many things to survive the heat. Some of us move to the suburbs, put bars on our windows, put locks on our hearts, and teach our children distrust for their own protection. Some of us believe the enemy is "out there" — and we can be safe "in here." Most of us never talk about what it means to be "in here" with other white people and why we are so afraid of people with darker skin colors "out there." When we don't talk about our fears, we are prevented from doing anything effective to put out the fire.

Poll after poll shows that most white Americans are scared. We are scared about violence; we are scared about the economy; we are scared about the safety, education, and future of our children. Much of the time those fears are directed toward people of color — long-term residents or recent immigrants. It is easy for us to focus on them, and yet doing so is devastating to our ability to address the critical national issues of jobs, education, social infrastructure, family violence, and economic development.

Since the uprising in South Central Los Angeles in 1992, white people are even more afraid than before. Once again people of color brought the injustice of racism to our national attention. We saw the fire flare up and again we were frightened. Many of us wanted to do something, to pick up a bucket and throw water on the flames, but the size of the blaze seemed to make our individual efforts useless. Besides, many of us thought that we were too far away from the cause of the fire to make a difference. People of color were defined as the problem and the inner cities as the site.

In fact, there are already flames in our (all too often predominantly white) schools, churches, neighborhoods, and workplaces. Poverty, family violence, crime, drugs, fear, suicide, and despair are not limited to somewhere "out there" nor to "those people."

Our houses are burning out from under us, and we need to pick up our buckets and start carrying water now. But just like the volunteer fire departments in rural communities and small towns, we need to be part of a fire line where everyone realizes that when the sparks are flying, anything can catch on fire. We need to be a community that is alert for the signs of sparks and embers so they can be put out before a bigger blaze develops.

We don't need scare tactics. They just reinforce the fear and paralysis. We don't need numbers and statistics. They produce numbness and despair. We need to talk with each other, honestly, simply, caringly. We need to learn how to talk about racism without rhetoric, which fans the flames; without attack, fear, or intimidation, which keep people off the lines. We need to share fire-fighting suggestions, advice, exercises, and approaches so that we can work together to fight the fire.

Racism is often described as a problem of prejudice. Prejudice is certainly one result of racism, and it fuels further acts of violence toward people of color. However the assumption of this book is that racism is the institutionalization of social injustice based on skin color, other physical characteristics, and cultural and religious difference. White racism is the uneven and unfair distribution of power, privilege, land, and material goods favoring white people. Another way to state this is that white racism is a system in which people of color as a group are exploited and oppressed by white people as a group. Although we can and should all become more tolerant and understanding of each other, only justice can put out the fire of racism. We will certainly have to examine our fears and misconceptions to see why we stay home while the fire sweeps our nation. Our primary purpose in doing so will be so that we can get as many strong, able, and committed bodies on the front lines as quickly as possible.

As we have witnessed many times in European and American history, the fires of racism include the flames of anti-Semitism. Most of the Jews in the United States are of European background. Sometimes these Jews are considered white and sometimes not, just as Asian and Arab Americans are sometimes considered white or not, depending upon the complex responses of white people. Jewish people are vulnerable to the same kinds of violence, discrimination, and harassment that most people of color have experienced. At the same time, those Jews who are of European descent are buffered from racism's worst aspects by the benefits of being white, as are many people of southern and eastern European heritage. Because of this complex dynamic in American society, understanding and confronting anti-Semitism is a crucial link in the struggle to end racism. In this book Jews of European descent will be referred to as white and as targets of racism. Jews of color are always targets of racism from white people and even from Jews of European descent. They are also vulnerable to anti-Semitism.

Anti-Semitism is similar to, different from, and intertwined with racism. Groups holding political power in Europe have exploited, controlled, and violated other groups of people based on religion, race, culture, and nationality (as well as gender, class, and sexual orientation) for hundreds of years. There is tremendous overlap in the kinds of violence that have been directed at these groups and the justifications used to legitimize political, economic, and cultural exploitation and dominance. Racism and anti-Semitism are two primary, closely related tools that groups in power have used to maintain their advantage. I will make connections between the two throughout the text. The section on Jews in Part IV will explore these complexities in more detail.

When I wrote my book Men's Work, I quoted a statement from Alice Walker in the preface. The statement was about how the fear of not being perfect can inhibit committing oneself to public action about a particular issue. She was talking about speaking out against cruelty to animals even though she occasionally ate meat. I referred to writing about sexism even though I wasn't perfectly non-sexist.

I think it is crucial that each of us speaks up about issues of injustice, violence, and inequality. It is true that our words have more moral credibility if we are leading the good, clean life and are totally consistent in what we say and what we do. We have to "walk the walk," not just "talk the talk."

However, issues of social justice are not fundamentally about individual actions and beliefs. This book is about white racism, which is a social system. Although my personal attitudes and actions can either support or confront racism, racism is completely independent of me. In fact, even if most of us were completely non-racist in our attitudes, there are many ways that unequal wages, unequal treatment in the legal system and segregation in jobs, housing, and education would continue.

Our beliefs and actions are important. You and I are responsible for how we treat the people around us and whether or not we are fighting against injustice or contributing to it. But as long as we focus only on individual actions and ignore community and organizational responses, we will leave the system of racism intact.

This book is about uprooting the system of racism. You may need to re-examine your individual beliefs and actions in order to participate effectively in that uprooting. This book will help you look at how you have learned racism, what effects it has had on your life, what have been its costs and benefits to you, and how you have learned to pass it on. More importantly, this book will help you become a member of a network of people who are committed to eliminating racism. It offers you connections, strategies, perspectives, and guidelines for becoming involved in the struggle.

Don't take it too personally. You did not create racism. You may have many feelings while reading this book. Confronting racism may trigger guilt, horror, embarrassment, defensiveness, anger, excitement, discovery, anxiety, inspiration, jealousy, competitiveness, loneliness, despair, or confusion. Acknowledge the feelings, talk about them with others, get support, but don't get stuck in the feelings. If our feelings immobilize us, we cannot strategically plan how to sabotage the system.

This book is not about unlearning racism.[2] It is fine for us to unlearn racism. But many of us live in highly segregated or highly stratified communities and we may have only limited opportunities to fight racism in our daily encounters. Unlearning racism makes it easier for people of color to live and work with us, but it doesn't necessarily challenge the system to change. Unlearning racism may or may not be a path to taking action to eliminate racism. In a society where individual growth is often not only the starting place but also the end point of discussion, strategies for unlearning racism often end in complacency and inaction.

Racism has existed in this hemisphere since Columbus and his crews invaded the shores of the West Indies and slaughtered, raped, enslaved, and exploited the Taino peoples living there. Since his arrival there has been continuous active resistance from people of color, beginning with the Taino and other indigenous peoples. Throughout that time there has also been a strong and steady stream of white people who have supported the resistance and contributed to the struggle to end racism. This book is an invitation to join that tradition of white people. It offers you some guidance about how to be more effective in that struggle.

This book does not document the existence of racism. There are many books and thousands of studies showing the direct, devastating impact of racism on the daily lives of the tens of millions of people of color in this country. That there are inequality and injustice in our educational, political, legal, medical, housing, and employment systems is amply documented and indisputable. I will present few statistics and little information proving racism exists. (There are some excellent resources listed in the bibliography which provide that kind of information.)

Instead, this book provides some suggestions and starting points based on the fact that racism exists, it is pervasive, and its effects are devastating. Because of this devastation we need to start doing everything possible to end racism. The first step is for us to talk together, as white people.

PART I

What Color Is White?

Let's Talk

I AM TALKING TO YOU as one white person to another. I am Jewish, and I will talk about that later in this book. You also may have an ethnic identity you are proud of, and you have a religious background, a culture, a country of origin, and a history. Whatever your other identities, you probably are not used to being addressed as white.

"Other" people are African American, Asian American, Pacific Islanders, Native American, Latino/as, or Muslims. "Other" people have countries of origin and primary languages that are not English. Rarely in this country do we identify ourselves or each other as white. It is an adjective that is seldom heard explicitly, but is everywhere implied. People are assumed white unless otherwise noted, much as people (and animals) are assumed to be male.

Read the following lines:

He walked into the room and immediately noticed her.

This new sitcom is about a middle-aged, middle-class couple and their three teenage children.

The average American drinks two cups of coffee a day.

Women today want to catch a man who is strong, but sensitive.

She didn't know if she would get into the college of her choice.

My grandmother lived on a farm all her life.

I have a friend who has AIDS.

He won a medal on the Special Olympics basketball team.

Are all these people white?

Read the sentences again and imagine the people referred to are

Chinese Americans. Does that change the meanings?

Try making them Native American. How does that change the meaning?

If you are of Christian background, what happens when you

make them Jewish or Muslim?

In reality, we would have to specify they are Chinese American or Native American or Jewish or Muslim because we would not automatically assume they were.

Similarly with you and me. We assume we are white. It can seem like we're stating the obvious. Yet there is something about stating the obvious that makes us feel uneasy, marked. Why notice? What's the point of saying I'm white?

We have been led to believe that racism is a question of particular acts of discrimination or violence. Calling someone a name, denying someone a job, excluding someone from a neighborhood — that is racism. These certainly are acts of racism. But what about living in a white suburb where people of color are excluded or harassed? What about working in an organization where people of color are paid less, have more menial work or fewer opportunities for advancement? What about shopping in a store where you are treated respectfully but people of color are followed or suspected of shoplifting? Racism affects each and every aspect of our lives all the time, whether people of color are present or not.

People of color know this intimately. They know that where they live, work, and walk; who they talk with and how; what they read, listen to, or watch on TV; their past experiences and future possibilities are all influenced by racism. As white people we also know this, but most of us do not talk about it. I will discuss why we don't talk about it later. Because we don't talk about it, naming whiteness can seem scary, foolish, unnecessary, pointless, or illegitimate.

Of course there are times when many of us talk with the unspoken assumption that we are white. When the subject is desegregation or integration or immigration or affirmative action we are clear about being white and speaking about "them," i.e., people of color.

> For the next few days notice how rarely you see or hear
> the words white, Caucasian, or Euro-American.
> Where is it implied but not stated specifically?
> Where is African American or Latino/a specified so you
> can infer who is white without it being named?

> Carry your whiteness with you. During the day, in each new situation,
> remind yourself that you are white. What difference has it made/does it
> make? Who is around you? What are they doing? Are they white or
> people of color? What difference do you notice that it makes?
> Write down what you notice. Discuss it with a friend.

> Particularly notice whenever you are somewhere
> where there are only white people.
> How did it come to be that there are no people of color there?
> Are they really not there, or are they only invisible?
> Did they grow some of the food, originally own the land,
> build the buildings, or clean and maintain the
> place where you are?

"I'm Not White"

Recently I was doing a workshop on racism. We wanted to divide the group into a caucus of people of color and a caucus of white people so that each group could have more in-depth discussion. Immediately some of the white people said, "But I'm not white."

I was somewhat taken aback because although these people looked white, they were clearly distressed about being labeled white. A white Christian woman stood up and said, "I'm not really white because I'm not part of the white male power structure that perpetuates racism." Next a white gay man stood up and said, "You have to be straight to have the privileges of being white." A white, straight, working-class man from a poor family then said, "I've got it just as hard as any person of color." Finally, a straight, white, middle-class man said, "I'm not white, I'm Italian."

My African-American co-worker turned to me and asked, "Where are all the white people who were here just a minute ago?" Of course I replied, "Don't ask me. I'm not white, I'm Jewish!"

Most of the time we don't notice or question our whiteness. However, when the subject is racism many of us don't want to be white because it opens us to charges of being racist and brings up feelings of guilt, shame, embarrassment, and hopelessness. There are others who proudly claim whiteness under any circumstances and simply deny or ignore the violence that white people have done to people of color.

Those of us who are middle class are more likely to assume we are white without having to emphasize the point, and to feel guilty when it is noticed or brought up. Those of us who are poor or working class are more likely to have had to assert our whiteness against the effects of economic discrimination and the presence of other racial groups. Although we share the benefits of being white, we don't share the economic privileges of being middle class and so we are more likely to feel angry and less likely to feel guilty than our middle-class counterparts.

Whatever our economic status, many of us become paralyzed with some measure of fear, guilt, anger, defensiveness, or confusion if we are named as white when racism is being addressed.

In this country it has always been dangerous even to talk about racism. "Nigger lover," "Indian lover," and "race traitor" are labels that have carried severe consequences. You probably know the names of white civil rights workers who were killed for their actions against racism, such as Goodman, Schwerner, and Luizzo. Many of us have been isolated from friends or family because of disagreements over racism. A lot of us have been called "racist."

Saying "I am white" may make us feel either guilty of being racist or traitorous toward other whites. We don't want to be labeled or stereotyped. Talking about racism has often occurred in the context of angry words, hostility, accusations, and divisiveness. We also may have fears about people of color separating from us if we are clearly identified as white.

In any case, some of us are quick to disavow our whiteness or to claim some other identity that will give us legitimate victim status. We certainly don't want to be seen as somehow responsible for or complicit in racism.

I want to begin here — with this denial of our whiteness — because racism keeps people of color in the limelight and makes whiteness invisible. To change this we must take whiteness itself and hold it up to the light and see that it is a color too. Whiteness is a concept, an ideology, which holds tremendous power over our lives and, in turn, over the lives of people of color. Our challenge in this discussion will be to keep whiteness center stage. Every time our attention begins to wander off toward people of color or other issues, we will have to notice and refocus. We must notice when we try to slip into another identity and escape being white. We each have many other factors that influence our lives, such as our ethnicity, gender, sexual orientation, class, personality, mental and physical abilities. Even when we're talking about these elements of our lives we must keep whiteness on stage with us because it influences each of the other factors.

What parts of your identity does it feel like you lose
when you say aloud the phrase "I'm white"?

Part of our discomfort may come from our own family's
ethnic and class background and its complex relationship to whiteness.
Was your ethnic or cultural group ever considered not white?
When they arrived in the United States or Canada, what did members of your
family have to do to be accepted as white? What did they have to give up?

How has pride in being white sustained you or your family?
Has that identification or pride ever allowed you or your family to tolerate
poverty, economic exploitation, or poor living conditions because you can say,
"At least we're not colored"?

If, when you move down the streets of major cities, other people assume, based on skin color, dress, physical appearance, or total impression, that you are white, then in American society that counts for being white. This is where we are going to start talking about what it means to say "I am white." I realize that there are differences between the streets of New York and Minneapolis, Vancouver and Winnipeg, and between different neighborhoods within each city. But in American society there is a broad and pervasive division between those of us who are treated as white people and those of us who are treated as people of color, and most of us know from a very early age which side we are on. If we are white we are told or learn in early childhood who to stay away from, who not to play with, who not to associate with, who isn't one of our kind. Several studies have shown that young children between the ages of two and four notice differences of skin color, eye color, hair, dress, and speech and the significance that adults give to those differences.[1] This is true even if our parents are liberal or progressive. The training is too pervasive within our society for anyone to escape. Anthropology and sociology professor Annie Barnes recounts the following interview with a parent who noticed how early in their lives white children learn racism.

> *I experienced it [racism] through my three-year-old daughter. One day at preschool, the students had a "show and tell." All the students had brought their toys to school. My daughter forgot her toys, so I had to go home and get them. My daughter told me specifically what to bring. She wanted her pretty black Barbie doll with the white dress. She loved this doll and thought that it was pretty and often said, "When I grow up, I want to look just like my Barbie.*
>
> *All the other children were white. While my daughter brought out her Barbie during show and tell, they screwed up their faces and said, "Yuck. That's not Barbie. She's ugly."...She cried for hours and never carried her doll to school again, I couldn't believe those little children's actions. That was racism by babies, so to speak.[2]*

Whiteness is about more than skin color, although that is a major factor in this country. People of color and Jewish people are also marked as different by dress, food, the smells of cooking, religious ceremonies, celebratory rituals, and mannerisms. These features are all labeled racial differences, even though they may be related to culture, religion, class, or country of origin. I'm sure you know whether you are treated as white or as a person of color by most of the people you meet.

Say "I am white" to yourself a couple of times.

What are the "buts" that immediately come to mind?

Do you quickly add on another identity, perhaps one where you might claim a victim status such as female, poor, lesbian or gay, Jewish or Italian?

Do you defend yourself with statements such as "I have friends who are people of color" or "My family didn't own slaves"?

Do you try to separate yourself from other white people ("I don't feel white" "I'm not like other white people")?

Do you try to minimize the importance of whiteness ("We're all part of the human race")?

We are understandably uncomfortable with the label "white." We feel boxed in and want to escape, just as people of color want to escape from the confines of their racial categories. Being white is an arbitrary category that overrides our individual personalities, devalues us, deprives us of the richness of our other identities, stereotypes us, and yet has no scientific basis. However, in our society being white is just as real and governs our day-to-day lives just as much as being a person of color does for African Americans, Latino/as, Asian Americans, Pacific Islanders, Native Americans, Arab Americans, and others. To acknowledge this reality is not to create it or to perpetuate it. In fact, it is the first step to uprooting racism.

Whiteness is problematic. All the fear, anger, frustration, helplessness, and confusion we experience about admitting that we are white are the results of racism. Many of these feelings are what keep us from recognizing and talking about the effects of racism in our own lives and the devastation that racism wreaks in our society.

We may claim that we aren't white because we simply don't (or refuse to) notice race. I sometimes like to think that I don't. But when I'm in an all-white setting and a person of color walks in, I notice. I am slightly surprised to see a person of color and I look again to confirm who they are and wonder to myself why they're there. I try to do this as naturally and smoothly as possible because I wouldn't want anyone to think that I wasn't tolerant. Actually what I'm surprised at is not that they are there, but that they are there as an equal. All of my opening explanations for their presence will assume they are not equal. "They must be a server or delivery person," I tell myself. It is usually not until another white person introduces me, or gives me an explanation, that my uneasiness is laid to rest. (And even then I may inwardly qualify my acceptance). I think that most of us notice skin color all the time, but we don't "notice" race unless our sense of the proper racial hierarchy is upset.

When I first meet someone I identify their gender (and get anxious when I can't), I identify as much about their class as I can figure out, and I identify what their racial identity is. I have two categories, white and other. I'm interested in the other. In fact, because of my assumptions about the commonness of whiteness, I often assume a person of color will be more interesting than another white person. But whether we value it positively or negatively, the difference counts and we notice it.

Since I've been taught to relate differently to people who are African American, Latino/a, Asian, or Arab American, I may need more information than appearance gives me about what "kind" of person of color I am with. I have some standard questions to fish for more information, such as: "That's an interesting name. I've never heard it before. Where's it from?" "Your accent sounds familiar but I can't place it." "You don't look American. Where are you from?"

Sometimes I ask these questions of white Americans who have unusual names or unfamiliar accents. But most often I have noticed that I use these questions to clarify who is white and who isn't and, secondarily, what kind of person of color I am dealing with.

I was taught that it is not polite to notice racial difference. I also learned that racial difference is an artificial basis used to discriminate against and exploit people of color, and therefore sometimes I overcompensate by pretending to ignore it. Occasionally I hear white people say, "I don't care whether a person is black, brown, orange, or green." Human beings don't come in orange or green. Those whose skin color is darker are treated differently in general and we, in particular, respond differently to them. As part of growing up white and learning racial stereotypes, most of us have been trained to stiffen up and be more cautious, fearful, and hesitant around people of color. These are physiological and psychological responses that we can notice in ourselves and see in other white people. These responses belie our verbal assurances that we don't notice racial differences.

There's absolutely nothing wrong with being white or with noticing the difference that color makes. You were born without choice into your family. You did not choose your skin color, native language, or culture. You are not responsible for being white or for being raised in a white-dominated, racist society in which you have been trained to have particular responses to people of color. You are responsible for how you respond to racism (which is what this book is about), and you can only do that consciously and effectively if you start by realizing that it makes a crucial difference that you are white.

"I'm Not Racist"

WHETHER IT IS EASY OR DIFFICULT TO SAY that we're white, the phrase we often want to say next is "But I'm not racist." There are lots of ways that we have learned to phrase this denial.

- I'm not racist.
- I don't belong to the Klan.
- I have friends who are people of color.
- I don't see color, I'm color blind.
- I do anti-racism work.
- I went to an unlearning racism workshop.

This book is not about whether you are racist or not, or whether all white people are racist or not. We are not conducting a moral inventory of ourselves, nor creating a moral standard to divide other white people from us.

To avoid being called racist we may claim that we don't notice color and don't treat people differently based on color. However, we all notice color in just about every situation we're in. It's not useful or honest for any of us to claim that we don't. It is too pervasive a construct of our society to avoid. When we say things like "I don't see color," we are trying to maintain a self-image of impartiality and fairness (and whiteness). Some of the motivation behind the claim that we are color neutral is to establish that we don't mistreat people or discriminate against them because of their race. Ultimately, this disclaimer prevents us from taking responsibility for challenging racism because we believe that people who see color are the problem.

The only way to treat people with dignity and justice is to recognize that racism has a profound negative effect upon our lives. Noticing color helps to counteract that effect. Instead of being color neutral we need to notice much more acutely and insightfully exactly the difference that color makes in the way people are treated.

Just as it's not useful to label ourselves racist or not, it is not useful to label each other. White people, individually and collectively, have done and continue to do some very brutal things in the name of whiteness. We may want to separate ourselves from the white people who commit these acts by claiming that they are racist and we are not. But because racism operates institutionally, to the benefit of all white people, we are connected to the acts of other white people.

Of course you're not a member of the Klan or other extremist groups. Of course you watch what you say and don't make rude racial comments. But dissociating from white people who do is not the answer. You may want to dissociate yourself from their actions but you still need to challenge their beliefs. You can't challenge them or even speak to them if you have separated yourself from them, creating some magical line with the racists on that side and you over here. This division leads to an ineffective strategy of trying to pull as many people as possible over to your (non-racist and therefore superior) side. Other white people will listen to you better, and be more influenced by your actions, when you identify with them. Then we can explore how to work from the inside out together.

Perhaps most importantly, the people who are more visibly saying or doing things that are racist are usually more scared, more confused, and less powerful than we are. (Or they are trying to increase their own power by manipulating racial fears.) It is amazing how, when we feel scared, confused, or powerless, we do and say the very same things. Since racism leads to scapegoating people of color for social and personal problems, we are all susceptible to resorting to racial scapegoating in times of trouble. Visible acts of racism are, at least in part, an indication of the lack of power that a white person or group of people have to camouflage their actions. More powerful and well-off people can simply move to segregated neighborhoods or make corporate decisions that are harder to see and analyze as contributing to racism. Since the racism of the wealthy is less visible to us, those of us who are middle class can inadvertently scapegoat poor and working-class white people for being more overtly racist.

We do need to confront words and actions that are racist when we encounter them because they create an atmosphere of violence in which all of us are unsafe. We also need to understand that most white people are doing the best they can to survive. Overtly racist people are scared and lack the information and skills to be more tolerant. We need to challenge their behavior, not their moral integrity. We also need to be careful that we don't end up carrying out an upper-class agenda by blaming poor and working people for being racist when people with wealth control the media, the textbooks, the housing and job markets, and the police. We need to stay focused on the institutions themselves.

What is Whiteness?

RACISM IS BASED ON THE CONCEPT OF WHITENESS — a powerful fiction enforced by power and violence. Whiteness is a constantly shifting boundary separating those who are entitled to have certain privileges from those whose exploitation and vulnerability to violence is justified by their not being white.

Racism itself is a long-standing characteristic of many human societies. For example, justifying exploitation and violence against other peoples because they are "inferior" or different has a long history within Greek, Roman, and European Christian traditions.

In more recent historical times in western Europe, those with English heritage were perceived to be pure white. The Irish, Russians, and Spanish were considered darker races, sometimes black, and certainly non-white. The white category was slowly extended to include northern and middle European people, but still, even 70 years ago, it definitely excluded eastern or southern European peoples such as Italians, Poles, Russians, and Greeks. In the last few decades, although there is still prejudice against people from these geographical backgrounds, they have become generally accepted as white in the United States.[1]

The important distinction in the United States has always been binary — first between those who counted as Christians and those who were pagans. As historian Winthrop Jordan has written:

> *Protestant Christianity was an important element in English patriotism .... Christianity was interwoven into [an Englishman's] conception of his own nationality, and he was therefore inclined to regard the Negroes' lack of true religion as part of theirs. Being a Christian was not merely a matter of subscribing to certain doctrines; it was a quality inherent in oneself and in one's society. It was interconnected with all the other attributes of normal and proper men.* [2]

As Africans and Native Americans were converted to Christianity, such a simple distinction was no longer useful, at least as a legal and political difference. In addition, because Europeans, Native Americans, and Africans often worked and lived together in similar circumstances of servitude, and resisted and rebelled together against the way they were treated, the landowning class began to implement policies to separate European workers from African and Native-American workers. Even in this early period, racism was used to divide workers and make it easier for those in power to control working conditions. Drawing on already established "popular" classifications, whiteness, separate from Christianity, was delineated more clearly as a legal category in the United States in the 17th century,[3] and the concept of life-long servitude (slavery) was introduced from the West Indies and distinguished from various forms of shorter-term servitude (indenture). In response to Bacon's rebellion and other uprisings, the ruling class, especially in the populous and dominant territory of Virginia, began to establish a clear racial hierarchy in the 1660s and 1670s. By the 1730s racial divisions were firmly in place legally and socially. Most blacks were enslaved and even free blacks had lost the right to vote, the right to bear arms, and the right to bear witness. Blacks were also barred from participating in many trades during this period.

Meanwhile in Virginia, whites had gained the right to corn, money, a gun, clothing, and 50 acres of land at the end of indentureship; could no longer be beaten naked; and had the poll tax reduced. In other words, poor whites "gained legal, political, emotional, social, and financial status that was directly related to the concomitant degradation of Indians and Negroes."[4] Typically, although poor whites gained some privileges vis-à-vis blacks and Indians, because of the increased productivity from slavery, the gap between wealthy whites and those who were poor widened considerably.

Although racism was long established in American society legally, socially, and economically, it was only defined "scientifically" as a biological/genetic characteristic about 150 years ago with the publication of Darwin's theory of species modification and Linnaeus's system of classification. Others combined these ideas into a pseudo-scientific theory, eventually called Social Darwinism, which attempted to classify the human population into distinct categories or races and put them on an evolutionary scale with whites on top.

The original classification consisted of three categories — Caucasoid, Negroid, and Mongoloid. These were not based on genetic differences, but on differences that Europeans and European Americans perceived to be important. They were in fact based on stereotypes of cultural differences and (mis)measures of physiological characteristics such as skull size.[5]

From the beginning the attempt to classify people by race was fraught with contradictions. Latin Americans, Native Americans, and Jewish people did not fit easily into these categories so the categories were variously stretched, redefined, or adapted to meet the agenda of the Europeans and Americans who were using them.

For example, in the last century Finns were doing most of the lowest-paid, unsafe, mining and lumbering work in the upper Midwest. Although logically they were white, in terms of political, cultural, and economic "common sense" they were black because they were the poorest and least respected group in the area besides Native Americans. The courts consistently ruled that they were not white, despite their skin color, because of their cultural and economic standing. In another case the courts ruled that a Syrian was not white, even though he looked white and had the same skin color as Caucasians, because "common sense" dictated that a Syrian was not white.[6]

On the West Coast during the constitutional debates in California in 1848–49, there was discussion about the status of Mexicans and Chinese. There were still Mexicans who were wealthy landowners and business partners with whites, while the Chinese were exclusively heavily exploited railroad and agricultural workers. It was eventually decided that Mexicans would be considered white and Chinese would be considered the same as blacks and Indians. This decision established which group could become citizens, own land, marry whites, and have other basic rights.[7]

Today people of Finnish background are considered white; Latino/as are considered not white; and Chinese Americans are conditionally white at times, not white at others, but clearly different from blacks and Native Americans.

There was a complex and dynamic interplay between the popular conception of race and the scientific categories, neither of which was grounded in physiological or biological reality, but both of which carried great emotional import to "white" people and devastating consequences to "people of color," regardless of how they were being defined.

Although a few scientists still try to prove the existence of races, most scientists have long ago abandoned the use of race as a valid category to distinguish between humans. There is such tremendous genetic difference or variation within "racial" groupings, and such huge overlap between them, that no particular racial groupings or distinctions based on skin color or other physical characteristics are useful or justified.[8] That hasn't stopped many people from believing that distinct races exist and from trying to use scientific language to buttress their arguments.[9]

There is likewise no scientific (i.e., biological or genetic) basis to the concept of whiteness. There is nothing scientifically distinctive about it except skin color, and that is highly variable. All common wisdom notwithstanding, the skin color of a person tells you nothing about that person's culture, country of origin, character, or personal habits. Because there is nothing biological about whiteness, it ends up being defined in contrast to other groups, becoming confused with ideas of nationality, religion, and ethnicity.

For example, Jewish people are not a "racial" grouping. Jewish people share cultural and religious beliefs and practices but come from every continent and many different cultural backgrounds. Jews range in skin color from "white" to dark brown. Because race was falsely assumed to be a scientific category, being Jewish has often been assumed to mean that a Jew is genetically different from non-Jewish people.

I grew up learning that racial categories were scientifically valid and gave us useful information about ourselves and other people. In other words, racism had a scientific stamp of approval. It is difficult for me to let go of the certainty I thought I had gained about what racial difference meant. And, of course, there are always new attempts to prove to us that race means something.[10]

What residual doubts do you have that there may be something genetic or biological about racial differences? ("But, what about ... ?")
How can you respond to people who say that there are specific differences between "races"?

I began to understand the artificial nature of racial categories more clearly when I examined how moral qualities were attached to racial differences. This confirmed my suspicion that there was a political, not a scientific, agenda at work in these distinctions.

The lack of a physical difference attached to whiteness hasn't prevented many people from assuming that they know what whiteness is, or what it is different from. Although some of these associations have changed or have had different prominence over time, they have generally been linked to moral qualities. These moral qualities have, in turn, been used to justify various forms of exploitation.

From the old phrase referring to a good deed — "That's white of you" — to the New Age practice of visualizing oneself surrounded by white light, white has signified honor, purity, cleanliness, and godliness in white western European and mainstream U.S. and Canadian culture. Because concepts of whiteness and race were developed in Christian Europe, references to whiteness are imbued with Christian values. We have ended up with a set of opposing qualities or attributes that are said to define people either as white or as not white.

The tendency to see the world in sets of opposites, either/or categories, is itself a core pattern of thinking developed in elite settings in western Europe and the United States. Many other cultures do not divide the world into opposing camps. The English phrase "black and white" reflects our desire to divide things into opposites even though everyday reality is rarely clearly defined or neatly categorized. Classical Greek either/or logic and a Christian theology of good versus evil were combined to impose a good/bad set of values based on selected categories of racial difference. Some of the most common pairings are listed below.

LIST OF "DARK" AND "WHITE" QUALITIES

"Dark" Qualities	"White" Qualities
superstitious	scientific
subhuman	human
crazy	sane
immoral	moral
animalistic	god-like (in the image of God)
tainted	pure
abnormal	normal
emotional, angry	calm
primitive, uncivilized, barbaric, savage	civilized
prone to dishonesty	well-intentioned, decent
subversive, rebellious	upholder of tradition
satanic	angelic
pagan	Christian
malicious	loving
godless	god-fearing, wholesome
rude	polite
evil	benign
low class	middle class
crude, brutish	refined
demanding	restrained
intellectually inferior	intelligent
impulsive	thoughtful

traitor	patriot
fanciful	level-headed
weak link	strong specimen
lacking self control	prudent
manipulative	sincere
irrational	rational
radical	conservative
undignified	respectable
sinful	innocent
out of control	in control
impure, contaminated	pure
tainted, poisonous	innocuous, harmless
dirty	clean
illegal	legal, law-abiding ·
needing permission	authorized
soulless, damned	saved
fringe, marginal	center
subjective	objective, detached
wild	calm
sexual, wanton	chaste
colorful	bland
disorganized	orderly
inefficient	effective
traditional	modern
impatient	patient
self-righteous	righteous
rhythmic	stiff
devious	straightforward
promiscuous	committed
cloudy	clear
disease-carrying	healthy
present-time-oriented	future-oriented
un-American	American
dark	fair, blond

Which words in each pair do you associate with white people?
Which words on the left do you use to discount people of color's demands
for fair and equal treatment ("they are too ... "), or to blame them for
how they are treated in our society
("They would be successful if they weren't so ... ")?

Qualities not associated with whiteness have been given negative meanings. They have become associated not only with people of color, but also with children, workers, lesbians, gays, bisexuals, Jews, and heterosexual white women — just those groups excluded from the political and scientific institutions that defined what normal should be.

In reality, individual character traits don't have anything to do with skin color, cultural background, age, gender, class, or sexual orientation. The personalities and character of members of any cultural group are highly variable, but the "good" qualities in the table have been claimed by white people and the "bad" ones attributed to people of color. White people have then claimed to be morally superior and our superiority has been used to rationalize the creation of a racial hierarchy with white people in positions of power.

Not all white people had an equal voice in defining racial differences. Those with most power — who had the most to gain or preserve — set the terms. White landowners, church leaders — the educated and successful — systematically, though not collusively, defined whiteness in ways that extolled and legitimized their actions and denigrated the actions of others.

These meanings are now many hundreds of years old. Today, none of us escapes the traps, lies, and emotional resonances of these dichotomies. They are passed on to us by parents, school, literature, TV, and the movies. It is difficult for any of us, powerful or less powerful, to dissociate "positive" qualities from white people and "negative" ones from people of color, no matter how "color blind" we would like to be.

White people who have challenged racism and the false dichotomies upon which it is based have been labeled in various ways to show that they don't really belong to the white group. Labels such as "nigger lover," "race traitor," "un-American," "feminist," "liberal," "Communist," "unchristian," "Jew," "fag," "lesbian," "crazy," "terrorist," and "thought police" have all been used to isolate and discredit people and to imply that they are somehow outside the territory of whiteness and therefore justifiably attacked. We can see from the moral virtues attached to whiteness that only those who are white will be able to speak with authority. A powerful way to discredit any critique of whiteness or racism is to discredit the speaker by showing that they are not really white. This is a neat, circular convention that stifles any serious discussion of what whiteness means and what effect it has on people.

This leaves most of us who are white on pretty shaky ground. If we bring attention to whiteness and racism, we risk being labeled not really white or a traitor to our "race." These accusations discredit our testimony and potentially lose us some of the benefits of being white such as better jobs and police protection from violence. Behind the names lies the threat of physical and sexual violence such as ostracism, firing, silencing, condemnation to hell, institutionalization, incarceration, deportation, rape, lynching, and other forms of mob violence that have been used to protect white power and privilege.

We could usefully spend some time exploring the history and meaning of any particular pair of words on the list above. I encourage you to do so. Each one reveals some vital aspect of whiteness and racism. Here I want to point out four concepts that many of these words cluster around: purity, Christian, American, and gender.

Appeals to group solidarity, particularly in the last 250 years during which political concepts of the nation-state have developed, have often focused on the "racial" purity of some particular group of people. In different European countries, in the United States, in Australia, and in South Africa, white people have attempted to claim a purity of racial stock and a genetic superiority that entitled them to control the land and other people around them in a particular geographical area. (Other groups of people have done the same thing; racism is by no means exclusive to white people.) They have then set up economic and psychological barriers to participation in that society for people defined as "other." People of color, Jews, Roma (often misnamed gypsies), people with physical or mental disabilities, homosexuals, Irish, southern Europeans, Slavic peoples, the poor — each group has been defined as outsiders who could contaminate white racial purity and the strength of the nation-state through corruption, contagion and disease, inferior intelligence, dirt and uncleanliness, and intermarriage. Segregation, anti-miscegenation laws, medical experimentation, concentration camps, and extermination have all been used at times to "cleanse" and "protect" whiteness and national identity. White people have considered anyone with even 1 percent African-American, Native, or Latino/a "blood" to be impure, not white, alien. The Nazis considered people to be Jewish if they had even one great-grandparent who was Jewish. Many of our fears today about intermarriage and mixed heritage children stem from these old misconceptions about racial difference and racial purity.

Another cluster of concepts and practices of whiteness centers on Christianity. Whiteness has often been equated with being a Christian in opposition to being a pagan, infidel, witch, heathen, Jew, Muslim, Native American, Buddhist, or atheist. Racial violence has been justified by a stated need to protect Christian families and homes. Pogroms, crusades, holy wars, and colonial conquests have been justified by the need to save the souls of "uncivilized" and "godless" peoples (often at the expense of their lives).

Jewish people have lived within Christian-dominated societies (when permitted to) for nearly 2,000 years. There is substantial Christian teaching and belief that Jewish people are dangerous and evil. These beliefs have been sustained even during periods of hundreds of years when Jews were not living near Christians.[11] Jews, along with Muslims, have become symbols to many Christians of the infidel. This anti-Semitism, originally based on religious and cultural differences, has become racialized over the centuries as Christian values were combined with racial exploitation and an ideology of white superiority. It has exposed Jews to the same harsh reality of Christian violence toward non-Christians that pagans, Roma, witches, and Muslims have experienced.

In addition, anti-Semitism has been passed on to Christians of color through Christian teachings. Religious leaders of both Eastern Orthodox and Catholic branches of Christianity, as well as most Protestant denominations, have accused the Jews of killing Jesus, using the blood of Christian children for Passover ritual, refusing to recognize the divinity of Jesus, and consorting with the devil. As Christianity was spread by Western colonialism and missionary practice, these teachings were incorporated into the beliefs of many Christians of color.

Christianity, particularly its Protestant versions, is equated with moral, virtuous, pure, hardworking, saved, civilized, decent, God-fearing, righteous, and, of course, white people. Today the majority of Christians in the world are people of color, but racism continues to be justified in Christian terms. Whiteness and Christianity remain inextricably entwined, targeting both people of color and white Jews for continued violence.

At the same time there are core Christian values of love, caring, justice, and fellowship that have inspired some Christians to work against white racism. For example, many white abolitionists were Christians inspired by religious teachings and values to work against slavery.

Yet another cluster of meanings centers on the concept of American. In the United States the concept of who is an American is often conflated with who is white. In fact, "All-American" is often used as a thinly disguised code word for white. A third-generation Swedish- or German-American child is considered an all-American kid in a way that a third-generation Japanese- or Chinese-American child is not.

In the same way, the patriotism of anyone with darker skin color is routinely questioned. Non-European citizens are continually suspected of having dual allegiances. During World War II, U.S. citizens of Japanese heritage were interned in concentration camps and U.S. citizens of German heritage were not. Even when they fought in the armed services in wartime, the loyalty of Asian-American, Latino/a, Native-American, Arab-American, and African-American soldiers was challenged.

For those of us who are white, immigrating to this country and giving up our native cultures and customs were equated with the process of becoming American. We were told that when we assimilated completely, whether it took two generations or five, we would have made it. As long as we held on to our cultures we were less American, un-American, perhaps even anti-American. On the one hand, the definition of who was white was broadened over time to include virtually all European Americans. At the same time, the boundaries keeping people of color out were firmly maintained. Immigration policies and quotas consistently favored Europeans and much of the time completely excluded people who were not considered white. Even when they have legally arrived here, non-Native-American people of color are routinely asked where they came from and told to go back home. For example, even though many Spanish-speaking citizens have roots in the Southeast, Southwest, and California going back more than three centuries, native-born Latinos are often stopped by police and immigration officials and asked to show proof of citizenship. The reluctance of many white Americans fully to accept Asian-American, Arab-American, and Latino citizens as patriotic Americans has meant that many feel "forever foreign" and wonder what it would take for them to be accepted as "all-American."

The final cluster of words centers on gender. Whiteness strongly leans toward "male" virtues and "male" values. While terms of whiteness apply to men and women, there are also significant differences in which qualities are associated with men and which with women.

Each of the particular virtues of whiteness has a gender version for men and women. White women are held to higher standards of chasteness, cleanliness, and restraint than white men. The basis of women's rationality, righteousness, and authority is supposed to lie with the white men they are related to. For example, white women are presumed to carry white authority over men and women of color. Their authority is derived from their association with white men whose backing they are assumed to have. White women hold onto whiteness by the authority and protection of white men or by their willingness to adapt to male roles and exert authority in traditionally male spheres to protect their white privilege as employers, supervisors, or teachers. They can also be cast out of the circle of white male "protection" by being rebellious or by violating racial or gender norms.

White women have been held to be the purest realization of white values. They have been locked up within this symbolism, and tremendous violence has been done in their name to "protect" them and to protect the white civilization they are supposed to embody. White women have both colluded with and resisted their role and the violence it has justified.

Whiteness is a many-faceted phenomenon, slowly and constantly shifting its emphasis, but all the time maintaining a racial hierarchy and protecting the power that accrues to white people. It is a powerful fiction with wide-ranging effects on our lives and on the lives of people of color. Although there are no natural or essential qualities or characteristics of whiteness, or of white people, it is not an easy fiction to let go of.

Words and Pictures

WHITENESS HAS BEEN A DEFINING PART OF OUR CULTURE for hundreds of years. We have embedded the idea that white people are good and people of color are bad and dangerous into our everyday language. Most words containing "black" have negative meanings (there are nearly 90 of them), while those containing "white" have positive meanings. Looking more deeply at our words and their current meanings, we can find hundreds that imply people of color and people of different cultures and ethnicities are dangerous, threatening, manipulative, dishonest, or immoral. In fact, anything foreign or alien has connotations of being not white, not pure, not American, and not Christian. We reinforce racism every time we use such language.

My goal in the following exercise is not to enforce some kind of political correctness. We are trying to understand how racism becomes embedded in our culture, our language, the way we see the world. And we are trying to develop ways of talking with each other that are respectful and that counter historical patterns of exploitation and domination.

Each of the following words and phrases contains a derogatory racial meaning in its definition or derivation, or puts a comparatively positive spin on whiteness, white people, or white culture. Can you list an alternative, racially neutral word you could use in its place?

LIST OF RACIALLY CHARGED WORDS

black deed	black hearted
blacklist	blackmail
black market	black sheep
white lie	white knight
white hope	black magic
dark (as in dark day)	Dark Ages
to gyp (from gypsy)	alien
yellow peril	red menace
to scalp	to Jew down
Jew's harp	yellow bellied
war paint	
(referring to women's makeup)	Indian giver
cotton-pickin'	Black Death

black mark	black flag
white wedding	white flag
whitewash	pure/white as snow
that's white of you	the dark side
to be in the dark	to be dim-witted
wampum	terrorist
gypsy blood	macho
barrio	manana
tribe	tribal warfare
natives	peace pipe
Indian giver	smoke signals
feather in your cap	on the warpath
banana republic	china doll
Chinese fire drill	far east
near east	middle east
dark continent	old world
third world	

What other words or phrases can you think of that are racially derogatory?

Racially demeaning usage also needs to be challenged in our visual images. When the good guys wear white hats and ride white horses and the bad guys wear black, the same racially tainted values are passed on. Advertisements, movies, and TV images rely on the development of images of darkness to convey danger and to provoke white fear.

One recent example is the Disney movie The Lion King. Throughout the movie lightness is associated with good, darkness with evil. Everything from the lightness or darkness of the manes of the lions, the colorings of different animals, the sunshine in the lions' kingdom versus the murky land of the hyenas, reflects the racial and moral hierarchy of the film. This is reinforced by the language of the characters: the lions talk in middle-class "white" English and the hyenas in a more colloquial street dialect. These racial, color-coded values can be found consistently in Disney movies going back to Sleeping Beauty and Dumbo (remember the crows) and introduce young children to our racial hierarchy in a way that seems natural and unremarkable (or at least is not remarked upon by adults).

What films have you seen where the use of images of white and black,
light and dark, or the racial casting of the heroes and villains was used
to reinforce white = good and dark = bad?

If we pay attention to the images around us we will notice the pervasive influence that racism has on our everyday lives. Racial difference and racial hierarchy, like gender hierarchy, are built into our spiritual values, our national identity, our language, our visual imagery, and our sense of who we are. So far we have looked at whiteness as a general social construct. Before going into more detail about how whiteness works in our lives, we need to look at the benefits and costs that whiteness brings to us.

White Benefits,
Middle-Class Privilege

IT IS NOT NECESSARILY A PRIVILEGE TO BE WHITE, but it certainly has its benefits.[1] That's why so many of us gave up our unique histories, primary languages, accents, distinctive dress, family names, and cultural expressions. It seemed like a small price to pay for acceptance in the circle of whiteness. Even with these sacrifices it wasn't easy to pass as white if we were Italian, Greek, Irish, Jewish, Spanish, Hungarian, or Polish. Sometimes it took generations before our families were fully accepted, and then it was usually because white society had an even greater fear of darker-skinned people.

Privileges are the economic "extras" that those of us who are middle class and wealthy gain at the expense of poor and working-class people of all races. Benefits, on the other hand, are the advantages that all white people gain at the expense of people of color regardless of economic position. Talk about racial benefits can ring false to many of us who don't have the economic privileges that we see others in this society enjoying. But though we don't have the economic privileges of those with more money, we do enjoy some of the benefits of being white.

We can generally count on police protection rather than harassment. Depending on our financial situation, we can choose where we want to live and choose neighborhoods that are safe and have decent schools. We are given more attention, respect, and status in conversations than people of color. We see people who look like us in the media, history books, news, and music in a positive (white) light. (This is truer for men than for women, truer for the rich than for the poor.) We have more recourse to and credibility within the legal system (again taking into account class and gender). Nothing that we do is qualified, limited, discredited, or acclaimed simply because of our racial background. We don't have to represent our race, and nothing we do is judged as a credit to our race or as confirmation of its shortcomings or inferiority. There are always mitigating factors, and some of us have these benefits more than others. All else being equal, it pays to be white. We will be accepted, acknowledged, and given the benefit of the doubt. Since all else is not equal, we each receive different benefits or different levels of the same benefits from being white.

These benefits start early. Most of them apply less to white girls than white boys, but they are still substantial. Others will have higher expectations for us as children, both at home and at school. We will have more money spent on our education, we will be called on more in school, we will be given more opportunity and resources to learn. We will see people like us in the textbooks. If we get into trouble, adults will expect us to be able to change and improve and therefore will discipline or penalize us less or differently than children of color.

These benefits continue today and work to the direct economic advantage of every white person in the United States. First of all, we will earn more in our lifetime than a person of color of similar qualifications. We will be paid $1.00 for every $.60 that a person of color makes. We will advance faster and more reliably as well.

There are historically derived economic benefits too. All the land in this country was taken from Native Americans. Much of the infrastructure of this country was built by slave labor, incredibly low-paid labor, or by prison labor performed by men and women of color. Much of the housecleaning, childcare, cooking, and maintenance of our society has been done by low-wage-earning women of color. Further property and material goods were appropriated by whites through the colonization of the West and Southwest throughout the 19th century, through the internment of Japanese Americans during World War II, through racial riots against people of color in the 18th, 19th, and 20th centuries, and through an ongoing legacy of legal manipulation and exploitation. Today men and women and children of color still do the hardest, lowest-paid, most dangerous work throughout the country. And we white people, again depending on our relative economic circumstances, enjoy plentiful and inexpensive food, clothing, and consumer goods because of that exploitation.

We have been taught history through a white-tinted lens that has minimized our exploitation of people of color and extolled the hardworking, courageous qualities of white people. For example, many of our foreparents gained a foothold in this country by finding work in such trades as railroads, streetcars, construction, shipbuilding, wagon and coach driving, house painting, tailoring, longshore work, bricklaying, table waiting, working in the mills, furriering, or dressmaking. These were all occupations that blacks, who had begun entering many such skilled and unskilled jobs, were either excluded from or pushed out of in the 19th century. Exclusion and discrimination, coupled with immigrant mob violence against blacks in many northern cities (such as the anti-black draft riots of 1863), meant that recent immigrants had economic opportunities that blacks did not. These gains were consolidated by explicitly racist trade union practices and policies that kept blacks in the most unskilled labor and lowest-paid work.

It is not that white Americans have not worked hard and built much. We have. But we did not start out from scratch. We went to segregated schools and universities built with public money. We received school loans, Veterans Administration (VA) loans, housing and auto loans when people of color were excluded or heavily discriminated against. We received federal jobs, military jobs, and contracts when only whites were allowed. We were accepted into apprenticeships, training programs, and unions when access for people of color was restricted or nonexistent.

Much of the rhetoric against more active policies for racial justice stem from the misconception that we are all given equal opportunities and start from a level playing field. We often don't even see the benefits we have received from racism. We claim that they are not there. I certainly did not think that I had benefited all that much from being white until I stopped to do a personal family inventory of those benefits.

White Benefits?
A Personal Assessment

WHEN I BEGAN to take careful stock of my family's history over the last 60 years, I could trace the powerful and long-lasting benefits that have accrued to me and to my family because of affirmative action programs for white people in general and white men in particular. I began to see the numerous ways that my father and I, and indirectly the women in my family, have benefited from policies that either explicitly favored or showed a preference for white men, or explicitly excluded people of color and white women from consideration altogether.

Let me begin with my father, who served overseas in a desk job in the military during World War II. When he returned he was greeted by many government programs specifically designed to reintegrate him into society and help him overcome the disadvantage of having given his time to defend the country. The three most substantial programs were the G.I. Education Bill, the Veteran Administration Housing Authority, and the Veteran Administration health care system.

The benefits from these programs were primarily (although not exclusively) available to white men. As one study concludes, "Available data illustrate clearly that throughout the post-WWII era the benefits provided by each and every component of the MWS [militarized welfare state] disproportionately accrued to whites. Jim Crow and related overt exclusionary policies ensured that African Americans' proportion of WWII veterans was significantly less than their portion of the total population. In the Korean War veterans population they were nearly as underrepresented."[1]

During most of World War II the armed services were strictly segregated. After the war, many people of color were denied veterans' benefits because they had served in jobs that were not considered eligible for such benefits. Many more were deliberately not informed about the benefits, were discouraged from applying when they inquired about them, or simply had their applications for benefits denied. The report cited above concludes "Thus, not only were far fewer blacks than whites able to participate in these programs, but those blacks who could participate received fewer benefits than their white counterparts.[2]

My father was able to continue his education on the G.I. bill (attending the nearly all-white and largely male University of Southern California). He was not unique. 2.2 million men received higher education benefits from the G.I. Bill. In fact, by 1947 half of all college students were veterans.[3]

My father applied to Merrill, Lynch, Pierce, Fenner, and Bean for a training program to become a stock broker —a program open only to white men. If he and the other white male job recruits had had to compete with white women and men and women of color, fewer than half of them would have ended up with those jobs. Being a stockbroker was just one of many lucrative professions reserved for white men. When my father completed his training and joined the firm, he was on the road to economic success with all the resources of a national financial corporation behind him.

Besides the immediate income from his wages and commissions as a stockbroker, there were other financial benefits he had privileged access to. The company had a generous pension plan. That had a significant effect later on in our family's life, but at the time it meant that my parents could save money for a car and for their children's college education because they knew their retirement was secure.

My father was also able to contribute to Social Security, which had been set up primarily to benefit white male workers during the Depression. My father (and mother and, indirectly, their children) benefited from the program when he retired. Although many people with jobs were eligible to contribute to Social Security, millions more were not eligible. President Franklin Roosevelt knew he could not pass the Social Security bill without the votes of Southern agricultural and Western mining interests that controlled key Congressional committees. These interests were unwilling to support the bill if people of color, particularly agricultural workers, were included.[4] The compromise was to create a system in which the benefits were specifically set up to exclude large numbers of people of color (and, incidentally, white women) by excluding job categories where they were concentrated, such as agricultural and domestic workers. Many hundreds of thousands more people of color were in job occupations that qualified for Social Security, but earned too little to be able to participate.[5]

My father had secured a good job and was eligible for a housing loan because of affirmative action. Of course, he still had to find a house that could be both a shelter for his family and an investment. Like most white Americans of the period, he wanted to live in a white suburban neighborhood with good schools, no crime, and rising property values. Many Americans, however, were excluded from buying houses in precisely those kinds of neighborhoods because they were not white males. People of color and unmarried women were not shown properties in those neighborhoods, government Veterans Administration (VA) and Federal Housing Authority (FHA) loan policies made it hard for them to get loans, banking red-lining policies denied them loans, and many real estate agents participated in exclusionary real estate covenants (agreements not to sell to people of color or, sometimes, Jews) – all of which gave my father and other white males with steady jobs non-competitive access to affordable and good-quality suburban housing.

For example, the FHA specifically channeled loans away from the central city and to the suburbs, and its official handbook even provided a model "restrictive covenant" to prospective white homebuyers and realtors.[6] The FHA and the VA financed more than $120 billion worth of new housing between 1934 and 1962, but less than 2 percent of this real estate was available to non-white families.[7] Some people of color did buy houses during this period but they were often restricted to living in poorer, racially segregated neighborhoods with inadequate schools, infrastructure, and community services. The initial investment that a black family made either did not grow or grew at a far less substantial rate than that of their white counterparts.

In addition, the federal home-mortgage interest tax deduction meant that the government subsidized my father's purchase of a house at the direct expense of people who did not have affirmative action programs or other means to help them buy a house and therefore were renters. This provided my father additional tens of thousands of dollars of support from the government over his adult lifetime. Researchers estimate that these affirmative action housing programs for white men have cost the current generation of African Americans alone approximately $82 billion.[8]

The results of all of this affirmative action provided my family with more than just financial benefits. For me, specifically, I was able to go to a public school with many advantages directed at me as a white male. These special programs included heavy investments in science programs, sports programs, college preparatory classes, and leadership programs. There were no students (or teachers) of color at my school, so these advantages were only for white people. And most of these programs were designed for the boys; girls were discouraged from participating or straightforwardly refused the opportunity.

Meanwhile the government was subsidizing suburban development, and my family enjoyed parks, sports facilities, new roads — an entire infrastructure that was mostly directed to the benefit of white men and their families, even though the entire population paid taxes to support it.

Of course my mother and my sister enjoyed substantial benefits from all of this white male affirmative action — as long as they stayed attached to a white male. They did not receive these benefits on their own behalf or because they were felt to deserve them. They received them because they supported and were dependent on a white man. Even though my father was verbally and emotionally abusive towards my mother, she did not contemplate leaving him, partly because she did not have the independent financial means to do so nor did she have access to the kinds of affirmative action that he did.

Conversely, not all white men could take advantage of many of these benefits. If they were too poor or too poorly educated, if they were gay or had a disability, they were seriously limited in how much of these affirmative action programs they could take part in. When it came to jobs, housing, and education, these men were not welcomed, discriminated against, screened out, or denied access to many of the benefits my father was able to enjoy.

Growing up as the son of a white male in a society in which affirmative action programs for white men were abundant in every area of community life, I viewed these benefits as natural and inevitable. I came to believe that because I lived in a democracy where equal opportunity was the law of the land, white men must be successful because they were superior to all others. They must be smarter, they must work harder, my father must be a much superior person to all the other people around him except similarly endowed white men. No one ever qualified his success to me by describing all the advantages he had been given or labeled him an affirmative action baby. The prevalent assumption was that he had worked hard for, and therefore deserved, what he had, and those who didn't have as much must not have worked hard enough.

My father made good, sound decisions in his life. He was intelligent and worked hard. He worked hard enough and was smart enough to take advantage of the social support, encouragement, and direct financial benefits that were available to him. Many white women, and men and women of color were just as smart and worked just as hard and ended up with far, far less than my father.

As a result of all of these white benefits, my father retired as a fairly wealthy and successful man at the age of 50. By that time I was already enjoying a new round of affirmative action programs.

My parents could afford private college tuition, but just in case they could not my father's company offered scholarships for white males, the sons of employees. When I looked at private colleges I received the impression that these colleges also provided affirmative action programs — most were only open to white people and had very strong preferences for white males. In fact, at that time, some of those considered the best were only open to men.

There was a more specific affirmative action program offered at many of these schools — legacy admissions. Children of alumni were given special preferences. I was told that if I wanted to go to my father's university, USC, I had an excellent chance of getting in regardless of my qualifications because my father had gone there.[9]

I ended up attending Reed College in the mid 1960s, a school that had no faculty of color, only one white woman faculty member, and barely a handful of students of color until my senior year. During my college years I was strongly encouraged in my studies and urged to go on to graduate school, which I could see was even more clearly a white male preserve.

By the late 1960s the United States was fully engaged in the Vietnam War. The U.S. government reinstated the draft and developed yet another affirmative action program for white males — especially white males from affluent families — the college draft deferment. Proportionately few students of color were attending college in those years, and large numbers of white males were. One way to keep well-off white male students from being drafted was to create a special policy that gave them preferred status in the draft. This naturally resulted in fewer young men being eligible for the draft, so the armed forces lowered its standards so it was able to recruit more men of color who had previously been rejected. The results of these policies were that in 1964, 18.8 percent of eligible whites were drafted, compared to 30.2 percent of eligible blacks. By 1967, when there was larger-scale recruitment, still only 31 percent of eligible whites were inducted into the military compared to 67 percent of eligible blacks. I was able to avoid the draft entirely because of affirmative action for white men and what Michael Eric Dyson has called the affirmative retroaction policies of the military, which targeted men of color for recruitment.[10]

If I had wanted to serve in the armed forces, I could have used my education to get a non-combat job, or I could have applied to West Point or Annapolis and been assured that, as a white man, I wouldn't have to compete with women or with most men of color for a position as an officer.

When I graduated from college I was presented with a wide variety of affirmative action options. In fact, corporate recruiters were constantly at my predominantly white college offering us job opportunities. The affirmative action pension policies of my father's company and the government Social Security system guaranteed that my father and mother had a decent and secure living through their retirement years. Many of my working-class friends had to take any job they could get to support themselves or their parents or younger siblings. Since I had no one else to support, I could pursue the career or profession of my choice.

When I eventually became involved in a long-term relationship, my partner and I could take advantage of another generation of affirmative action programs since I had such a secure financial base. For example, when we wanted to buy a house we were given preferred treatment by banks when we applied for loans in the form of less paperwork, less extensive credit checks, and the benefit of the doubt about our financial capacity to maintain a house. Our real estate agent let us know that we were preferred neighbors in desirable communities and steered us away from less desirable areas (meaning neighborhoods with higher concentrations of people of color). In addition, because of my parents' secure financial position, they could loan us money for a down payment and co-sign our loan with us.[11] At every step of the way we benefited from the preference for well-off white males and their families. Subsequently, we could take full advantage of the home-mortgage tax deduction — the same tax benefit (i.e., public subsidy) for those who can afford to buy a house that my father had used. Poor and working-class people, including a large percentage of people of color, have not had the wealth or the "creditworthiness" to buy homes and therefore don't receive the substantial financial benefits the home mortgage interest tax deduction offers.[12]

Most of the government programs and institutional policies described above were not called affirmative action programs. Programs that benefit white men never are. They were seen as race and gender neutral, even though most or all of the benefits accrued to white men. These programs were not contested as special preferences nor were the beneficiaries stigmatized as not deserving or not qualified.

Think about your grandparents and parents and where they grew up and lived as adults. What work did they do? What are some of the benefits that have accrued to your family because they were white?

WHITE BENEFITS CHECKLIST

L ook at the following benefits checklist.[13] Put a check beside any benefit that you enjoy that a person of color of your age, gender, and class probably does not. Think about what effect not having that benefit would have had on your life. (If you don't know the answer to any of these questions, do research. Ask family members. Do what you can to discover the answers.)

- ❑ My ancestors were legal immigrants to this country during a period when immigrants from Asia, South and Central America, or Africa were restricted.
- ❑ My ancestors came to this country of their own free will and have never had to relocate unwillingly once here.
- ❑ I live on land that formerly belonged to Native Americans.

❏ My family received homesteading or landstaking claims from the federal government.

❏ I or my family or relatives receive or received federal farm subsidies, farm price supports, agricultural extension assistance, or other federal benefits.

❏ I lived or live in a neighborhood that people of color were discouraged or discriminated from living in.

❏ I lived or live in a city where red-lining prevents people of color getting housing or other loans.

❏ My parents or I went to racially segregated schools.

❏ I live in a school district or metropolitan area where more money is spent on the schools that white children go to than on those that children of color attend.

❏ I live in or went to a school district where children of color are more likely to be disciplined than white children, or are more likely to be tracked into non-academic programs.

❏ I live in or went to a school district where the textbooks and other classroom materials reflected my race as normal and as heroes and builders of the United States, and where there was little mention of the contributions of people of color to our society.

❏ I was encouraged to go on to college by teachers, parents, or other advisors.

❏ I attended a publicly funded university or a heavily endowed private university or college, and/or I received student loans.

❏ I served in the military when it was still racially segregated, or achieved a rank where there were few people of color, or served in a combat situation where there were large numbers of people of color in dangerous combat positions.

❏ My ancestors were immigrants who took jobs in railroads, streetcars, construction, shipbuilding, wagon and coach driving, house painting, tailoring, longshore work, bricklaying, table waiting, working in the mills, furriering, dressmaking, or any other trade or occupation where people of color were driven out or excluded.

❏ I received job training in a program where there were few or no people of color.

❏ I have received a job, job interview, job training, or internship through personal connections of family or friends.

❏ I worked or work in a job where people of color made less for doing comparable work or did more menial jobs.

❏ I have worked in a job where people of color were hired last or fired first.

❏ I work in a job, career, or profession or in an agency or organization in which there are few people of color.

❏ I received small business loans or credits, government contracts, or government assistance in my business.

❏ My parents were able to vote in any election they wanted without worrying about poll taxes, literacy requirements, or other forms of discrimination.

❏ I can always vote for candidates who reflect my race.

❏ I live in a neighborhood that has better police protection and municipal services, and is safer than one where people of color live.

❏ The hospital and medical services close to me or which I use are better than those of most people of color in the region in which I live.

❏ I have never had to worry that clearly labeled public facilities, such as swimming pools, restrooms, restaurants, and nightspots were in fact not open to me because of my skin color.

❏ I see people who look like me in a wide variety of roles on television and in movies.

❏ My skin color needn't be a factor in where I choose to live.

❏ My skin color needn't be a factor in where I send my children to school.

❏ A substantial percentage of the clothes I wear are made by poorly paid women and children of color in this country and abroad.

❏ Most of the food I eat is grown, harvested, processed, and/or cooked by poorly paid people of color in this country and abroad.

❏ The house, office building, school, hotels and motels, or other buildings and grounds I use are cleaned or maintained by people of color.

❏ Many of the electronic goods I use, such as TVs, microwave ovens, VCRs, telephones, CD players, and computers, are made by people of color in this country and abroad.

❏ People of color have cared for me, other family members, friends, or colleagues of mine either at home or at a medical or convalescent facility.

❏ I don't need to think about race and racism every day. I can choose when and where I want to respond to racism.

What feelings come up for you when you think about the benefits that white people gain from racism? Do you feel angry or resentful? Guilty or uncomfortable? Do you want to say "Yes, but ... "?

Again, the purpose of this checklist is not to discount what we, our families, and foreparents have achieved. But we do need to question any assumptions we retain that everyone started out with equal opportunity.

You may be thinking at this point, "If I'm doing so well how come I'm barely making it?" Some of the benefits listed above are money in the bank for each and every one of us. Some of us have bigger bank accounts — much bigger. According to 1998 figures, 1 percent of the population controls about 47 percent of the net financial wealth of this country, and the top 20 percent own 91 percent.[14] In 2000, women generally made about 74 cents for every dollar that men made.

Benefits from racism are amplified or diminished by our relative privilege. People with disabilities, people with less formal education, and people who are lesbian, gay, or bisexual are generally discriminated against in major ways. All of us benefit in some ways from whiteness, but some of us have cornered the market on significant benefits from being white to the exclusion of others.

The Economic Pyramid

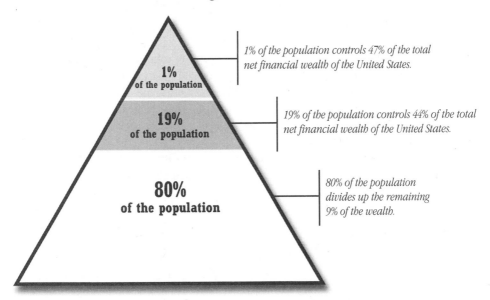

1% of the population controls 47% of the total net financial wealth of the United States.

19% of the population controls 44% of the total net financial wealth of the United States.

80% of the population divides up the remaining 9% of the wealth.

As THE ECONOMIC PYRAMID SHOWS, wealth is tremendously unequally distributed in our country.[1] People of color are preponderantly on the bottom and in the middle of the pyramid. The top of the pyramid is almost exclusively white. There are also large numbers of white people in the middle and on the bottom of the pyramid. With wealth so concentrated in the top 20 percent, most white people have much to gain from working with people of color to redistribute wealth and opportunity. However racism often keeps poor, working-, and middle-class white people from seeing common struggles with people of color. Feelings of racial solidarity keep many of us focused on our racial connections with people at the top rather than our economic connections with others lower down. The small amount of benefits we receive from being white can distract us from recognizing the amount of exploitation we receive at the hands of those at the top. For example, many poor and working-class white men fought in alliance with landowning whites in the Civil War, and substantial numbers died to protect white supremacy. However the landowning class of the South used the slave-based economy to ensure poor whites remained disenfranchised, to keep their wages low, and to dramatically curtail their civil rights.[2]

The Costs of Racism
to People of Color

THE OPPOSITE OF A BENEFIT is a disadvantage. People of color face distinct disadvantages, many of which have to do with discrimination and violence. If we were to talk about running a race for achievement and success in this country, and white people and people of color lined up side by side as a group, then every white benefit would be steps ahead of the starting line and every disadvantage would be steps backwards from the starting line before the race even began.

The disadvantages of being a person of color in the United States today include personal insults, harassment, discrimination, economic and cultural exploitation, stereotypes, and invisibility, as well as threats, intimidation, and violence. Not every person of color has experienced all the disadvantages, but they each have experienced some of them, and they each experience the vulnerability to violence that being a person of color in this country entails.

Institutional racism is discussed in detail in Parts IV, V, and VI, but the personal acts of harassment and discrimination committed directly by individual white people can also take a devastating toll.[1] People of color never know when they will be called names, be ridiculed, or have jokes and comments made to them or about them by white people they don't know. They don't know when they might hear that they should leave the country, go home, or go back to where they came from. Often these comments are made in situations where it isn't safe to confront the person who made the remark.

People of color also have to be ready to respond to teachers, employers, or supervisors who have stereotypes, prejudices, or lowered expectations about them. Many have been discouraged or prevented from pursuing academic or work goals or have been placed in lower vocational levels because of their racial identity. They have to be prepared to receive less respect, attention, or response from a doctor, police officer, court official, city official, or other professional. They are likely to be mistrusted, accused of stealing, cheating, or lying, or stopped by the police because of their racial identity. They may also experience employment or housing discrimination or know someone who has.

There are cultural costs as well. People of color see themselves portrayed in degrading, stereotypical, and fear-inducing ways on television and in the movies. They may have important religious or cultural holidays that are not recognized where they work or go to school. They have seen their religious practices, music, art, mannerisms, dress, and other customs distorted, "borrowed," ridiculed, exploited, used as mascots, or otherwise degraded by white people.

If they protest they may be verbally attacked by whites for being too sensitive, too emotional, or too angry. Or they may be told they are different from other people of their racial group. Much of what people of color do or say, or how they act in racially mixed company, is judged as representative of their race.

On top of all this they have to live with the threat of physical violence. Some are the survivors of racial violence or have close friends or family who are. People of color experience the daily toll of having to plan out how they are going to respond to racial discrimination and racist comments whenever they might occur.

In the foot race referred to above for jobs, educational opportunities, or housing, each of these disadvantages would represent a step backward from the starting line before the race even started.

Although all people of color have experienced some of the disadvantages mentioned above, other factors make a difference in how vulnerable a person of color is to the effects of racism. Economic resources help buffer some of the more egregious effects of racism. Depending upon where one lives, women and men with different racial identities are treated differently. Discrimination varies in form and ranges from mild to severe depending on one's skin color, ethnicity, level of education, location, gender, sexual orientation, physical ability, age, and how white people and white-run institutions respond to these factors.

Is it hard for you to accept that this kind of pervasive discrimination still occurs in this country? Which of the above statements is particularly hard to accept?

There is ample documentation of the frequency and the effects on people of color of each form of racism listed above. In many workshops I lead an exercise using a list of disadvantages for people of color to respond to. Those of us who are white are often surprised and disturbed by how many people of color stand when asked if they have experienced these things.

Most of us would like to think that today we have turned the tide and people of color have caught up with white people. We would like to believe (and are often told by other white people) that they enjoy the same opportunities as the rest of us. If we honestly add up the benefits of whiteness and the disadvantages of being a person of color, we can see that existing affirmative action programs don't go very far toward leveling the playing field.

The Culture of Power

WHY DON'T WHITE PEOPLE SEE WHITE BENEFITS? Whenever one group of people has benefits at the expense of another group, the privileged group creates a culture that places its members at the center and other groups at the margins. People in the in-group are accepted as the norm, so if you are in that group it can be very hard to see the benefits you receive.

Since I'm male and I live in a culture in which men have more social, political, and economic power than women, I often don't notice that women are treated differently than I am. I'm inside a male culture of power. I expect to be treated with respect, to be listened to, and to have my opinions valued. I expect to be welcomed. I expect to see people like me in positions of authority. I expect to find books and newspapers that are written by people like me, that reflect my perspective, and that show me in central roles. I don't necessarily notice that the women around me are treated less respectfully, ignored, or silenced; that they are not visible in positions of authority nor welcomed in certain spaces; and that they are charged more for a variety of goods and services and not always safe in situations where I feel perfectly comfortable.

Remember when you were a young person entering a space that reflected an adult culture of power — a classroom, store, or office where adults were in charge? What let you know that you were on adult turf, that adults were at the center of power?

Some of the things I remember are that adults were in control. They made the decisions. They might be considerate enough to ask me what I thought, but they did not have to take my concerns into account. I could be dismissed at any time, so I learned to be cautious. I could look around and see what was on the walls, what music was being played, what topics were being discussed, and most important, who made those decisions, and I knew that this was an adult culture of power.

I felt I was under scrutiny. I had to change my behavior — how I dressed, how I spoke, even my posture ("Sit up, don't slouch") – so that I would be accepted and heard. I couldn't be as smart as I was or I'd be considered a smart aleck. I had to learn the adults' code, talk about what they wanted to talk about, and find allies among them — adults who would speak up for my needs in my absence. Sometimes I had to cover up my family background and religion in order to be less at risk from adult disapproval. And if there was any disagreement or problem between an adult and myself, I had little credibility. The adult's word was almost always believed over mine.

The effects on young people of an adult culture of power are similar to the effects on people of color of a white culture of power. As an adult I rarely notice that I am surrounded by an adult culture of power, which often puts young people and their cultures at a severe disadvantage as they are judged, valued, and given credibility or not by adults on adult terms. Similarly, as a white person, when I'm driving on the freeway I am unlikely to notice that people of color are being pulled over based on skin color. Or when I am in a store I am unlikely to notice that people of color are being followed, not being served as well, or being charged more for the same items. I assume that everyone can vote as easily as I can and that everyone's vote counts. I am never asked where I am from (and this would be true even if I had stepped off the boat yesterday). In a society that proclaims equal opportunity I may not even believe that other people are being paid less than I am for the same work, or being turned away from jobs and housing because of the color of their skin. When I am in public spaces, the music played in the background, the art on the walls, the language spoken, the layout of the space, the design of the buildings are all things I might not even notice because, as a white person, I am so comfortable with them. If I did notice them I would probably consider them bland, culturally neutral items. Most of the time I am so much inside the white culture of power, it is so invisible to me, that I have to rely on people of color to point out to me what it looks like, what it feels like, and what impact it has on them.

We can learn to notice the culture of power around us. Recently I was giving a talk at a large Midwestern university and was shown to my room in the hotel run by the university's hotel management department. When I had put my suitcase down and hung up my clothes, I looked around the room. There were two pictures on the wall. One was of a university baseball team from many years ago — 22 white men wearing their team uniforms. The other picture was of a science lab class — 14 students, 13 white men and 1 white woman dressed in lab coats and working at lab benches. In total I had 35 white men and 1 white woman on the walls of my room. "This clearly tells me who's in charge at this university," I said to myself, and it would probably send a message to many people of color and white women who stayed in that room that they could expect to be excluded from the culture of power in this institution. I mentioned the composition of the pictures to the hotel management and referred to it again in my talk the next day. A few years ago I would not have "seen" these pictures in terms of race and gender. The pictures themselves, of course, are only symbolic. But as I walked around the campus, talked with various officials, and heard about the racial issues being dealt with, I could see that these symbols were part of the construction of a culture of power from which people of color were mostly excluded. I have learned that noticing how the culture of power works in any situation provides a lot of information about who has power and privilege, and who is vulnerable to discrimination and exclusion, and this institution of higher education was no exception.

The problem with a white culture of power is that it reinforces the racial hierarchy. As white people, many of us expect to have things our way, the way we are most comfortable with. We may go through life complacent in our monoculturalism, not even aware of the limits of our perspectives, the gaps in our knowledge, the inadequacy of our understanding. We remain unaware of the superior status and opportunities we have simply because we're white. Of course a white culture of power also dramatically limits the ability of people of color to participate in an event, a situation, or an organization.

They are only able to participate on our terms, at our discretion, which puts them at a big disadvantage. They often have to give up or hide much of who they are to participate in our culture. And if there are any problems it becomes very easy to identify the people of color as the source of those problems and blame or attack them rather than the problem itself.

It is important that we learn to recognize the white culture of power in our society so that we can challenge the hierarchy of power it represents and the confinement of people of color to its margins. Use the previous paragraphs and the questions below to guide you in thinking about the white culture of power around you.

ASSESSMENT:
The Culture of Power

1. Is there a white culture of power and, if so, what does it look like —
  a. In your office or area where you work?
  b. In your school or classroom?
  c. In your living room or living space?
  d. In your congregation?
  e. Where you go out to eat?
  f. Where you shop for clothes?
  g. In agencies whose services you use?

2. Some questions you might ask yourself to identify the culture of power and its appearance include:
  a. Who is in authority?
  b. How is the space designed?
  c. What is on the walls?
  d. What language(s) are used? Which are acceptable?
  e. What music and food is available?
  f. Who has credibility?
  g. Who is treated with full respect?
  h. Whose experience is valued?
  i. Whose voices are heard?
  j. Who decides?

(These questions may identity cultures of power based on gender, class, sexual orientation, religion, age, or physical ability as well as race.)

In your workplace, insofar as you have control over it,
what changes can you make to diminish the impact of the
white culture of power on people of color?

Every person in this country should enjoy the benefits that white people enjoy. Our public spaces should represent a multicultural power so that no individual or group is disadvantaged. No one should have to endure the disadvantages that people of color and others experience from being left out of the culture of power. In leveling the playing field we don't want to hold anyone back. We want to push everyone forward so that we all share the benefits.

When we talk about the unequal distribution of benefits and disadvantages, we may feel uncomfortable about being white. We did not choose our skin color. Nor are we responsible for the fact that racism exists and that we have benefited from it. We are responsible for acknowledging the reality of racism. We are accountable for the actions that the government and other institutions commit in our name and that benefit us. And we are responsible for the daily choices we make about how to live in a racist society. We are only responsible for our own part, and we each have a part.

Sometimes, to avoid accepting our part, we want to shoot the bearer of bad news. Whether the bearer is white or a person of color, we become angry at whoever points out a comment or action that is hurtful, ignorant, or abusive. We may accuse the person of being racist. (You may be having some of those feelings right now about me or about the content of this book.) This evasive reaction creates a debate about who is racist or correct or good or well-intentioned, but it does not create a debate about what to do to eliminate racism. It is probably inevitable that, when faced with the reality of the benefits and the harm of racism, we will feel defensive, guilty, ashamed, angry, powerless, frustrated, or sad. These feelings are healthy and need to be acknowledged.

Recognize and accept your feelings and any resistance you have to the information presented above. Keep reading through this book and doing the exercises. Yes, it can be hard and sometimes discouraging. For too long we have ignored or denied the realities of racism. In order to make any changes, we have to start by facing where we are and making a commitment to persevere and overcome the injustices we face.

We can support each other through the feelings. We need a safe place to talk about how it feels to be white and know about racism. It is important that we turn to other white people for this support.

Who are white people you can talk with about racism?

When people say, "We all have it hard," or "Everyone has an equal opportunity," or "People of color just want special privileges," how can you use the information in this book to respond? What might be difficult about doing so? What additional information or resources will you need to be able to do this with confidence? How might you find those resources?

You will find more information about racism in many of the resources listed in the bibliography. The exercises in this book will also help you begin to think more clearly about racism, about typical white reactions, and about how to respond to them. Many organizations and websites can provide further information about particular issues. Be creative and don't become discouraged — later sections of this book offer more advice about how to be a strong anti-racist ally to people of color.

Entitlement

HAVING BENEFITS AND BEING PART OF THE CULTURE OF POWER very often encourages a person to develop a sense of entitlement to special treatment.

A sense of entitlement is the sense that you are owed certain rights, privileges, services, or material goods because of who you are. In Western countries a person's race, class, and gender strongly influence what that person feels entitled to.

Of course, there are some entitlements that we might all agree are legally or morally good. A right to a decent job, to food and housing, to free speech, to be able to vote — we might call these basic rights or entitlements.

But I use entitlement here in a different way: as the feeling that one is entitled to certain goods or services more than others are, or that is one is entitled to be served by others because of one's class, race, and/or gender. When people grow up in a society where, despite rhetoric about equal opportunity, they are given more access to power, status, goods, and services, they will come to think that they or their group is superior and that they deserve more than others. And they may become upset, bitter, and resentful if they don't receive what they see as their due. In fact, when they are treated the same as everyone else, because of their expectations they will perceive themselves to be victimized or to be at a disadvantage, simply because they have lost the unacknowledged advantage they had. When you don't expect to have to wait your turn or wait in line or take a number, when you do have to do these things and you see other people being served ahead of you, you may feel angry at these people for being given preference. In fact, it is simply your sense of entitlement that is being challenged.

A sense of entitlement is also visible when people don't acknowledge the humanity and worth of the people who serve them. Class, race, and gender hierarchies lead us to dehumanize others who are "beneath" us, which in turn dehumanizes us and isolates us from others.

When I was younger there were times when I would walk past a receptionist and into my office without saying anything to her. There were times when I did not acknowledge or talk with the people maintaining the building in which I went to school, or the people who cleaned my dorm room in college or my motel room when I traveled. When this behavior was pointed out to me and I began to notice it in myself, I realized that I felt entitled to other people's services and assumed that they were there to take care of my needs. At first I thought that to correct this I had to become friends with people who provided services for me. However, I soon saw that what was required from me was not friendship, but acknowledgement of and respect for the people who were contributing to my well-being and the well-being of the community. I needed to see them differently, as full human beings, rather than as support staff for my life and activities.

As I noticed my sense of entitlement, I began to see other ways that it played out. I expected people in "lower" status roles to take care of my needs without my having to take responsibility for the mess I made in a room, in a building, in a park, etc. I expected that people would clean up after me, and I was upset when it wasn't done.

Anyone with wealth and status in society can develop a sense of entitlement, but I think it is particularly common in white people because of our cultural history of having Native Americans, African Americans, Asian Americans, and Latino/as working for us as slaves or as extremely low-paid workers. We generally expect people of color to take care of our physical and emotional needs. To rationalize this exploitation we also have a history of telling ourselves that we are a superior culture, far more morally and technologically advanced than any other. Because white men have been seen as the leaders of that culture, this sense of entitlement is highly developed in white men, who therefore expect to be treated better than people of color, better than white people of a "lower" class, and better than women.

How does this sense of entitlement show itself? I have noticed it in the following ways. (I have put the word white in parentheses because although I think that it is usually white people exhibiting these behaviors, with people of color or people of a lower class on the receiving end, this is not always the case. There are certainly people of color, especially those with economic means, who do these things as well.)

- (White) People cutting in line in front of others because they think their needs have a priority
- (White) Drivers cutting in front of other cars because they are in a hurry
- (White) People saying to a receptionist "Don't put me on hold!"
- (White) People walking by or ignoring people like receptionists, maintenance staff, or cleaning staff
- (White) People not noticing and appreciating the large numbers of people who spend time taking care of their needs.
- (White) People feeling okay about paying childcare workers, au pairs, gardeners, in-home attendants, and other workers less than a living wage
- (White) People feeling justified paying organizational staff much less than they themselves make
- (White) People who become impatient when they don't receive the prompt service or the attention they feel entitled to and direct abusive comments at the staff who are dealing with them
- (White) People who leave a paltry tip when they can well afford to tip generously
- (White) People quickly judging the motives and behavior of people they don't know, and holding their own group up for comparison
- (White) People expecting that their need for acknowledgment and service is more important than that of others in the room/office/classroom, etc.
- (White) People taking up more time and attention than their fair share in conversations, in classrooms, in meetings, and in public events

- (White) People speaking for others, about others, or using phrases like "we," "they," or "that group" rather than "I think," "I feel," "In my opinion"

These behaviors can all be signs of entitlement. They are the direct result of an internalized sense of the superiority of white people and white culture, which leads to racism and other forms of exploitation and discrimination. I know that I have done many of these things, but because I grew up believing in equal opportunity and equal rights, I had to develop a rationale for my behavior. I had to explain to myself why I deserved better treatment, quicker access, prompter service, and more airtime in meetings. As a result I have consciously or unconsciously told myself that I deserve this preference because:

- I am better educated
- I have more experience
- I am more rational
- My time is more valuable
- I earn more money
- Everyone will get served so I might as well be in front
- I worked hard to get to where I am
- I work harder than others
- They probably don't need as much to live on
- They are used to getting by with less
- They probably get lots of tips from other people
- I don't actually have direct contact with them so I am not responsible
- I need to get there on time.

I have only just begun to see the sense of entitlement that these excuses mask and the degree to which they are rationalizations for inequality.

ASSESSMENT:
ENTITLEMENT

1. Look over the list of entitlements above and note the ones that you have felt at times.
2. Which others would you add to the list?
3. Which of the rationalizations have you used to explain the preference you felt you deserved?
4. Has your sense of entitlement ever led you to ignore the needs or rights of others?
5. What impact does it have on others and on the community when you act out of a sense of personal entitlement?
6. How can you better notice the impact of entitlement on your family, work, and school environments?

Besides lessening our own sense of entitlement, we can also challenge the behavior of those around us. In a public place we can ask people to wait their turn. In a meeting we can ask those who have spoken not to speak again until everyone has had a turn. We can ask co-workers what impact they think it has on a receptionist when they walk past without acknowledging his or her existence. We can ask people to use "I" statements and not make generalizations about, or speak for, others. And we can challenge people's rationalizations for unequal and inadequate wages, benefits, tips, and other forms of monetary compensation.

When we challenge behavior based on a sense of entitlement in white people we counter the negative impact such behavior has on people of color. We also counter one of the costs to white people of racism, a mistaken belief that white people and their culture are superior to all others. This is only one of many costs that white people pay for the racial benefits we receive.

The Costs of Racism
to White People

W E TEND TO THINK OF RACISM as a problem for people of color and something we should be concerned about for their sake. It is true that racism is devastating to them, and if we believe in justice, equality, and equal opportunity for all, then we should be trying to end it. As we saw in the last sections, racism does produce material benefits for white people. However, the costs of racism to white people are devastating, especially to those of us without the money and power to buffer their effects. They are not the same costs as the day-to-day violence, discrimination, and harassment that people of color have to deal with. Nevertheless, they are significant costs that we have been trained to ignore, deny, or rationalize away. They are costs that other white people, particularly those with wealth, make us pay in our daily lives. It is sobering for us as white people to talk together about what it really costs to maintain such a system of division and exploitation in our society. We may even find it difficult to recognize some of the core costs of being white in our society.

For example, one of the costs of assimilating into white mainstream culture is that we are asked to leave behind the languages, foods, music, games, rituals, and expressions that our parents and/or grandparents used. We lose our own "white" cultures and histories. Sometimes this loss leads us to romanticize the richness of other cultures.

We have been given a distorted and inaccurate picture of history and politics because the truth about racism has been excluded, the contributions of people of color left out, and the role of white people cleaned up and modified. We also lose the presence and contributions of people of color to our neighborhoods, schools, and relationships. We are given a false sense of superiority, a belief that we should be in control and in authority, and that people of color should be maids, servants, gardeners and do the less valued work of our society. Our experiences are distorted, limited, and less rich the more they are exclusively or predominantly white.

There are many ways that racism affects our interpersonal relationships. We may have lost relationships with friends, family members, and co-workers to disagreements, fights, and tension over racism. At the same time we may have lost relationships with people of color because the tensions of racism make those relationships difficult to sustain.

Racism distorts our sense of danger and safety. We are taught to live in fear of people of color. We are exploited economically by the upper class and unable to fight or even see this exploitation because we are taught to scapegoat people of color. On a more personal level, many of us are brutalized by family violence and sexual assault, unable to resist it effectively because we have been taught that people of color are the real danger, never the white men we live with.

There are also spiritual costs. Many of us have lost a connection to our own spiritual traditions, and consequently have come to romanticize those of other cultures, such as Buddhism or Native American beliefs. Our moral integrity is damaged as we witness situations of discrimination and harassment and do not intervene.

Our feelings of guilt, shame, embarrassment, or inadequacy about racism and about our responses to it lower our self-esteem. Because racism makes a mockery of our ideals of democracy, justice, and equality, it leads us to be cynical and pessimistic about human integrity and about our future, producing apathy, blame, despair, self-destructive behavior, and acts of violence, especially among our young people.

Costs of Racism to White People Checklist[1]

It can be hard for us to be honest with ourselves about the costs of racism in our own lives. The following is a checklist you can use to evaluate the costs of racism to white people. Check each of the items that apply to you.

❏ I don't know exactly what my European American heritage is, what my great-grandparents' names were, or what regions or cities my ancestors are from.

❏ I grew up, lived, or live in a neighborhood, or went to school or a camp, which, as far as I knew, was exclusively white.

❏ I grew up with people of color who were servants, maids, gardeners, or babysitters in my house.

❏ I did not meet people of color in person, or socially, before I was well into my teens.

❏ I grew up in a household where I heard derogatory racial terms or racial jokes.

❏ I grew up in a family or heard as a child that people of color were to blame for violence, lack of jobs, or other problems.

❏ I have seen or heard images, in magazines, on TV or radio, on cassettes and CDs, or in movies of (check all that apply.):

- Mexicans depicted as drunk, lazy, or illiterate
- Asians depicted as exotic, cruel, or mysterious
- Asian Indians depicted as excitable or "silly"
- Arabs depicted as swarthy, ravishing, or "crazed"
- African Americans depicted as violent or criminal
- Pacific Islanders depicted as fun-loving or lazy
- American Indians depicted as drunk, savage, or "noble"
- Any character roles from non-white cultures depicted by white actors

❏ I was told not to play with children of particular other ethnicities when I was a child.

❏ I have sometimes felt that "white" culture was "wonderbread"[2] culture — empty and boring — or that another racial group had more rhythm, more athletic ability, was better at math and technology, or had more musical or artistic creativity than mine.

❏ I have felt that people of another racial group were more spiritual than white people.

❏ I have been nervous and fearful or found myself stiffening up when encountering people of color in a neutral public situation (for example, in an elevator, on the street).

❏ I have been sexually attracted to a person from another racial group because it seemed exotic, exciting, or a challenge.

❏ I was in a close friendship or relationship with a person of color, where the relationship was affected, stressed, or endangered by racism between us or from others.

❏ I am not in a close significant relationship with any people of color in my life right now.

❏ I have been in a close friendship or relationship with another white person where that relationship was damaged or lost because of a disagreement about racism.

❏ I have felt embarrassed by, separate from, superior to, or more tolerant than other white people.

❏ I have worked in a job where people of color held more menial jobs, were paid less, or were otherwise harassed or discriminated against and I did nothing about it.

❏ I have participated in an organization, work group, meeting, or event which people of color protested as racist or which I knew to be racist and did nothing about it.

❏ I have had degrading jokes, comments, or put-downs about people of color made in my presence and did not protest or challenge them.

❏ I have felt racial tension or noticed racism in a situation and was afraid to say or do anything about it.

❏ I have seen a person of color being attacked verbally or physically and did not intervene.

❏ I am concerned that there is not enough attention paid to family violence and sexual assault in my community because of the focus of police and criminal justice resources on communities of color.

❏ I am concerned that drug abuse in my white community is not taken seriously enough because disproportionate attention is on drug use in communities of color.

❑ I experience a heightened and intrusive state of surveillance and security in my neighborhood, where I shop, in my school, when I cross borders, or when I use airports because of social fears of the dangers of people of color.

❑ I have had to accept unnecessary limits on my basic civil liberties because of social fears that people of color are dangerous.

❑ I have felt angry, frustrated, tired, or weary about dealing with racism and hearing about racial affairs.

❑ I live in a community where, for whatever reason, no people of color are present, so that some of these questions don't apply.

When I use this list in an exercise with a group of white people, and every person answers "yes" to a substantial number of the questions, I can clearly see that we have all paid some of the costs of racism. Realizing what those costs are can easily make us angry. If we are not careful, we can turn that anger toward people of color, blaming them for the problems of white racism. Sometimes we say things like "If they weren't here we would not have these problems." But racism is caused by white people, by our attitudes, behaviors, practices, and institutions. How is it that white people in general can justify retaining the benefits of being white without taking responsibility for perpetuating racism? How do you justify it for yourself?

Retaining Benefits,
Avoiding Responsibility

W E HAVE SEEN HOW PEOPLE OF COLOR experience acts of violence such as rape, battery, economic discrimination, lack of police protection, police brutality, and poor health care due to racism. There is no time that a person of color is immune to harassment, discrimination, or the possibility that she or he will be attacked. Money and other accoutrements of power afford some protection, but not completely and not always.

During the first few years that I worked with men who are violent, I was continually perplexed by their inability to see the effects of their actions and by their ability to deny the violence they had done to their partners or children. I only slowly became aware of the complex set of tactics that men use to make violence against women invisible and to avoid taking responsibility for their actions. These tactics are listed below in the rough order that men employ them.

LIST OF TACTICS TO AVOID RESPONSIBILITY

Tactic	Typical Statement
Denial	"I didn't hit her."
Minimization	"It was only a slap."
Blame	"She asked for it."
Redefinition	"It was mutual combat."
Unintentionality	"Things got out of hand."
It's over now	"I'll never do it again."
It's only a few men	"Most men wouldn't hurt a woman."
Counterattack	"She controls everything."
Competing victimization	"Everybody is against men."

These tactics are part of a cycle in which these claims, particularly those of blame, counterattack, and competing victimization, lead to a justification of further violence.

As the battered women's movement tried to bring the prevalence and destructiveness of male violence to national attention, it became clear that these tactics were used not only by individual men, but were also in general use in our society to avoid naming and responding to male violence.

As I began to understand the interconnection between the systems of gender, race, class, and sexual orientation, I came to see how these tactics are used, consciously and unconsciously, by those in power to cover over the violence that is directed toward groups of people with less power. These are not gender specific tactics. They are the tactics of those who seek to retain their power and the privileges they have accrued.

Although these tactics follow a logical progression from outright denial to competing victimization, they are often used in combinations that make it confusing to argue against them. It is important to remember that although they appear as logical reasoning, all of the tactics are part of a strategy for explaining or justifying already existing injustice and violence.

We can learn to recognize and counter these tactics. I am going to use the history of the relationship between white Europeans and Native Americans to illustrate how these tactics have been (and still are) used to cover up the violence that white people commit toward people of color. There is more detailed information about that history in Part IV in the section on Native Americans. A brief summary here will have to suffice.

DENIAL

Denial is usually the first tactic employed and works very simply. The batterer says, "I didn't hit her."

European Americans say that Columbus was just looking for a trade route, the Pilgrims found a vast wilderness, and the early colonists befriended the Indians and exchanged presents with them. At this level there is absolute denial that violence occurred and therefore of any responsibility for it.

Today we are using the tactic of denial when we say, "It's a level playing field," "Discrimination is a thing of the past," or "This is a land of equal opportunity."

MINIMIZATION

If the denial doesn't hold up because of the evidence — for instance, she has a broken arm — then the violence is minimized. The batterer says, "I didn't hit her. Well, it was only a slap."

Native Americans were killed and their land taken. In response we say, "A few Indians died because they didn't have immunity to European diseases." We try to minimize the presence of the 12 to 15 million Native Americans in North America prior to 1492 and to minimize the violence we committed against them.

Today we continue to minimize racism by saying, "Personal achievement mostly depends on personal ability," "Racism isn't prevalent anymore," or (about slavery) "There were a lot of kind slave owners."

BLAME

If the minimization doesn't hold up because the victim is in the hospital, then the batterer's effort shifts to a combination of justifying the violence and blaming the victim. "She asked for it." "She should have known not to say that to me." If the discussion is more general, then men might make statements like "Women are too emotional/manipulative/backstabbing."

Similarly, we know that millions of Native Americans died, not only from intentional transmission of diseases, but also from being shot, tortured, and enslaved. Since the blame has to fall on entire societies, we make statements like "Indians were primitive." "They had not developed the technology to compete." "They were not physically able to resist the diseases, hold up under slavery [they didn't make good slaves!]." "They were naive, simple, heathens."

These justifications rely on a series of biological and psychological justifications for the abuse. Historically there have been continual attempts to "explain" away white violence against people of color as the inevitable result of genetic, biological, chemical, physiological, or psychological differences. These differences often do not exist. Where they do, they are seldom related to real differences in behavior. In any case they never justify injustice and violence. What they do is shift the focus from the perpetrators of violence to the victims, subtly blaming them for being inferior or vulnerable to violence.

When we describe what happened in terms of the agency of the person or people with power, the uses of these explanations become clearer. He hit her. He broke her arm. He put her in the hospital. Columbus invaded, killed, enslaved, and tortured the Taino/Arawak peoples. The U.S. Army at Fort Clark deliberately distributed smallpox-infected blankets to the Mandan in order to kill them.[1]

Today we blame people of color for racism by saying, "Look at the way they act," "If they weren't so angry ... ," or "They are immoral, lazy, dumb, or unambitious."

REDEFINITION

We want to hold adults responsible for what they do. Therefore we must carefully and accurately investigate what happened so that we can stop violence. If we don't look at the overall context and take differentials of power into account, we can be susceptible to the tactic of redefinition. For example, he says, "It was mutual combat." "She hit me first." "It takes two to fight."

If we can no longer claim that Columbus simply and innocently discovered America, we try to redefine that event too. The 1992 quincentennial museum exhibit in New York was called "Encounter," a word implying some level of mutuality, equality, and neutrality. In the same vein we say, "The settlers had to protect themselves from Indian attacks."

Today we redefine racism as a mutual problem by saying, "This country is just a big melting pot," "Anybody can be prejudiced," or "People of color attack white people too."

IT WAS UNINTENTIONAL

At this point in the battle the group or individual with more power, who has clearly done something that resulted in some kind of devastation, might claim that the damage was unintentional and therefore their responsibility was minimal. The batterer says things such as "I didn't intend to hit her." "I didn't mean to hit her so hard." "Things got out of hand."

First of all, claims of innocence by someone who has hurt you are always suspect. Adults are responsible for their actions and for the results of those actions. "I didn't mean to" is not an acceptable legal or moral excuse for being violent toward another person. Secondly, actual intent is often discernible from the pattern of action of the perpetrators of violence. When a man systematically tries to control a woman and then says, "I didn't mean to hit her," he is saying that he hoped to control her by non-physical means. When all else failed, he resorted to hitting. The issue is power and control. Intent is clearly evident in the entire pattern of behavior.

We have said that the near-eradication of Native Americans and their food supplies, hunting areas, and natural resources was the unintended result of European immigration. We now know that the complete elimination of Native Americans from the United States was government policy as well as part of the general, everyday discourse of white Americans (see Part IV for details).

Today we continue to claim racism is unintentional by saying, "Discrimination may happen, but most people are well intentioned." "She probably didn't mean it like that." "It was only a joke."

IT'S ALL OVER NOW

Another way to defuse responsibility is by claiming that the violence happened in the past and is no longer an issue. The batterer says, "It's over with" or "I'll never do it again." He may finally claim responsibility (often indirectly), but he asserts that things have changed. Part of his claim is that the effects of the violence are similarly in the past and shouldn't influence us anymore. The trauma, pain, mistrust, fear, disrespect, and vulnerability should just be forgotten. This discounts the seriousness of the violence, blames the survivor for not being able to let go of it and move on, and focuses on the perpetrator's words, not his actions. All we have is his promise that it won't happen again.

White people often claim that genocide, land grabbing, and exploitation are things of the past. Most of our images of Indians reinforce that belief by focusing on Native Americans who lived 100 to 300 years ago. The reality is that the effects of colonial violence are still readily apparent today. The small number of remaining Native Americans, the poor economic conditions, the alcoholism, the shattered traditions and devastated communities are the direct result of 500 years of systematic oppression.

Furthermore, the same policies are in play today as they were hundreds of years ago. The violence did not magically stop at some point. White civilization did not back off and allow the Native nations to heal and recover. Across the country, land is still being taken; treaties are still being broken; Native culture, religion, and artifacts are still being stolen and/or exploited; Native-American nations are still denied sovereignty; Native Americans are still being killed by whites with some degree of impunity; and their land, including their sacred sites, is still being exploited and laid waste on a massive scale. Some of the violence takes different forms than it did a hundred years ago. It is important that we not use those differences to claim that we are not responsible for the violence that occurs today, or to blame Native Americans for the results of violence that white people committed in the past and continue to commit today. When we are dealing with structural violence, the proof of change is structural change, not claims of innocence.

Today we claim racism is all over by saying, "Slavery was over a long time ago." "The days of land grabbing are long gone." "That was before the civil rights era." "There aren't any Indians left."

IT'S ONLY A FEW PEOPLE

If we are unable to maintain that the violence was all in the past, we may switch to another tactic to make a current situation seem isolated. We might say that it's really only a few people who are like that — it is not systemic or institutionalized. In the case of domestic violence we contend that only a few men are batterers; most men treat women well. However, if in 25 to 33 percent of all heterosexual relationships there is an incident of the man hitting the woman — 3 to 5 million such incidents a year — then we are clearly talking about a social issue, not the isolated anger of a few men.[2]

Similarly, it wasn't just rogue officers like Custer disobeying orders, or cruel, greedy men like Columbus, or a few cowboys who killed Native Americans. Slavery, genocide, and racism were built into the structure of all the institutions of our society and were everyday occurrences. We have inherited, perpetuated, and benefited from these actions. All of us are implicated.

Today we continue to use this tactic when we say, "Housing and job discrimination are the result of a few bigoted people." "The Far Right is behind the scapegoating of immigrants." "It's only neo-Nazis and Skinheads who do that sort of thing."

COUNTERATTACK AND COMPETING VICTIMIZATION

When all else fails and responsibility for the violence is inexorably falling on the shoulders of those who committed the acts themselves, there is a counterattack, an attempt to claim a reversal of the power relationships. This approach is usually combined with the final tactic, competing victimization. An individual batterer might say, "She really has all the power in our family." "If I didn't hit her she would run all over me." On a national level there are more and more claims that women batter men too, that women win child custody and men don't when divorce occurs, and that there is too much male-bashing.

To counter this tactic we must go back to what happened, who has power, and what violence is being done. Who ended up in the hospital, and who remained in control of the family resources? In the claims above we find that in about 95 percent of domestic violence cases the woman is the victim of a pattern of abuse, and in 5 percent of the cases the man is the victim.[3] The reality is not what the men would claim, nor what media reporting would have us believe.

We now have a national debate about multiculturalism which claims that people of color and women have so much power that American society itself is threatened. We are told that Native Americans and other people of color are a danger and a threat to our national unity and to our "American" way of life. White people are filing a competing claim of victimization, claiming to be the victims of multiculturalism.

We need to ask ourselves who was killed and who ended up with the land base of this country? Today, who has the jobs, who gets into the universities, who earns more pay, and who gets more media attention for their concerns, white people or people of color?

Some white people are counterattacking today by saying, "Political correctness rules the universities." "We just want our rights too." "They want special status." "They're taking away our jobs." Some of the things we say when we claim to be victims include: "White males have rights too." "I have it just as bad as anybody." "White people are under attack."

Those with power have many resources for ensuring their view of reality prevails, and they have a lot at stake in maintaining the status quo. They will employ the tactics described above to defend their interests. We must be aware of these tactics and able to counter them. When unchallenged, they can be used to justify further inequality and violence. If we keep our eyes clearly on the power and the violence, we can see that these tactics are transparent attempts to prevent placing responsibility on those who commit and benefit from acts of injustice. Our strongest tools are a critical analysis of who has power and an understanding of the patterns and consequences of present actions and policies. Parts IV, V, and VI of this book will help sharpen your analysis of racism and increase your understanding of how racism plays out in current institutional and interpersonal practices so that you can counter the tactics described above.

"Thank You for Being Angry"

A PERSON OF COLOR WHO IS ANGRY about discrimination or harassment is doing us a service. That person is pointing out something wrong, something that contradicts the ideals of equality set forth in our Declaration of Independence and Bill of Rights. He or she is bringing our attention to a problem that needs solving, a wrong that needs righting. We could convey our appreciation by saying, "Thank you, your anger has helped me see what's not right here." What keeps us from responding in this way?

Anger is a scary emotion in our society. In mainstream white culture we are taught to be polite, never to raise our voices, to be reasonable, and to keep calm. People who are demonstrative of their feelings are discounted and ridiculed. We are told by parents to obey "because I said so." We are told by bosses, religious leaders, and authorities not to challenge what they say, "or else" (or else you'll be fired, go to hell, be treated as "crazy"). When we do get angry we learn to hold it in, mutter under our breath, and go away. We are taught to turn our anger inward in self-destructive behaviors. If we are men we are taught to take out our frustrations on someone weaker and smaller than we are.

When we have seen someone expressing anger, it has often been a person with power who was abusing us or someone else physically, verbally, or emotionally. We were hurt, scared, or possibly confused. Most of us can remember a time from our youth when a parent, teacher, coach, boss, or other adult was yelling at us abusively. It may have made us afraid when those around us became angry. It may have made us afraid of our own anger.

A similar response is triggered when a person of color gets angry at us about racism. Many of us become scared, guilty, embarrassed, confused; we fear everything is falling apart and we might get hurt. If the angry person would just calm down or go away, we could get back to being happy, friendly, and relaxed.

Relationships between people of color and whites often begin as friendly and polite. We may be pleased that we know and like a person from another cultural group. We may be pleased that they like us. We are encouraged because, despite our fears, it seems that it may be possible for people from different cultures to get along together. The friendships may confirm our feelings that we are different from other white people.

But then the person of color becomes angry. Perhaps he or she is angry about something we did or said, or about a comment or action by someone else, or about racism in general. We may back off in response, fearing that the relationship is falling apart. We aren't liked anymore. We've been found out to be racist.

For a person of color, this may be a time of hope that the relationship can become more intimate and honest. The anger may be an attempt to test the depths and possibilities of the friendship. The person may be open about his or her feelings to see how safe we are, hoping that we will not desert them. Or the anger may be a more assertive attempt to break through our complacency to address some core assumptions, beliefs, or actions.

Many white people have been taught to see anger and conflict as a sign of failure. They may instead be signs that we're becoming more honest, dealing with the real differences and problems in our lives. If it is not safe enough to argue, disagree, express anger, and struggle with each other, what kind of relationship can it be?

We could say, "Thank you for pointing out the racism because I want to know whenever it is occurring," or "I appreciate your honesty. Let's see what we can do about this situation." More likely we get scared and disappear, or become defensive and counterattack. In any case, we don't focus on the root of the problem, and the racism goes unattended.

When people of color are angry about racism, it is legitimate anger. It is not their oversensitivity but our lack of sensitivity that causes this communication gap. They are vulnerable to the abuse of racism every day. They are experts on it. White society, and most of us individually, rarely notice racism.

It is the anger and actions of people of color that call our attention to the injustice of racism. Sometimes that anger comes from an individual person of color who is talking to us. At other times it is the rage of an entire community protesting, bringing legal action, or burning down buildings. Such anger and action is almost always a last resort, a desperate attempt to get our attention when all else fails.

It is tremendously draining, costly, and personally devastating for people of color to have to rage about racism. They often end up losing their friends, their livelihoods, even their lives. Rather than attacking them for their anger, we need to ask ourselves how many layers of complacency, ignorance, collusion, privilege, and misinformation have we put into place for it to take so much outrage to get our attention?

The 1965 riots in Watts, as never before, brought our attention to the ravages of racism on the African-American population living there. In 1968 a national report by the Kerner Commission warned us of the dangers of not addressing racial problems. Yet in 1992, when there were new uprisings in Los Angeles, we focused again on the anger of African Americans, on containing that anger, protecting property, and controlling the community, rather than on solving the problems that cause poverty, unemployment, crime, and high drop-out rates. As soon as the anger was contained, we turned our attention elsewhere and left the underlying problems unaddressed. The only way to break this cycle of rage is for us to seriously address the sources of the anger, the causes of the problems. And in order to do that, we need to talk about racism directly with each other.

It's Good to Talk about Racism

R ACISM IS AN EVERYDAY INFLUENCE ON OUR LIVES. It has great power partly because we don't talk about it. Talking about racism lessens its power and breaks the awful, uncomfortable silence we live within. Talking about it makes it less scary.

Talking about racism is an opportunity to learn about people of color and to reclaim our lives and true histories. We can ask questions, learn, and grow in exciting ways that have been denied us.

Racism is a gross injustice that kills people of color, damages democracy, and is linked to many of our social problems. Talking about it helps make our society safer for people of color and safer for us as well. Talking about racism keeps us from passing it on to our children. Talking about racism allows us to do something about it. Because it seems scary or confusing to talk about racism, we can forget that there are lots of good sound reasons for doing so. You can probably think of reasons I haven't mentioned. It is a useful group exercise to brainstorm the reasons it is good to talk about racism.

We actually talk about race all the time, but we do it in code. Much of our discussions about economics, military issues, neighborhood affairs, public safety and welfare, education, sports, and movies are about race. Some of the code words we use are "underclass," "welfare mothers," "inner city," "illegal aliens," "terrorist," "politically correct," "invasion," and "model minority."

These color-coded words allow white people to speak about race or about people of color, whether in the United States or abroad, without having to admit to doing so. We don't have to risk being accused of racism; we don't have to worry about being accountable for what we say. We can count on a mutual (white) understanding of the implications of the words without having to specify that this comment is about race. In order to be allies of people of color, we need to break the code of silence and subterfuge between white people in our talk about racism. Dealing with racism, then, is not just talking about it, but talking about it openly, intentionally, with the goal of ending it. It calls for us to demystify and analyze our coded interactions.

I want to look briefly at the eight words and phrases mentioned above to decipher the meanings they contain, including the ways that class perceptions are intertwined with racial ones. This analysis should help us challenge other white people when they fall back on racial code words.

"Underclass" generally stands for African Americans who are poor. It suggests they are a separate group from other poor people, a class by themselves that is "below" the rest of us. It connotes hopelessness, desperation, and violence and implies that this group lives by values that are different from ours and is therefore immune to efforts to change its economic circumstances.

This word operates, like most racially coded words, by labeling a particular group as a group of color and then creating or exaggerating its characteristics so that we feel completely separate from the group's members. The negative qualities attributed to this group then become justifications for our treatment of "them."

African Americans have no monopoly on poverty in this country. There are over twice as many poor whites as poor blacks.[1] Nor is there a special "culture of poverty" (another racially coded phrase). There are certainly significant negative effects of poverty, but well-paying jobs, access to decent housing, and schooling would mitigate most of these effects very quickly.

"Welfare mothers" is another phrase that seems to have a clear definition but actually has several layers of racial meaning. For most white people the word represents African-American women and teens who have children without being married. Our image is of a woman with several children who lives rather well for long periods of time on welfare to avoid working for a living. In turn, the expense of providing for welfare mothers is said to be draining our country financially, contributing to the national deficit, and providing a disincentive for African-American teens to work.

The reality is quite different. The majority of welfare recipients are white. Welfare recipients are primarily women who have, on the average, two children and stay on welfare for less than two years. Only 20 percent of welfare recipients stay on the rolls for five years or more. The percentage of African-American women on welfare had actually dropped in the last two decades before the welfare system was drastically restructured.[2]

Welfare does not provide more than poverty-level support. The average payment in 1996 for a family of three was $499 per month, or $5,988 per year. If you had two children, would you give up a job for this amount of money? With these meager payments, currently being cut back further, we can see why welfare accounts for less than 1 percent of the federal budget. Social Security, in contrast, accounts for about 20 percent.[3]

Both of the terms examined above come together in the phrase "inner city." This is supposedly where the underclass, including most welfare mothers, lives. The inner city is more a site in our minds than in our cities. For most white people, "inner city" means anywhere there are large concentrations of people of color, regardless of their economic status. The central sections of most large metropolitan areas in this country are highly diverse economically and racially. In many cities there are now neighborhoods of upper-income whites in gentrified houses and condos. Communities of color also have much economic diversity because of housing and lending discrimination and family ties, which keep middle-income people of color close to where they grew up. Conversely, many poor people of color live in rural or suburban areas. Poor people in general, and welfare mothers in particular, can be found throughout the country, not just in urban areas. There are white communities of people who are poor, such as in Appalachia, which have longer histories than those in "inner city" areas and as severe impediments to economic recovery. All of this racial and economic complexity is concealed and distorted by the phrase "inner city."

Each of these terms attempts to create a division between white people and African Americans, giving us the illusion they are different from us and lower than we are. The facts are distorted to make it seem as if white people and people of color live in different worlds with different cultures and moral values. In this framework it becomes easy to blame them for their poverty and to fail to see the interconnections between their lives and ours.

Following are five other racially coded words in common use.

- Illegal aliens: Deciding which immigrants are legal or illegal has always been a function of racially determined immigration policies. Throughout most of our history, Europeans have been welcomed and immigrants from Africa, Latin America, and Asia have been excluded or discouraged. Today, discussion about illegal aliens focuses on Mexicans, Central and South Americans, and Asians rather than on Canadians or Europeans. Talk of illegal aliens justifies control of Spanish-speaking communities by extending discriminatory policies to legal residents and long-standing citizens who are Spanish-speaking, while claiming that this is a legal and non-racial issue.

- Terrorist: This has become a code word for Arabs. When using it we can mask anti-Arab statements and policies while ignoring the terrorist acts of white people and of European and U.S. governments, such as the bombings of civilian areas in Panama, Bosnia, the Sudan, and Iraq.

- Politically correct: Progressives have long been challenging language that is disrespectful and abusive as well as policies and practices that are discriminatory. People opposed to racial progress use this phrase to divert attention from racism by counterattacking the people who are challenging it. The people who use these words claim to be concerned about freedom of speech while avoiding addressing issues of discrimination and harassment.

- Invasion: Why don't we say that Europeans invaded North America? Or that settlers invaded the West? Most of the time we use the word invasion to set ourselves up as victims, describing how we — white Americans — are being invaded by Japanese investment, illegal aliens, people of color moving to the suburbs, or Haitian refugees. We avoid the word when it might accurately focus attention on our role in attacking others.

- Model Minority: White people use this phrase the way we refer to well-behaved children. Implicit in the statement is a comparison to badly behaved children. Groups labeled model minority, often Asian Americans, are judged by white people to behave well (by white standards) and are contrasted with groups that are unruly, ungrateful, or unsuccessful by our standards. This label, while seemingly positive, is still a stereotype applied indiscriminately to an entire community. It overlooks the complexity of Asian-American communities, judges the entire group by white standards of obedience, docility, and accommodation, and then is used to berate African Americans or Latino/as for not being as successful.

We can only develop effective strategies for uprooting racism with a language that reflects reality. Racially coded words make it easier for us to focus on people of color as the problem and ourselves as the victims to allow us to avoid taking responsibility for ending racism. In effect, they give us excuses for not being allies to people of color.

Who Is a Victim?

S OME OF US BELIEVE that there is a certain glamour to being a victim. We may think victims get more attention, more respect, more care, or simply have some inherently virtuous quality. We may even believe that some people would prefer to be victims and take active steps to achieve victim status. And sometimes, those of us with more power or privilege or less vulnerability to violence may think that the way to redirect attention, resources, or virtue back to ourselves is to claim that we are victims too.

Men are doing this in custody cases, counter-harassment and discrimination suits, and in charges of reverse discrimination. White people do this routinely when they protest affirmative action and special programs for people of color.

There is nothing, absolutely nothing, good about being a victim. Being a victim means you were not powerful enough to protect yourself from someone else's abuse. It means your life, livelihood, or family was threatened and possibly taken away. Those of us who have been raped, robbed, battered, harassed, or discriminated against know how painful and long-lasting the effects can be. Nor is it necessarily safe to step forward and describe one's victimization. Survivors of abuse are routinely blamed, not believed, and revictimized.

Claiming to be victimized is not the same as being victimized. Who is the victim and who is the perpetrator of abuse in any particular situation depends on what actually happened and who has the power. In order to understand clearly who was victimized, we must ask the questions, "Who has the power?" and "Who did what to whom?"

Actual claims of reverse discrimination are rare, and many of them lack merit. A 1995 Labor Department draft report reviewing opinions by U.S. District Courts and Courts of Appeal found that between 1990 and 1994, of the 3,000 discrimination cases brought forward, only 100 were charges of reverse discrimination. Of the 100, only six were found to have merit. Relief was provided in those six cases.[1]

What is going on when white people claim reverse racism or claim to be victimized by people of color? Often we are being victimized, but not by people of color. We are economically exploited by white-owned corporations that move jobs overseas, leaving our communities stranded and some of us unemployed. Then we are deceived about the true cause of our exploitation and are incited to blame people of color, Jews, and recent immigrants.

An individual white person can be abused by a person of color. This is unfair and needs to be stopped and addressed. Any person can decide to hurt other people. We have seen in the sections on white benefits and the costs of racism that whites are not victims of people of color in any way similar to how people of color are hurt by racism every day, in every aspect of their lives. Charges of reverse racism are usually part of a white strategy to deny white racism and to counterattack attempts to promote racial justice.

So far we have been looking at the broad picture of whiteness and racism. In the next section we will look at some of the misunderstandings that prevent us from challenging racism effectively.

PART II

The Dynamics of Racism

The Enemy Within

ONE OF THE PRIMARY PURPOSES and effects of racism and anti-Semitism is to keep people of color and Jewish people at the center of attention while keeping white people in general and white Christians in particular at the center of power, at the top of the economic pyramid, and in control of most of the wealth. The majority of Americans have been abused, economically exploited, harassed, and discriminated against. We experience tremendous physical, economic, and emotional loss from social inequity and personal abuse. Like the proverbial thief who points off in the distance to get you to look away and then deftly picks your pocket, racism and anti-Semitism divert our attention from those who have the power to rob and hurt us. In our pain and anger we often rely on traditional scapegoats and blame anyone around who is less powerful than we are.

People of color and Jewish people have long been portrayed as economic threats to white Americans. We have heard and perhaps used phrases like "They will do anything." "They work for less." "They take away our jobs." "They are a drain on our economic system, eating up benefits." "They drive wages down and unemployment up." Or about Jewish people, "They control everything." "They are unscrupulous." "They rob us blind."

In fact, people of color and Jewish people don't make most of the economic decisions that affect our jobs and livelihoods. Closing factories and moving them to "cheaper" parts of the country or abroad, busting unions, blocking increases in the minimum wage, decreasing health care and other benefits — these are all intentional attempts by the wealthy, who are also predominantly white and Christian, to increase profits and personal gain. Corporate leaders lower wages, increase prices, and increase their salaries and corporate profits with impunity. This results in real decreases in our standard of living. Racism and anti-Semitism are major distractions in our lives, keeping our attention on people of color, Jewish people, and immigrants and diverting our attention from the people who have been getting richer while we have been getting poorer.

There has been an enormous redistribution of income toward the rich in the last 30 years in this country, while the standards of living for the rest of us have decreased. Simultaneously, our national infrastructure has deteriorated, decent health care is beyond the reach of millions (34 million at last count), our retirement funds have eroded, and our schools are falling apart. We are right to be wary of any leader who says we need to tighten our belts and sacrifice. We don't have anything to spare. The wealthy do. To rebuild our country they should be taxed at least to the level they were in 1970. We are not doing this for people of color; we are doing it for ourselves. We are being ripped off, not by welfare mothers earning $6,000 a year, but by corporate executives earning $4 million a year. Blaming immigrants, illegal workers, welfare mothers, or other poor or less powerful groups diverts our attention from the people who own the power and wealth. We hurt ourselves and make it impossible to solve our economic problems when we don't understand the nature of racism. And the rich keep getting richer.

ASSESSMENT:
WHERE DOES ECONOMIC POWER LIE?

In order to address racism effectively, we need to become better at analyzing where real power lies. Which groups are making important political and economic decisions and which are being blamed or scapegoated? The questions below can guide you in making such an analysis.

1. In your community, which corporations are the largest employers?
2. What decisions has this group made in the last few years that have affected employment levels and wages (e.g., opening or closing offices or plants, downsizing, moving production abroad, etc.)?
3. Which companies were taken over or bought out? Who took over and what happened to jobs, wages, and working conditions after the takeover?
4. How would you describe the people who own these companies? Are they mostly or exclusively white? Are they primarily Christian? Are they men? (The fact that those who gain most are well-off Christian white men does not mean that most Christian white men benefit from these actions.)
5. Which particular racial groups are being blamed for these decisions in your local area? In your state?
6. How much money have businesses put into promoting this scapegoating through political contributions, lobbying, political ads, or public campaigns?
7. How do you benefit and what do you lose from those actions?

Racism makes us vulnerable to economic exploitation and violence from other white people. The relationship between these issues is complex, and I have only sketched the briefest outline here. Even so, it should be clear that effective action against racism makes the white community stronger, safer, and more effective in fighting for economic justice and safety for all. It also allows us to join as allies with people of color in the struggle for economic justice and democracy. Most white people have as much to gain as people of color from the struggle to redistribute wealth to poor, working-, and middle-class people. Most white people have as much to gain as people of color from making our families and communities safer. Rather than letting racism divide us, we need to work together to address these issues.

Fear and Danger

MANY OF US IN THE UNITED STATES TODAY ARE AFRAID. We worry about crime, drugs, our children's future, and our own security. Our fear is a result of many economic, social, political, and personal factors. It is also linked to violence in news media, TV, and the movies.

In a society where we are constantly presented with tales of danger and violence and told how vulnerable we are, it is not surprising that most of us are fearful. Racism produces a fear-based society in which no one feels safe. However being afraid is not the same as being in danger.

For example, white people often fear people of color, and most people of color fear white people. White people are not usually in danger from people of color. People of color are in danger of individual acts of discrimination, hate crimes, and police brutality at the hands of white people, as well as of institutional practices that kill people due to lack of health care, lack of police protection, and unequal legal prosecution. White people are rarely killed, harassed, or discriminated against by people of color.

To understand whiteness, we need to look at how fear of people of color is manufactured and used to justify repression and exploitation of communities of color.

Have you ever been in your car when a person of color drove past? Did you reach over to lock your car door? When a man of color walks by do you touch your wallet or purse or hold it tighter? Have you ever closed a window, pulled a blind, or locked a door when you saw a person of color in your neighborhood?

Have you ever had an adult or young person of color in your house and wondered, ever so briefly, if valuables were out? Have you ever seen a person of color with quality clothes, an expensive car, or other valuable items and wondered how they got the money to buy them?

I have done all of these things. I was taught to fear people of color. I was told that they were dangerous and that they would steal, cheat, or otherwise grab whatever I had.

Many of these motions were practically involuntary. My hand was on my wallet before I realized it. Of course I tried to turn the gesture into a casual motion so it wouldn't be apparent what I had done. For many years I did not realize I was doing this. Then I listened to people of color, particularly African-American men (who we have been trained to fear the most), describe how white people were always afraid of them. I began to notice my own and other people's gestures — the tensing, the guardedness, the suspicion, the watchfulness.

White fear is primarily fear of men of color. (We also have fears about women of color, but they are not as visceral or pervasive.) For example, I grew up playing cowboys and Indians, always wanting to be the brave cowboy who protected the innocent homesteaders and settlers from the vicious (male) Indians ready to sweep down and destroy white outposts. I was learning that as a man I would have to protect (white) womanhood and (white) civilization.

Growing up in Los Angeles in the 1950s and early 1960s, I heard repeated stories about the masses of Mexican and Central-American people pushing against our borders, pressing to get in, to overwhelm us. I remember a discussion with my parents in which I said I didn't think I ever wanted to have children because there were already so many people in the world. My parents tried to convince me that it was important that I have children because I was smart and educated and we needed more of our kind. I understood "our kind" to be white. Again I was getting the message that we had to defend ourselves, reproduce ourselves, and protect what was ours because we were under attack.

Many of the racial images that we hear today such as "illegal alien," "border patrol," "drug wars," and "the invasion of Japanese capital" are based on images of protection, defense, borders, and danger. Many of us feel besieged. We talk as if we are under attack in many areas of our lives where we used to feel safe. We complain that we can't say what we want with impunity, we can't go where we want. We notice that people of color in the United States and abroad are demanding a more equitable distribution of the world's wealth. To counter these attacks on white power and to divert attention from the benefits we have accrued, we have created a fear of potential retaliatory violence from people of color.

This pattern has a long history. Individual white settlers who took Native-American lands feared retaliation. But many white people lived in cities and were not worried about Indian attack. White settlers, in conjunction with the U.S. government, which wanted to "open up" Native-American land, had to convince the public that Native Americans were dangerous and needed to be exterminated. A campaign, using books, pictures, and the media, created images of Indians as primitive, cruel savages who wanted to kill white men and rape white women. This campaign made it easier to justify the appropriation of Native-American lands and the killing or removal of Native Americans themselves. In the process, generations of us learned to fear Indians. Many children growing up today still do, even though there are only about 3 million Native Americans in all of the United States and Canada.[1] They are the ones who have suffered the effects of racial violence.

Over the course of 240 years of slavery, white slave owners created the illusion that African Americans were dangerous to justify the harshness of their treatment and to scare other white people into supporting their subjugation. White people feared African Americans even though they were so thoroughly dominated and brutalized as to offer little threat to whites. Slaves were brutalized publicly and routinely. Some fought back, but most were more interested in escaping than in retaliation.

This pattern of white fear and violence continues today. We still see selected news coverage that presents African-American men as the embodiment of danger itself. It is difficult for any white American not to have an immediate feeling of fear in the presence of an African-American male. This fear, in turn, has justified massive and continuous control of the African-American community through the schools, police, legal system, jails, prisons, and the military. This control starts in pre-school or elementary school. It limits educational opportunities, jobs, skills, and access to health care. It is enforced by police brutality and various forms of discrimination. These conditions produce stress, despair, and desperation for African-American young men, leading to their killing each other and themselves at high rates, living six years less than white men on the average. White violence leads to fear, which is used to justify further white violence. African-American men, not white people, are the victims of this cycle of violence.

Similarly Arabs and Arab Americans are portrayed as fanatical terrorists who will stop at nothing to kill us. After the bombing of the Oklahoma City Federal Building, law enforcement officials and the media immediately began talking about the possibility of Arab terrorists being involved. On the one hand, Arab Americans are victims of discrimination, stereotyping, and hate crimes. On the other hand, the U.S. government continues to bomb Iraq and to maintain a blockade that prevents food and medical supplies from being shipped to that country, leading to the deaths of thousands of Iraqi children every month. Within recent years the United States has also bombed Libya, the Sudan, and Afghanistan and American arms are being used by Israelis to subjugate the Palestinians. While the fear between Arabs, Arab Americans, and white Americans may be mutual, white Americans are in little danger. But the fear is used to justify the scapegoating, abuse and violence directed against Arabs and Arab Americans. The misrepresentation and demonization is so extreme that I cannot remember the last time I saw a positive image of an Arab or Arab American in the media.

Many times we use stories to justify the fear that we feel toward people of color. We might introduce them by such phrases as "I was attacked once by ... " "I don't want to sound prejudiced, but I know someone who had a bad experience with ... " or "It's unfortunate, but my one negative experience was ... " We then use these single examples to reinforce a stereotype about a whole category of people and to prove the legitimacy of our fear of them.

Is there a story that you use to justify your fears of people of color?
What are stories that you've heard other white people use?

These shared stories can be a way to strengthen white solidarity by implying that we share a common danger. They reinforce our desire to be with white people and to avoid people of color. They also raise the stakes if we challenge racism, because to do so seems to threaten our own security. How can we challenge other whites when we may need them in case of an attack?

Sometimes, when I realize the extent of the stereotypes I have learned and act from, I want to disavow the fear altogether and convince myself that there is nothing to be afraid of. Or, to counter the stereotype, I try to assume that all men of color are safe and all white men are dangerous. Yet I know that I am foolish if I simply reverse the stereotypes. In a society in which many people are dangerous and violence is a threat, we need to evaluate the danger from each person we're with. Any preconceived notions of danger or safety based on skin color are dysfunctional — they can actually increase our danger and make us less able to protect ourselves. For example, even as white women have moved to the suburbs, put locks on their doors and windows, and avoided urban streets at night, they have remained vulnerable to robbery and assault from white male friends, lovers, neighbors, and co-workers.

This example shows how racism turns our attention away from real exploitation and danger as we create myths about family violence and sexual assault. We are taught that men of color and men from other cultures are dangerous. We have stereotypes about rapists being dark (i.e., black) strangers in alleys, about Asian men being devious and dishonest, about Latinos being physically and sexually dangerous. Racism has produced myths about every group of non-white, non-mainstream men being dangerous to white women and children.

The reality is that approximately 80 percent of sexual violence is committed within the same racial group by heterosexual men who know their victim.[2] If we and our children are beaten up, sexually assaulted, or abused it is most likely to be by heterosexual white men, but we continue to believe that we need to protect ourselves from men who are different. We justify public policies that disproportionately lock up men of color, primarily Latino and African-American men, but these changes do not make it appreciably safer for us. Because we are led to believe that we need "our" men to protect us from men "out there," we are slow to recognize the violence of men in our family and dating relationships.

Was there ever a time when you heard about violence that a white man committed and said to yourself, "I never would have imagined that so-and-so could have done something like that"?

We are often awarded a presumption of innocence if we are white. This works to our benefit when we are stopped by the police, shopping in a store, walking down the street, or renting equipment such as cars, tools, or movies. Other white people assume we are safe until we are proven dangerous.

Have you ever been surprised that an African-American or Latino man could commit a particular act of violence?

We expect men of color to be dangerous. When Susan Smith killed her two children, she claimed that an African-American man had kidnapped them. When Charles Stuart killed his pregnant wife in Boston, he stabbed himself and claimed an African-American man had attacked them. When the federal building in Oklahoma City was bombed, most people immediately suspected Arab men as the culprits. Many of us accepted these statements without question because they fit with our expectations. In each situation the search for the guilty white man was temporarily diverted toward men of color.

We fear people of color in great disproportion to any danger they may hold for us. We trust white men in spite of the danger some of them pose. These fears become expectations that influence whom we trust and how we evaluate danger. Our personal vigilance is often increased when people of color are present and relaxed when only white people are around.

These expectations translate into feeling uneasy whenever there are significant numbers of people of color around us. Statistics show that whites are most comfortable in interracial situations where people of color constitute a small percentage of the population. When the percentage rises to 15 or 20, white people often begin to feel that "they" are dominating or are unfairly represented. When people of color constitute 20 or 25 percent of the population, white people begin to describe people of color as the majority or as having taken over.

This tendency to fear people of color also leads white people to exaggerate wildly how many there actually are in our society. According to a Gallup Poll, the average American thinks that 21 percent of all Americans are Hispanic, when the real number is 8 percent [now 10 percent]; that 32 percent of all Americans are black when the real figure is 12; and that 18 percent of all Americans are Jewish when the real figure is 3 percent. Not even counting Asian Americans, Arab Americans, and Native Americans, many Americans think that people of color constitute a large majority of the American population when the actual total figure is 26.4 percent, of which 22 percent is black and Latino/a; 3.5 percent is Asian and Pacific Island; and 0.7 percent is Native American. Jews constitute another 3 percent of the population in the United States, bringing the total non-white, non-Christian population to less than 30 percent.[3]

As white people we can start by acknowledging the violence we have done to people of color throughout our history. We must understand how we have demonized them to justify that violence. Our fear of violence to ourselves is related to the violence we have done and continue to do to people of color. Therefore one way to lower our fear is to acknowledge and reduce our own violence.

Jewish people have likewise been portrayed as dangerous — economically dangerous. Stereotypes that Jews own the banks and are crafty, unscrupulous, and untrustworthy contribute to such anti-Semitic fears. Age-old Christian teachings that Jews killed Christ, and false documents like the "Protocols of the Elders of Zion," are additional currents in this river of fear.

Jewish people in the United States have been subject to verbal and physical attack, bombings, desecration of cemeteries, intimidation, and murder by white Christians. Jews have not attacked Christians for being Christian. Again we can see that although the fear is mutual, Jewish people are in some danger from Christians whereas Christians are in no danger of being attacked by Jews.

Economically, most banks, major corporations, and other institutions that make the financial decisions about jobs, pensions, and health care are owned by Christians. They make the decisions to close down factories in our cities, steal from the government, move jobs overseas, create unsafe working conditions, bust unions, and dump cancer-producing toxins into our rivers and lakes. Christian fear works, like all racial fear, to divert people from the source of danger — people inside the mainstream who hold political, economic, and social power. Jews are blamed for economic problems for which they are not responsible, and they become the targets of further anti-Semitic violence.

All Jews experience the stereotypes and fear that white Christians and other non-Jews have of them. Jewish people know what it's like to be attacked because others have been trained to fear you. Jews who are white are feared and are taught to fear people of color.

Many white Jewish concerns about violence focus on danger from African Americans, even though most anti-Semitic violence is committed by white Christians. Anti-Semitism should be challenged wherever it occurs, but primary energy should always go to defend against those with most power to do harm. Meanwhile, Jews of color are attacked from all sides, by white Christians and Jews, and by Christian people of color.

The focus by white Jews on external danger from people of color also helps conceal the significant levels of domestic violence, sexual assault, and child abuse within the Jewish community. When Jewish family violence is denied and minimized, and Jewish family values are held up as better than those of African Americans, then racism is perpetuated. This racism justifies violence against African Americans while obscuring violence against Jewish women and children.

All of us who are white need to recognize just how deeply we have been trained to fear and distrust people of color and how much that fear guides our behavior, because that fear is easily manipulated by politicians, the media, or corporate leaders. Christians need to acknowledge their fear and distrust of Jews for the same reasons. Our fear often leads us to misconstrue our own best political interests because our racial fear overrides our best thinking.

Our fear of African Americans is such that a single person can come to represent the danger we feel from an entire community. Since the beginning of the civil rights movement, many different individuals have been held up by politicians and the media to represent the "danger" of African Americans to white people. Malcolm X, Huey Newton, Eldridge Cleaver, Martin Luther King, Jr., Angela Davis, "Willie" Horton, Ice Cube, Jesse Jackson, and Sister Souljah have all been used to symbolize danger and to manipulate white people's fears. As our fears of people of color increase, we are more easily deceived by white leaders who have an aura of trustworthiness simply because they are white.

The Geography of Fear

T HERE IS ALSO A GEOGRAPHY OF FEAR. We fear being in certain places and certain kinds of spaces. The geography of fear is built on perceptions of race, class, and gender. For example, we are all taught to fear violence in the inner city. Here "inner city" is a code word for "where African Americans and Latino/as live."

There is certainly more street crime in low-income neighborhoods. There is not necessarily more family violence, drugs, or economic crime. In any case, most of the crime and violence in low-income neighborhoods is not racially motivated. People of color are the most common targets of crime by people of color, and white people are the most common targets of crime by white people. We tend to think that we are particularly vulnerable in inner-city neighborhoods because of the racism of people of color. There is no evidence that this is so.

There are many areas in which straight white males feel fairly safe. They can roam the countryside and the suburbs and generally are not worried they'll be attacked. They can be alone in the woods, at the beach, or in the hills and not worry about being assaulted. White women alone are much less safe than white men alone, but white women with other women or with a man are not usually attacked. White lesbians, gay men, and bisexuals are less safe than heterosexual white people.

In what areas do you routinely feel safe? Why? How safe do you think people of color feel in those areas you feel safest in?

Except in neighborhoods that are predominantly populated by people of their own ethnic group — where they are still vulnerable to higher levels of street crime and the threat of police brutality — people of color are not safe alone or in groups. In other areas they are verbally attacked; harassed by police; "mistaken" for gardeners, servants, or delivery people; and shunned or followed by shopkeepers. They are questioned and mistrusted by whites, who assume that their own neighborhoods are inner-city ghettos. This is true even for people of color who live in suburban or rural areas. Women of color cannot assume they are safe and free from harassment and violence anywhere.

To sum up, there is nowhere that men and women of color are safe from crime, violence, or white racism. Whites, on the other hand, are seldom vulnerable to violence from people of color and can generally avoid high crime areas unless forced by economic circumstances to live or work in one. As white people we have been trained to see danger in the very presence of people of color. This will not change until we alter the negative images and portrayals of people of color in our society and learn to value positively their presence and participation.

Exotic and Erotic

Have you ever imagined it was exotic, erotic, or exciting to have sexual relations with a person of color or with a Jewish person? Have you ever been in a dating or longer-term relationship with a person of color or Jewish person where these elements were present?

ANOTHER WAY THAT RACISM AND ANTI-SEMITISM OVERLAP is in the eroticization of difference. White people's images of people of color and of Jewish people make them seem not only dangerous, but also exotic and erotic. Men of color, including Irish men and men from southern and eastern Europe at times when they were not considered to be white, and Jewish men, have been portrayed as wild, bestial, aggressive sexual beings with little or no restraint and insatiable appetites for white (Christian) women. White men have been trained to see men of color and Jewish men as sexual rivals and are supposed to protect white women from them.

Similarly, women of color and Jewish women are portrayed as more passionate and sensual than white women. Through economic systems of exploitation, women of color and sometimes Jewish women have been available to white men as slaves, domestic help, factory workers, childcare workers, prostitutes, and sex industry workers. White men have been able to sexually exploit women and then justify their abuse by citing the sexual nature of their victims. In fact, sexual exploitation of women who are vulnerable says more about the sexual nature of white men than of anyone else.

Traditional Christian sexuality permits only a narrow range of sexual behavior within a heterosexual marriage relationship focused on childbearing. Christian concepts of virtue and sin, good and evil are heavily intertwined with those limitations. White European society proscribed all practices that were not sanctioned by the church, labeled them as bad, and projected them first onto Jews and later onto people of color. Everything that was unwanted — such as lust; passion; non-procreative sex; female assertion, sensuality, and pleasure; titillation; and non-marital sex — was labeled sinful, evil, and not truly white. White Christian sexuality was portrayed as pure, chaste, procreative, and restrained, at least in its ideal form.

White people experience all the varieties of sexual desire that any other group does. Whenever there has been dissent or rebellion within the white community, one way those with most power try to maintain control is to impose white, Christian, sexual standards on those who are too independent. White women and poor and working-class people, as well as lesbian, gay, and bisexual whites, have always been persecuted for sexual trespass even when, as is usually the case, the real issue is independence and challenge to authority.

White people have eroticized African Americans more than any other group. Black has been seen as the opposite of white, and therefore the sexuality of black people has been perceived as directly opposite the "chaste and controlled" sexuality of white people. In addition, African-American slaves were seen as sexual commodities, particularly after the slave trade was declared illegal. The ability of African-American women to reproduce and increase the slave owner's capital was nearly as important as their ability to work. Many came to be defined by the sexual role that they were forced to play in the plantation economy. White people have since used these sexual projections to justify violence — most prominently, but certainly not exclusively, in the form of lynchings, castrations, and rape.

In most discussions of masculinity we underestimate the role that racism plays. Training in white, primarily male, violence against people of color starts early. Many young men are challenged by other white men to prove they are real (white) men by participating in physical, sexual, or verbal abuse of men of color and Jewish men. White male bonding at work, at school, or in the extended family includes significant levels of racism toward men of color ranging from sitting around joking about men of color (or Jews or lesbians or gays of all colors), to bonding as a team against an opposing team of color, to participating in an attack upon a specific person of color, to joining an explicit white supremacist group. Not participating in such "rites of passage" makes white men vulnerable to physical and sexual aggression from their white peers. Those who challenge racist (or sexist or homophobic) jokes or comments risk derision, attack, and exclusion. Members of some sports teams, gangs, hate groups, and clubs have beaten up members who threatened group solidarity.

White men also bond with others and "prove" their heterosexuality by verbally and sexually assaulting women of color and Jewish women. Having sex with a woman of color or a Jewish woman is often seen as the mark of the most (hetero)sexually experienced white men because these women are stereotyped as the most erotic, wild, and dangerous women available. (There are other, less sexual, stereotypes of women of color and Jewish women as well.) The ability to have sex with, but not to be undermined or entrapped by, "exotic" and "dangerous" women is a sign of success and reaffirms that a man is in control, is one of the (white Christian) boys, and that he knows the sexual and racial order.

When a young man is pushed by white male peers to assault or harass women or men of color, a lot is riding on the line — and he knows it. It is hard for most young men to avoid such pressure because the threat of violence from other white men is real and immediate. We can help young men refuse to participate by giving them tools for resisting male gender role training and for creating different options. These options can make the entire community safer.[1]

The eroticization of people of color has been used to justify the control of entire communities. After the Civil War, when African Americans were no longer protected or valued as slaves, lynching became one form of repression against the African-American community. Before that time there were almost no reports of African-American men raping white women. During the first years that lynching was prevalent, rape was not a frequent justification. Lynching was used as a method to control an unruly, potentially dangerous ex-slave population, a way to terrorize them into not using their newly won freedom.

After the Reconstruction period, African Americans were no longer a credible threat to white people because of the dismantling of post-Civil War rights and the beginning of Jim Crow segregation. Lynching began to be justified by appeals to white people's fear of sexual aggression by African American men. Even then, rape of white women was only alleged in about a third of the situations where men were lynched. It was only after many more years that lynching became almost exclusively justified by claims of African American men's sexual aggression toward white women.[2] Throughout all those years, in all the thousands of lynchings that took place, white people committed eroticized violence against African-American men by castrating, mutilating, and lynching them in public, to the entertainment of the white community.

The disproportionate criminalization and punishment of African-American men for violence against women continues today. It is evident in media images of African-American men as sexual predators and in the disproportionate arrest, sentencing, and incarceration of African-American men for sexual offenses. These patterns are directly tied to attacks on the sexual explicitness of African-American musical lyrics, when similarly sexist language from white groups goes unnoticed.

White women don't have the same social, political, or economic power as white men. They haven't been as influential in setting up people of color as either dangerous or erotic. Nonetheless, they have gained some of the benefits of racism and many have colluded in maintaining these stereotypes. White women have also been vocal critics of them, at least partly because of the stereotypes' negative effect on the power and position of white women themselves.

White women are taught that men of color are highly sexual beings whose very gaze will assault them. They are told that they "need" white men who are strong, aggressive, and armed to protect them from this menace. These beliefs have directed the attention of white women to danger outside of their families, diminishing their ability to defend themselves against rape, domestic violence, incest, and murder committed by white men closer to home.

White women are also taught to regard women of color as competitors — temptresses and seducers of white men. This training adds to the general images of danger associated with people of color and makes it difficult for white women to regard women of color as allies. The solidarity between women needed in the struggle against sexism is undermined by racial violence and by white women's fear and mistrust.

At times, white women's groups have supported attacks against the African-American community in the name of women's safety. In the late 19th century the National American Woman's Suffrage Association refused to take a stand against lynching and mob violence and asked Frederick Douglass, a black man and a staunch NAWSA supporter, not to come to meetings in the South because they did not want to jeopardize white southern support. The association also did not support the organizing of chapters by black women for the same reason. Eventually the arguments within the organization became more explicitly racist. White women argued that if they could vote, it would buttress the supremacy of the white race against the demands of black people, Indians, and newly colonized Spanish-speaking people.[3]

More recently, in the 1970s, 1980s, and 1990s, the rape prevention and domestic violence prevention movements have called for stronger police and criminal justice response to violence against women. However, of the 455 men executed between 1930 and 1967 on the basis of rape convictions, 405 were black.[4] At times these movements have inadvertently contributed to the targeting of African American men insofar as they have not taken into account the racial bias in the legal system and the use of rape and assault charges against men of color as a means of social control.[5]

At other times white women's groups have been strong, if belated, allies to African-American women and men in the fight against lynching, mob violence, and false accusations of rape. The Association of Southern Women for the Prevention of Lynching did important and effective work through petition drives, letters, and demonstrations. It was formed in 1930, after decades of pioneering work by black women organizers such as Ida B. Wells, Mary Church Terrell, and Mary Talbert.[6]

Similarly, there have always been some strong and vocal white women in the rape prevention and domestic violence prevention movements working for complete inclusion of women of color and their needs, paying attention to racism, supporting women of color in leadership positions, reexamining police and criminal justice responses to violence against women, and developing an analysis that includes an understanding of race and gender.[7]

The issues of race and gender intersect in African-American women's lives. This crucial perspective has given them the ability to challenge the limited focus of much political work in this country. For example, in the mid-19th century, Sojourner Truth challenged the suffrage movement to take racism and racial violence seriously with statements such as "If you bait the suffrage-hook with a woman, you will certainly catch a black man."[8] Ida B. Wells continued that tradition in conversations with Susan B. Anthony and statements to suffrage organizations at the end of the century.

African-American women have long provided challenges to men and white women in political leadership to sort out the myths and the realities of race- and gender-based violence. Sojourner Truth, Ida B. Wells, Josephine St. Pierre Ruffin, Mary Church Terrell, Lucy Parsons, Claudia Jones, and Frances E.W. Harper were some of the African-American women leaders in the abolition, anti-lynching, and women's suffrage movements who understood the connections between gender and racial violence and provided constant challenges to the exclusive focus of each of these three movements.

Today some of the most nuanced analyses of the intersections of race, gender, and class issues are in the writings of women of color and Jewish women. Not only from African-American women such as Angela Davis, Paula Giddings, Patricia Hill Collins, Beth Richie, Joy James, and bell hooks, but also women from other cultural backgrounds including Cherrie Moraga, Gloria Anzaldua, Andrea Dworkin, Janice Mirikitani, Beth Brant, Chrystos, Trinh T. Minh-ha, Paula Gunn Allen, Melanie Kaye-Kantrowitz, Pat Mora, Winona LaDuke, M. Annette Jaimes, and Huanani-Kay Trask.

The dictates of racism, anti-Semitism, and sexism teach us to devalue the experience of women of color and Jewish women and give them little credibility, but we would do well to support their leadership and draw on their experience and insight so that our tactics in fighting against one "ism" don't lose us the war against another.

The previous section on fear and danger and this section on sexuality are even more intertwined than I have discussed so far. Because of the merging of sex and violence with racism in our society, images of people of color, which are seen as dangerous, are also seen as erotic. Because of prohibitions about sexual expression, erotic projections onto people of color make them seem more dangerous. This added danger then makes them seem more erotic.

One way that people can challenge the authority of a society is to violate its sexual taboos. For young white people the taboos against interracial or interfaith sexual relationships, coupled with the eroticized stereotypes of people of color and Jews, makes having such relationships a gesture of rebellion against white norms. A sexual relationship with a person outside the norm becomes attractive — both arousing and dangerous — because of the characteristics projected onto people of color. Given the stereotypes and symbolism involved, any person of color or Jewish person — male or female, lesbian, gay, or heterosexual — will provide some "risk." Because white people have characterized blacks as the most dangerous and sexually "other," they represent the most risk.

Not all interracial relationships are based on projections, stereotypes, and symbolic value, but these facets are part of all white people's conceptual baggage and do affect our actual relationships with people of color. Some white people have used people of color to make their sexual lives more exotic, erotic, or thrilling or to defy white (and parental) standards. There are residues of these erotic elements in our relationships with people of color even when we are not sexually involved with them. These residues interfere with our ability to treat them as valued and respected people.

This sense of the erotic and dangerous nature of people of color gets attached not only to their bodies, but also to their music, art, and other elements of their culture. Music like rock and roll and rap have been sources of intergenerational conflict in white families, connected with issues of sexuality. National discussion about gender and family issues such as rape, domestic violence, teenage sexuality, sexual harassment, marital infidelity, interracial dating, and miscegenation often have explicit and implicit racial references built into them.

I have used our beliefs about African Americans as examples in this section. Asian Americans, Latino/as, Native Americans, and Jews are each eroticized somewhat differently. Despite the tremendous differences in these other cultures, however, there are remarkable similarities in white sexual beliefs and stereotypes about them because the hidden but central focus is whiteness and white sexuality, much of it derived from Christian teachings.

The sexuality we project onto people of color tells us a great deal about white concepts of virtue and immorality, good and evil, but little about white practice, and nothing at all about people of color. As long as we don't examine the sexual ideology of (Christian) whiteness, we will continue to be directed by our sexual fears and fantasies, leading us to commit injustice in the name of virtue.

The Myth of the Happy Family

B ESIDES OUR UNDERSTANDING OF SEXUALITY, we have certain understandings of what a family is and what family relationships should be like. These too are affected by racism.

What did you learn as a child about what a family was?

What did your parents convey? What did you learn from TV and movies?

The word "family" probably brings up images of people caring about each other, doing their part to make the whole group work well for everyone. Even when our own family was violent or otherwise dysfunctional, we may have felt that everyone else's was close to the norm. We talk about the human family, our extended family, a network of people or friends who feel like family, and our biological/created family.

The word "family" conveys good feelings, although we know that many families lack these qualities. It is perhaps easier today than in the past to acknowledge the existence of incest, domestic violence, marital rape, alcoholism or other drug abuse, and neglect. But it remains hard to see that some families "work" because they provide caring, support, and nurturing for some members at the expense of others.

Because of violence and unequal power we are not equally privileged or equally safe within our families. Those of us who are safe, cared for, and thriving, or at least not vulnerable to physical or sexual violence (often men and/or adults), can pretend that everything is all right because it is all right for us. It could be better, but from our perspective it certainly could be worse. Other people may tell us that it looks good from the outside as well, reinforcing our sense of the rightness of things. All too often what is working for us is not working for other family members. We have a sense of being part of a happy family, but some members of the family may be being abused.

The myth of the happy family is common in our culture. Many slave owners in the South shared this myth. Men in families where there is incest and domestic violence often share this myth. Communities where there are people who are poor or homeless share this myth. Most white people share this myth.

The myth allows us to attack anyone who speaks out. When someone says, "This arrangement is not working for me because I am being abused, discriminated against, having my land taken away, being denied my freedom," we immediately respond by saying, "You are creating a problem with your complaints. Everything was okay until you brought this up. After all, we're really one big happy family and we care about each other."

The idea of family usually implies that if everyone plays their part, then the whole unit works. Each person has a role, with a set of responsibilities and privileges within the family. For most of us this means a hierarchy where some people — such as parents, men, or elders — have more power and authority than others, such as children, women, and younger people. The title of an old TV show, "Father knows best," probably best captures this feeling. People don't know best for themselves, the saying goes, so they should defer to father/authority. Many of us assume that father will take into consideration everyone's needs and interests and benevolently make decisions that are good for all.

People who say they are unhappy in the family or who reject this hierarchy are labeled homewreckers who are breaking up the family, creating divisions, and disrupting the smooth functioning of the organization. They are called names such as rabble-rouser, complainer, whiner, rebel, or teenager and are described as too shrill, harsh, angry, loud, and aggressive. The presumption is that everything was okay until this person started complaining. In the 1970s and 1980s men used these terms to silence or discount women who were challenging incest, domestic violence, and inequality in the family.

Racial relations in this country are often described as if we were all a big family. If people of color point out racism in our neighborhoods, offices, schools, or churches, white people generally react with one of two responses. The first is to defend the family and cast out the troublemaking person of color. "Things were just fine before you got here and made it into a problem. You can just go back to where you came from if you don't like it." (This response also makes it seem like those who are dissatisfied are the ones with no right to be here.)

The second response is to reassert white people's role as the benevolent fathers of the family who know what's best for everyone involved. People of color are seen as rebellious or ungrateful children. Our perspective is the overview, the dispassionate consideration of everyone's interests. If the children weren't so angry and rebellious and would just leave decisions to us, we would work it out and take care of their needs too.

A more useful assumption is that complaints mark issues that need changing. Rather than labeling people complainers, we need to take what they say seriously. Most people do not speak up easily in the face of authority or power. Most of us have been mistreated by people in authority, and few people joyously or enthusiastically create problems where none exist. When people object to what is happening, it is because someone is being exploited or abused or placed in an unsafe situation. Some kind of injustice is occurring.

People and groups bring up problems in different ways. The less powerful and less listened to need to be more forceful when bringing up the fact that the family system is not working for them. (In the extreme case where it is completely unsafe, then the problems may be turned inward in self-destructive behavior or acted out. This is true for both individuals and communities.) The more forcefully people act up or act out, the more loudly, forcefully, and repressively we respond by saying that they are the problem.

White people, especially those with at least middle-class incomes or financial security, have always said that the system works. We live in a democracy, there is equal opportunity, hard work is rewarded, and there are no special privileges.

Just as child assault, incest, domestic violence, and marital rape are denied and covered over by the myth of the happy nuclear family, so too racism, poverty, and discrimination are covered over by the myth of the happy social community. Our "families" will always look happy to those with more power, privilege, or prestige, and will always be dangerous for those of us with less. A happy family can only exist when justice prevails and when everyone in the family has an equal and adequate amount of power, safety, participation, and autonomy.

We must reject any notion of a family that has a (white) father at the top making benevolent decisions for everyone else. This is not a democratic image of human relations.

Have you ever been in a situation that was formerly all white and subsequently integrated? Did the person (or people) of color raise issues of racism? How were they responded to? Did the racism they identified exist before they arrived?

I worked at a small non-profit community agency at a time when all the staff was white. After some discussions about racism we decided that the next person we hired would be a person of color.

We subsequently hired a Latina (I'll call her Sylvia) to join our staff. We felt very satisfied with what we had done. After all, we felt we were taking a risk in order to do the right thing.

After working with us for a while, Sylvia began to bring to our attention various ways that we were discounting her experience and excluding her from decision-making. In addition, she pointed out how we were not serving Latino/a clients well.

Some of us became very upset and felt attacked and discounted. It seemed like we had more racism now that Sylvia was on staff. It was easier before she came because we didn't have to watch what we said or did. She was labeled a troublemaker by some and called ungrateful by others. But neither she nor the problems would go away. We were eventually forced to take Sylvia's complaints seriously and decide what to do about them. Even then, we did not include her or other Latino/as in that process.

All of our responses had elements of the happy family syndrome in them. The racism Sylvia identified existed before she arrived, but we blamed her. Paternalistically, we felt she was unappreciative of all we had done for her. When we acknowledged racial problems, we still felt that we, the white people, should decide how best to fix things. We were the parents and she was the child, and the parents knew what was best.

Sylvia didn't stay long with this organization. We did learn some lessons about how our expectations regarding her and our roles prevented us from acting effectively to identify and solve racial problems.

Many of us will be in all-white situations that become racially integrated. What can you do to support people of color if they are attacked for pointing out racism?

Beyond Black and White

I GREW UP IN A HOUSE in which an African-American woman came once a week to clean. She was the only person of color that I knew personally as a child. Later, when I was in high school, a single African-American student transferred to my apparently all-white high school. He was the object of tremendous attention and comment, much of it negative. For years we had talked about the prowess of the African-American football and basketball teams in South Central Los Angeles, and now we had a black person among us.

These years were the 1950s and early 1960s, and the civil rights struggle was often in the news. African American athletes were integrating sports, and students were integrating schools, lunch counters, department stores, and recreational facilities.

When I became an adult and looked back on my childhood, I thought that these public events and personal experiences defined my exposure to racism. Racism meant black-white relations. When I began to read about racism, I came across books about the civil rights struggle, slavery, and the black power movement. Even today, the books I can most easily find about racism have titles like *Black Lives, White Lives: Three Decades of Race Relations in America; Black Children, White Dreams;* and *Race: How Blacks and Whites Think and Feel about the American Obsession* (by Bob Blauner, Thomas J. Cottle, and Studs Terkel respectively).

When I looked more closely at my childhood, I began to notice other people of color in my life who were less visible but still present. I played cowboys and Indians with my friends; my food was grown by Latino farmworkers; the parks I played in were maintained by Japanese-American gardeners; the high school I went to employed black custodians and used a Native-American reference (the Birmingham Braves) for its sports teams, mascot, and logo; and when my parents sold our house in West Los Angeles to a Japanese family, they received hate calls because of it.

In the United States we tend to identify racism with the relationship between African Americans and whites. Even within the Jewish community, black-Jewish discussion groups and questions about black-Jewish relations are the primary racial focus. There are rarely white–Asian American or Jewish-Latino groups.

There are important reasons why the African-American struggle for justice and equality is at the forefront of our consciousness. The existence of slavery and Jim Crow segregation, and the struggles for justice led by African Americans have been defining historical forces in our development as a nation. African Americans have powerfully and unrelentingly challenged the myths of American democracy and economic opportunity.

The world is not just black and white. It is simple to say we shouldn't forget Spanish-speaking, Native-American, Asian-American, and Arab-American peoples when we discuss race. In reality, it takes more than tacking on the names of each group to address adequately the issues that a multiracial society raises. We cannot build a stable multicultural society on only two legs. Using the African-American experience as the model for all communities of color in the United States distorts the history of the African-American struggle for justice and full participation and renders invisible the identities and issues of other communities.

When anything is divided into black and white it makes it seem as if there is a clear dividing line between the two groups — no gray, no fuzziness, no gradations. Many people in this society are bicultural. Many people of color and white people are of racially mixed heritage. Some people of color are so light that they can pass as white.

The black-white division makes it seem as if white people are homogeneous. On the contrary, what counts as white has been contested throughout our country's history. At times the Irish were not white; Spanish, Italians, and Greeks were not white; Russians and Poles were not white. There is tremendous complexity, intermingling, struggle for inclusion, and resistance to incorporation within our European heritages and histories. At times, for example, Jewish people have been considered white and at other times as clearly not white.

Nor has African-American culture been homogeneous. Some African-American people have been free for hundreds of years; others remained virtual slaves until just a generation ago. African Americans came from complex and very different African cultures and retained some of those differences for long periods in this country. Ethnic differences, regional differences, and class differences have made most generalizations about African Americans tenuous at best. Many African Americans have intermarried with Native Americans or with members of other ethnic groups.

The division of racial discussion into black and white is misleading in other ways. It obscures the long and devastating struggle of Native Americans for survival, cultural autonomy, and sovereignty. Their struggle is largely misunderstood because it is so different from the African-American struggle.

The struggle of Spanish-speaking peoples, which is heavily intertwined with Native American struggles since both include resistance to colonization, is ignored and trivialized.

In a similar way, the presence, diversity, achievements, and defeats of the many different Asian, Pacific Islander, and Asian-American communities are lumped together as one and are oversimplified. Asian Americans are invisible in much of white American culture and are usually excluded from political representation and social power.

Another result of black-white thinking is that we are unable to understand and develop truly multicultural environments. Many of us claim our communities are all white if there are no African Americans visible. This can make it seem like racism is a problem "over there," in urban, inner-city areas.

Racism is not only an issue for large metropolitan urban areas. Most communities in the United States, including those in the Midwest, Northwest, and Southwest, are multiracial. There are often Native-American, Spanish-speaking, Asian-American, and Arab-American people in our communities where no African Americans are present.

Which communities of color are routinely ignored or not seen by white people you know? What groups are habitually left out in your thinking?

Conversely, we believe we have integrated an event, neighborhood, or workplace if there are African Americans present, even though other groups are absent. This belief creates an opportunism in which we can choose to deal with the African-American community and ignore other communities, or choose other communities and ignore African Americans at our convenience. On the one hand, we claim that if we are addressing African-American concerns we are speaking about the concerns of all people of color. On the other hand, we can avoid dealing with the harsh effects of racism on the African-American community by pointing to examples of the integration or progress of other non-white groups such as Asian Americans.

There are other negative results of perceiving racism as a problem of black and white. We maintain the illusion that whites are the majority and therefore deserve a disproportionate share of the national resources. Conversely, we fear that "people of color" are becoming the majority and that a monolithic group of darker-skinned people will take over. In addition, racial tension, economic divisions, and hate crimes between different communities of color are misunderstood and ignored because white people are unable to distinguish the complex relationships between these groups.

We must delve into the complexity: we cannot be satisfied with what has been achieved. We have to keep asking the questions "Who is still excluded?" "Who remains unseen?" "Who is still being exploited?" When new groups of immigrants arrive, we cannot conveniently forget that long-established communities of color still face racism every day.

Nor can we say that there is more of a certain group so we should put our attention there. Racist actions and policies in the past have determined the numbers of people in particular communities of color living today in the United States. The breeding of slaves, the killing of Native Americans, the restrictions on Asian immigration — all determined how many people of color are currently in this country. Human dignity and opportunity are not measured in quantities of people. Relatively small population groups such as Native Americans may deserve large amounts of compensatory reparations

Complexity also exists within the categories we use. "People of color," "Asian American," or even "Korean American" are examples of categories that can confuse and mislead us more than they help. We need to be talking about inclusion within particular communities. If we are talking about the Korean-American community or the Lakota community or the Salvadoran community, we need to ask, "Are the women of that community included? Are the young people included? Are the elders included? Are the poor included? Are the lesbians and gays and bisexuals included? Are the physically challenged included?"

Democracy means the inclusion of all people in the process of making decisions that affect their lives. Our society is undemocratic to the extent that anyone is excluded from the decision-making process. Racism is fundamentally undemocratic and makes a travesty of our democratic ideals. Fighting racism means extending democracy to include all people of color and moving beyond a black-white, or even a simple white–people of color focus.

What's in a Name?

THE WORDS WE USE TO DESCRIBE groups of people have developed within the system of racism as it has changed historically. These words have changed and continue to change, partly in response to the struggle to end racism, and partly in the resistance to and backlash against that struggle. All of our vocabulary is inadequate and frustrating. However, there is much to learn from attempts to use accurate and respectful language. It is important that we pay attention to the words we use because language itself is used to maintain racism.

The phrase "people of color," which I use in this book, is one such problematic term. Every human being is a person of color. The word "white," which has been used to describe European Americans, does not reflect anyone's skin color so much as a concept of racial purity that has never existed. I use the phrases "people of color" and "communities of color" to suggest the multitude of peoples and cultures that have been exploited by European-American society for the last 500 years. However, if we are not careful this term will also allow whiteness to stay neutral, unmarked, and at the center of power, while all other groups are "colorful" and marked as different. (Even the phrase "European-American" as a substitute for white is a problem because there have been communities of different skin colors, origins, and cultures in Europe for centuries. Used as a racial descriptor, the phrase denies non-white Europeans their history and presence.)

Other troublesome words used to refer to people of color include "minority" (people of color are a majority of the world's population and a majority in some of our communities); "third world" (it implies they come from somewhere else and don't belong in our communities; third also implies less worth than first or second); and "non-white" (this term equates white as the norm or standard and everything else as different or "non," i.e., negative).

The phrase "people of color" itself covers over so much complexity and diversity that it's sometimes more useful to state explicitly the group of people being referred to, whether African American, Asian American, Arab American, Native American, or Latino/a. However, these terms are also abstractions, engulfing the specific lives of tens of millions of people.

More specific referents like Japanese American, Hopi, or Lebanese are still generalizations that hide significant differences while giving a false appearance of inclusiveness. The male bias of our society gives most racial terms a male identification. I keep the masculine/feminine form of Latino/a precisely to remind us that women and men are included in each of these categories.

Who else is excluded from these categories? Does the word "African American" connote "poor" to white people? Does "Latino" mean "heterosexual"? Does "Asian

American" assume "able-bodied"? Racial referents are coded for specific meanings relating to class, sexual orientation, and physical ability, reflecting broad patterns of inequality within our society.

Language is important not because it should or can be "correct," but because it should convey respect for and dignity to the people referred to. Everyone should have the choice to name themselves. Many Native Americans, African Americans, and immigrants from around the world had their names taken from them and were renamed by ignorant and insensitive missionaries, immigration officials, slave owners, military officers, teachers, and representatives of government agencies. Reclaiming lost names, rejecting demeaning names, or renaming oneself is a powerful step for an individual or group to take because it challenges the presumed subordination when others have dictated your name.

Sometimes there is not agreement within a community about what people want to be called, often because there is really no coherent community in the first place. Nonetheless, there is always a clear difference between respectful terms and disrespectful ones.

Within the African-American community there are differences over whether to retain use of the word black, or to use African American. Neither term is without problems, although both terms are respectful. Similarly, in the Native-American community there is disagreement over whether Native American or American Indian is the better term. These discussions reflect concerns about cultural pride, historical roots, the meaning of multiculturalism, and strategies for resisting racism. We can learn a lot about the concerns of people of color by listening to their discussions of the issues raised by different terms of self-identity. It is more important that we support those concerns than that we use the most correct words.

How have different communities of color renamed or redefined themselves during your lifetime?

It can be hard for white people to accept new terms because they represent challenges to long-standing social relationships. Different words call forth different behavior. We may feel less secure that we know the racial rules — what to say and how to act. This alone can cause anxiety for many middle-class Americans, for whom knowing and following the rules is important.

Some of our resistance to new words reflects our desire to control racial boundaries and maintain power. We may take advantage of changing terminology to try to discredit people of color with comments such as "Why can't they make up their minds about what they want to be called?" Focusing on the terminology is a way to divert attention away from the underlying challenge to white power and control that the changing vocabulary represents.

In the United States we have always been concerned about politeness and good breeding. Upper-class and successful middle-class people have long prided themselves on using correct language and being well behaved and respectful. The use of correct racial terminology has been a signifier of class or breeding and has been used to disparage poor and working-class people. In the South, respectable whites, deriving great advantage from segregation, referred to African Americans as "Negroes" and looked down on people who used words like "nigger." Being overtly polite or respectful in language or personal encounters made these whites no less complicit in white racism.

When we criticize other white people today for not using the right language, we may be showing our good breeding, masking our complicity with racism, and using our own educational or class advantages to put down those with less opportunity. Language that is obviously derogatory or abusive should be challenged. But we need to be concerned with much more than language in fighting racism.

Some of us wonder why people of color want to be called African American, Chinese American, or Mexican American. Why can't they just be Americans? Are they holding something back? Do they owe allegiance to another country or continent?

Sometimes people of color use these names as a response to the lack of acceptance and inclusion that they have experienced from white people in this country. At other times, people use them to indicate cultural and social connections that they feel to the countries or continents from which their foreparents emigrated. These names can indicate feelings of connection to distinct cultural communities, especially in response to the strong pressure in this country to give up one's culture in order to be accepted. Such naming can also be a call to a collective political identity. None of these practices has anything to do with one's loyalty to the United States.

We have adopted the word American for people who are citizens of the United States. (Literally, anyone born in North, Central, or South America is an American.) It is not an ethnicity or culture. There are many different kinds of Americans, and our country encompasses thousands of distinct cultures and communities. Being an American doesn't mean denying one's culture, ethnicity, or community. There is no single, national culture that defines what it means to be an American, however much some of us wish there were.

Being able to acknowledge and value one's cultural background is vital to personal and community health. This is even more necessary in a society that devalues most forms of popular cultural expression and minimizes historical roots and cultural development as ours does.

Part of the American myth, the frontier myth, was that we could create ourselves anew here. We portrayed the United States as a virgin territory where people could come and discover or create new selves. We conveniently "forget" that we had to kill off Native Americans to make that frontier empty. We had to chop down the vegetation to make it tillable. We had to deny our own cultural histories, practices, and customs to fit in. Some of our families did deny or cover up their cultural practices. The traditions of others were lost over time. Today many of us can hardly identify with any specific ethnic identity or culture.

Many of our foreparents resisted assimilation and carried on strong and proud Italian, Greek, Irish, Swedish, German, Russian, or Portuguese traditions. But most of us grew to believe that this was a land of newness, separated from the old tired traditions of other, primarily European countries. This mythology makes it difficult to acknowledge the strengths and contributions of people from various cultures, particularly non-European ones, to our American mix.

American culture has come to mean white European-American norms, values, beliefs, and traditions. Patriotism has become overlaid with a national chauvinism that reinforces white racism. We have used our national borders, immigration policies, literary canons, and patriotic homilies to maintain the dominance of white norms. It is ironic that in this time of a global economy, international trade, world sports competitions, and global cultural communication, our appeals to nationalism and protectionism have increased.

We face a challenge that is even larger than incorporating all Americans into our national identity. We must fundamentally question why we give so much credence and importance to our national identity. Whose interests does it serve? Nationalism in many countries has led to protectionism, aggression, xenophobia, internal repression, and war. Who has benefited from these patterns?

There is no reason we can't be proud of being American and of the positive achievements of our fellow citizens. And we can be proud of being New Yorkers or Texans or from the Northwest. We can take pride in our cultural, religious, ethnic, and other identities. However, when that pride fosters feelings of superiority, arrogance, competition, or the denigration of others who are not part of our group, we are breeding intolerance and violence. Further, when we use "American" as a code for who we, white people, consider good or rich or smart or successful enough to be part of "our" country, we are maintaining racism in disguise. When we blame our problems on non-Americans, whether they are immigrants without papers, Japanese capitalists, Arab oil producers or South American drug cartels, we are again refusing to look at our own complicity in these situations and are failing to take responsibility for our own problems. It then becomes easy for our economic and political leaders to stir up fear and anger against "foreigners," which fuels more militarism and racial violence.

Nationalism can be used to reinforce racism in the opposite direction as well. If we try to pretend that we have all assimilated into one large melting pot and that differences of culture, tradition, and community no longer exist, we can maintain white norms and white racism by pretending to have transcended them. Saying "We're all just Americans and therefore nobody should claim to be Asian American" can be a way to deny the inequality and injustice that still operate in this country. This false inclusion is just as strong a support to racism as exclusionism is. In both cases we are using nationalism to speak about and reinforce white dominance.

There is no natural or homogeneous national community in this country. Nation states are complex. Ours was created over centuries and includes diverse peoples and communities. Any attempt to define or create a single national culture will inevitably disenfranchise and oppress many of us. It can only be done with power, control, and violence, to the benefit of some and the detriment of others.

Discussion of racism inevitably focuses on boundaries and divisions. Who is on "our" side and who is not? Making our boundaries more inclusive doesn't eliminate this competitive and exclusive kind of thinking. Our national borders are arbitrary constructions of historical circumstance influenced by wars, colonization patterns, trade, treaties, and resistance struggles. We have seen countries throughout the world break up, consolidate and change borders, and redefine "national" identity. These transitions have generally fueled nationalism, racism, and religious fanaticism.

Nationalism in the United States has been used not only to exclude some people from our national identity, but also to control all those who live within the national boundary, and to persecute for disloyalty those who are labeled traitors or "un-American." Our challenge is to accept and embrace the full diversity of who we are and strive for inclusion without expecting people to think or act like we do.

People will always make choices about what traditions to keep or discard, and what to name themselves. They deserve respect for the choices they make. Many Americans have cultural or social ties to other countries — some Italians to Italy, some Irish to Ireland, some Jews to Israel, some Vietnamese to Vietnam, some Bolivians to Bolivia, some Palestinians to Palestine, some Filipinos to the Philippines, and some African Americans to Ghana, Benin, Egypt, or South Africa. We each live within complex webs of international culture and communication, and no U.S. border stops or limits these kinds of cultural connections. Connecting to traditions and cultures that reach beyond U.S. borders is a source of strength, inspiration, creativity, and support for many Americans. We need to encourage those connections, not use them to persecute people for having "divided" loyalties.

One of the purposes of maintaining whiteness is to construct a normative set of values that defines who is entitled to certain resources and privileges. In response, people of color come together to juxtapose their numbers and their social and political influence against that entitlement. They define themselves as people of color against the ultimate dividing line that white racism creates. In small groups in which white people are dominant, people of color may band together for similar reasons.

At a different level, because the binary discussion of race relations puts everything in a black-white framework, Asian Americans, Arab Americans, Latino/as, and Native Americans have formed broad coalitions to strengthen their political bargaining power for the distribution of resources, services, and political representation. In earlier historical periods, for example, there were no Asian Americans; there were only Japanese Americans, Chinese Americans, and Korean Americans. Now these groups have come together, downplaying their differences for strategic reasons, to claim resources and representation against white or African-American claims.

At the same time as they work in coalition as Asian Americans, however, particular ethnic and national groups are reasserting the uniqueness of their experiences and the importance of their needs for resources, recognition, and political representation as Korean Americans, Filipino/as, or South Asians. This is a strategic response because white culture denies the importance of cultural identity on the one hand, and on the other hand tends to see all people of color as "other," without recognizing their specificity.

Finally, many people from particular ethnic groups want simply to be "American." The force of racism in this society makes it nearly impossible for a Latino/a or Asian American to be "just American." White Americans regularly perceive them to be Latino/a or Asian and therefore not completely, 100-percent-loyal Americans.

Each of these levels of self-definition and coalition is an important and valid strategic response to the realities of racism in U.S. society. Each tells us something about whiteness as it is currently understood and perceived.

There is nothing "essential" about any of these forms of identity. They are each historical responses to the politics of white society. That doesn't mean these identities are not real. They are real, important, serious, and significant in the struggle to end racism. They will not go away when racism is eliminated, although they might look very different at that time. As white people, we need to respect the ability of people of color to name themselves. We also need to support the forms their struggles against racism take and learn about the resistance of white racism to change.

We cannot forget that communities of color are trying to survive in a white-controlled society. They have constantly to redefine their strategies for survival and resistance. Many of their words are bought out, co-opted, and commercialized or lose their meaning over time. The slogan "Black is beautiful," originally coined to strengthen pride and self-esteem in the African-American community, is now being used by advertisers to market shampoo, skin cream, alcohol, and clothes. We can learn much about ourselves and about tactics of resistance to cultural domination by listening to the language of resistance of people of color.

Resistance to white racism might appear to white people to recreate clearly delineated, separable groups and thus be racist itself. The terms "people of color," "African American," "Korean American," "Latino/a" — all self-chosen labels in reaction to white racism — reflect real, but not necessarily stable or long-term, cultural or political groupings. They demarcate broad currents within certain groups that are part of their resistance to white domination and racism.

Individual responses to the fluctuating dynamics of resistance are varied. Particular people of color may herald new forms of resistance, hold on to traditional patterns, or emphasize or de-emphasize racial identity at different points in their lives. There is much debate within communities of color about tactics of resistance, including naming practices. And these communities themselves are large and complex, without the clearly defined boundaries that we white people want to ascribe to them.

Finally, to add one last complicating but crucial factor: race/ethnicity is only one of the factors in the makeup of our identities. At times other factors, such as geographical origin, gender, sexual orientation, parental or work role, may supersede ethnicity as a primary focus. It is important to respect the choices individual people of color make about when and how much to identify with their "racial" identity, and how to understand it, knowing that our society gives a distorted and overemphasized meaning to racial identity.

Separatism

MANY WHITE PEOPLE BECOME UPSET when people of color get together without us. In our workshops my colleagues and I sometimes separate people into racial groups. There are always white people who protest by saying, "I want to know what they have to say." "How can we deal with racism without people of color?" "How come they get their own group?" "I think their group will be more fun." "This is reverse racism."

Racism is divisive. Each of these responses reflects some of the pain and confusion of that divisiveness. Although being white – with all the privileges and benefits, costs, limits, and opportunities that entails – has heavily influenced our lives, it is difficult for us to admit that we are white. It is difficult to look around and identify other white people and to recognize that we are in this together. We can learn from each other. We need to learn from each other.

It is particularly hypocritical for us to complain about people of color being separatist. For the last 500 years it is white people who have excluded people of color from our homes, "our" schools, "our" workplaces, "our" neighborhoods, and from "our" country. Even today people of color are routinely excluded or harassed or told to leave and go home by white people in all kinds of circumstances. Most of us don't want to be excluded, but we are not so great at inclusion either. It is only in the last 35 years that people of color have been able to meet in and control their own space without the threat of intrusion by white people of authority, and even that privilege is commonly violated because of our fears of people of color "banding together."

People of color have been controlled and segregated throughout U.S. history. There are strategic reasons why they might want to meet together without white people. They may want to be in a safe environment, to enjoy each other's company, to talk about racism, to congregate with people who share certain things, and not to have to focus attention on white people and white culture. Some of these are the reasons that any group of people with shared interests or concerns get together. Others are particular to the needs of a minority group in a larger social setting.

Physical and emotional safety is a crucial concern. Women know they aren't necessarily safe with men just because the men say "I'm liberated" or "I'm a feminist." For the same reasons, people of color know that they aren't necessarily safe when white people say similar things. At least in terms of racial abuse, it is generally safer for people of color when white people are not around. It is also safer for them to talk about difficult issues, to be vulnerable, and to acknowledge conflicts and disagreements within their community without the danger that white people will use the things they say against them.

Congregating in a group without white people is also less distracting for people of color. Rarely do we whites sit back and listen to people of color without interrupting, without being defensive, without trying to regain attention for ourselves, without criticizing or judging. People of color can't talk with and listen to each other with the same amount of attention and respect when white people are present.

Most people of color spend a tremendous amount of time and energy taking care of white people. This has been true historically as people of various ethnic groups cared for our children, took care of our homes, cooked our food, and made our clothes. It has also been true emotionally. People of color have often counseled us, nurtured us in our old age, been our teachers, assuaged our guilt about racism, covered over their pain and anger to protect us, assured us that we were okay even though we were white, and, out of economic necessity, put aside the needs of their families and communities to take care of ours. One of the assumptions of whiteness, particularly for people of middle-class economic status or higher, is that people of color will put our needs before theirs. They have been dependent on jobs and goodwill from white people for so long that many have learned how to do it well. It occurs so commonly and routinely that few of us notice it going on.

In separated groups, people of color don't have to take care of white people and therefore can take care of themselves and each other. They can talk about their experiences of racism, they can talk about white people and white society, without worrying about or having to respond to the questions, insecurities, misinformation, and defensiveness of white people.

There are many reasons people congregate. Safety, shared interests, and mutual support are primary ones. These are the same reasons white people congregate. If you look around a school cafeteria you might see white students, Latino/a students, and Asian-American students sitting in separate groups. If you looked closer and knew more about the groups, you might discover that most of the social groupings had to do with shared interests, experiences, and concerns. Yet many of us who are white might say that the people of color are cliquish or separatist, and we might feel offended. We probably would not question the white students' sitting together in a similar manner.

Since so many public spaces in our society are white in tone, structure, and atmosphere, people of different ethnic groups need space to enjoy their own cultural uniqueness, strengths, and styles. They are not necessarily rejecting individual white people, or plotting revenge or revolution. White society has controlled communities of color while all the time fearing that their members would rebel. Any time we see even a few of them together, we become afraid. This fear reflects our own understanding and guilt about the inequalities of the past, as well as the fears we have been taught about people who are different.

Our fear of separation can also lead us to ignore our responsibility for most of the separation. People of color are still routinely and persistently denied access to much public and most private space in this country. There is tremendous and undeniable segregation in housing, schools, jobs, and recreational facilities. People of color do not choose to live in barrios, ghettos, and reservations any more than white people do. Those who do, do so out of lack of choice. White-controlled institutions and individual discrimination have created this lack of choice. We segregate communities of color and rarely notice or challenge it. But when a group voluntarily congregates, we oppose its right to do so.

It is to our advantage when people of color congregate voluntarily without whites. None of us wants to be racist or to see racism perpetuated. But most of us are not very adept at noticing racism when it occurs, or responding vigorously to it. When people of color come together for discussion and support, they become more able to point out and challenge racism.

We can also benefit from the opportunity to talk with other white people. Seldom do we consciously get together with other whites and talk about racism, about being white, and about working for racial justice. We need this time together.

All too often we let people of color take responsibility for challenging racism. We may describe it as their issue. We may fail to see how seriously and continuously it affects us. In an all-white group we have a chance to explore our questions, concerns, and fears about racism. We have an opportunity gently to challenge other white people about it. We have an opportunity to develop plans for confronting racism and becoming better allies for people of color. Let's take advantage of it!

How could you bring together white people you know to think about
some of the issues raised in this book?
Who are some white people who can help you do this?

Intervening with other white people about racism is an important way that we become allies for people of color. The next part of the book looks in detail at the ways we can be strong, effective allies in stopping racism.

PART III

Being Allies

What Does an Ally Do?

BEING ALLIES TO PEOPLE OF COLOR in the struggle to end racism is one of the most important things that white people can do. There is no one correct way to be an ally. Each of us is different. We have different relationships to social organizations, political processes, and economic structures. We are more or less powerful because of such factors as our gender, class, work situation, family, and community participation. Being an ally to people of color is an ongoing strategic process in which we look at our personal and social resources, evaluate the environment we have helped to create, and decide what needs to be done.

This book is filled with things to do and ways to get involved. These suggestions are not prioritized because they cannot be. Times change and circumstances vary. What is a priority today may not be tomorrow. What is effective or strategic right now may not be next year. We need to be thinking with others and noticing what is going on around us so we will know how to put our attention, energy, time, and money toward strategic priorities in the struggle to end racism and other injustices.

This includes listening to people of color so that we can support the actions they take, the risks they bear in defending their lives and challenging white hegemony. It includes watching the struggle of white people to maintain dominance and the struggle of people of color to gain equal opportunity, justice, safety, and respect.

We don't need to believe or accept as true everything people of color say. There is no one voice in any community, much less in the complex and diverse communities of color spanning our country. We do need to listen carefully to the voices of people of color so that we understand and give credence to their experience. We can then evaluate the content of what they are saying by what we know about how racism works and by our own critical thinking and progressive political analysis.

It is important to emphasize this point because often we become paralyzed when people of color talk about racism. We are afraid to challenge what they say. We will be ineffective as allies if we give up our ability to analyze and think critically, if we simply accept everything that a person of color states as truth.

Listening to people of color and giving critical credence to their experience is not easy for us because of the training we have received. Nevertheless, it is an important first step. When we hear statements that make us want to react defensively, we can instead keep the following points in mind as we try to understand what is happening and determine how best to be allies.

We have seen how racism is a pervasive part of our culture. Therefore we should always assume that racism is at least part of the picture. In light of this assumption, we should look for the patterns involved rather than treating most events as isolated occurrences.

Since we know that racism is involved, we know our whiteness is also a factor. We should look for ways we are acting from assumptions of white power or privilege. This will help us acknowledge any fear or confusion we may feel. It will allow us to see our tendencies to defend ourselves or our tendencies to assume we should be in control. Then we may want to talk with other white people both to express our feelings and to get support so our tendencies towards defensiveness or controlling behavior don't get in the way of our being effective allies.

We have many opportunities to practice these critical listening and thinking skills because we are all involved in a complex web of interpersonal and institutional relationships. Every day we are presented with opportunities to analyze what is going on around us and to practice taking direct action as allies to people of color.

People of color will always be on the front lines fighting racism because their lives are at stake. How do we act and support them effectively, both when they are in the room with us and when they are not?

Being a Strong White Ally

WHAT KIND OF ACTIVE SUPPORT does a strong white ally provide? People of color that I have talked with over the years have been remarkably consistent in describing the kinds of support they need from white allies. The following list is compiled from their statements at workshops I have facilitated. The focus here is on personal qualities and interpersonal relationships. More active interventions are discussed in the next part of the book.

WHAT PEOPLE OF COLOR WANT FROM WHITE ALLIES

"Respect us"

"Find out about us"

"Don't take over"

"Provide information"

"Resources"

"Take risks"

"Don't take it personally"

"Understanding"

"Teach your children about racism"

"Speak up"

"Don't be scared by my anger"

"Listen to us"

"Don't make assumptions"

"Stand by my side"

"Don't assume you know what's best for me"

"Money"

"Make mistakes"

"Honesty"

"Talk to other white people"

"Interrupt jokes and comments"

"Don't ask me to speak for my people"

"Support"

"Your body on the line"

Basic Tactics

EVERY SITUATION IS DIFFERENT and calls for critical thinking about how to make a difference. Taking the statements above into account, I have compiled some general guidelines.

1. **Assume racism is everywhere, every day.** Just as economics influences everything we do, just as our gender and gender politics influence everything we do, assume that racism is affecting whatever is going on. We assume this because it's true and because one of the privileges of being white is not having to see or deal with racism all the time. We have to learn to see the effect that racism has. Notice who speaks, what is said, how things are done and described. Notice who isn't present. Notice code words for race, and the implications of the policies, patterns, and comments that are being expressed. You already notice the skin color of everyone you meet and interact with — now notice what difference it makes.

2. **Notice who is the center of attention and who is the center of power.** Racism works by directing violence and blame toward people of color and consolidating power and privilege for white people.

3. **Notice ho wracism is denied, minimized, and justified.**

4. **Understand and learn from the history of whiteness and racism.** Notice how racism has changed over time and how it has subverted or resisted challenges. Study the tactics that have worked effectively against it.

5. **Understand the connections bet ween racism, economic issues, sexism, and other forms of injustice.**

6. **Take a stand against injustice.** Take risks. It is scary, difficult, and may bring up feelings of inadequacy, lack of self-confidence, indecision, or fear of making mistakes, but ultimately it is the only healthy and moral human thing to do. Intervene in situations where racism is being passed on.

7. **Be strategic.** Decide what is important to challenge and what's not. Think about strategy in particular situations. Attack the source of power.

8. **Don't confuse a battle with the war.** Behind particular incidents and interactions are larger patterns. Racism is flexible and adaptable. There will be gains and losses in the struggle for justice and equality.

9. **Don't call names or be personally abusive.** Since power is often defined as power over others — the ability to abuse or control people — it is easy to become abusive ourselves. However, we usually end up abusing people who have less power than we do because it is less dangerous. Attacking people doesn't address the systemic nature of racism and inequality.

10. **Support the leadership of people of color**. Do this consistently, but not uncritically.

11. **Learn something about the history of white people who have worked for racial justice.** There is a long history of white people who have fought for racial justice. Their stories can inspire and sustain you.

12. **Don't do it alone.** You will not end racism by yourself. We can do it if we work together. Build support, establish networks, and work with already established groups.

13. **Talk with your children and other young people about racism.**

Getting Involved

I T CAN BE DIFFICULT FOR THOSE OF US who are white to know how to be strong allies for people of color when discrimination occurs. In the following interaction, imagine that Roberto is a young Latino student just coming out of a job interview with a white recruiter from a computer company.[1] Let's see how one white person might respond.

> *Roberto is angry, not sure what to do next. He walks down the hall and meets a white teacher who wants to help.*
>
> ***Teacher:*** *Hey, Roberto, how's it going?*
>
> ***Roberto:*** *That son of a bitch! He wasn't going to give me no job. That was really messed up.*
>
> ***Teacher:*** *Hold on there, don't be so angry. It was probably a mistake or something.*
>
> ***Roberto:*** *There was no mistake. The racist bastard. He wants to keep me from getting a good job. Rather have us all on welfare or doing maintenance work.*
>
> ***Teacher:*** *Calm down now or you'll get yourself in more trouble. Don't go digging a hole for yourself. Maybe I could help you if you weren't so angry.*
>
> ***Roberto:*** *That's easy for you to say. This man was discriminating against me. White folks are all the same. They talk about equal opportunity, but it's the same old shit.*
>
> ***Teacher:*** *Wait a minute. I didn't have anything to do with this. Don't blame me, I'm not responsible. If you wouldn't be so angry maybe I could help you. You probably took what he said the wrong way. Maybe you were too sensitive.*
>
> ***Roberto:*** *I could tell. He was racist. That's all. (He storms off.)*

What did you notice about this scene? The teacher is concerned and is trying to help, but his intervention is not very effective. He immediately downplays the incident, discounting Roberto's feelings and underestimating the possibility of racism. He seems to think that racism is unlikely — that it was just a misunderstanding, or that Roberto was being too sensitive.

The teacher is clearly uncomfortable with Roberto's anger. He begins to defend himself, the job recruiter, and white people. He ends up feeling attacked for being white. Rather than talking about what happened, he focuses on Roberto's anger and his generalizations about white people. He threatens to get Roberto in trouble himself if Roberto doesn't calm down. As he walks away, he may be thinking it's no wonder Roberto didn't get hired for the job.

You probably recognize some of the tactics described in Part I. The teacher denies or minimizes the likelihood of racism, blames Roberto, and eventually counterattacks, claiming to be a victim of Roberto's anger and racial generalizations.

This interaction illustrates some of the common feelings that can get in the way of intervening effectively where discrimination is occurring. First is the feeling that we are being personally attacked. It is difficult to hear the phrases "all white people" or "you white people." We want to defend ourselves and other whites. We don't want to believe that white people could intentionally hurt others. Or we may want to say, "Not me, I'm different."

There are some things we should remember when we feel attacked. First, this is a question of injustice. We need to focus on what happened and what we can do about it, not on our feelings of being attacked.

Second, someone who has been the victim of injustice is legitimately angry and may or may not express that anger in ways we like. Criticizing the way people express their anger deflects attention and action away from the injustice that was committed. After the injustice has been dealt with, if you still think it's worthwhile and not an attempt to control the situation yourself, you can go back and discuss ways of expressing anger.

Often, because we are frequently complacent about injustice that doesn't affect us directly, it takes a lot of anger and aggressive action to bring attention to a problem. If we were more proactive about identifying and intervening in situations of injustice, people would not have to be so "loud" to get our attention in the first place.

Finally, part of the harm that racism does is that it forces people of color to be wary and mistrustful of all white people, just as sexism forces women to mistrust all men. People of color face racism every day, often from unexpected quarters. They never know when a white friend, co-worker, teacher, police officer, doctor, or passerby may discriminate, act hostile, or say something offensive. They have to be wary of all white people, even though they know that not all white people will mistreat them. They have likely been hurt in the past by white people they thought they could trust, and therefore they may make statements about all white people. We must remember that although we want to be trustworthy, trust is not the issue. We are not fighting racism so that people of color will trust us. Trust builds over time through our visible efforts to be allies and fight racism. Rather than trying to be safe and trustworthy, we need to be more active, less defensive, and put issues of trust aside.

When people are discriminated against they may feel unseen, stereotyped, attacked, or as if a door has been slammed in their face. They may feel confused, frustrated, helpless, or angry. They are probably reminded of other similar experiences. They may want to hurt someone in return, or hide their pain, or simply forget about the whole experience. Whatever the response, the experience is deeply wounding and painful. It is an act of emotional violence.

It's also an act of economic violence to be denied access to a job, housing, educational program, pay raise, or promotion that one deserves. It is a practice that keeps economic resources in the hands of one group and denies them to another.

When a person is discriminated against it is a serious event and we need to treat it seriously. It is also a common event. For instance, the government estimates that there are over 2 million acts of race-based housing discrimination every year — 20 million every decade.[2] We know that during their lifetime, every person of color will probably have to face such discriminatory experiences in school, work, housing, and community settings.

People of color do not protest discrimination lightly. They know that when they do, white people routinely deny or minimize it, blame them for causing trouble, and then counterattack. This is the "happy family" syndrome described earlier.

People of color are experts in discrimination resulting from racism. Most experience it regularly and see its effects on their communities. Not every complaint of discrimination is valid, but most have some truth in them. It would be a tremendous step forward if we assumed that there was some truth in every complaint of racial discrimination, even when other factors may also be involved. At least then we would take it seriously enough to investigate fully.

How could the teacher in the above scenario be a better ally to Roberto? We can go back to the guidelines suggested earlier for help. First, he needs to listen much more carefully to what Roberto is saying. He should assume that Roberto is intelligent, and if he says there was racism involved then there probably was. The teacher should be aware of his own power and position, his tendency to be defensive, and his desire to defend other white people or presume their innocence. It would also be worthwhile to look for similar occurrences because racism is usually not an isolated instance but a pattern within an organization or institution.

Let's see how these suggestions might operate in a replay of this scene.

> *Teacher:* Hey, Roberto, what's happening?
>
> *Roberto:* That son of a bitch! He wasn't going to give me no job. He was messin' with me.
>
> *Teacher:* You're really upset. Tell me what happened.
>
> *Roberto:* He was discriminating against me. Wasn't going to hire me cause I'm Latino. White folks are all alike. Always playing games.
>
> *Teacher:* This is serious. Why don't you come into my office and tell me exactly what happened.
>
> *Roberto:* Okay. This company is advertising for computer programmers and I'm qualified for the job. But this man tells me there aren't any computer jobs, and then he tries to steer me toward a janitor job. He was a racist bastard.
>
> *Teacher:* That's tough. I know you would be good in that job.

This sounds like a case of job discrimination. Let's write down exactly what happened, and then you can decide what you want to do about it.

Roberto: *I want to get that job.*

Teacher: *If you want to challenge it, I'll help you. Maybe there's something we can do.*

This time the teacher was being a strong, supportive ally to Roberto.

An Ally Makes a Commitment

NOBODY NEEDS FLY-BY-NIGHT ALLIES, those who are here today and gone tomorrow. Being an ally takes commitment and perseverance. It is a lifelong struggle to end racism and other forms of social injustice. People of color know this well because they have been struggling for generations for recognition of their rights and the opportunity to participate fully in our society. The struggle to abolish slavery took over 80 years. Women organized for over 60 years to win the right to vote. I was reminded about the long haul recently when my sister sent me a news clipping about my old high school in Los Angeles, Birmingham High.

The clipping was about the 17-year struggle to change the "Birmingham Braves" name and caricatured image of an "Indian" used by the school teams to something that did not insult Native Americans. I was encouraged to hear that the name and mascot were now being changed, but was upset to read that there was an alumni group resisting the change and filing a lawsuit to preserve the old name.

Soon after receiving the article I had the good fortune to talk with a white woman who had been involved with the struggle over the mascot. The challenge had originated with a group of Native Americans in the San Fernando Valley. This woman decided to join the group — the only white person to do so. She started attending meetings. For the first two or three years all she did was listen, and the group hardly spoke to her. After a time, members of the group began to acknowledge her presence, talk with her, and include her in their activities. This woman learned a tremendous amount about herself, the local Native cultures, and the nature of white resistance during the 15 years she was involved with this group. They tried many different strategies and eventually, because they met with so much intransigence at the high school, they went to the Los Angeles school board.

When the school board made its decision to eliminate Native-American names and logos in school programs, it affected every school in the Los Angeles area. Subsequently the decision became a model for the Dallas school district's policy and is being considered for adoption in other school districts across the country.

This was a long struggle, but much public education was accomplished in the process. This work is part of a national effort by Native Americans and their allies to get sports teams and clubs to relinquish offensive names and mascots.

If the woman I talked with had been discouraged or offended because nobody welcomed her or paid her special attention during those first meetings, or if she felt that after a year or two nothing was going to be accomplished, or if she had not listened and learned enough to be able to work with and take leadership from the Native American community involved in this struggle, she would have gone home and possibly talked about how she had tried but it hadn't worked. She would not have been transformed by the struggle the way she had been; she would not have contributed to and been able to celebrate the success of this struggle for Native-American dignity and respect. Her work as an ally reminded me of what commitment as an ally really means.

I Would Be a Perfect Ally If ...

WE LEARN MANY EXCUSES AND JUSTIFICATIONS for racism in this society. We also learn many tactics for avoiding responsibility for it. We have developed a coded language to help us avoid even talking about it directly. Our training makes it easy to find reasons not to be allies to people of color. In order to maintain our commitment to being allies, we must reject the constant temptation to find excuses for inaction.

What reasons have you used for not taking a stronger stand against racism, or for backing away from supporting a person of color?

Following are some of the reasons I've recently heard white people use. I call them "if only" statements because that's the phrase they usually begin with. Our real meaning is just the reverse. We are often setting conditions on our commitment to racial justice. We are saying that "only if" people of color do this or that will we do our part. These conditions let us blame people of color for our not being reliable allies.

I would be a committed and effective ally —

- *If only people of color weren't so angry, sensitive, impatient, or demanding.*
- *If only people of color realized that I am different from other white people. I didn't own slaves. I treat everyone the same. I don't see color. I'm not a member of the KKK. I've even been to an unlearning racism workshop.*
- *If only people of color would give white people a chance, hear our side of things, and realize that we have it hard too.*
- *If only people of color didn't use phrases like "all white people."*
- *If only people of color didn't expect the government to do everything for them and wouldn't ask for special treatment.*

Being a white ally to people of color means to be there all the time, for the long term, committed and active. Because this is hard, challenging work, we often look for ways to justify not doing it. Rather than finding ways to avoid being allies, we need to look at what gets in our way. Where does it get hard? Where do we get stuck? We use many of the reasons listed above to justify withdrawal from the struggle against racism.

Another way we justify our withdrawal is to find a person of color who represents, in our minds, the reason why people of color don't really deserve our support. Often these examples have to do with people of color not spending money or time the way we think they should. "I know a person who spends all her money on ... "

We often set standards for their conduct that we haven't previously applied to white people in the same position. "Look what happened when so-and-so got into office." In most instances we are criticizing a person of color for not being perfect (by our standards), and then using that person as an example of an entire group of people.

People of color are not perfect. Within each community of color, people are as diverse as white people, with all the human strengths and failings. The question is one of justice. No one should have to earn justice. We don't talk about taking away rights or opportunities from all white people because we don't like some of them or because we know some white people who don't make the decisions we think they should. Even when white people break the law, are obviously incompetent for the position they hold, are mean, cruel, or inept, it is often difficult to hold them accountable for their actions. Our laws call for equal treatment of everyone. We should apply the same standards and treatments to people of color as we do to white people.

Not only are people of color not perfect, neither are they representatives of their race. Yet how many times have we said:

"But I know a person of color who ... "
"A person of color told me that ... "
"So and so is a credit to her race ... "
(Turning to an individual) "What do people of color think about that ... ?"
"Let's ask so and so, he's a person of color."

We would never say that a white person was representative of that race, even if that person were Babe Ruth, Mother Teresa, Hitler, John Lennon, or Margaret Thatcher, much less the only white person in the room. When was the last time you spoke as a representative for white people?

Imagine yourself in a room of 50 people where you are the only white person. At one point in the middle of a discussion about a major issue, the facilitator turns to you and says, "Could you please tell us what white people think about this issue?" How would you feel? What would you say?

Would it make any difference if the facilitator said, "I know you can't speak for other white people, but could you tell us what the white perspective is on this issue?" What support would you want from other people around you in the room?

In that situation would you want a person of color to be your ally by interrupting the racial dynamic and pointing out that there isn't just one white perspective and that you couldn't represent white people? Would you want someone to challenge the other people present and stand up for you? Being a white ally to people of color calls for the same kind of intervention — stepping in to support people of color when we see any kind of racism being played out.

It's Not Just a Joke

"**D**ID YOU HEAR THE ONE ABOUT THE CHINAMAN WHO ... " What do you do when someone starts to tell a joke that you think is likely to be a racial putdown? What do you do if the racial nature of the joke is only apparent at the punchline? How do you respond to a comment that contains a racial stereotype?

Interrupting racist comments can be scary because we risk turning the attack or anger toward us. We are sometimes accused of dampening the mood, being too serious or too sensitive. We may be ridiculed for being friends of the group being attacked. People may think we're arrogant or trying to be politically correct. They may try to get back at us for embarrassing them. If you're in an environment where any of this could happen, then you know that it is not only not safe for you; it's even more unsafe for people of color.

People tell jokes and make comments sometimes out of ignorance, but usually knowing at some level that the comment puts down someone else and creates collusion between the speaker and the listener. The joke teller is claiming that we're normal, intelligent, and sane, and others are not. The effect is to exclude someone or some group of people from the group, to make it a little (or a lot) more unsafe for them to be there. Furthermore, by objectifying someone, it makes it that much easier for the next person to tell a joke, make a comment, or take stronger action against any member of the objectified group.

The reverse is also true. Interrupting such behavior makes it less safe to harass or discriminate, and more safe for the intended targets of the abuse. Doing nothing is tacit approval and collusion with the abuse. There is no neutral stance. If someone is being attacked, even by a joke or teasing, there are no innocent bystanders.

As a white person you can play a powerful role in such a situation. When people of color protest against being put down in an atmosphere where they are already disrespected, they are often discounted as well. You, as a white person interrupting verbal abuse, may be listened to and heeded because it breaks the collusion from other white people that the abuser expected. If a person of color speaks up first, then you can support that person by stating why you think it is right to challenge the comments. In either case, your intervention as a white person challenging racist comments is important and often effective.

What can you actually say in the presence of derogatory comments? There are no right or wrong answers. The more you do it the better you get. Even if it doesn't come off as you intended, you will influence others to be more sensitive and you will model the courage and integrity to interrupt verbal abuse. Following are suggestions for where to start.

If you can tell at the beginning that a joke is likely to be offensive or involves stereotypes and putdowns, you can say something like: "I don't want to hear a joke or story that reinforces stereotypes or puts down a group of people," or "Please stop right there. It sounds like your story is going to make fun of a group of people and I don't want to hear about it," or "I don't like humor that makes it unsafe for people here," or "I don't want to hear a joke that asks us to laugh at someone else's expense." There are many ways to say something appropriate without attacking or being offensive yourself.

Using "I" statements should be an important part of your strategy. Rather than attacking someone, it is stronger to state how you feel, what you want. Other people may still become defensive, but there is more opportunity for them to hear what you have to say if you word it as an "I" statement.

Often you don't know the story is offensive until the punchline. Or you just are not sure what you're hearing, but it makes you uncomfortable. It is appropriate to say afterwards that the joke was inappropriate because … , or the story was offensive because … , or it made you feel uncomfortable because … Trust your feelings about it!

In any of these interactions you may need to explain further why stories based on stereotypes reinforce abuse, and why jokes and comments that put people down are offensive. Rather than calling someone racist or writing someone off, interrupting abuse is a way to do public education. It is a way to put what you know about racial stereotypes and abuse into action to stop them.

Often people telling racial jokes are defensive about being called on the racism and may argue or defend themselves. You don't have to prove anything, although a good discussion of the issues is a great way to do more education. It's now up to the other person to think about your comments and to decide what to do. Everyone nearby will have heard you make a clear, direct statement challenging verbal abuse. Calling people's attention to something they assumed was innocent makes them more sensitive in the future and encourages them to stop and think about what they say about others.

Some of the other kinds of reactions you can expect, and your potential responses, include the following.

- "It's only a joke." "It may 'only' be a joke, but it is at someone's expense. It creates an environment that is less safe for the person or group being joked about. Abuse is not a joke."

- "I didn't mean any harm." "I'm sure you didn't. But you should understand the harm that results even if you didn't mean it, and change what you say."

- "Is this some kind of thought patrol?" "No, people can think whatever they want to. But we are responsible for what we say in public. A verbal attack is like any other kind of attack; it hurts the person attacked. Unless you intentionally want to hurt someone, you should not tell jokes or stories like this."

- "This joke was told to me by a member of that group." "It really makes no difference who tells it. If it is offensive then it shouldn't be told. It is sad but true that some of us put down our own racial or ethnic group. That doesn't make it okay or less hurtful."

Sometimes the speaker will try to isolate you by saying that everyone else likes the story, everyone else laughed at the joke. At that point you might want to turn to the others and ask them if they like hearing jokes that are derogatory, do they like stories that attack people?

Sometimes the joke or derogatory comment will be made by a member of the racial group the comment is about. They may believe negative stereotypes about their racial group, they may want to separate themselves from others like themselves, or they may have accepted the racial norms of white peers in order to be accepted. In this situation it is more appropriate, and probably more effective, to talk to that person separately and express your concerns about how comments reinforce stereotypes and make the environment unsafe.

Speaking out makes a difference. Even a defensive speaker (and who of us isn't defensive when challenged on our behavior?) will think about what you said and probably speak more carefully in the future. I have found that when I respond to jokes or comments, other people come up to me afterwards and say they are glad I said something because the comments bothered them too but they didn't know what to say. Many of us stand around, uneasy but hesitant to intervene. By speaking out we model effective intervention and encourage other people to do the same. We set a tone for being active rather than passive, challenging racism rather than colluding with it.

The response to your intervention also lets you know whether the abusive comments are intentional or unintentional, malicious or not. It will give you information about whether the speaker is willing to take responsibility for the effects words have on others. We all have a lot to learn about how racism hurts people. We need to move on from our mistakes, wiser from the process. No one should be trashed.

If the speaker persists in making racially abusive jokes or comments, then further challenge will only result in arguments and fights. People around them need to take the steps necessary to protect themselves from abuse. You may need to think of other tactics to create a safe and respectful environment, including talking with peers to develop a plan for dealing with this person, or talking with a supervisor.

If you are in a climate where people are being put down, teased, or made the butt of jokes based on their race, gender, sexual orientation, age, or any other factor, you should investigate whether other forms of abuse such as sexual harassment or racial discrimination are occurring as well. Jokes and verbal abuse are obviously not the most important forms that racism takes. (Analysis of organizational or institutional racism, and steps you can take to intervene against it, are the subjects of Part V.) However, we all have the right to live, work, and socialize in environments free of verbal and emotional harassment. In order to create contexts where white people and people of color can work together to challenge more fundamental forms of racism, we need to be able to talk to each other about the ways that we talk to each other.

Talking and Working with White People

ONE OF THE RESPONSIBILITIES OF A WHITE ALLY is to work with other white people. But what does this really mean? If we look at Western history we can see that members of exploited groups have rarely gained political or economic change by converting more and more members of the group in power to their side. Groups in power don't generally make concessions to disenfranchised groups just because they understand that it is the right, moral, or just thing to do. Social change comes when people organize to challenge the everyday practices and policies of the organizations and institutions in society. Popular opinion is important at certain times in efforts to create change, but I believe it is unrealistic to think that most white people will become active participants in the struggle for racial justice in the near future. We could spend all of our time talking with other white people, trying to convince them that racism is indeed a problem and that they should do something about it, but I don't think this is an effective or strategic use of our time or energy.

Training, workshops, talks, and other forms of popular education are important. I do a lot of each of these things. But to what end? In many of the workshops I find there are a few white people — often young or adult males — who resist even acknowledging that racism exists. They are sometimes loud and vociferous, sometimes soft-spoken, but they demand lots of time and attention from the group. They assume that they and their concerns deserve center stage. When I talk with other trainers around the country, our discussion sometimes gets bogged down as we try to figure out how to reach these people. What magic exercise, response, or group activity can we develop to reach the most resistant white people? What are we doing wrong?

I think that self-criticism is useful. But I also wonder if we should be paying so much attention to these people. A workshop group can easily spend too much time taking care of the feelings of white people rather than attending to the concerns of the people of color present.

I know that when white people express such common responses to discussions of white behavior as "I am feeling unsafe," "White people are under attack," "Nobody wants to hear our side of the story," "What I said was misunderstood or misinterpreted," or "I didn't intend to hurt anyone," I want to take care of them by giving them time and attention. It can be difficult for me to set limits with them, to ask them to stop responding and just listen for a bit, to acknowledge their feelings but to juxtapose their perceptions to the greater reality in the room. There are a lot of things I could say.

- I may need to say, "I recognize that you don't feel safe, but this is not about safety. Many of us don't feel safe, but we have to keep addressing the structures that put us at risk and that may mean operating out of our comfort level."
- I may need to say that although it is, of course, personal, it is not personal. The problem under discussion is institutional racism, not their personal behavior, although they have a responsibility for their personal behavior and for addressing racism.
- I may need to say, "Rather than defending yourself, I encourage you to just take in what was said, understand the spirit in which it was offered, and take some time to reflect upon it before responding."

I have never found that getting into a long discussion with someone who is defensive is useful. It just increases their defensiveness and my frustration. I get caught up in attempting to win them over to the anti-racist side, converting them by the power of my arguments and reasoning.

I've decided that I don't want to be an anti-racist missionary trying to convert white people to a belief in racial justice. My goal is not to neutralize, overcome, persuade, convince, overwhelm, or seduce them if they are resistant.

This decision has increased my effectiveness as a facilitator because it means I don't get locked into a passionate debate with participants as often, and I no longer try to meet their every defense with an effective response. I can listen to them and move on to working with other participants and, more importantly, with the group itself.

Make no mistake, my goal is partly to motivate white people to take a stand against racism. But there are plenty of well-intentioned white people who want to move forward in this work. I find it more effective to help them find the understanding and tools to make their work more effective than to spend large quantities of time trying to convert the unconvertible.

I also try to be clear with myself that I am not invested in how many white people I win over. My role as a facilitator is to provide the safety, information, and exercises that allow people to understand their role as community members and to figure out how to address injustice. I have no control over what they do with the opportunity, and much as I would like to have the magic dust that would turn everyone I spoke with into anti-racism activists, I know that every individual makes his or her own moral choices. When I work with people I am trying to send them out the door more connected to each other as part of a community, more aware of injustice in their midst, and committed and better equipped to go out of the room and take some specific actions to challenge racism. If there are white people in the room who are unable or unwilling to do so, I am not going to spend huge amounts of time and energy trying to convince them they should.

When the goal of a group is organizing against racism, then we are not talking about winning people over. We are trying to achieve some concrete changes in the institutional practices we confront, and that requires some combination of social, economic, and political pressure. We are not trying to change the minds of government officials, judges, or corporate executives; we are trying to change public policy, judicial practice, or corporate behavior. Being persuasive is rarely a tactic that works in achieving organizational change.

There were large numbers of African Americans involved at all levels of the civil rights movement, but perhaps not even a majority of African Americans were active participants. There were a substantial number of white allies in the struggle, but certainly they were far from a majority of whites. But those that were active were effective enough in confronting white power that the country could not continue to operate without attending to some of the most glaring aspects of racism at the time.

There are ongoing struggles today to end racism. The question I hope to leave white people with is "Which side are you on?" The side of resistance and backlash, the side that protects white interests and perpetuates injustice? Or the side that works as allies to people of color in the fight to end racial discrimination, racial violence, and racial exploitation? I can challenge others with the question, but I can only answer it for myself.

What About Friends
and Family Members?

W E MAY HAVE A LOT MORE AT STAKE PERSONALLY when confronted with friends or family members who are outspokenly racist. Our ability to continue the relationship or to spend time with that person may be at issue. Here again, unfortunately, there is no magic dust that will help them change their minds. In this situation I have had to decide whether to challenge their opinions, set limits to what they can say around me, end the relationship, or agree to disagree. Obviously it depends partly on how close and/or important the relationship is to me. Even in those rare times when I have decided to end a relationship, I have tried to make it clear that it is because of my values and because of my commitment to my friends and colleagues of color that I could not continue to spend time with that person's attitude, comments, and behavior. I want them to know that it is specifically because of their racism that I can't be around them, not because of personality differences or different interests.

However, in most relationships there are grounds for engagement. All of us who are white have work to do on racism, all of us who are men on sexism, all of us who are straight on heterosexism. Rather than feeling superior or righteous because "I'm not racist," we can gently but seriously challenge each other. I try to engage people in open discussion with questions like:

"Why did you say that?"

"Why do you say such stereotyped and negative things about people of color?"

"I've known you a long time and I know you're not as mean-spirited as that comment makes you sound."

"I love you a lot, but I can't let these things that you do around people of color go unchallenged."

"You may know a great deal about … But when it comes to talking about this issue you're wrong, misinformed, inaccurate, not looking at the whole picture, etc."

"I've been told by Asian Americans that when you use that word it is very offensive. Are you trying to hurt people?'

I find that I can quickly tell if someone is well-intentioned but unaware of the effects of their words, or if they are resistant and not likely to change their behavior.

When relating to friends and family I speak up because I can no longer remain silent. I refuse to bond or collude with other white people in maintaining racism. I hope my actions make it easier for people of color to be around these particular white people.

But I also try to be clear with myself that my efforts at this level, as necessary as they are for me, are not going to contribute to ending racism. This realization keeps me from spending all my time in discussions with Uncle Max and Aunt Jane about how they talk about people of color.

I think it is crucial that as white people we work with other white people. But not every white person, not all of the time, perhaps not even most of the time.

QUESTIONS AND ACTIONS:
WORKING WITH WHITE PEOPLE

1. What is your personal investment in converting white people?

2. Which white people in your personal network of family and friends do you think it makes sense for you to talk with? And which white people would it not be useful or productive for you to talk with?

3. Does talking with white people sometimes divert your time and attention from organizing white people or participating in anti-racist activities? How can you change that?

4. What long-term anti-racist goals are you trying to achieve in your organization, institution, or community?

5. Which white people do you need to work with, influence, and organize to achieve those goals?

6. What kind of education will raise white people's awareness and understanding to provide an environment that will support those goals?

7. Which people of color will you talk with to help you answer the previous questions?

8. Which individuals or groups of white people do people of color around you want you to talk or work with?

Allies, Collaborators, and Agents

A S WE HAVE SEEN, an ally takes an active but strategic role in confronting racism. A collaborator, on the other hand, is someone who follows the rules (which are set up to benefit white people), doesn't make waves, and makes sure that most people of color don't have the information and resources they need to move ahead. They don't have to be overtly racist (although some are) because the organization or institution they work in maintains racism without their active contribution. They simply collude with the status quo rather than challenging it. A collaborator says, "I'm just doing my job, just getting by, just raising my family. Racism doesn't affect me." But they continue enjoying the benefits of being white and ignore the costs of racism.

In reality, most of us are more actively complicit in perpetuating racism than collaborators. Many of us find ourselves in situations in which, because of racism, we have more status, seniority, experience, or inside connections than the people of color we are around. This may be in the PTA, in a civic group, in a church, in a recreational program, on the job, at school, in a store, or in a neighborhood. As an ally we can be welcoming, sharing information, resources, and support. Or as an agent we can be unwelcoming. We may treat people of color a little bit differently, as outsiders, so that they know their place. We may not share all of the information or resources we have with them. We might set limits on their participation by failing to provide culturally appropriate outreach and opportunities. In many small and large ways we may not reach out to people of color to the same degree as we do to white people. We may give them the message that they are not as welcome, not as legitimate, not as qualified, not as acceptable as friends, neighbors, shoppers, members, or classmates. In this way many of us act as agents to maintain a white culture of power.

But there is a stronger sense in which I use the word "agent" — to refer to the way that many of us have become agents of the ruling class in maintaining racism through the roles we play in the community.

People in the ruling class — those who are at the top of the economic pyramid — have never wanted to deal directly with people on the bottom of the pyramid and they have always wanted to prevent people at the bottom of the pyramid from organizing for power. Thus they have created a series of occupations that buffer them from the rest of the population. I will call this the buffer zone. The buffer zone consists of all the jobs that carry out the agenda of the ruling class without ruling class presence. The buffer zone has three primary purposes.

The first function is to take care of people on the bottom of the pyramid. If there were a literal free-for-all for the 9 percent of the wealth that 80 percent of us have to fight over, there would be chaos and many more people would be dying in the streets (instead of dying invisibly in homes, hospitals, prisons, rest homes, homeless shelters, etc.). So there are many occupations to sort out which people get how much of the 9 percent, and to take care of those who aren't really making it. Social welfare workers, nurses, teachers, counselors, case workers of various sorts, advocates for various groups – all these workers (who are mostly women) take care of people at the bottom of the pyramid.

The second function of jobs in the buffer zone is to keep hope alive, to keep alive the myth that anyone can make it in this society, that there is a level playing field, and that racism and other forms of discrimination no longer exist. These jobs, often the same as the caring jobs, determine which people will be the lucky ones to receive jobs and job training, a college education, housing allotments, or health care. The people in these jobs convince us that if we just work hard, follow the rules, and don't cause waves, we too can get ahead and gain a few benefits from the system. Sometimes getting ahead in this context means getting a job in the buffer zone and becoming one of the people who hands out the benefits.

The final function of jobs in the buffer zone is to maintain the system by controlling those who want to make changes. Because people at the bottom keep fighting for change, people at the top need occupations that keep people in their place in the family, in schools, in the neighborhood, and even overseas in other countries. Police, security guards, prison wardens, soldiers, deans and administrators, immigration officials, and fathers in their role as "the discipline in the family" — these are all primarily male roles in the buffer zone designed to keep people in their place in the hierarchy. (These distinctions are not always so distinct. For instance, many caring roles, such as social worker, also have a strong client control element to them, and the police are now trying to soften their image by including a caring component, using community policing strategies to build trust in the community.)

Buffer zone jobs are the largest category of working- and middle-class jobs. Each of us in one of those jobs should ask ourselves critical questions.

Am I an agent of the ruling class or am I an ally to people at the bottom?
As a white person, am I an agent of the racism that reinforces the racial hierarchy,
or am I an ally to people of color at the bottom of the pyramid?

We all need a job and therefore we have to work in the pyramid that is designed to keep power and money flowing to the top. Most of us want our work to benefit people at the bottom. Our heartwork has led us to choose work that will make a contribution to society and not just help the rich get richer. But who really benefits from our work?

Some of us are in more powerful positions, where we supervise people of color; allocate benefits to people of color such as jobs, housing, welfare, educational opportunities; or control people of color. We are paid agents of the ruling class, instructed to use racism to insure that although a few people of color may advance individually to keep hope alive, people of color as a group don't advance and the racial hierarchy does not change.

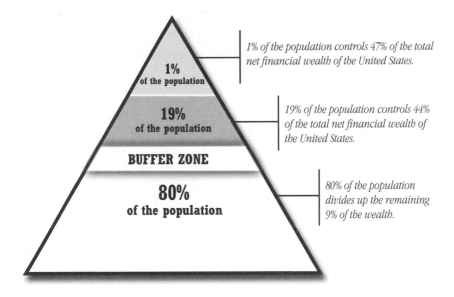

1% of the population controls 47% of the total net financial wealth of the United States.

19% of the population controls 44% of the total net financial wealth of the United States.

80% of the population divides up the remaining 9% of the wealth.

To quote Taiaiake Alfred, substituting the word racism for colonialism:

The challenge, and the hope, is for each person to recognize and counteract the effects of [racism] in his or her own life, and thus develop the ability to live in a way that contests [racism]. We are all co-opted to one degree or another, so we can only pity those who are blind or who refuse to open their eyes to the [racial] reality, and who continue to validate, legitimate, and accommodate the interests of that reality in opposition to the goals and values of their own nations.[1]

ASSESSMENT:
THE BUFFER ZONE

1. Is the work you do part of the buffer zone, either taking care of people at the bottom of the pyramid, keeping hope alive, or controlling them?
2. Historically how has your job, career, profession, or occupation developed in relationship to communities of color? What impact has it had on different communities of color at different times?
3. How have people in your line of work protected white privilege and excluded people of color?
4. How have individuals and communities of color resisted these actions either from within your work/occupation/profession or from the community?
5. Who are white people who have challenged racism in your work?

6. Who benefits from the work that you do — people at the top of the pyramid, people in the buffer zone, or people at the bottom?

7. What could you do to become less of an agent of the wealthy and more of an ally to people of color?

8. What will you do?

The next section of this book looks at how whiteness has been defined in terms of particular racial groups and how we can be more effective allies to each one.

PART IV

The Effects of History

Introduction

THE FOLLOWING SECTIONS GIVE A BRIEF HISTORY of white people's relationships to particular "racial" groups. I include this information for several reasons. First, most of us are woefully misinformed about the actual history of interracial relationships, particularly their more devastating aspects. We have been taught lies beginning with the benign story of Columbus's "discovery" of America.

Second, our history affects our current situations and experiences. The effects of slavery, the genocide of Native Americans, the conquest of Mexico, and the banning of Chinese and later all Asian immigration continue to influence our lives and the lives of people of color.

Third, we cannot build trust and an honest commitment to creating equality in this country if we are denying the injustices of the past. Our good faith efforts to change the system will not be taken seriously if we continue to deny or distort the record of white racism.

Fourth, the past, even with all its horror, can give us hope for the future. White Americans did contribute to abolishing slavery and ending coolie labor. We expanded the vote to people of color and women and allowed them to hold elected office. We ended legally sanctioned segregation and broadened the democratic base of this country. We can easily be defeated by the challenges of the present if we don't understand the progress we have made in the past.

Finally, we have a long history of white people speaking out for economic and political justice, and we need to reclaim those heroes and continue that commitment.

These brief histories will focus on what white people did. The history of people of color's strong, determined, and diverse resistance to racism is beyond the scope of this book. There are many good sources for that history, some of which are listed in the bibliography.

Unfortunately, when we focus on white racism and its effects on people of color it can seem as if the lives of people of color are determined by racism, that they are nothing but victims of injustice. Nothing could be further from the truth. They are creators of their own lives and cultures. Racism is one of the social constraints that influence how people of color live, but racism does not determine how they lead their daily lives.

In this book, because the focus is on white racism, there could be the false perception that I am ignoring the cultural, political, economic, and personal achievements of people of color. White people do this all the time, even those who are committed to anti-racist work. To counter this tendency it is important for you to supplement the information in this section with the writing, music, dance, speeches, and history of people of color themselves in all the diversity they represent.

The following sections are more than very brief (and inadequate) lessons about a part of our white history. They break down the monolithic racial terms we have developed for large conglomerations of different peoples. They hint at the richness of culture, creativity, and community that lies behind the simple-minded stereotypes and misinformation we have about other groups of people.

These sections allow us some insight into how white racism has defined and controlled specific other groups. All of these sections are about white people and what we have done to people of color, even though they seem to focus on particular groups of people of color. If we keep this emphasis in mind, each section will help us think more creatively about how to be better allies to Native Americans, African Americans, Asian Americans, Latino/as, Arab Americans, Jews, and people of mixed heritage, as well as groups not discussed here, such as South Pacific Islanders and South Asians.

People of Mixed Heritage

NOTHING CHALLENGES OUR PERCEPTIONS OF RACE more than the millions of people of mixed heritage in the United States. Still largely invisible in our culture, their presence is in sharp contradiction to our expectation that racial difference is binary, clear, and simple. People of mixed heritage pose difficult challenges not only for white people, but for people of color as well. Many people of color have been pushed to claim sharply delineated identities in resistance to white racism. They have minimized the complexities of their own identities and cultures for strategic reasons. At the same time, fear and lies about people of color have pushed white people to disown and persecute white people in racially mixed relationships and people of mixed heritage — even members of their own families.

It is estimated that 30 to 70 percent of African Americans are multiracial. Virtually all Latino/as and Filipinos are multiracial, as are the majority of American Indians and Native Hawaiians. A significant proportion of white-identified people are of multiracial origins.[1] Racial identity is still a crucial determinant of one's opportunities in life. In the United States, a person is considered a member of the lowest status group from which they have any heritage. Therefore it is unsafe for most white people to acknowledge any part of a mixed heritage. Although the numbers are substantial, we have no way of knowing how many white people are actually of mixed heritage.

The myth of biological race and the desire to maintain the boundaries (and attendant divisions of wealth) between white people and people of color sustain white people's fear of interracial relationships and mixed heritage children. Often the justification for discrimination and persecution of interracial couples is that the difficulties of living "like that" are so bad because of the racist response of other white people. Present racial prejudice becomes the justification for continued racist practices against people of mixed heritage.

It was only in 1967 that the U.S. Supreme Court ruled remaining miscegenation laws illegal. Even today it is commonly assumed that members of interracial relationships and mixed heritage children lead harder lives, meet more prejudice, and have higher rates of divorce, suicide, and other personal problems. There is no proof that this is so, and indeed there are indications that such people are more resilient and have higher self-esteem than monocultural people.[2]

People in interracial relationships and people of mixed heritage belie many of our common justifications for racism and racial segregation. Their health and success challenge the biological and cultural justifications commonly used for the separation and inferior treatment of people of color. They emphasize the futility of searching for genetic justification for social and political distinctions between people.

We are becoming a nation with a substantial population of people of mixed heritage. The links between physical characteristics such as skin color and either the continent of origin of one's foreparents or the cultural roots of one's ancestors will eventually become nearly indistinguishable. People of mixed heritage challenge our assumptions about racial difference and the naturalness of our "racial" categories.

The presence of large numbers of people of mixed heritage does not mean that we are moving toward the elimination of racism through the withering away of racial differences. It is perfectly possible to replace a racial hierarchy of discrete groups with a racially continuous hierarchy that still has white people on top, such as is found in Brazil. Unless we eliminate white power and privilege, people with lighter skin color, regardless of racial heritage, will be more highly valued than people with darker skin.

Racism is resilient. White people have constantly shifted the vocabulary of racism and the ways that we justify our power. There are many other ways to justify racism besides the religious and scientific reasons we have used in our past. The current force of institutional racism in our society may eventually make such justifications completely unnecessary. The large numbers of visible people of mixed heritage challenge our present justification of racism, but they do not necessarily challenge the ongoing force of racism itself.

In reading the sections below, keep in mind the mixed heritage of many Americans in all "racial" groups. This should be one more reminder of the arbitrariness of referring to entire groups of people as single coherent entities.

Native Americans

I GREW UP WATCHING ROY ROGERS, Gene Autry, and the Lone Ranger kill Indians. I played cowboys and Indians every chance I had. We fought over who got to be the cowboys because they always won. Native Americans, for me, were reduced to one generic Indian male who was worth about 1/20th of a white cavalry officer. I "knew" what they looked like, what they wore, where they lived, and how sneaky, brave, and clever they were. I knew that part of my responsibility as a white man in the past would have been to protect white women from Indian savages.

Most of all, I "knew" that they were all dead. It was precisely because they were history that we dressed up as Indians on Halloween and in Thanksgiving plays. In Cub Scouts I learned to yell and pat my mouth in the "Indian" war cry, and I was given toy tomahawks so I could pretend to scalp my opponents. I had no understanding that I was recreating a distorted and painful history, and I certainly had no idea that Native Americans were still alive in the United States.

Today there are over 500 federally recognized Native-American nations in the United States. At the time that Columbus arrived in the West Indies there were approximately 15 million indigenous people in North America. Today, after reaching a low point around 1900, the population of Native Americans in the United States is around 3 million according to U.S. government census figures, although these figures are highly contested.[1]

The population of the Taino people and other local inhabitants of the West Indies decreased from several million to 22,000 by 1514, only 22 years after Columbus arrived. The population of Native Americans in the continental United States decreased from 12 million to 237,000 during the first four centuries of our history. During that time white people expropriated 97.5 percent of Native-American land.[2]

Please read these last two paragraphs again and stop to consider the magnitude of this genocide.

For many of us, Native Americans are largely invisible in our daily lives and are dead, romantic figures in our imaginations. They have been replaced by slogans, chants, mascots, historical replicas, and new age imitations.

All the land of North America, including the land that you are on at the moment, originally belonged to Native Americans. They did not use the same legal concepts of ownership as we do, but they knew that they had rights to use it in exchange for caring for it.

There are no generalizations that we can make about Native Americans except insofar as we describe the ways that they have been exploited, and even these vary tremendously. Various Native-American nations are still struggling for recognition of their sovereignty; for control over what little land they have retained; for an end to interference in their affairs;

for an end to mining, logging, and toxic waste dumping that are destroying their lands; for an end to the belittlement, stereotyping, and mockery of their culture; and for full respect and civil rights within American society.

The enslavement of Native Americans occurred on both coasts of the North American continent and was carried out by early explorers, wealthy landowners, priests, and local governments. Early in its history, the United States government systematically killed Native Americans in this country to remove them from land that colonists wanted, often with the stated intention of committing genocide. This policy was consistent, from the highest levels of government down to the ordinary citizens who carried out much of the destruction.

The Catholic Church officially justified the destruction of Native Americans in the papal bulls of 1452 and 1493. The bull of May 4, 1493, "Inter Cetera," states that "barbarous nations" be "subjugated and over-thrown" as a means of converting them to the Catholic faith and Christian religion. (There is currently an international movement to get this papal bull rescinded.)

But the church did more than sanction the destruction of Native Americans. Priests and other representatives of the church were often the people who carried it out. For example, the missions set up along the California coast by the church were death camps for the Indians captured and forced to be there by the Spanish. Between 1779 and 1833, twice as many deaths as births occurred at the missions, often prompting padres to call in Spanish soldiers to raid distant villages for replacements. In reality the missions were often slave labor camps, and an early ethnologist, Alfred Kroeber, remarked, "The brute upshot of missionization, in spite of its kindly flavor and humanitarian root, was only one thing: death."[3]

The church was just one of many participants in the process of destroying Native-American peoples. Ward Churchill gives a vivid description of this period in our nation's history in his book *Indians Are Us?* and includes the following quotes and events. Cotton Mather, a noted colonial minister, referred to the burning of Indians as "a barbecue" and to Indians themselves as "wolves — both being beasts of prey, tho' different in shape." In 1783 George Washington ordered that those remaining within the areas of the initial 13 states be "hunted like beasts" and that a "war of extermination" be waged against those barring U.S. access to certain desired areas, notably the Ohio River Valley.[4] Washington himself fought for the British against the Indians, and as payment he received thousands of acres of native peoples' land. He also owned shares in the Mississippi Company, a land speculation group that claimed 2.5 million acres of native land in the Ohio Valley where native people were still living. On May 31, 1779, Washington wrote to General Sullivan, who was leading an expedition against the Iroquois: "The immediate object is their total destruction and devastation and the capture of as many person of every age and sex as possible .... ruin their crops ... and prevent their planting more .... lay waste all settlements around that the country may not be merely overrun, but destroyed."[5]

Or, as Thomas Jefferson put it in 1812, Euro-Americans should drive every Indian in their path "with the beasts of the forests into the stony mountains"; alternatively, as he'd already stated in 1807, the United States should "pursue [the Indians] into extermination, or drive them to new seats beyond our reach;" national policy should be to wage war against each native people it encountered "until that tribe is exterminated, or driven beyond the Mississippi." Andrew Jackson characterized Indians as "wild dogs" and supervised the mutilation of about 800 Creek Indian corpses — the bodies of men, women, and children that he and his men had massacred. "Scalp bounties paid better than buffalo hides for 'enterprising citizens' in Texas and the Dakotas until the 1880s."[6]

Racism against Native Americans, like all racism, is gendered. White women were said to need protection from rape by Indian men, who were portrayed as sexual animals. Images of white women ravished by Native-American men were used to incite white men to kill them. Native-American women were extolled when they served white men (i.e., Pocahontas, Sacajawea) and were otherwise portrayed as exotic, shy, and reserved sexual creatures. White family norms and attitudes were projected onto Native Americans, whose families were then destroyed by forced adoption, residential schooling, and federal policies breaking up tribal ownership of land.

As with slavery or any policy of violence and exploitation, we are not responsible for what our forefathers and foremothers did. We are responsible for acknowledging what happened, what it cost, and who participated. The annihilation of Native Americans in the United States happened. It was systematic, sanctioned by all levels of society, and carried out by ordinary citizens as well as by the military and state militias. Most of our predecessors participated, and every single one of them and all of us gained enormously because of this mass murder.

White people have denied the extent of the genocide by minimizing estimates of the number of Native Americans who lived here. Although now discredited by most historical research, there are still attempts to describe the country as an empty wilderness with a few bands of "Indians" here and there.

Another way to deny what happened is to make it appear to be a natural phenomenon with a momentum of its own. Americans have talked about "manifest destiny" as if there were not real white people involved in the process of killing Native Americans and appropriating their land, as if white people were not manifesting and manufacturing that destiny.

White people also justified the genocide by saying that Native Americans died from diseases they were biologically unable to resist. We know that white people introduced diseases to Native-American populations intentionally and systematically as part of a policy of extermination. For example, "In 1763 Lord Jeffrey Amherst ordered a subordinate to distribute items taken from a smallpox infirmary as 'gifts' during a peace parley with Pontiac's Confederacy .... Upwards of 100,000 Indians died of smallpox in the ensuing epidemic."[7]

Yet another justification white people have used for their violence is that Native Americans were simple and unsophisticated and that, by implication, their culture was not really a loss because they were unable to compete in the modern world. In fact, there were long-term, stable, complex, and sophisticated cultures in all parts of this country including the Southwest, Northwest, South, Southern Mississippi Valley, Northeast, and the Great Plains. Furthermore, a people's right to exist, control their land, and maintain their culture is not contingent on their sophistication.

Besides, Native societies were not primitive and unsophisticated. They were so developed that westerners continually took their ideas and practices and incorporated them into their institutions. White American settlers exploited Native-American agricultural, medicinal, hunting, and various craft techniques, land-use patterns, trade routes, and the genetic development of foods and were also heavily influenced by Native-American social and political arrangements. Early political leaders, including Thomas Jefferson, Thomas Paine, and Benjamin Franklin, acknowledged the Native-American origin of many of the practices they incorporated into the Articles of Confederation and the American Constitution.[8] Early women suffragists such as Elizabeth Cady Stanton, Matilda Joslyn Gage, and Lucretia Mott also were inspired by the respectful gender relationships, the lack of violence against women, and the strong role that women played in native societies to challenge the lack of women's participation in social and political life in American and Canadian society.[9]

Of course, European Americans rarely acknowledged the source of these ideas when the very existence of native nations was under attack. Today our children are not taught, and few adults even know about, the achievements and contributions that Native Americans have made to our lives. Contemporary Native-American healing, spiritual, agricultural and land use, and medicinal practices continue to be exploited by corporations and individuals with no recognition of the source of these practices, no compensation, and continued attack upon the Native-American communities that produced them.[10] The cultural appropriation (possibly cultural imperialism is a better term) of Native-American cultural and spiritual beliefs and practices is part of the continuing exploitation of Native-American nations and communities.

We cannot change the past, but if we are honest with ourselves, and if we want to stop the injustices occurring in the present, we have to acknowledge what happened. It is hard to face. It makes me sad and angry, depressed and frustrated. I feel guilty over what white people have done and are doing to Native Americans, yet it doesn't help them or me to remain stuck in these feelings. Many of us feel saddened by the past, while remaining ignorant of the present reality of continued exploitation and destruction of Native people, land, and culture.

Throughout the United States today, in every state, Native Americans are struggling to regain control of land, to end centuries of colonization, and to stop cultural exploitation. Native-American lands are being mined, logged, hunted, and developed without permission or adequate compensation. Native Americans are fighting for recognition of their sovereignty, return of appropriated cultural artifacts, recognition of their status as Native Americans, protection of sacred religious sites, an end to police and military interference with traditional hunting and fishing rights, culturally appropriate education for their children, and the end of stereotyping, inaccuracies, and lies about American history and present realities.

At the same time that white people have vilified and annihilated Native Americans, we have constructed a mythologized image of them. We hold them up as natural, ecologically wise, at one with nature, enduring, skillful, brave, and in possession of rituals, stories, and beliefs that we need to adopt to counter the destructiveness of our modern industrialized lives. Boy Scouts and Campfire Girls, men's lodges and men's movement retreats, new age spiritual groups — all mimic our generic version of Native-American culture.

Our stereotypes are so strong that very often we, or our children, don't believe that someone who is wearing contemporary clothing is a Native American because he or she "doesn't look like one." These stereotypes allow us to talk about how Native Americans were, without addressing who they are. Such symbolic annihilation is devastating to Native Americans because it renders them invisible and their struggles for sovereignty incomprehensible.

There are many simple and immediate ways that we can counter the continued attacks on Native Americans in our society. The following questions suggest some places to start.

QUESTIONS AND ACTIONS:
NATIVE AMERICANS

1. What people lived on the land you presently inhabit? How were they removed? Where do they live now? Are there any land or tribal recognition claims still pending? Where else in your state are these struggles going on?

2. Do Native Americans have full access to jobs, social services, and community resources in your community? For example, what is the unemployment rate for Native-American adults and young people?

3. Are Native Americans in your area harassed for exercising, or prohibited from exercising, traditional hunting and fishing rights?

4. Is there corporate mining, logging, or land devastation occurring on Native lands in your region? Are toxic dumps located on Native lands?

5. Is there a climate of hatred toward Native Americans in your area? How do white people talk about them? Is there police harassment or brutality directed toward them?

6. What forms of government, foods, medical treatments, products, names, and customs have white people adopted from Native Americans? How much has their contribution been recognized? How has it been exploited?

7. Are local Native-American historical sites, relics, and burial grounds preserved in your community? Are museums being asked to return sacred Native-American objects to the people from whom they came? If so, how do they respond?

8. Are you part of a spiritual or growth community that has appropriated Native-American rituals, artifacts, or customs? Have you ever borrowed Native-American spiritual practices? How might it feel to Native Americans when people from different religious backgrounds take their sacred rituals and use them as recreational activities or mix them in with traditions from other cultures?

9. Are there schools, universities, or companies in your vicinity that use Native-American names or figures as mascots, slogans, or product or team names?

10. Do you hear people refer to Native Americans in derogatory ways, make jokes about Indians, or make generalized statements about all Native Americans? How can you respond when someone does a tomahawk chop or war whoop, or otherwise contributes to perpetuating a caricature of a Native American?

11. What do you remember about portrayals of Indians in film and TV when you grew up? How do you think these portrayals affected you?

12. Do your children play with toys and video games or watch TV shows or movies where Native Americans are stereotyped, portrayed as the enemy of white people, or otherwise degraded? Are there books, pictures, or artifacts in your house that degrade, make fun of, or stereotype Native Americans?

13. Do textbooks in your local schools accurately and truthfully describe what white settlers and government troops did to Native Americans? Do any romanticize them? Do any speak of a generic Indian? Is the full story of Columbus's and the colonists' practices and policies told?

14. Do you and your children know about Native Americans in contemporary America?

15. When talking about Native peoples do you refer to Native Americans generically, assuming there are valid generalizations you can make about all Native Americans, or do you name the nation or culture you are referring to and give specific examples?

16. How would Columbus Day and Thanksgiving activities have to be changed so they did not disguise the genocide of Native Americans in the West Indies and New England?

African Americans

A S WITH ANY OTHER "RACIAL" IDENTITY, the term "African American" hides tremendous diversity. In the United States there are Africans, native-born African Americans, and immigrants from the West Indies and South America. There are African Americans with hundreds of years of history as "free blacks" and others whose grandparents were slaves. Many, if not most African Americans have Native-American, white, and Latino/a ancestors. Differences in class, gender, sexual orientation, physical ability, and geographically specific cultures are also vitally important in the African-American community. There are no biological, economic, cultural, or physiological generalizations that hold for them except for the existence of white racism itself, which they must all deal with. Even here they are vulnerable in different ways based on their gender, class, age, sexual orientation, location, and other factors. Generalizations about the effects of white racism and the modes of African-American resistance to it are false and reflect the beliefs of the white people involved.

Since the early 17th century the presence of an at first enslaved and then subjugated population of African Americans in the United States has challenged the truth of white people's claim that the country operates from democratic values. The history of white racism toward African Americans can help us understand how white people have justified racism.

The first Africans were brought to what is now the United States in 1619. In the earliest days of colonial America, most Africans and 75 percent of white Europeans were indentured servants and were treated similarly if not equally.[1] Many whites and African Americans fraternized, some intermarried, and others worked together to revolt against or escape from servitude.

By and large, in the early days of the colonies, Africans were seen by whites as different, but not innately inferior. Differences in economic status were explained by reasons of class and religion, the result of qualities that related to being poor and non-Christian.

By the early 1700s there were over a million slaves in the West Indies and South America, as well as a long tradition in enlightenment Europe of treating darker skinned people as inferior. These factors, combined with a decrease in the number of indentured servants arriving from Europe, led to the gradual expansion of slavery and increasingly rigid distinctions between white servants and African slaves. After the scare of Bacon's Rebellion in 1676, in which white and African workers united in arms to challenge the landowning class, those in power moved quickly to consolidate slavery in the mid-Atlantic region. Over the next 25 years Virginia passed a series of laws that legalized slavery, producing a racially subordinate and stigmatized class below that of all whites. The white landowning class systematically codified the separation of African Americans and poor European Americans by legalizing lifetime servitude (slavery) to control the former and by using the latter as a buffer to protect themselves from rebellion. As historian Ronald Takaki describes the process, "the Virginia elite deliberately pitted white laborers and black slaves against each other. The legislature permitted whites to abuse blacks physically with impunity: in 1680, it prescribed thirty lashes on the bare back 'if any Negro or other slave shall presume to lift up his hand in opposition against any Christian.' Planters used landless whites to help put down slave revolts."[2]

From 1619 until slavery ended officially in 1865, 10 to 15 million Africans were brought to North America, and another 20 to 30 million died in transport — a journey called the Middle Passage.[3] In all, 30 to 45 million Africans were abducted or killed by our white American and European foreparents.[4]

Please pause a moment and take in the magnitude of these numbers.

During slavery, white people did everything possible to dehumanize, demoralize, and degrade African Americans. White society systematically tried to destroy any vestige of the language, culture, spirituality, religion, and family structure of the slave community. This cultural genocide was practiced throughout what was then the United States, and all white Americans, in the North and the South, benefited materially from the economic system of slavery.

Most of the early leaders of our country, including Washington and Jefferson, owned slaves. During the 18th and 19th centuries the slave-based agricultural prosperity of the South fueled the industrial expansion of the North. New waves of immigrants came to a land of opportunity partly supported by the jobs this prosperity generated. For example, jobs in the textile mills and shipbuilding companies of New England and in the clothing sweatshops and trading centers of New York and other large cities were dependent on the cheap cotton produced by slave labor in the South. White immigrants prospered not only while African Americans were enslaved, but because they were, benefiting from the many jobs and trades from which African Americans were excluded.

Not all white people supported slavery. There was a longstanding minority tradition of public outcry for the abolition of slavery, particularly among white women in the 19th century.

The Civil War and the end of slavery occurred because of economic tensions between North and South and because of political differences about state's rights and the expansion of slavery, more than as an outcry against slavery itself. The Civil War was a complicated political, economic, and social event, and while the extension of slavery was a key issue, the abolition of slavery was not a strong concern of the American public. As Lincoln wrote in a letter to Horace Greeley:

> *Dear Sir: I have not meant to leave any one in doubt .... My paramount object in this struggle is to save the Union, and is not either to save or destroy Slavery. If I could save the Union without freeing any slave, I would do it; and if I could save it by freeing all the slaves, I would do it; and if I could do it by freeing some and leaving others alone, I would also do that. What I do about Slavery and the colored race, I do because it helps to save this Union.[5]*

Slavery raises issues for white people that we are not yet finished dealing with. We commonly say that slavery is a thing of the past. Putting an injustice behind us is one of the tactics we looked at in Part I of this book. This tactic is not useful for several reasons.

First, we have not yet fully acknowledged as a society the extent of the devastation that white people perpetrated on West African civilization and on African Americans in this country during the period of slavery. We don't talk about the horrors of the Middle Passage, the systematic attempt to eradicate African culture, and the everyday participation of common white folks in supporting slavery. We still refer to slavery as something that most people survived. We don't talk about the millions dead, the maimed, the tortured, the broken families, the rape, and daily violence. We still talk about good slave owners and pretend that some slaves had it pretty good. One indication of our lack of acknowledgement is that there is still no national or regional museum on slavery and the Middle Passage.

We don't talk about the benefits of slavery to white people. Most of our families did not own slaves. Most of our families did participate in and benefit from slavery, even if our foreparents arrived here after slavery ended. Immigrants benefited from the presence of a group of people that had less respect and status than they did, from being able to take jobs that African Americans were not allowed to do, and from economic development based on agricultural profits from slave labor.

The second problem with "moving on" from slavery is that we rarely acknowledge the long-lasting aftereffects of more than 200 years of slavery. Although slavery was officially abolished by the 13th Amendment in 1865, economic and cultural exploitation; everyday violence including lynching, rape, physical attack, and other forms of mob violence; political disenfranchisement; and almost total segregation in the South and the North continued into recent times. We have had over 350 years of economic and cultural enrichment of the white community at the expense of African Americans. The effects of that exploitation are in the present.

As white people we take credit for the achievements of the past. We are proud of the democratic traditions, the struggle for independence, and the scientific and industrial achievements of our foreparents. We cannot be hypocritical and deny the full complexity of our heritage, including the negative aspects of it. We retain false feelings of superiority and justify further exploitation of African Americans when we deny or minimize the actions of our foreparents. It is even more of an affront and part of our denial when we hold on to symbols and re-enactments that extol white supremacy. The Confederate flag, for example, was the flag of the army that was defending slavery. The Civil War was not just a complex and fascinating military campaign, but also the struggle to liberate large numbers of slaves throughout the country. By continuing to flaunt representations of the defense of slavery we admit that we are unwilling to acknowledge, and in fact continue to deny or minimize, the pain and horror of those whose families and communities have been scarred by hundreds of years of enslavement.

This minimization of the horrors of the past contributes to our denial of present injustices. Some of us lived through the lynchings of the 1930s and 1940s. Many of us lived through the civil rights struggles of the 1950s and 1960s. All of us are living through the criminalization of African-American men, the scapegoating of African-American women, and the police and state brutality of the 1970s, 1980s, and 1990s. Many of us have supported and benefited from segregation in this country during our lifetimes. Many of us and our parents fought against the dismantling of segregation and are still resisting the integration of schools, country clubs, recreation centers, neighborhoods, and businesses. Until we have enough integrity to acknowledge our role and the role of our families, friends, and neighbors in these injustices, we will continue to stand in the way of progress toward full equality. There is no dividing line between slavery, other forms of white exploitation of African Americans, and the present. Until we deal with the past we will not lessen its overpowering influence on the future.

Although white people have systematically tried to destroy African-American culture in this country by not allowing African Americans to learn how to read and write; by withholding public funding for schools; by withholding public means to disseminate music, dance, games, writing, and religion; by preventing religious freedom; and by forced breakup of families, there has always been resistance to that destruction. Enslaved African Americans taught each other to read and write, passed on musical and religious traditions, and resisted their dehumanization.

With the end of slavery and the beginning of migration to Northern cities in significant numbers in the 1940s, the direct assault on African-American culture diminished. It was replaced by the exploitation of that culture by white society. The appropriation of music, dance, fashion, and various elements of "style" from African Americans has enriched white culture and individual white people. For example, blues, jazz, rock and roll, and rap are all African-American musical forms that white people have listened to, copied, and profited from. Even elements of culture that cannot be exported outside the African-American community — for example, concepts such as "Black is Beautiful" and "Black Pride" — have been repackaged by white-owned corporations and marketed back to African Americans.

White racism is not just a system of economic exploitation. It is also a struggle for cultural and ideological domination. African-American cultural resistance has always been strong and persistent. It continues today, constantly taking new and diverse forms.

The impact of African American cultural resistance and resilience reaches far into the American mainstream, even affecting the relationships in white families, most noticeably between young people and adults and between men and women. Intergenerational conflict over clothes, music, patterns of socialization, and interracial dating often trigger parents' or other adults' fears of the perceived subversive, scary, or eroticized elements of African-American people and culture. Young people manipulate these fears to create more space for their personal autonomy and individual creativity. Of course, the icons of African-American culture used by white youth — for example, music and clothing styles — have already been bought by white adults and repackaged for consumption by white youth. This intergenerational "discussion" about lifestyles and personal choices tells us more about white racism and about contests of authority within white families than it does about the virtues and values of rock, jazz, or rap music.

Our national discussions about gender roles and male-female relationships, especially their more difficult and troubling aspects, often use the projected fear of African-American men as a framework. For example, in the late 19th century, debates about women's independence often referred to the need for white men to protect white women and for white women to depend upon and to be loyal and deserving of such white male protection from sexual predators, who were assumed to be black. In other words, the sexual protection that white men demanded white women accept was framed in the context of fear about African-American men.

More recently, national media attention has focused our discussion of contemporary male-female issues on prominent African-American men such as Clarence Thomas (sexual harassment), Mike Tyson (rape), Michael Jackson (child sexual assault), and O.J. Simpson (domestic violence). Each of these issues is current, volatile, and contested. Each strikes deep chords of anger, fear, and pain among white people. The lives of these individuals can be held up in white Americans' conversations about these issues because African-American men are presumed to represent naturally male, but less civilized or controlled sexuality, because they have less protection in a white society, and because they are perceived to be clearly outside the boundaries of whiteness. These issues are less threatening to us when they are framed by white racism. If the debate gets hot and we can't reach an understanding, we can write the whole issue off to the perversions of African-American sexuality.

This pattern continues a tradition of demonizing African-American men, pretending they are aberrant, and condoning further violence toward them. When we use the actions of African-American men as examples (regardless of what they may have actually done), we are furthering the pretense that white men are not violent. The sexual harassment, rape, child sexual assault, and domestic violence committed by white men remain less visible.

The relationship between race and gender issues as they have played out in our country's history has focused on African-American men and white women. The concerns of African-American men have been seen as opposed to the needs of white (generally middle-class) women in the struggle for the right to vote, in many affirmative action programs, and in concerns about women's safety from male violence.

As noted earlier, these dynamics are complex. White women have been active in fighting racism on specific issues such as abolition, education for African Americans after Reconstruction, and voting rights during the civil rights movement. White male resistance to their participation in these struggles motivated the women to organize around specific women's issues. Their work in these movements provided them with organizing skills, political models, inspiration, and experience that they subsequently used in feminist struggles. But often these feminist movements ended up pursuing racist policies that subverted some of the gains they had been working for in their earlier abolition or civil rights work.

The focus on fear of African-American male sexuality leaves the lives and concerns of African-American women unacknowledged. This is despite the fact that African-American women have been in the forefront of the fight against racism and the fight for safety and equality for women. This lack of respect for African-American women has meant that they have not been acknowledged for the particular needs, concerns, insights, skills, and experience they consistently provided both to the struggle to end racism and to the struggle to end sexism.[6]

Two other factors have been at work in white racism against African-American women. White women's roles and relationships have been taken as the norm for all women (even though these norms were, in fact, constructed by racism), and African-American women's lives are not seen or understood. White people have assumed that because many white women did not work outside the home, women of color did not either. We have assumed that because large numbers of white women were falling into poverty (the "feminization of poverty"), so were many women of color. In reality, most were already living in poverty and had nowhere to fall from. We have assumed that since white women were primarily domestic workers, taking care of children and the home, that slave women were also. In fact, most female slaves were field workers and did the same work as men. Since slavery, African-American women have continued to work outside the home, often in the homes of white women.

These are examples of the assumption that African-American lives mirror white lives. Overlaying the patterns of white women's lives on those of African-American women, in conjunction with the lack of opportunity for African-American women to describe their own experience, has contributed to their invisibility and exploitation. (A parallel dynamic occurs for other women of color and poor and working-class white women as well.)

These patterns have also contributed to the exploitation of white women. The wages paid to African-American women as domestics have always put a ceiling on wages paid to white women domestics. The expectations and attitudes of white men toward African-American women will always limit the respect and equality accorded white women. This relationship between the exploitation of African-American and white women has been particularly damaging to poor and working-class white women.

White exploitation of African Americans will always have a boomerang effect on white people, particularly on the poor and working class. We will not be able to recognize the source of those costs as long as our attention is focused on African Americans and not on white people.

Racial exploitation continually takes new forms as white social and economic systems change and as people of color and concerned whites resist. What remains constant is that white lives and norms remain central and opposed to those of African Americans.

When we project personal qualities onto African Americans, it reflects our images of who we think ourselves as white people to be. Statements that African Americans are lazy, promiscuous, or stupid are simultaneously statements that white people are hardworking, monogamous, and smart. Hardworking and monogamous refer to fundamental Christian values. Our statements about people of color tell us how we want to perceive ourselves as white Christians.

Our stereotyped statements about African-American relationships, families, and community structure similarly tell us what we want to believe about white social organization. When we describe African-American families as matriarchal and violent, and their communities as filled with drugs and violence, we are implying that white families are patriarchal and peaceful, and our communities are not filled with drugs and violence.

These characterizations set up a false norm for each community. In fact, there are all kinds of family and community structures in both white and African-American communities, with much more overlap than difference. These dichotomies also establish white valuations of what should be accepted as normal. In the examples above, patriarchal is assumed to be normal and is valued over matriarchal. Matriarchal family structures are seen as abnormal, needing to be analyzed. Eventually they become an explanation for lack of success in the African-American community. Drugs and violence are seen as natural to the African-American community — allowing us to be complacent about them — and they only become problems when we find them in the white community or when their effects in the African-American community spill over into our white neighborhoods.

The ideological systems we use to justify racism tell us a great deal about the legitimizing structures of different historical periods. The original white European settlers of this country were Protestant. Some were missionaries and others were fleeing religious persecution. People of color were demonized as pagan and "soulless." As substantial numbers of people of color were converted to Christianity, and as religion itself lost much of its power as a legitimizing agent, justifications for the brutality of slavery changed.

At the same time as the agricultural South developed into a slave-based economy, biological, zoological, and botanical theories about the natural world were extended to explain human difference and to justify the extreme exploitation and degradation of slavery. Because these theories could be used to justify economic arrangements, they enhanced the status of these sciences in particular and the public valuation of science in general. It became persuasive to call upon scientific theory to certify the naturalness of political and economic arrangements.

Within Christianity there were values of compassion, fellowship, and acceptance of other Christians that provided a base from which Christians could resist slavery and refute scientific explanations. There were also subversive scientific currents that contested the scientific "proof" of biological superiority. These countercurrents within religion and science undermined those belief systems from within even as they were pitted against each other. Together with the remarkable achievements and resistance of free blacks and slaves, these currents created space for a great national debate about the abolition of slavery.

When slavery was abolished, the justification for the exploitation of African Americans continued to be scientific (i.e., biological) for several decades. As the scientific theories were discredited, the explanations became more historical, often using the effects of slavery itself as the reason why African Americans were experiencing difficulties in the United States.

In more recent times, biological and historical justifications for racism have been discredited, although not without many pockets of resurgence. It is now the social sciences that have become a stronger legitimizing force for the status quo in our society. Sociological and psychological explanations of the economic disparities between whites and people of color have proliferated. They deal with issues of family structure, community breakdown, individual psychology, and the internalized effects of racism itself. They translate into discussions of the black family, the role of women in the black community, the devastation of community infrastructures, ghetto psychology, black rage, issues of self-esteem in African-American children, and "internalized oppression." Within these disciplines, as well, there are currents of resistance, even as they continue to challenge biological and religious justifications of racism.

These theories and explanatory models tell us about white society. They provide keys to understanding white intellectual history and how white society thinks about itself. They describe how we have wanted to see ourselves over the centuries as first morally right, then scientifically superior, then historically justified, and finally sociologically and psychologically insightful. What has remained constant is the dominance of white people in power and privilege and the subordination of African Americans.

The resistance and resilience of African Americans in the face of white racism have been defining characteristics of American history and contemporary life. They force us ultimately to see that all our attempts to explain and understand racism fail to change it. These explanatory projects are, in effect, efforts to divert our attention from the practical challenge of creating a society in which African Americans have full political, economic, and cultural equality. However critically they analyze the past history of white–African-American relationships, each theory reinforces and legitimizes white racism by focusing on African Americans.

White people are not directly mentioned in our discussions of African Americans and "their" problems. We are the invisible narrator as well as the only participants in the discussion. We talk to ourselves about African Americans, we describe and then "explain" their problems, and then we blame them and prescribe solutions that have to do with their changing themselves, their attitudes, and their behavior.

Finally we look for people of color to testify to our conclusions. Because communities of color contain people from the full spectrum of moral and political beliefs, it is not hard for white people to find some person of color who says things that validate our theories. These people are paraded as seals of approval for white agendas.

Here again our understanding of white racism should immediately tell us to turn our attention back to white people. What are we saying and doing? How are we implicated in this situation? What privileges, power, and moral virtue are we trying to hold on to?

African Americans have been a numerically large and important part of this country's culture and economy for several hundred years, particularly in the South and on the East Coast. They have been the center of racial attention, and the struggles of other peoples of color have been defined against theirs. Yet most white people know little about them because layers of whiteness overlay our perceptions, and African Americans have had little opportunity to describe their own experience. Even today we hear the voices of few African Americans. Those we do hear are generally well educated, successful, and professional. A white-controlled news and publishing network is still the gatekeeper, deciding which African-American voices are acceptable. (On March 7, 1995, for example, the Oakland Tribune reported that 51 percent of the newspapers in the country didn't have any minority employees. By 2000, when people of color represented 28 percent of the population of the U.S., they still made up less than 12 percent of newsroom staff at daily newspapers across the country according to the American Society of Newspaper Editors' annual survey.)

Whites have created a fictitious and mythologized African-American community that we use for our convenience. African Americans are either problem or victim, aggressive or dependent, natural or barbaric. We rarely listen to what they themselves say or give them credit for the substantial contributions and leadership they have provided our society.

Beyond ending false generalizations about African Americans, there is much we can do to end racism against them. Below are some questions and activities to use as a starting point.

QUESTIONS AND ACTIONS:
AFRICAN AMERICANS

1. List ways that at one time or another you or your family have downplayed, minimized, or denied the effects of slavery and post-slavery Jim Crow segregation on the African-American community.

2. List ways your family may have colluded with or benefited from the economic exploitation of African Americans.

3. What are ways that, actively or through inaction, you have resisted the full integration of African Americans into your workplace, school, social organizations, or congregation?

4. Notice which contemporary national problems are blamed predominantly on African Americans. What national policies are being discussed to blame and punish African Americans for these problems?

5. Analyze your community. Which parts — schools, recreational facilities, job sectors, clubs — are presently de facto segregated?
    a. Which of these do you participate in?
    b. What could you do to challenge this segregation?

6. Notice what specific institutional practices contribute to de facto segregation in your community (for example, red lining, real estate covenants, school district borders, suburban incorporation). List one that you are going to work with others to change.

7. Notice what kinds of individual acts of discrimination keep the segregation in place (decisions by landlords, real estate agents, employers, teachers, etc.). What is one thing you can do to support public policies against discrimination, and their strong and consistent enforcement?

8. Work to make sure the police are adequately supervised and monitored.

9. Listen to African Americans define their own lives and problems, and push for their involvement at every level in every situation you are involved in. Support their leadership.

10. Find out what you can do to work against the dismantling of affirmative action and other anti-discrimination programs and policies.

11. Find out about the agencies, local government offices, and community organizations working against racism in your community.
    a. Support them financially.
    b. Support them with your time and energy.

12. Notice the sports you watch and the music you listen to. Are there any in which African Americans are major performers?
    a. Who benefits financially and who benefits culturally from the performances of African Americans in these areas?

b. What are the economic factors that led African Americans to be major participants in those areas?

c. What are the stereotypes that white people use to justify these concentrations?

d. Support the efforts of African Americans to become more powerful in these arenas through participation in management, through ownership arrangements, through less exploitive recruitment practices, etc.

13. How can you challenge other white people when stereotypes of African Americans are used to blame them for social problems? What information or other preparation do you need to be able to do this well?

14. Introduce your children to the complexities, history, and accomplishments of African Americans.

15. Make sure schools and children's programs in your area are multicultural and that African-American youth are not singled out for punishment, disproportionately tracked into lower-level academic classes, or harassed.

Many of these suggestions apply to being an ally to Latino/as, Asian Americans, Arab Americans, and Native Americans as well. Others are specific to African Americans. We cannot focus on African Americans to the exclusion of other people of color, nor avoid dealing with racism against African Americans by focusing on other communities of color.

Asian Americans

WHEN I WAS TEN, growing up in West Los Angeles in 1958, my parents were able to buy a house in the San Fernando Valley. We put our old house on the market, and the real estate agent received a bid from a Japanese family. As soon as my parents accepted their offer we began getting angry and threatening phone calls from neighbors for selling to "outsiders," "foreigners," and "Japs." This was my first experience of white hate and discrimination. My parents did not discuss the situation with my sister and me. It wasn't until years later that I realized what we had experienced, and what the Japanese family may have experienced, was the equivalent of what was happening in the South to African Americans. At the time our attention was focused on black-white interactions in the South. Racism toward other groups, in other parts of the country, was invisible to most of us.

Asian Americans have emigrated from over 20 countries and an even greater number of distinct cultures. Like every other referent for a racial group, the term "Asian American" lumps together vastly different cultural groups and subsumes the class, gender, and diversity of millions of people.

The role of Asian Americans has always been ambiguous in a country that sees race as a polarity between black and white. The skin color of many Asians is not much different than that of many "white" people. White people have used other markers — dress, food, religious beliefs, customs, and even cooking smells — to identify and justify the exclusion of Asian Americans. These differences have then been explained as biologically or genetically based and as a sign of inferiority.

We have viewed Asian Americans as inferior for much of our history. At other times we have accorded honorary white status to those who have assimilated most completely. For example, white ambiguity about the racial status of Chinese immigrants (the majority of Asians in the West and South in the late 19th century) was reflected in constant shifts in how they were officially categorized. Gary Okihiro describes Louisiana's census:

> In 1860, Chinese were classified as whites; in 1870, they were listed as Chinese; in 1880, children of Chinese men and non-Chinese women were classed as Chinese; but in 1900, all of these children were reclassified as blacks or whites and only those born in China or with two Chinese parents were listed as Chinese.[1]

White people's relationship to Asian Americans is deeply anchored in Eurocentric beliefs that Euro-American culture and development are central in the world. We have a tradition of seeing people from Asia as irrevocably different and inferior. Although the presence of Asian Americans in the United States dates back only 200 years, the West has had a nearly 3,000-year history of relations with Asia. Early Greeks such as Hippocrates, Herodotus, and Aristotle had negative things to say about Asians, and these were commonly accepted stereotypes of their times.[2]

It was Asia that Columbus was headed for. At first this fact clouded Europeans' perceptions of Native Americans more than it did their perceptions of Asians, with whom there was little contact. But when Asian Americans did arrive here, they faced an already deeply entrenched system of white racism and a long-standing set of beliefs and practices toward "Asians."

White people have seldom been able to step far enough out of a Eurocentric focus to understand Asian Americans as part of Asian history and culture. In the European and American invasions of Asia in the 19th and early 20th centuries we met peoples who had 3,000 to 5,000 years of highly sophisticated and continuously recorded history. Despite this history, or perhaps in response to it, we only acknowledge Asians from the time they arrive here; we only accept them once they give up, renounce, or betray their broader historical culture.

Our current anti-Asian rhetoric claims that we are under attack or being besieged. We cite Japanese, Chinese, or Vietnamese imperialism to feed our fears that Asian Americans have come to overrun our country and take away our jobs and industries. It is best to remind ourselves that it was we who forcefully opened up Japan and China to American trade in the 19th century after they refused to have anything to do with us.

> *Asians, it must be remembered, did not come to America; Americans went to Asia. Asians, it must be remembered, did not come to take the wealth of America; Americans went to take the wealth of Asia. Asians, it must be remembered, did not come to conquer and colonize America; Americans went to conquer and colonize Asia.[3]*

And we might add that, more recently, Vietnamese, Cambodians, and Laotians did not come to invade the United States, but to escape the invasion and disruption of their countries by U.S. military and economic forces.

Substantial numbers of Chinese were encouraged by American business interests to come and work in this country in the mid-19th century to replace African Americans after slavery was abolished and African Americans began to gain power during Reconstruction. When Reconstruction ended and African Americans were forced back to the fields, Asians became less desirable as field hands. Chinese workers were used to compete with African-American labor, and this use of Asian workers against African Americans continued for decades. For instance, soon after African Americans organized the Brotherhood of Sleeping Car Porters in 1925, Filipino men were brought in and were given the jobs African Americans had formerly held. The struggles of African-American and Chinese workers intertwined, and whites played one group against the other. White business leaders employed Chinese and other Asian workers when they needed them and excluded them when they didn't.[4]

From the beginning, their presence was highly contested. Control of immigration from Asia was a touchstone for immigration battles that continue today. African Americans, Native Americans, and Latino/as have always been solidly present in our society, despite practices that killed them in massive numbers and disrupted their cultures. With Asian Americans the battle has been whether to let them come to the United States at all and, once they are here, whether to let them stay and become part of our society.

Beginning in 1882 with the Chinese Exclusion Act, and only ending with the 1965 Immigration Act, Asian immigration was either illegal or so sharply limited as to be virtually nonexistent. During periods in which immigration was allowed, often only men were permitted to come. We did not permit Asians who were living here to become naturalized citizens for most of that time. In the late 19th and early 20th centuries, whites passed more than 600 separate pieces of anti-Asian legislation limiting or excluding persons of Asian ancestry from citizenship.[5] Non-citizens had no legal rights. Whites could kill Asians with impunity because Asians could not testify against them. It was only in 1952 that the last bars to Asians becoming citizens were lifted.

Although white people feared that Asians would overwhelm the white majority and contaminate white culture, such fears did not prevent government and business leaders from importing Chinese as cheap and disposable laborers whenever it was convenient to do so.

All white immigrants benefited tremendously from the restriction of Asian immigration, even those who were only subsequently accepted as "white." In addition, they benefited from the expanding industrial economy in the Northeast and Midwest based on tin, rubber, and other raw materials arriving from European and U.S. colonies in Asia such as Malaysia, the Philippines, China, and India.

We allowed few Asian women into this country in the 19th and early 20th centuries. Those women who did settle here have been nearly invisible to us. We tend to see Asian Americans as men, while portraying Asian women as passive, dependent, sensual, sexy, and obedient — sexual objects for the use of white American men. Through our limited focus on Asian-American men and Asian women, we have tried to understand Asian-American history without connecting it to the home countries from which people came. This perspective has distorted our understanding of Asian family structure, male life here, and the lives of women who remained in Asia. There are still almost no contemporary portrayals of Asian Americans in the full complexity of their gender and class relationships spanning both continents. In fact, Americans relate to Asian Americans as if their cultures and countries of origin were irrelevant except when we want to compare ourselves favorably to them.

We like to think that (white) Americans are modern and forward-looking. We often describe Asian cultures as tradition-bound. We think that innovations and "progress" come from us, and resistance to change comes from Asians. Because we have a positive regard for innovation and modernness, it is difficult for us to respect alternatives to our way of doing things. When Asian Americans propose different ways of approaching problems, we reject their ideas and describe their communities as more traditional than ours. Thus we reinforce our stereotypes that Asian Americans are conservative and tradition-bound, and that we are modern, progressive, and forward-looking.

Indian, Thai, Malaysian, Indonesian, Japanese, Korean, and Chinese cultures have survived for thousands of years and contain traditional elements that contribute stability, and innovative elements which promote change. These cultures would not have been able to adapt to changing historical circumstances if they weren't innovative and changing. Stereotypes give us static images of other people, which we often use to generalize and say their lives are static and unchanging.

We have also done the opposite, taking these same stereotypes of other cultures and turned them into virtues. Sometimes we romanticize particular Asian traits and put down American (or African-American) culture for lacking them. We may say that Asians are hardworking, patient, industrious, meditative, and steady. Recently U.S. business leaders have held up the Japanese as innovative and hardworking and used them as examples to pressure U.S. workers to work harder and be more adaptable to the needs of business. These stereotypes have also been used to justify quotas on Japanese products and "Buy American" campaigns.

Our statements about Asian Americans and Asian culture reflect more on the uses we want to put them to than the qualities of the people we are describing. They also reflect our ignorance of the differences between different Asian-American peoples and cultures.

Most white Americans cannot distinguish between Chinese, Korean, and Japanese peoples or languages, much less between Indians from Bangladesh or Sri Lankans. We know little at all about Filipino culture, even though Filipinos are one of the oldest and largest Asian-American communities and the United States occupied the Philippines as a colony for many years. We also lump together recent immigrants from Southeast Asia, often unable or unwilling to distinguish between Thais, Cambodians, Vietnamese, and Laotians.

Most Asian Americans have been eager to assimilate into American society so they would be less subject to violence and exclusion and more able to reap the advantages that being white has always meant. White Americans' discrimination and violence have prevented them from doing so. Partly in response to our lack of differentiation and blanket discrimination, Asian Americans have joined together in political unity for economic and political clout.

National and cultural identification is highly variable among Asian Americans. Some individuals have virtually no connections with a country of origin; others maintain substantial personal and community ties. Some practice primarily "white" American customs; many practice mixtures of culture derived from their own, white, and African-American traditions. Since it often seems that participating in any culture outside the bounds of what has been pronounced acceptable by popular mainstream media is grounds for being considered un-American, it is easy for Asian Americans to feel that only if they completely "whitewash" their lives will they be accepted. So many white people believe in the primacy of white skin, blue eyes, "European" features, and blond hair that it is understandable Asian Americans might not believe integration and acceptance will ever be truly forthcoming. The large number of us who bleach our own hair blond while fearing anyone who doesn't look white confirms the truth of their fears.

A good illustration of how white people's lack of acceptance, suspicion, and fear of

Asian Americans lead to violence and discrimination is the death of Vincent Chin in 1982. Chin was a Chinese American living in Detroit who was killed by two white, unemployed auto workers who believed he was Japanese. He had lived in the United States all his life. His killers had been led to believe that they couldn't get work because of the import of Japanese cars. They believed that Japanese corporations were responsible for their unemployment and that any Japanese American was complicit with the Japanese government. And they couldn't tell a Japanese American from a Chinese American. The sentence they each eventually received for killing Chin was three years' probation and a $3,000 fine.[6]

Vincent Chin is dead, one of many Asian Americans blamed for economic problems and then attacked. His murderers were barely reprimanded. We must ask ourselves how many decades, generations, centuries, even, people must live here before they are accepted as American if they are not white.

White people have used the success of some Asian Americans to demonstrate the lack of racism in this country and the opportunity that African Americans have supposedly had and not used. Some white people label them a "model minority," a code phrase (see Part I) that implies Asian Americans are hardworking, industrious, thrifty, future oriented, and law-abiding, as all good white Christians are (or at least should be). However, this is just another example of projecting our own stereotypes onto Asian Americans, and it says more about our self-perception and our manipulation of racism (and of statistics) than it does about Asian Americans.

Statistics for a group as diverse as the Asian-American community are not useful for comparison with other groups. Average family income figures for Asian Americans hide large disparities in the distribution of wealth. Substantial groups of Asian Americans live in poverty. Generalizations about average income lump together different communities, some long established and some very recent, as well as covering over gender and class differences in income and opportunity. The unique histories and diversities of each large racial grouping (Asian American, Latino/a, African American, Jewish, Native American, white) make such comparisons invalid. They are also particularly insidious because the historical circumstances of each group are so different.

This overgeneralizing is itself a manipulation of white racism to instill fear of Asian-American success and divert the attention of poor and working-class people away from white economic and political control.

That control is most evident when a "model minority" becomes too successful. At universities in California and in other parts of the country where Asian-American students have been outperforming white students, quotas have been placed on the number of admission slots available to Asian Americans. These quotas were enacted to ensure room for white students, not to preserve slots for African Americans or Latino/as.

The example of Asian-American "success" shows not that racism doesn't exist, but that it is more than a system of economic exploitation. Racism systematically exploits people culturally and spiritually as well as materially. It keeps some people the targets of violence (physical, emotional, or economic) regardless of their financial success, and it keeps other (white) people safe and protected. Many Japanese Americans were highly successful in the Western United States but were still attacked, locked up in concentration camps, and subjected to mob violence during World War II. Economic success may offer some protection against the worst effects of racism, but many white Americans still consider Asian Americans (and other people of color and Jews) as different and inferior. White-controlled institutions continue patterns of white racism, and without the dismantling of white control and domination, no amount of economic success will protect people from continued attack and injustice. Vincent Chin could have been rich or poor, a citizen or non-citizen — what mattered to the two men who killed him was that he was Asian American.

Different groups of Asian Americans have often been held up to "prove" that this is a country where even recent immigrants can get ahead. Koreans are one of the latest groups to be used in this way.

In media portrayals of the 1992 uprising in Los Angeles, Koreans and African Americans were pitted against each other. This opposition distorted the reality of what took place in the uprising. It also shifted attention away from the huge role that white society has had in creating the conditions that sparked the uprising. The biggest immediate obstacles to success in both the African-American and Korean communities are the exploitation and oppression experienced as a result of white social practices such as housing and job discrimination, and the restructuring of the economy by large corporations, not the actions or personal prejudices of blacks and Koreans toward each other's communities.

These practices set up Koreans and other Asian Americans (as well as Jews and some Arab Americans) to be buffers between white neighborhoods and African-American ones. For example, structural discrimination and anti-foreign bias force well-educated Koreans to become small shop owners in African-American and Latino/a communities, where they face small profits and vulnerability to violence. Deteriorating economic conditions, coupled with media attention to their "success," direct people's anger toward them rather than toward economic policymakers. Koreans were clearly set up to be sacrificed to the rioters. Their calls to the Los Angeles Police Department and to state and local officials for protection were unanswered.[7]

White people, on the other hand, could sit back and watch the show, perhaps temporarily uneasy about things getting out of hand, but nevertheless buffered from the direct effects of the violence. When rioters attacked major shopping malls in white Culver City, they were quickly stopped by police.[8]

What does it mean for an Asian American to be successful, compared to a white American or to an African American? Why do we hold up an average income for one community and use that figure to put down or extol another one? Does economic success measure the presence or absence of racism for a particular group?

We don't need to accept the simple dichotomies of success and failure, Korean and black. We don't need to accept simplified and misleading statistics about complex groups of people. We must not accept the false conclusion that because some groups are economically successful, any group can be, or that economic success itself is a sign that exploitation and injustice are no longer a problem.

In order not to accept these lies we need to be considerably better informed about the particular histories and complexity of Asian-American communities in this country. We need to break down our simplified stereotypes by going beyond an awareness of the Chinese New Year and the Japanese internment. We have to analyze critically any information we are given and counter it with a better understanding of the actual dynamics both within and between different communities.

Within particular Asian-American communities there have been accomplishments and much resistance to racism. There have been many kinds of cross-influences and effects — a constant exchange and mutual influence between many different Asian-American cultures. The cross-influences between different Asian cultures and African-American, Latino/a, and white cultures are also dynamic and important and have a major impact on our lives.

The complexity of these dynamics defies simple generalizations about economic success or model minorities. As is always the case, such generalizations actually reflect back on what we want to think about ourselves as white people.

QUESTIONS AND ACTIONS:
ASIAN AMERICANS

1. What specific Asian-American cultural communities live in your area? How can you find out more about the uniqueness of each particular community?

2. List four key Asian-American concerns in your community. If none come to mind, why might you not know about them? How could you find out?

3. How have parts of the Asian-American community organized to address these concerns?

4. What has been the response from the mainstream white community?

5. Are different Asian-American groups represented in your city and county governments, school boards, and other local political institutions?

6. What are some of the "positive" stereotypes that you hear about Asian Americans? What complexities and problems do these stereotypes cover up? What can you learn about white self-images from these stereotypes?

7. How have different Asian-American groups been scapegoated for economic problems in your community? How have non-American Asians been blamed?

8. What is demanded of Asian Americans for acceptance into the white community? Are there hidden reservations or conditions for that acceptance?

9. How are Asian-American and Asian culture and history represented in the schools in your community?

10. Do you and your children have accurate knowledge about the struggles for independence from colonialism of the Filipinos, Chinese, Koreans, Vietnamese, and Indians?

11. How has our relationship with particular Asian countries affected the immigration of Asians to the United States and their treatment once here?

Latino/as

IN THE OFFICIAL 2000 CENSUS, Latino/as, or native Spanish-speaking Americans, made up about 12.5 percent of the population in the United States, approximately 35 million people. They comprised 32 percent of the populations of California and Texas, 15 percent of New York's population, nearly 17 percent of Florida's, over 13 percent of New Jersey's, 25 percent of Arizona's, 42 percent of New Mexico's, over 12 percent of Illinois's, 5.5 percent of Nebraska's, and 17 percent of Colorado's.

The variations of Spanish spoken are many, and the differences between communities of Latino/as are large. Some groups, such as Cuban Americans or Puerto Ricans, have kept strong national identities. Others are from families that have been here for hundreds of years and have Spanish-derived cultures but no connection with another country.

The very terminology used to describe Latino/as has been in great dispute over the years. I use Latino/a because it is broadly inclusive and tends to be preferred by Spanish-speaking people when speaking in very general terms. I use the masculine/feminine ending to remind us that we tend only to recognize the men in other cultures. The problem with "Hispanic" and "Latino/a," which derive their meaning from Spain, is that the culture no longer has much connection to Europe. These words conceal the connections to North and South American land struggles and the intermingling of Spanish-derived culture with Native-American cultures.

I also use the term "Spanish-speaking" because most Latino/as in this country are connected to longstanding and complex Spanish language cultures that span the hemisphere. This term also emphasizes that many of the issues we are addressing are cultural as well as economic or political.

There is no national identity or set of interests uniting Latino/as except their concern for the end of white racism toward Spanish-speaking people. Many Latino/as prefer to be called Cubanos, Mexicanos, or Puertoriqueñosor boricuans. These are the three largest groups of Spanish-speaking people in the United States; many Latino/a identities are formed primarily within these communities.

The first permanent European settlement within the current United States borders was established at St. Augustine, in what is now Florida, in 1565. From settlements in Florida, Mexico, and the West Indies, approximately one-third of the present territory of the continental United States was invaded by Spanish soldiers and missionaries and conquered in the most brutal way. A combination of Spanish (male) administrators, conquistadors, ranchers, and missionaries killed, tortured, and enslaved most of the Native-American men and killed, raped, and intermarried with the Native-American women in what are now the states of California, Utah, Nevada, Arizona, New Mexico, Texas and parts of Colorado and Wyoming.

Part of our white "creation" story (which we tell on Thanksgiving) relates how our roots are deep in this country and how we were the original European settlers. Contrary to our story, descendants of Spanish colonists have lived in the Southeast, Southwest, and West for considerably longer than most English-speaking people. Spanish-speaking Americans and many Africans arrived in this country from the very earliest period of colonization. Some were here before any northern Europeans.

When our ancestors arrived in this country — whether 400 years ago or last week — should not be important. But we can probably agree that misrepresenting the facts of our history is morally wrong and reflects on our integrity as a people. It also fuels anti-immigrant violence because we conveniently forget that many of us were immigrants ourselves not so long ago, and many of the people we target as unwelcome have roots far back into our history.

White people whose foreparents have arrived within the last hundred years lay claim to the false history that white people were the original colonists in this country. We then look at recent immigrants from Asia and Central and South America and forget that we haven't been here that long ourselves.

Most white people don't distinguish between recent immigrants and people whose foreparents preceded ours, lumping all Latino/a people together. Our attacks on recent immigrants or immigrants without papers become abuse of all Latino/as. Cracking down on immigrants without papers promotes police harassment, job and housing discrimination, and denial of health and educational services to anyone who a white person "mistakes" for an undocumented immigrant.

A substantial number of Latino/a Americans in the United States are here because they were conquered and colonized by U.S. forces seeking new territories to provide markets for U.S. goods. Most white Americans also felt they had a mandate from God to spread Christianity and white hegemony over the rest of the continent and overseas. President William McKinley's explanation of his decision to take the Philippines illustrates the mixture of economic, nationalist, racist, and moralistic reasoning involved in justifying U.S. expansion throughout the Spanish-speaking world.

> *Before you go I would like to say just a word about the Philippine business .... The truth is I didn't want the Philippines, and when they came to us as a gift from the gods, I did not know what to do with them .... I went down on my knees and prayed Almighty God for light and guidance .... I don't know how it was, but it came: 1) That we could not give them back to Spain — that would be cowardly and dishonorable. 2) That we could not turn them over to France or Germany, our commercial rivals in the Orient — that would be bad business and discreditable. 3) That we could not leave them to themselves — they were unfit for self-government — and they would soon have anarchy and misrule over there worse than Spain's was: and 4)*

*That there was nothing left for us to do but to take them all and
to educate the Filipinos, and uplift and civilize and Christianize
them, and by God's grace do the very best we could by them, as
our fellow men for whom Christ also died.[1]*

At the turn of the century, Mark Twain offered a contrasting and more honest appraisal of American imperialism. On December 30, 1900, the New York Herald published Twain's commentary "A Greeting from the 19th Century to the 20th Century," which denounced the blood-drenched colonial forays of England, France, Germany, Russia, and the United States. "I bring you the stately matron named Christendom, returning bedraggled, besmirched and dishonored from pirate-raids in Kiao-Chou, Manchuria, South Africa and the Philippines, with her soul full of meanness, her pocket full of boodle and her mouth full of pious hypocrisies. Give her the soap and a towel, but hide the looking-glass." He suggested a new flag for the Philippine province — "just our usual flag, with the white stripes painted black and the stars replaced by the skull and cross-bones."

The Monroe Doctrine, written in 1823, was the first attempt to articulate the American perception that all of the Western Hemisphere was our "backyard" and we could control what happened there. Since then we have initiated hundreds of invasions and interventions in Central and South American countries, leading to the deaths of tens of thousands of people and wreaking havoc on the lives and economies of local populations.

For example, in 1830, when the Mexican government outlawed slavery and prohibited further American immigration into Texas, Americans were outraged and thousands continued to move into Texas as illegal aliens. They rose against Mexican rule in 1836 and, although initially defeated, were eventually victorious, claiming independence as the Lone Star State. Texas was annexed by the United States in 1845. U.S. instigated border skirmishes led to a brutal invasion of Mexico in 1846, resulting in the Treaty of Guadalupe Hidalgo in 1848 in which Mexico ceded all of California, New Mexico, Nevada, and parts of Colorado, Arizona, and Utah. As one congressman wrote at the time about our "manifest destiny" to rule the hemisphere, "This continent was intended by Providence as a vast theatre on which to work out the grand experiment of Republican government, under the auspices of the Anglo-Saxon race.[2]"

In 1898 the U.S. declared war on Spain and took over a war of independence that Cubans had started in 1895. Within three months we defeated the Spanish forces and required them to turn over control of Cuba to us, completely ignoring the Cubans who had been fighting for their freedom. We also took over Puerto Rico, annexed Hawaii, occupied Wake Island and Guam in the Pacific, and claimed the Philippines. Filipinos had been engaged in a long-term war of independence with Spain, and in 1899 they rose up against U.S. rule. President McKinley sent in 70,000 troops. Three years later one-sixth of the Philippine population was dead and the war was over.[3]

More recently, many Spanish-speaking people have arrived from Cuba, Dominican Republic, and many Central and South American countries. These immigrations have been connected with U.S. foreign policy and economic expansion. The blockade of Cuba, support for dictatorships in Central and South America, economic dislocation in Mexico due to U.S. corporate development, and the need for agricultural laborers in the fields of California and the Southwest have all contributed to large numbers of people being uprooted, exiled, or forced to migrate. Groups of refugees came to the United States seeking asylum and economic opportunity. U.S. government and corporate policy also directly encouraged migration through the Bracero program, which brought more than 5 million Mexican workers to the United States between 1942 and 1964 as cheap agricultural labor.[4]

We are clearly hypocritical when we blame recent Spanish-speaking immigrants for our economic problems and when we try to enforce a rigid border separation between Mexico (or Cuba or Haiti) and the United States. Corporate interests want to have free movement of capital and resources throughout the Americas and have pushed through the North American Free Trade Agreement (NAFTA), the General Agreement on Tariffs and Trade (GATT), and other policies conducive to their ends. But they want the rest of us to blame low-wage Mexican and Central-American workers for the lack of jobs and economic dislocation that result from those policies.

White Americans have long been concerned with both expanding and maintaining our national borders. The expansion is seen in terms of economic opportunity, while the maintenance consists of keeping Spanish-speaking people on the fringes of our society and not allowing them into centers of power and control — maintaining white privilege. The struggles of many Latino/a people in this country have therefore been focused on the borderlands, both physical and figurative, between Anglo and Spanish land and culture.

I don't think it is accurate to say that people of color within the United States make up internal colonies. Concentrations of Spanish-speaking peoples in Florida, New York, Chicago, and the U.S. Southwest don't have the same dynamics and issues as colonies such as Puerto Rico. While there are some similarities to the colonial process, by and large this model doesn't help us to understand how racism works in this country nor to develop strategies to end it. We do have to understand and take responsibility for the history and dynamics of colonialism because the presence of people of color, and particularly of Spanish-speaking people, in the United States is intertwined with the colonial expansion of the United States during the 19th century and the continuation of those patterns in the 20th.

Latino/a Americans have occupied various positions in the overall racial hierarchy of the United States depending upon economic and cultural factors. After the annexation of the Southwest in 1848, Mexican people had enough economic clout and "civilized" habits that they were accepted as white and given the rights of citizenship in California.[5] This was in contrast to the few blacks there, who were ranked far below Mexicans; to the Chinese, who were ranked slightly above Native Americans and had no rights; and to the Native Americans, who were considered barely human and were killed indiscriminately.[6] California's racial hierarchy still has white people on top, but today Spanish-speaking people are considered, along with African Americans, to be at the bottom, and Asian Americans are held up as closer to white and treated far better.

Latino/as are underrepresented, undercounted, and underestimated. Their lives, culture, and the deprivations they have suffered are invisible to us. For example, in the Los Angeles uprising in 1992, the greatest number of people killed from any ethnic group were Latino/as. The greatest damage done was to property owned by Latino/as.

Immediately following the uprising there was an immigration crackdown and hundreds of Spanish-speaking Los Angeles residents were deported, most without trials or legal recourse. Very few non-Latino/a Americans know these facts because the media was focused on African Americans as the villains and on black-white and black-Korean interactions.

Latino/a communities are exploited and oppressed by white-controlled political, economic, and cultural practices. I will focus on some of the cultural dimensions of racism in this section because our relationship to Latino/a communities illustrates some salient features.

Spanish-speaking people can participate in literary, musical, dramatic, political, and popular developments throughout the Spanish-speaking world. They have access to a major international culture that is largely invisible to monolingual white people. The Spanish-speaking people of this country could bring these dynamic, cosmopolitan, and creative currents into mainstream U.S. culture. Some of them obviously have been introduced, yet most of the time they are resisted. White people have fought against the use of Spanish in schools and workplaces, and have ignored, denigrated, and attacked Spanish language culture as being inferior, uncivilized, rural, traditional, monolithic, subversive, and dangerous. What are white people trying to maintain, and what do we fear, when we attack a vital, international culture of which we are ignorant?

We are saying that English is the language of culture and achievement, and European-based civilization is the source of all beneficial contributions to the world. We are also saying that the lives, thoughts, feelings, and cultures of Spanish-speaking people are insignificant and do not count. We are, in addition, demonstrating that white racism is not only about economic and political domination, but is also about cultural hegemony. It is about white people and white institutions being able to define what culture is, who gets to participate in it, and what language, literature, art, and music are included in it. White racism is about control of the cultural content of people's lives.

It is crucial for us to understand the importance of white racism as a system of cultural domination. White people have long denied or minimized the importance of culture to people's everyday lives. We have appealed to universal, international, and human standards and values in our politics, science, and philosophy. This makes it very difficult for us to recognize the value of culture in our own lives, much less in other people's. We don't want to understand the crucial and devastating role culture plays in white racial domination. We fail to see the inspirational role that culture plays in resistance to that domination by people of color. Even the cultural aspects of our everyday "white" lives are impossible for us to see or understand.

When we aren't remotely familiar with the music, literature, and dance of people we live with, we cannot expect to understand what they experience or what moves and guides them. We cannot honor and respect their concerns and life choices. In addition, using music as an example, when we are unfamiliar with the contributions of Reuben Blades, Celia Cruz, Tito Puente, Carlos Santana, Flaco Jimenez, Los Lobos, Selena, and Villa-Lobos we deny ourselves access to the richness, creativity, and inspiration that their culture could provide us. Instead of maintaining cultural borders, we need to become much better at crossing them.

Today's international cultures are complex, without clear boundaries, in constant flux. Boundaries and borders are permeable. Nothing we do — the food we eat, the words we use, our gestures, rituals, music, or celebrations — is purely white, Latino/a, African American, Asian American, or Native American. There are no traditions unchanged by contact with others.

We cannot eliminate racism without understanding its cultural dimensions. White racism is supported by economic, political, and cultural practices that operate partly by marketing other people's cultures to us and packaging them as exotic, original, natural, and authentic. Their cultures are distorted by this marketing and packaging and by the separation of their cultures from themselves as people living those cultures. At the same time, white cultural practices are rendered invisible by our focus on other people's practices. In this sense the border keeping Spanish-speaking people out of the mainstream of our society is maintained by economic and cultural domination, language barriers, and geographic segregation.

Use the following questions and the suggestions in the sections on Native Americans, African Americans, and Asian Americans to guide your work as an ally to Latino/as.

QUESTIONS AND ACTIONS:
LATINO/AS

1. Which groups of Latino/a people live in your town, city, or rural area?
2. Which groups of Latino/a people provide labor or services on which you personally or the economy are dependent (farm workers, low-wage manufacturing workers, or workers in factories near the Mexican border)?
3. What do you gain and what do you lose when these workers are poorly paid, work in unsanitary conditions, are exposed to dangerous chemicals, and have unsafe working conditions?
4. In what ways are Latino/a groups under attack at this time? Which social problems are they being blamed for?
5. How well are Latino/a communities represented in your local governments?
6. Are there adequate support services for Spanish-speaking families and Spanish-speaking youth in your area? How could you find out?
7. How has the history of U.S. involvement with Mexico, Cuba, Puerto Rico, and El Salvador influenced the status and position of the immigrant communities that arrived here from those countries?
8. How have stereotypes of Latino/as helped prepare for or justify invasions and control of South and Central American countries?
9. Have you been involved with solidarity work with Spanish-speaking countries? How might that work have been connected to the exploitation of Latino/a communities closer to home?
10. Did your foreparents speak a native language that has been lost in your family or community? What other losses accompanied the pressure to be a monolingual community?

11. How has the emergence of English as the language used in international communication been an advantage and a disadvantage to us?

12. How has this role of English in world discourse affected people whose primary language is not English?

13. Do you speak Spanish? If not, what might be reasons for learning to do so? Why haven't you learned it in the past?

Arab Americans

O<small>N</small> M<small>AY</small> 24, 2001, I came across the following two sentences in two different articles on the front page of *The New York Times.*

>*Like most Afghan men he wore a turban coiled around his head like a holy bandage.*

>*Afghanistan, known these days as a womb for global jihad ...*

Our images of Arabs, and our images of Islam are primarily filtered through a Western media lens filled with stereotypes, disrespect, misinformation, and emotionally laden descriptions. Images of Arabs and of Islam are conflated, producing a confusing and distorted picture of both, and tainting Arab Americans with the residue of these misrepresentations. Just as one example, until very recently almost all Arabs in America were Christians, and Christian Arabs still constitute the majority of Arabs in America.[1]

The stereotypes of Arab and Arab-American men as terrorists, fanatics, sheiks and traders riding camels, and untrustworthy and deceptive businessmen, and of women as seductive or submissive are still so pervasive that sometimes I find it difficult to imagine more mundane images. Have you seen images recently of —

- an Arab-American father playing catch with his son or daughter?
- an Arab-American woman in a business suit?
- Arab-American youth doing community service?
- an Arab-American community celebrating a birth or marriage?

As with other communities of color, Arab-Americans are very diverse coming from such countries as Algeria, Egypt, Iraq, Jordan, Kuwait, Lebanon, Libya, Palestine, Mauritania, Morocco, Qatar, Saudi Arabia, Yemen, Sudan, Syria, Tunisia, and the United Arab Emirates. (Iran and Turkey are not Arabic-speaking countries and their citizens are not considered Arabs.) There are about 4 to 6 million Arab Americans in the United States today, living in communities throughout the country. The first wave of Arab-American immigrants came to the Western Hemisphere during the late 19th century (beginning around 1870) through the end of World War I. They were mostly from what was called the Greater Syria area, which included Lebanon, homeland to the majority of them. These immigrants were primarily Christian, and substantial numbers of this first generation became peddlers, shopkeepers, and traders. Later waves of immigrants came from a variety of Arab-speaking countries and were mostly Sunni Muslims.

Early Arab-American immigrants were yet another group that the legal system attempted to place within its rigid racial classification system. At first they were denied citizenship in the U.S. and Canada because they were labeled Asian and therefore, in the early 20th century, were not considered white. In 1914 a man named George Dow was denied permission to become a U.S. citizen because he was a Syrian of Asiatic birth, and the law (the 1790 U.S. Statute) stated that only free white persons could become citizens. The following year a different court ruled that 19th-century laws allowed Syrians, because they were so closely related to "white persons," to become citizens.

In 1942 the difficulty with arbitrary racial classifications was again apparent in divergent court rulings based on race and religion. One court decision ruled that Yemenis were not eligible for citizenship "especially because of their dark skin and the fact that they are 'part of the Mohammedan world,' separated from Christian Europe by a wide gulf."[2] Two years later another Arab was granted citizenship because the judge considered Arabs to share an Aryan culture with whites. Generally they have been seen by white Americans as not quite white and not quite colored.

The reference to "a wide gulf" between Arabs and Christians is especially ironic because it was primarily Christian Arabs who immigrated to North America. However, to many white people, any Arab is a Muslim, and their religion, Islam, has often been portrayed by Westerners as antithetical to Christianity and the West. The conflation of Arab and Muslim, along with prevailing anti-Muslim stereotypes, have confirmed many white Americans' distrust of and hostility towards Arab Americans.

Most Muslims are neither Arab nor Middle Eastern. Of the over 1 billion Muslims in the world, the majority live in countries as diverse as Indonesia, Malaysia, Pakistan, Sudan, China, Nigeria, Kenya, India, and the Philippines. However, Islam is often portrayed as a monolithic, militaristic religion, unchanged since the seventh century, hostile to Christianity, and inimical to all things modern and Western. Muslims themselves are assumed to be mindless adherents, devoid of any individuality, and fanatical, blind followers of extremist clerics.

The result of hundreds of years of these stereotypes, dating back to the demonization of Muslims during the Crusades, is extreme hostility towards Arab Americans today. George McGovern in 1972, Jimmy Carter in 1976, Ronald Reagan in 1980, Walter Mondale in 1984, and Hillary Clinton in 2000 all rejected political and financial support from Arab Americans and even returned contributions that had been previously received, denying them the opportunity as Americans to support the candidates of their choice. The demonization continues, as the quotes beginning this section indicate. It is represented in books with titles such as Sacred Rage or In the Name of God, in Hollywood movies such as Delta Force and True Lies, and in the PBS documentary Jihad in America. Political statements and media portrayals contribute directly to a social climate that fosters violence against Arab Americans.

Such a climate of anti-Arab racism was much in evidence during the Gulf War against Iraq. For example, in a nationally televised news briefing on NBC, February 27, 1991, General Norman Schwarzkopf, head of our military operations, stated that the Iraqis "are not part of the same human race we are." Time magazine, the New York Times, and many other media carried editorials, articles, and cartoons describing Arabs as less than human.

During this period Islamic mosques in the United States were broken into or bombed; shots were fired into the homes of known Arabs; a taxi driver in Fort Worth, Texas, was attacked and killed; some Muslim schools and Islamic societies were vandalized; and Arab Americans received hate calls.

Arab Americans have reached the highest levels of professional achievement throughout the United States and Canada, have been political and social leaders, and have contributed to the arts and sciences. However, they continue to be vilified in the media, left out of mainstream political and social affairs, misrepresented in textbooks, and excluded from multicultural curricula. They are also readily blamed for the actions of Arabs or Muslims in any part of the world, and are vulnerable to verbal and physical attack simply for being of Arab descent.

The targeting of Arab Americans for violence makes us all less safe in two ways. First of all, the extreme violence of white American men is not responded to as quickly or as thoroughly as it should be because our attention is on "Arab terrorists." For example, since the Oklahoma City bombing by white men, white extremist groups have hatched conspiracies to bomb buildings, banks, refineries, utilities, clinics and bridges; to assassinate politicians, judges, civil rights figures, and others; to attack Army bases, National Guard armories, and a train; to rob banks and armored cars; and to amass illegal machine guns, missiles, and explosives. The FBI domestic terrorism docket has increased from 100 cases to nearly 1,000.[3] Although the government is clearly paying some attention to these threats, the diversion of substantial resources for the surveillance, harassment, and racial profiling of Arab Americans leaves us more vulnerable to terrorism from white extremists. In a similar vein, racist policies that have led to the deployment of thousands of immigration officials and the militarization of the U.S.-Mexican border have not stopped a single terrorist. All the known terrorists involved in the September 11, 2001, attacks came into the United States directly from Europe or the Middle East, most, if not all, with legal passports and visas. Not one is alleged to have arrived illegally via the Mexican-U.S. border.

We are also put at risk because, in the name of combating terrorism against Arabs, our civil liberties are compromised through such legislation as the Illegal Immigration Reform and Immigrant Responsibility Act and the Anti-Terrorism and Effective Death Penalty Act of 1996. This latter legislation contains sections which state that the government may deport an immigrant even if she or he has not committed any crime. It creates a new class of persons who are vulnerable to being deported simply because of their association with a list of "terrorist" groups. The creation of a set of removal courts, free from judicial review, also sets a chilling precedent for the legal protections of all Americans. This bill harks back to the McCarthy-era witch-hunts of the early 1950s, during which thousands of Americans were penalized merely for association with groups proscribed by the American government.

These bills and others like them fuel anti-Arab discrimination. They erode our civil rights without necessarily making us safer from terrorists, whether they come from other countries or are citizens of our own country.

A final issue to consider is how American anti-Arab racism allows us to be manipulated around foreign policy issues. In the last few years we have bombed Iraq, the Sudan, and Afghanistan, invaded Somalia, and supplied arms and other supplies to Israel, which has invaded Syria, Lebanon, and Palestine. At the same time our government has supported dictatorships and ruling elites in Saudi Arabia, Egypt, Jordan, Kuwait, Yemen, and the United Arab Emirates. Without a high level of anti-Arab feeling in the United States it would be impossible for our government to justify destroying a civilian hospital in a foreign country (Sudan); invading and occupying a country we were not at war with (Somalia); maintaining a boycott of food and medical supplies that international observers report kills up to 5,000 children a month (Iraq); or ignoring the occupation of, settlements in, and violence against the civilian population of yet another Arab country (Palestine) — all in clear breach of international law. We will continue to be manipulated by government and military propaganda until we understand the complexities of Arab societies, understand the distinctions between Islamic cultures and Arabic ones, and overcome our anti-Arab racism so that we can see Arab peoples and Arab-Americans as distinct, fully human members of our communities.

QUESTIONS AND ACTIONS:
ARAB AMERICANS

1. What is the composition and location of the Arab-American and Muslim communities in your local area?
2. What are some of the cultural traditions, community organizations, and political issues of the Arab-American and Muslim communities in your local area?
3. Who are some of the national Arab-American and Muslim leaders and what organizations are prominent nationally?
4. Do you know some of the fundamental beliefs of Islam and something about the major organizational branches? Where can you find out more about Islam?
5. How can you respond when people around you make anti-Arab or anti- Muslim comments?
6. Have there been anti-Arab or anti-Muslim harassment, racial profiling, or hate crimes in your area?
7. What can you do to join efforts to combat such harassment and hate crimes?
8. How can you join with others to challenge media stereotypes, misinformation, and lack of positive coverage of Arab Americans and Muslims?
9. Western nations contribute billions of dollars a year in arms and other resources to Saudi Arabia, Egypt, Israel, Pakistan, and other countries in the Middle East, supporting war and repression and, ultimately, fueling anti-western feeling and terrorism. How can you work to insure that some of that money is diverted from arms to efforts to build a foundation for peace in that region?

Jewish People

WHEN I'M IN A WORKSHOP ON RACISM and the facilitators tell everyone to break up into a white group and a people of color group, I immediately want to say, "Wait a minute. I'm not white."

To some extent this gut-level response is similar to the "I'm not white" response of other white people as described in the first part of this book. When the subject is racism, nobody wants to be white because being white is "bad" and brings up feelings of guilt, shame, embarrassment, and hopelessness.

There are other reasons why I want to say "I'm not white" which have to do with the particularities of being Jewish. I want to explore these other reasons because to understand them is to understand some of the complexities of being Jewish and of the ways racism and anti-Semitism operate as systems of power and domination.

When I say that I'm not white, there are many white people in the United States and throughout Europe who would immediately agree. "Of course you're not white. Jewish people are part of the contamination of the white Christian race, along with people of color, Roma, the mentally challenged, and lesbian, gay, and bisexual people." These attitudes are based on the conjunction of whiteness with Christianity.

Jews were considered inferior and a threat to Christians because they rejected Jesus as the son of God from the beginning of Christian church history. In addition, they were falsely accused of killing Jesus because of stories in the New Testament. Various anti-Semitic stereotypes were disseminated by early Church leaders such as St. John Chrysostom, who wrote:

> *The Jews are full of hatred for the rest of mankind and are the enemies of all gentiles: they are parasites on the gentile societies that harbor them; they are addicted to money, and through the power of money, they aspire to be rulers of the world.*[1]

Early Christian church leaders continually attacked Jews on theological grounds and condoned the actions of Christians who vandalized synagogues and killed Jews. When Christianity became the official religion of the Roman Empire in the early fourth century, Jews became even more vulnerable to violence from Christians. They were banned from public office and from many occupations, and some were forced to become tax collectors. They were subject to special taxes, prohibited from practicing their religion and building or repairing synagogues, not allowed to intermarry with Christians, and prohibited from holding any civil or economic position higher than any Christian. They were subject to forced conversions and commonly referred to as a source of religious pollution, contagion, and disease, setting the stage for later racially based anti-Semitism.[2]

Large-scale attacks on Jews by Christians occurred during the Crusades, when Jews were seen as the European agents of the Muslim/Arab "infidels" who controlled the Holy Lands. Although the goal of the church was to attack Arabs and reclaim Jerusalem, most crusaders never left Europe. As they pillaged their way toward Jerusalem, they rounded up and killed thousands of Jews and destroyed their communities.

In the following centuries Jews were forced to convert or were banished from such regions as England (1290), France (1306, 1322, 1394), Hungary (1367), Strasbourg (1381), Austria (1421), and Cologne (1426). Jews fought to protect themselves, fled, converted, or looked for protection from secular rulers, but were generally not powerful enough to protect themselves from Christian violence.

On July 1, 1492, the Spanish monarchs, pressed by the Inquisition, gave all Jews 30 days to pack up whatever they could and leave the country they had lived in for centuries. A month later Columbus had to depart from a different port than originally planned because of the congestion caused by the Jews' departure. Some of their confiscated possessions were used to finance his voyages.

Even after the Spanish expulsion, the Inquisition continued to persecute those suspected of idolatry. Under the laws of purity of blood, any person with even one drop of Jewish blood was condemned. To prove their innocence, suspects had to display genealogical charts proving they had no Jewish ancestry. The Inquisition, drawing on anti-Semitic stereotypes from early church teachings, combined religious and biological justifications for persecution, setting the stage for the later development of biologically based theories of racism.

Many Jews fled from Spain to Portugal, but within a few years were forced to flee again after being given the choice of forced baptism or death. Subsequently they faced persecution and expulsion from the Italian peninsula and from many German cities and principalities in the 16th century, as well as pogroms in the Ukraine in the mid-17th century.[3]

Anti-Semitism became rooted in Protestantism during the "Enlightenment" through the writings of such key figures as Martin Luther. In 1543 Luther wrote "Against the Jews and Their Lies," in which he accused the Jews of being not only the bloodthirsty murderers of Christianity, but also of the German people. He wrote:

> *We are at fault in not avenging all this innocent blood of our Lord and Churches and the blood of the children which they have shed since then, and which still shines forth from their Jewish eyes and skin. We are at fault in not slaying them.[4]*

He goes on to suggest that Germans burn the houses and synagogues of the Jews, ban their rabbis under pain of death, withdraw Jewish safe-conduct on the highways, prohibit usury, institute manual labor for young Jews, and finally, confiscate their wealth and expel them from Germany.

Protestantism imbued whiteness with a set of Christian values that included belief in Jesus, original sin, and individual salvation through one's work; the equation of sex with procreation; a belief in heaven and hell; and the condemnation of those who are not Christian.

Jews were held to be a nation of outcasts who had killed Christ, rejected Christianity, used the blood of Christian children in Passover rituals, and prevented the Second Coming by their failure to convert. Even before biological theories of race, they were believed automatically to pass on these traits to each succeeding generation regardless of where they lived, what they practiced, and even, in many cases, whether or not they converted to Christianity.

These were official policies of the Catholic Church and many Protestant denominations and the common beliefs of many Christians. It was only in 1965, for instance, that the bishops of Vatican Council II voted to absolve contemporary Jews of any guilt for the crucifixion of Jesus and to repudiate the belief that God rejected the Jews because they refused to accept Jesus as the savior.[5]

Because of the conjoining of whiteness, Christianity, and various forms of nationalism, Jews were prohibited from becoming part of the general community in many European countries and were often forced to relocate elsewhere on short notice. No matter how long Jews lived within a country or principality, or how successful they were economically, they were not immune to persecution and violence. For example, Jewish people lived in Germany for over a thousand years, were financially and socially successful, but were still subject to mass murder during the Holocaust.

Jewish people were originally Arabs. Whatever their original distinguishable Arab or "Semitic" characteristics, through rape, intermarriage, forced exile, conversion, and assimilation, Jews today are part of many cultural groups on several continents. Jewish people are not only not a race — we have seen how this is not a meaningful concept — but they also come in many shades and colors, from nearly black Ethiopian Jews, to dark brown Jews from the Cochin coast of India, to light brown Jews from Argentina and Morocco, to blond and light-skinned Jews in Denmark and England. While this diversity is a refutation of racial stereotypes, it can make Jews more vulnerable when another group of people is claiming some kind of national identity, religious unity, or genetic purity.

Dark skinned by northern European standards, light skinned by standards in the United States, in either case, Jews of European origin are not Christian. And even if Jews have the right color skin, many Christians still believe they can contaminate the "purity" of white Christian culture. The membership application of the Invisible Empire of the Knights of the Ku Klux Klan requires one to "swear that I am a White Person of Non-Jewish ancestry."[6]

When Jews walk down the street, their skin color is immediately visible, while their cultural practices and religious beliefs are not. If they pass for white and don't voluntarily give away the fact that they're Jewish, they enjoy the same respect and privilege that other white people are given in our society. Their presence is accepted, their words are listened to, and they have more police and judicial protection. If their name is recognizably Jewish, if they are wearing traditional clothes or religious objects, or if their appearance or mannerisms fit certain stereotypes of what it means to be or look or act Jewish, then passing is not an option. If they can't or don't want to pass, they are vulnerable to the same jokes, harassment, discrimination, and violence that other non-white, non-Christian people are vulnerable to. That in itself is a strong incentive to try to pass.

In order to pass they have to give up, minimize, or downplay any aspects of their life and appearance that are visibly Jewish. They can't say or do anything that will give away to people that they are really Jewish. Since being Jewish is inherently a range of ways of being, talking, and doing things that are not Christian, the more they pass the less they are who they are. They have to give up parts of themselves and become more Christianized and "white" in order to pass. At any time they might be found out and lose everything they thought they had gained in compensation for giving up their core identity.

It also becomes dangerous for them to be associated in any way with other Jewish people who are visibly Jewish. Either they fear they might be condemned along with them, or they fear they might pick up "Jewish" speech or mannerisms, which would make it harder for them to pass. If they are in any way visibly Jewish, they know that many of the white Christians they encounter will treat them as non-white and they will face mistrust, ignorance, discrimination, or outright abuse.

When I say in that workshop that I'm not white because I'm Jewish, there are lots of people who would agree with me. There are others who would not. People of color often say, "What do you mean you aren't white? You look white, you act white, and you enjoy all the privileges of being white, including the direct benefits of exploiting people of color such as better jobs, better schooling, and better housing." They are right too. As a Jew descended from eastern European Jews, I am white.

I am white in the sense that my particular Jewish ancestors lived in Europe for nearly a thousand years before coming to the United States. During that time we assimilated a tremendous amount of European culture in order to survive. We have learned how to adapt, camouflage, assimilate, sabotage, resist, and undermine some of that culture. During that entire time we have never been safe from spontaneous and systematic violence and exploitation. Sometimes we have even had to exploit other people in order to stay alive or to be allowed to stay in a place where we had lived for hundreds of years. And sometimes we have come to believe the lies of racism, the justifications for economic and cultural exploitation that European culture is built on.

In the United States, besides the threat of violence and the constant pressure to assimilate, one of the prices people pay to be accepted as white is to collude in perpetuating racism. This is a price that many southern and eastern Europeans as well as assimilated Jews have paid. They come to believe that economic improvement for themselves is different than economic justice for everyone. Some Jewish people, probably no fewer or no more than in other groups, have paid that price. Today in this society there is some privilege attached to being white, or, we might say, conditionally white. We will accept you as white on the condition that you support the racial hierarchy which keeps people of color on the bottom. Jewish people who are "white," like Irish, Polish, Finnish, or Spanish people, are safer, have greater educational and economic opportunity, and are generally more accepted than African Americans, Latino/as, Asian Americans, Arab Americans, and Native Americans. That is what being white is all about.

Many Jewish people have accepted this racial hierarchy in exchange for feelings of safety and acceptance. Consequently, they have established, in this country and in Israel, parallel race-based systems within the Jewish community. Jewish people of color are the majority of Jews in the world and in Israel. Despite this fact, European-descended Jews dominate culture and politics in the Jewish communities of both Israel and the United States. This has rendered non-white Jewish people invisible and made it seem that racism is an issue that Jewish people are separate from, something out there in American society. Yet we carry the pain, violence, and confusion of racism within our own bodies and in the distribution of economic and cultural power within our Jewish communities.

Many Jewish people have also accepted the American bipolar focus on black-white relationships. In this book we have seen how the bipolar perspective is a distorted one. Yet most within the Jewish community do not understand or pay attention to the Latino/a, Asian-American, or Native-American communities, maintaining a focus only on black-Jewish relationships.

That binary focus is itself distorted because there is no monolithic black or Jewish community. What does it mean for a people of millions — including conservatives, liberals, radicals and fundamentalists, old and young, women and men, rich and poor — to have a relationship with another people of millions with similar diversity? We need to ensure that we don't let journalistic representation simplify and distort the complexities of the interactions of two diverse peoples because it can only lead to more stereotypes, misunderstanding, racism, and anti-Semitism. This dynamic focuses attention on blacks and Jews and encourages us to attack each other rather than challenge white, Christian racism.

It is important to challenge anti-Semitism wherever it occurs. However, there is a clear difference in who has the power to carry out anti-Semitic violence in our society. One way white people retain power is by attacking strong and powerful individuals of color who are mobilizing people. Whether it's Louis Farrakhan, Sister Souljah, Jesse Jackson, or Malcolm X, we can expect that white people will try to set up Jewish people to attack African-American leaders and vice versa. Then they don't have to take the heat directly. If we are challenging Louis Farrakhan's anti-Semitic statements but not Pat Buchanan's or Rush Limbaugh's, then we are contributing to racism and being strategically ineffective. White Christian leaders like nothing better than to see groups taking potshots at each other.

Some people argue that racism and anti-Semitism are different because one is based on skin color and the other on religious and cultural differences. It is true that historically the two have taken on different characteristics. Ruling classes have always used cultural differences to exploit people and to determine the roles that outside groups would play in the economic system. Racism and anti-Semitism are strategies ruling classes use —

- to divide people, exploiting some groups more heavily than others;
- to strengthen white cultural solidarity and chauvinism;
- to make white workers feel lucky they have some privilege or status no matter how heavily exploited they are; and
- to divert working- and middle-class attention from the wealthy by focusing on scapegoats "above" them (Jews) and "below" them (people of color).

Colluding with anti-Semitism, even through silence, contributes to inequality and racial injustice. European and American political and economic elites have set up Jewish people as scapegoats for their economic and political decisions. Fighting against anti-Semitism is fighting for economic justice. Whenever the stereotypes of Jewish money or power go unchallenged, the injustice of our economic system is strengthened and racism is continued. Blaming Jewish bankers or African-American women on welfare are parallel strategies to divert our attention from the corporate elite that makes the economic decisions that affect our lives. These strategies give the majority of white people the mistaken impression that they are controlled by Jews and in competition with people of color — squeezed on both sides.

There are other complex strands in anti-Semitism. People of color who are Christian have adopted and passed on anti-Semitic lies about the role of the Jewish people in Western history. Many Christians of color are capable of condoning violence against Jews even while they are themselves the targets of racism. This leads many people who are fighting racism, whether they are people of color or white people, to downplay the importance of anti-Semitism and not respond vigorously when Jews are attacked.

Muslims also have a long history of anti-Jewish practices and justifications. At the same time, in Europe and America, Jews and Arabs have been categorized together as infidels and as threats to Christianity and to Western civilization. The word anti-Semitic itself points to the intertwined history of anti-Jewish and anti-Arab violence in Western countries. Jews and Muslims were both exiled from Spain in 1492. Although it is beyond the scope of this book, we have much to learn about how racism operates by analyzing the ways anti-Arab racism is part of anti-Semitism, how Arab societies have contributed to anti-Jewish violence, how European-based parts of Jewish-American and Israeli society have contributed to anti-Arab racism, and how white Christian-dominated Western societies have set up Jews and Arabs to fight each other in the eastern Mediterranean region.

Looking in detail at how anti-Semitism operates gives us further insight into the dynamics of racism. It helps us see that racism is not simply a religious, biological, or cultural persecution. It rests, instead, on a hierarchy and on institutionalization of power and violence. Those who benefit most from that power use economic, religious, cultural, biological, historical, or sociological justifications as needed to maintain their control. They can offer safe haven, economic success, voting rights, tolerance, and even status as honorary whites to various groups when their support is needed. Just as quickly they can withdraw those favors and set the wrath of the rest of the populace against selected scapegoats when a diversion is called for. The only long-term corrective to anti-Semitism and racism is the democratic dispersion of political, economic, and social power to all people within a society and the creation of a democratic, anti-racist, anti-sexist, and secular multicultural state.

Sometimes in a workshop it is useful to divide into a white caucus and a people of color caucus. If we don't acknowledge the differences between those who have access to material benefits from being "white" and those who don't, we are not adequately addressing racism. But if we don't acknowledge the issues of Jewish people's lives we aren't adequately addressing racism either. We need to do both.

I need non-Jewish people to recognize that my participation in the struggle against racism is part of my identity as a Jewish person fighting for justice, equality, the end of exploitation, and my personal and group safety. To ask me to fight racism as a white person without recognizing my Jewish identity renders me invisible, at risk for further violence from white Christians and from non-Jewish people of color, and ultimately renders me ineffective.

I am not a white Christian, I am a white Jew. I can fight racism best by understanding that it is a strategy, like anti-Semitism, used to justify economic and cultural exploitation and to keep power and control in the hands of white people, particularly the white Christian upper class. Racism exists within that part of the Jewish community that accepts economic and cultural exploitation. We need to challenge racism within the Jewish community, racism directed toward both Jewish and non-Jewish people of color. Since Jewish people know directly the results of racist ideology, institutionalized violence, and economic injustice, we can do that best by drawing on our own history and experience.

European-descended Jews can be powerful allies to people of color because we are often in positions to intervene or interrupt racism among white people. We don't need to overlook anti-Semitism in order to do this. We can't. We are often the targets of anti-Semitism as soon as we raise concerns about racism! Our fears of arousing anti-Semitism when challenging racism give us a deep understanding of how both oppressions work. We need to confront anti-Semitism wherever it occurs, including from people of color, because racism cannot be eliminated unless anti-Semitism is as well.

Bringing up anti-Semitism does not distract from the struggle to end racism; it enhances it. Dealing with anti-Semitism makes it clearer how racism works and how Christian values are a cornerstone of racism. My greatest effectiveness as an ally to people of color comes from my history and experience as a Jew.

I will return to the subjects of Christianity, religion and racism in Part V. For now, consider the following questions as they apply to you.

QUESTIONS AND ACTIONS:
JEWISH PEOPLE

If you are Christian or of Christian background:

1. What did you learn in religious school or church or from the Bible about Jewish people? What did you learn about people of color?

2. What non-explicit messages did you receive about both groups from your Christian heritage?

3. In what ways is it true and in what ways is it not true to say "America is a Christian country?" How would you respond if someone said this in your presence?

4. What are some of the ways that Jews are blamed for social problems?

5. Beginning with the fact that Jesus and Mary were Arab Jews with skin coloring, hair, and facial features that were clearly not European, in what ways has Christianity "whitewashed" its origins?

6. How can you challenge anti-Semitism expressed by other Christians and within your church?

If you are Jewish:

1. Are you generally treated as white or as non-white in Jewish society? In gentile society?

2. What forms does racism take within the American-Jewish community?

3. What kind of support do you need from Christian allies when anti-Semitic statements or actions are being committed?

4. How can you draw on your Jewish identity, history, and experience to be an ally to (other) people of color?

5. When you or other Jewish people raise issues of racism, do you find yourselves targets of anti-Semitism? What support do you need from Christians when this happens? What support do you need from other Jewish people?

6. How could you challenge racism within the Jewish community?

Recent Immigrants

IMMIGRATION IS A RACIAL ISSUE. Immigration and Naturalization Service (INS) officials do not stop white Americans to stem the flow of large numbers of illegal Canadian, Russian, and eastern European immigrants. There are not hundreds of miles of barbed-wire fencing between Canada and the U.S. And vigilante groups do not patrol that border.

Obviously, one of the great strengths of Canada, the United States, New Zealand, and Australia as nations has been their ability to welcome the presence and contributions of new immigrants. But not all immigrants and not all the time. Recent immigrants have always been both feared and disdained by older residents. And immigrants of color, during periods when they were allowed to enter the country, have always been treated differently than lighter skinned arrivals.

Some of this history is referred to in the preceding sections on particular racial groups. Throughout most of the history of the United States the immigration of Asians, Africans (except those enslaved), South and Central Americans, and people from the Middle East has been restricted if not totally excluded. Not all Europeans were welcomed either, and many returned to their countries of origin because of the harsh treatment they received here. But over the last 400 years there has been almost continuous opportunity for Europeans to arrive and settle in the U.S., find jobs, establish families, and build communities.

Many of us in the West like to think of our countries as magnets for immigration because of the opportunity to be found here. Many of us believe that our countries are the most civilized in the world, with coveted resources that everyone else is desperate to gain access to. This misperception has allowed us to construct a fantasy about alien invasion — hordes of people massed at our borders, frantically trying to sneak across only to overrun our communities, take our jobs, and use up our social services. To complement this image we have constructed metaphors of immigrants as disease, infection, plague, varmints, infestation, or simply as invaders. Nothing could be further from the truth.

Most immigrants from underdeveloped countries migrate to other underdeveloped countries, not to industrialized ones. Less than 2 percent of the world's migration ends in the United States.[1] Many factors fuel immigration including war, natural disaster, famine, and lack of work. The United States is a major cause of migration around the world because its foreign and economic policies have disrupted stable social and economic systems in many countries. There are many Southeast Asians here because we engaged in war in Southeast Asia and then welcomed those who supported our cause. There are immigrants from Cuba and Haiti here because we have supported dictatorships in those countries in the past and our economic policies led to their impoverishment as a result of corporate exploitation and trade embargo. There are Mexicans and Central Americans here because of the invasion of corporate agribusiness, manufacturing, and extraction industries that have severely disrupted both rural and urban economies, concentrated wealth among an elite, and forced people to migrate to urban areas and out of the country in search of jobs to support themselves and their families.

In addition, the United States has been a major promoter of International Monetary Fund (IMF) structural adjustment policies, World Bank loans for large-scale agricultural modernization projects, and "free trade" agreements that have forced millions of people to move from rural areas into cities and from one nation to another in search of food, work, and safety. Women in developing countries have been particularly hard hit by these practices. When women are displaced from their land or unable to continue farming because of policies emphasizing export agriculture, they end up migrating to cities to work in textile, manufacturing, or electronic industries, or travel overseas to do nursing, domestic, textile, or sex work.

First England, then the United States and other developed countries have used overseas economic interventions and immigration policies to extract resources and exploit people. The United States has generally not been against immigration as much as it has been against the long-term development of non-white immigrant communities. English and Irish immigrants were brought over to clear and settle the East Coast, Chinese laborers were brought over to build the railroads, and Mexican labor was brought in to work the fields of the Southwest in the Bracero program. The labor of all groups was exploited, but there was still a color line at the border. People of color were not expected or encouraged to stay. During the limited period when Chinese men were given permission to immigrate, no Chinese women were allowed into the country, and Mexicans were only given short-term visas during periods of great labor shortages. No such restrictions applied to English and Irish immigrants.

If we don't take into account the governmental and corporate policies that both push people out of their countries of origin and pull them towards our own, we end up blaming immigrants for making choices based upon circumstances that those in power in our country have created. Unless we analyze where the economic and political decision-making power lies, we will continue to have our attention directed towards people of color on the bottom of the economic pyramid rather than towards those white people in power at the top.

Once they arrived here, why did "white" immigrants fare better than immigrants of color? Immigrants from Ireland, Italy, Spain, Greece, and various regions of Eastern Europe faced violence, discrimination, social prejudice and stereotypes, and limited access to jobs, housing, and education, just as immigrants from other regions of the world did. However there were substantial differences as well. Immigration from Asia, South and Central America, the Middle East, and Africa was severely restricted from the 17th century until the mid-20th century, whereas immigrants from southern and eastern Europe, both men and women, were able to come in significant numbers. Although they faced discrimination, these immigrants were not driven out of trades, professions, and other occupations the way immigrants of color were. "White" immigrants were able to become citizens, could vote, and therefore were able to develop political strength. There were few laws preventing them from participating in civil society or from owning land and businesses. The government established public schools, hospitals, and other services specifically to help them assimilate into American society. And while they did occasionally face violent attack, it was nowhere near as brutal and sustained, nor was it supported by the government as was the violence experienced by immigrants of color. Immigrants of color had as little status and government protection as African Americans and Native Americans, and therefore were subject to discrimination, exploitation, hate crimes, mob violence. They were often killed with impunity in many areas of the country. Oftentimes this occurred with state or national government collusion or active participation.

Today the selective control of immigration to serve economic needs continues, as technology workers from South and East Asia enter the country on special visas to serve the interests of the computer industry, and women of color are imported from economically exploited countries as nurses under the Nursing Relief Act of 1989. The large communities of Mexican, Central-American, and Asian immigrants provide the labor force for the textile, computer, food harvesting, and service sectors of our economy. Businesses are not interested in eliminating illegal immigration — heavily exploited immigrant labor is a source of great profit to them. They are interested in controlling immigration, using the system to undermine immigrants' ability to organize against their exploitation, and keeping citizen workers alienated from and unable to unite with immigrant workers. As writer and historian Grace Chang notes, "immigration from the Third World into the United States doesn't just happen to a set of factors but is carefully orchestrated — that is, desired, planned, compelled, managed, accelerated, slowed, and periodically stopped — by the direct actions of U.S. interests, including the government as state and as employer, private employers, and corporations."[2]

Immigrants do not increase unemployment or reduce wages for citizens. Studies show that high levels of immigration do not increase joblessness even among the lowest-paid workers, and there is no correlation between immigration and wage level. Nor do immigrants bring disease or reduce health standards. Even though most immigrants come from countries poorer than the United States, recent immigrants are healthier than the U.S.-born population in general, and babies born to immigrant mothers are healthier than those born to U.S.-born mothers.[3]

Nor do immigrants drain our social services. In fact, just the opposite is true. In general, children, the elderly, the infirm, and those with disabilities do not emigrate. Immigrants come as adult workers, having been raised and educated at the expense of their country of origin. In addition, language barriers, fears of deportation, and the generally poor level of social services offered in the United States mean that immigrants use fewer public services than comparable groups of citizens. One study has shown that even legal immigrants use less than their share of medical care, unemployment insurance, food and educational programs, aid programs for families with dependent children, and retirement programs.[4] Julian Simon, professor of business administration at the University of Maryland, concludes that "illegal" immigrants provide the greatest economic bonus to the economy of any group because they use practically no welfare services, while about three-quarters pay Social Security and income taxes.[5]

The result is that American citizens of all races benefit significantly from the contributions of recent immigrants. A comprehensive study by the National Research Council of the National Academy of Sciences found that immigrants raise the incomes of

U.S.-born workers by at least $10 billion each year and that in 1997, immigrant households paid at least $133 billion in direct taxes to federal, state, and local governments. Over their lifetimes, immigrants and their children will each pay an average $80,000 more in taxes than they will receive in local, state, and federal benefits combined.[6]

If immigration is good for our country why do we have 100,000 Immigration and Naturalization Service (INS) officials operating as one of the largest bands of armed police in the world? If the business community profits from immigration, why does the INS raid our workplaces and summarily send workers back to their country of origin? Business leaders want immigrant workers but they want them on their terms. They want them as poorly paid, fearful, easily intimidated, non-unionized, fragmented, and easily controlled workers so that they can reap the highest level of profits from them. Many employers do not generally comply with immigration laws or report illegal workers unless those workers are demanding higher wages, safer working conditions, basic benefits, or the right to form a union and bargain collectively. The INS is used as the threat and enforcement tool to deport workers who are asserting worker's rights. If immigration laws were vigorously and consistently enforced, much of the dirtiest and poorest-paid agricultural fieldwork, manufacturing work, textile work, meat packing work, and maintenance work throughout our country would immediately come to a halt. The intent of immigration laws is not to stop the work, however, but to maintain it.

The only way fully to incorporate immigrants into our communities is to provide them with full rights and benefits. Until this occurs, employers' ability to exploit them will continue to depress wages and set working people against each other, contributing to the further exploitation of all workers and the continuing harassment of Latino/a and Asian-American communities under the guise of immigration enforcement.

We are heavily indebted to immigrants, both those with and those without legal papers, for our daily well-being. At the same time, these workers are some of the most highly exploited people in our society. To change this we can begin to work for full rights and protections for immigrants. The basic rights that all immigrants should have include:

- Full legal rights for all immigrants and refugees regardless of status
- Access to education and health care programs for all immigrants and refugees and their children regardless of status
- Access to permanent residency for all immigrants and refugees
- Clear and uniform standards for the granting of refugee status regardless of country of origin
- Standards that include vulnerability to domestic violence, femicide, and female genital mutilation as criteria for refugee status
- Elimination of employer sanctions and an end to visas tied to employment
- Release of all immigrants who are being held without charges or who have been denied legal rights

We should also work for:
- Resolution of the backlogs of visa applicants
- Demilitarization of the U.S.-Mexico border
- Non-governmental oversight of the Immigration and Naturalization Service

Conclusion

THE PRECEDING SECTIONS HAVE BEEN CURSORY, but again I remind you that this entire section was about white people and our treatment of people of color. People of color are not just the result of what white people have done to them or even of how they have resisted racism. The lives and cultures of people of color can only be conveyed through their own voices, and I encourage you to listen to those voices. Your life will be changed as a result.

To broaden our narrow thinking, which constrains our worldview and understanding, we need to promote the thinking, creative expression, and leadership of people of color. We should do this not because the result will be better than white thinking, but because we have systematically controlled, exploited, and stymied such expression for hundreds of years. We have an historic responsibility to work for the end of white cultural, political, and economic exploitation. We shall certainly gain from the process.

Some of the benefits we can expect include the fact that the burden of guilt, blame, shame, and sadness will be lifted from our shoulders. We will no longer be standing on the backs of other people with all the precariousness that position entails. We will have an active role to play in the end of injustice. We will gain immeasurably from the contributions that people of color make to the world without exploiting them for it. And we will have a more accurate assessment of the contributions of white people. We will better see that leadership, wisdom, and creative expression have nothing to do with racial groupings, but are the result of the rich interplay between individual creativity, culture, circumstances, politics, and history, and that they defy categorization of any kind.

The final part of this book looks at the structures and values we need to put in place to build a democratic, anti-racist, multicultural society. But first, in Part V, we look at institutional racism and how we can take more effective social action to end it.

PART V

Fighting Institutional Racism

Institutional Racism

RACISM IS NOT JUST THE SUM TOTAL of all the individual acts in which white people discriminate, harass, stereotype, or otherwise mistreat people of color. The accumulated effects of centuries of white racism have given it an institutional nature that is more entrenched than racial prejudice. In fact, it is barely touched by changes in individual white consciousness. We often find it difficult to see or to know how to challenge institutional racism because we are so used to focusing on individual actions and attitudes.

One example of institutional racism is that professors of color (and white women) make considerably less money than their white (and male) counterparts. Prejudice and acts of discrimination by individual white faculty and administrators contribute to this disparity. But even if all white people were completely racially neutral, the disparities would persist.

Some of the reasons for these systemic disparities are that past discrimination excluded students of color from academic programs. Segregated and inferior schools have forced students of color to play catch up in college, taking longer to complete their studies. Established networks of white academics have made it easier for white students, particularly males, to get into the best universities, thereby getting better training, credentials, and research opportunities. These networks help them to find out about scholarship opportunities and to find postdoctoral positions, thus advancing their careers faster.

People of color have only recently been allowed into many academic professions. The factors mentioned above result in white professors being hired at higher starting salary levels than corresponding professors of color. Lack of peers of color for support, racism from white colleagues, and pressure on the limited number of professors of color to advise students of color contribute to higher workloads and less support than for their white peers. In addition, recent cutbacks and salary and hiring freezes in many universities have prevented faculty of color from catching up with white faculty who have already reached the highest salary levels.

The result of these patterns is that faculty of color earn approximately 75 percent of what white faculty with comparable qualifications earn. A faculty member of color, working in the same department, who was equally qualified, the same age, and with the same years of experience as her white colleague could be making $10,000 to $15,000 less a year and have considerably less job security and fewer other benefits. This could be true without a single overt act of discrimination in the department or the university.

Nor is this pattern of institutional racism eliminated in one generation, as some of us might hope. There are few professors of color in most disciplines and therefore few role models, mentors, and advisors for current students of color, discouraging some and making it harder for others. This situation reproduces many of the above effects into the next generation.

Differences in public school funding by race are another example of institutional racism. Although in most states there is a standard reimbursement per student to school districts, the actual amount spent on students' education depends on many factors including local property taxes, contributions from parents, volunteer hours from community members, and business and foundation contributions. The average spent per pupil in the same metropolitan area varies enormously from $3,500 to $15,000.[1]

Most students in the United States go to schools that are highly segregated by race because of discriminatory housing and lending practices, and estate tax laws which promote the transfer of wealth through generations. Predominantly white schools spend much more per student than schools in which the majority of students are of color. The average difference in spending is probably about 2 to 1, although in many areas the greatest differences can run 8 to 1 or 10 to 1. An additional $1,500 per year per student gives a class of 30 children $45,000 more a year. Without a single overt act of discrimination, the educational opportunities of most children of color in our country are greatly deficient when compared to those of white children. Today we have an educational system that is nearly as racially segregated and unequal as it was before the Supreme Court's Brown vs. Board of Education ruling outlawed intentional school segregation. This is institutional racism.

We could take examples from any area of contemporary American society. White Americans no longer need to discriminate overtly against people of color to maintain a racial hierarchy. Because of the differences in wealth, power, and privilege and the historical injustices upon which that wealth and power are built, we cannot rely on neutral legal remedies, on bans against overt acts of discrimination, or on individual white people unlearning prejudice as sufficient means to overcome racism — although these are all important. Racism is self-sustaining. It can allow white people to be friendly to people of color, support the policies listed above, and still collude with institutional policies that continue racial injustice. The patterns are so well set in place that we can even allow some people of color to become successful, and little will change.

We can only stop racism by taking present and past institutional racism into account (as well as sexism, classism, and other historically significant injustices). We must judge our efforts at justice by the justice they produce. Public policy should be directed at producing equality of opportunity and justice for all Americans, regardless of race. The rest of this book considers how we can be more effective in combating racism in institutional settings and in public policy arenas.

Public Policy

PUBLIC POLICY REFERS TO GOVERNMENT PLANNING, decision-making, and allocation of public resources. Government officials and the public are constantly confronted by an array of issues affecting our lives and communities. Which issues are addressed, how they are addressed, who gets to participate in the discussion, and what solutions are considered viable are all influenced by racism. As informed and active citizens, we can influence the nature of public policy discussion and decisions.

Americans can influence public policy at several levels. We are most powerful when we organize around particular issues or programs and create pressure that public officials must respond to. The civil rights movement, women's movement, disability rights movement, lesbian and gay movement, American Indian movement, Chicano movement, and anti-Vietnam War movement are examples of large scale organizing that led to new laws, executive orders, funding appropriations, federal guidelines, and other specific results.

Another way to influence public policy is by electing officials who represent our interests. This is always complex because candidates run on a platform of interests, some of which may be progressive and others of which may not be. They also make promises during elections and then do not or cannot follow through. Unless there is public pressure while they are in office, they don't have the leverage to fight entrenched interests.

We are also able to respond to proposed legislation, state initiatives, nominations of public officials, and public planning documents. Here again, concerted mobilization of people dramatically increases our effectiveness in responding to issues.

We are asked to respond to a constant barrage of proposals, budgets, elections, special-interest agendas, and planning documents. Unless we analyze the issues carefully and critically, keeping a focus on how they affect racism and race relations, we will not be able to marshal our forces effectively. In Part VI I look at some current public policy issues in a way that can be used as a guideline for critically analyzing others not covered here.

We will not get very far in the struggle for racial justice unless we have significant national public support and leadership for addressing racial injustice directly and forcefully. This calls for no less than massive reinvestment in communities of color to begin to redress the long-term effects of racism on those communities. Some might call it reinvestment for what was taken out of communities of color by white people. Others might call it restorative justice. The concept is often referred to as reparations. Particularly within the African-American community, the demand for reparations for slavery and its aftermath has been gaining momentum in recent years. Senator Bill Owens introduced the first reparations bill in the Massachusetts state senate. More recently John Conyers, a Democrat from Michigan, has introduced several bills to put the issue of reparations on the table. These bills would establish a commission to examine the institution of slavery and economic discrimination against African Americans and recommend appropriate remedies. There have also been public conferences, books, talks, and lawsuits. These are relatively new developments, but the idea of reparations for African Americans has a long history.

On January 16, 1865, General William T. Sherman issued Special Field Order No.15, which awarded all the Sea Islands south of Charleston, South Carolina, and a significant portion of coastal lands, to newly freed slaves to homestead. Each freedman was eligible for 40 acres of tillable ground. The order became a proposed law that was passed by both houses but ultimately vetoed by President Andrew Johnson.

In this century we have seen other national and international examples of reparations. The German government paid reparations both to individual Jews who suffered losses during the Holocaust, and to the state of Israel. The American government paid reparations to Japanese Americans for the losses they suffered from the confiscation of their property and their forced relocation during World War II. We also saw investment in devastated communities through the Marshall Plan and the reconstruction of western Europe after World War II when the U.S. government devoted $13.3 billion (about 10 times that amount in today's dollars) to renovate 16 war-torn countries.

The principle under which Germany paid reparations was stated in the 1952 Luxembourg Agreement, which said that a state that victimized inhabitants on the basis of group membership has an obligation to compensate that group on the same basis. Slavery was a system legitimized in the Constitution and enforced through local, state, and federal statutes. The genocide of Native Americans, the destruction of their cultures, and the establishment and failure of the treaty system were acts of the U.S. government. In both cases individuals were targeted simply because of their membership in a particular group, and the damages from those systems continues to this day.

One form that reparations for Native Americans could take would be the return of land. For example, there is much federal land that is no longer being used as military bases. The government has promised to give priority to the claims of Native Americans for such land, but in practice this policy has not been carried out. Returning unused land would be a first step in restoring an economic base to Native communities at little cost to the government.[1]

Whether we call it reinvestment, retribution, redistribution, or reparations, it is a process by which American society takes responsibility for killing millions of people, stealing the land, and exploiting the labor and culture of Native Americans, African Americans, Latino/as, and Asian Americans during the last 500 years of European settlement in North America. We can't make up for the lives, communities, land, and culture lost. But we can acknowledge our responsibility and make a commitment to ending racism and other forms of injustice.

Public reinvestment needs to be focused and accountable. It needs to be controlled by the people whose lives it will affect and be directed toward building infrastructures that will promote personal and community development.

People of color do not want handouts. They say they want an end to racial exploitation; they want the same opportunities white people have. These opportunities include meaningful and effective education for themselves and their children, decent jobs, adequate health care, safe streets, quality childcare, adequate social services, and the chance to be represented by people who truly share their interests. These are opportunities that all people deserve and that, according to our founding documents, we are honor bound to provide equally for all Americans. We can certainly afford to do so, and we cannot afford not to.

How do we pay for reinvestment? It is no secret, but still little discussed among us, that wealth is concentrated among a relatively few in the United States. In 1998 the top 20 percent of the population owned 91 percent of the financial wealth of the entire country. The wealth of the top 1 percent of the population of the United States averages over $10 million per household.[2] The astoundingly high concentration of wealth in this country is the direct result of hundreds of years of exploitation of poor, working-, and middle-class people by the rich, and of people of color by white people. We need to put the redistribution of that wealth at the very top of our agenda.

In the last two decades the concentration of wealth has increased. In 2001 a tax-cut bill was passed in the United States that will further consolidate wealth, primarily benefiting the top 1 percent of the population and allowing them to pass on even greater amounts of wealth to their children. We have corporate welfare policies, such as unlimited deduction for interest on corporate debt, intangible asset write-offs, foreign tax credits, and write-offs for banks for foreign debt losses, costing us over $160 billion a year. In addition, it is estimated that corporate fraud costs us $200 billion a year. In contrast, the FBI puts the loss from burglary and street robbery at a comparatively small $4.64 billion in 1992.[3]

One example of widespread corporate fraud is the Savings and Loans debacle in which hundreds of millions of dollars were transferred to the rich at a cost to the country of over $500 billion (that's over $2,000 for each of us, which adds up to $10,000 for my family of five). We will be paying this off for another decade. Congress passed a bill that made it impossible to prosecute individual corporate officers or others who had been instrumental in the failure of Savings and Loans and who had benefited from those failures. This law was passed in 1996 at the same time as the Omnibus Crime Bill, which ostensibly cracks down on crime. Clearly white-collar crimes by the rich are treated differently than crimes committed by the poor and people of color.

Such government policy favors the rich over the rest of us, and white people over people of color. To end racial injustice we need to take money from where it has accumulated and move it to where we need to invest for our future.

This is an economic and a racial issue. Racial justice cannot be achieved when there are such huge disparities in wealth, much of which has been created through racial exploitation. Economic democracy and redistribution of wealth will not necessarily end racial injustice unless white people end the practices that exploit and oppress people of color.

We need to tax the income and accumulated wealth of the small percentage of individuals, families, and corporations that control our economy and our communities. Then we need to reinvest that money in community-controlled and racially just development. Poor, working-, and middle-class people of all races, women and men, young and old, people with disabilities, rural, urban, and suburban dwellers would benefit if we did so.

The tax structure of the United States is complex, at least partly to protect the tremendous accumulation and concentration of wealth. A detailed analysis of it is beyond the scope of this book. We could make the entire system simpler and substantially more just with a few major changes. Following are some suggestions that are adapted from Barlett and Steele's *America: Who Really Pays the Taxes?*[4]

- Eliminate all tax credits and exemptions except the personal exemption.
- Eliminate all itemized deductions.
- Lower the lowest rates and raise the highest rates in a simple scale.
- Eliminate special treatment for capital gains.
- Impose the income tax on the increase in value of all holdings at death.
- Withhold taxes on all income, regardless of source.
- Have a means test for all individual government benefits such as social security.
- Impose a 1 percent excise tax on all securities and options trading.
- Eliminate corporate tax preferences and increase corporate taxes to generate about 31 percent of total income tax collections.
- Tax income earned in the United States regardless of the filer's country residence.
- Eliminate write-offs for taxes paid to foreign governments.
- Raise taxes on overseas investors.
- Raise taxes on foreign companies earning money in the United States.

There are many areas of public policy that we need to address to end racial injustice, but redistribution of the wealth of this country should be the first and primary one.

We must stop exploiting and start rebuilding what we have devastated. We need to invest publicly in the creation of meaningful, safe, and well-paid jobs for everyone; universal and comprehensive health care; safe, challenging, and democratic schools for all young people; the end of discrimination based on gender, race, sexual orientation, age, physical or mental ability, religion, or other "differences"; the participation of every person in the decisions that affect their lives; and the reconstruction of our devastated urban and rural environments.

Public policy issues change over time, but every public policy issue in the United States is at least partly an issue of race. We must always pay attention to the racial consequences of any issue that is being considered. We must also be sensitive to the racial implications of any "progressive" policy we are advocating so it doesn't have racist effects.

At the same time we need to be aware that white politicians develop public policy from a white perspective to benefit their white majority constituents, and then give a racial spin to the policies to cement their support. We have already seen how public policy responses to issues of inner-city decay, poverty, welfare reform, and teenage pregnancy are coded for race. Both Republicans and Democrats routinely use these codings to build support based on our shared interests and fears as white people.

We can do three things to take strategic action on public policy issues. We should assume that there are substantial racial implications for every issue before us. We should understand the ways that issues are framed in racial terms, in code or openly, to build support for an upper-class agenda. And we must keep revisiting issues that we thought were once settled, because our gains are subject to erosion and counterattack.

Issues that were important to pursue a few years ago may not be so vital today. Stands that were originally progressive may be co-opted very quickly. Battles won can subsequently be lost when opponents regroup and counterattack. That is why we must strategically evaluate current realities — political, cultural, and economic — and keep in mind that our goal is effective action for racial justice.

It is easy to become mesmerized by public policy debates because the personalities and issues are fascinating. We can forget that the point of understanding the issues is to be able to influence the decisions that get made. Some of us are tremendously well informed on current affairs, passionately hold progressive opinions, and take a principled stand on issues — but we don't translate that stand into public action.

We want to respond effectively to public policy initiatives through public action. More importantly, we want to shape public policy through educational and organizing efforts. Public action is what influences and shapes public policy debates in the first place. During the first two-thirds of the 19th century, African Americans and white people worked to make abolition an issue that could not be avoided. Civil and voting rights for African Americans became public policy issues as a result of grassroots organizing that occurred during the civil rights movement. Japanese Americans struggled for many years to make reparations for the internment of Japanese-American citizens during World War II an issue the government had to address. These are the kinds of campaigns we can support. This is the kind of public action we need to take.

QUESTIONS TO ASSESS PUBLIC POLICY ISSUES

Here are some questions to ask yourself when responding to public policy issues.
1. How is the problem being defined? Who is defining the problem? Who is not part of the discussion?
2. Who is being blamed for the problem? What racial or other fears are being appealed to?
3. What is the core issue?
4. What is the historical context for this issue?
5. What is being proposed as a solution? What would be the actual results of such a proposal?
6. How would this proposal affect people of color? How would it affect white people?
7. How would this proposal affect the rich?
8. How would it affect women? Young people? Poor and working people?
9. What are other options?
10. How are people organizing to address this problem in a more progressive way? How are people organizing to resist any racial backlash this issue might represent?
11. What is one thing you could do to address this problem?

Any public policy issue can be analyzed using these and other questions. They stimulate our critical thinking so we are not misled into colluding with an agenda that benefits a few and distracts us from the source of our problems

Critical Analysis of Immigration Policy

Tʜʀᴏᴜɢʜᴏᴜᴛ ᴛʜɪꜱ ʙᴏᴏᴋ we have seen how people of color are routinely scapegoated for social problems over which they have little influence. Recent immigrants make up one of the most vulnerable groups of people of color (see the section on "Recent Immigrants" in Part IV). Although some immigrants come to this country highly skilled, highly trained, or with family and economic resources, most are poor, isolated by language and culture, and disoriented by a new society. Many are fleeing war, poverty, or political repression. Many of our own foreparents faced similar conditions when they arrived one, five, or ten generations ago. Recent immigrants, especially those without legal papers, are currently being attacked as a cause of economic deficits, the lack of jobs, and the deterioration of American values and cultural unity.

Who has legal papers and who doesn't, who is welcome here and who isn't, are not questions of impartial legal standards. Immigration policy has always been an arm of foreign policy as well as an instrument of white racism. Cubans fleeing Castro have been preferred over Haitians fleeing Duvalier; Vietnamese fleeing communism have been preferred over Salvadorano/as fleeing U.S.-supported dictators; and Europeans have been preferred over people of color. These are examples of how political factors influence immigration policy, which in turn determines who is here legally or illegally. The current debate over services to residents without papers, reflected in the 1994 California ballot initiative 187, can be analyzed using the questions posed above. It provides a good case study of how to look at public policy issues.

The following are answers to the questions posed on page 178.

1. The problem is defined as: "illegal" immigration places a disproportionate burden on the states that have to pay for the services provided to these immigrants. State politicians say this produces state budget deficits when the federal government mandates services but doesn't pay for them. White political leaders, the media, and states' rights advocates are primarily defining the problem while poor and working people, people of color, and immigrants are excluded from the discussion.

2. Recent immigrants without papers are being blamed for these problems. This becomes a way to blame the entire Latino/a and Asian-American immigrant communities, allowing the government to keep them under tight control and surveillance and to further cut back social services to the poor. Defining immigrants without papers and the Latino/a and Asian-American immigrant communities as the problem appeals to white people's fear of people of color

and immigrants, our fear of losing jobs, and our fear of budget deficits and further cutbacks.

3. The stated issues are: the federal government is not funding federally mandated services; politicians want to reduce federal and state budget deficits; and corporations are moving jobs overseas causing loss of jobs in the United States. The primary issue, however, is a white backlash against the increasing size, influence, and eventual majority status of communities of color. This backlash uses "illegal alien" as a racially coded word for immigrant of color, playing into the economic and racial fears of working- and middle-class whites.

4. Historically, white people have used issues of states' rights to fight against relinquishing white power. The Civil War was fought over whether the states or the federal government had the right to set policy on slavery, not on whether slavery per se was right or wrong. Much of the resistance to the civil rights movement was based on similar arguments about states' rights and the role of the federal government in enforcing desegregation, voting rights, and access to education. Once again white people are trying to roll back gains in government policy that benefit the poorest and most vulnerable members of our society by claiming that the federal government has no right to tell the states what services they must provide. This is a familiar pattern in which communities of color are attacked indirectly through a challenge to the government's role in enforcing their rights. The specific proposals being advanced would cut off all services to immigrants lacking legal papers. The intended result is a net savings from not providing services to them.

5. Not surprisingly, the cost of services to immigrants with or without papers is often inflated, and the contributions they make are ignored or minimized. Most studies indicate that they actually contribute more to the community in taxes, job creation, and the revitalization of neighborhoods than they require from it in economic support. Over time their contribution increases and costs decrease further. They do take jobs — usually those that whites don't want or won't do — but their need for services creates jobs as well.

6. In the long term this proposed "solution" would affect people of color in several ways. It would further impoverish the Latino/a and Asian-American immigrant communities while holding them responsible for declining employment, wages, and benefits in the U.S. economy. It would cut them off from schooling, health care, and other essential public services while targeting them for further police and Immigration and Naturalization Service harassment and intimidation as well as violence from individuals. (According to the Los Angles County Commission on Human Relations, hate crimes against Latinos increased sharply [in 1994]. The Commission attributed the 23.4 percent increase in hate crimes against Latinos in Los Angles County to the passage of Proposition 187." [5])

7. Anti-immigrant bills would further segregate white people from people of color, reinforce our racial stereotypes, and contribute to further racial injustice. These proposed solutions would focus our attention on the immigrant community

rather than on the true source of the loss of jobs, decreased earning power, and economic dislocation we are currently experiencing. The increasing concentration of wealth, and the source of the economic decisions that have impoverished many of our lives, would continue to be covered up. Businesses would have an increased ability to exploit immigrants because of their fear of being deported or of being mistakenly identified as illegal.

8. Under these proposals, certain groups would be hit particularly hard. Bearing primary responsibility for the health and welfare of the family, immigrant women would have less access to work, education, safety, and health care, and fewer resources for raising children. These proposals make all Asian-American and Latina women more vulnerable to sexual and racial harassment at work, and to physical and sexual violence within the family. The proposals would prevent children of immigrants without papers from accessing schooling and health care, and would intensify the two-tier system in which some children have opportunities and other children are without future prospects of work.

9. There are many options for balancing state budgets and paying for social services, if that is the concern, other than blaming and punishing immigrants of color. We could increase taxation of the rich and of corporate wealth. We could use some of that money to create jobs, job training, school programs, and social services to integrate immigrants more quickly into the economy.

10. A great deal of organizing against anti-immigrant proposals and policies has already occurred. Some programs provide services and legal assistance to immigrants without papers. Some are organizing immigrant workers so they will have a stronger voice in the political system. There are organizations addressing economic dislocation and redevelopment, while others are organizing and doing educational work against ballot initiatives and legislative proposals that attack immigrants. There are also campaigns of non-compliance with initiatives already passed, coordinated by teachers and health care workers.

11. There are many ways to become involved. You can join an organization supporting immigrant rights, and you can make a financial contribution to an organization working with immigrants and refugees. You can write letters, phone, or send faxes and e-mail to policymakers, and you can work with others to protest the enforcement of policies that discriminate against immigrants. You can challenge other people when you hear racially prejudiced or misinformed statements about this issue. You can help others think critically about how racism operates in an issue like this.

With this as an example of critical analysis of social issues, take a current public policy debate and scrutinize it using the questions listed on page 178.

Voting

We value our right to vote and to elect our public officials. We know that without democratic elections, and the ability of every citizen to participate in those elections, dictators and bureaucratic elites make public policy. Many of us have come to take our right to vote for granted, forgetting our foreparents' long struggles to achieve it. Originally only white men with property could vote. People have fought for hundreds of years to extend the right to vote first to poor and working-class white men, then to men of color, and finally to women.

It was during the civil rights movement, nearly one hundred years after the passage of the 15th Amendment, that many came to realize that what we as white people took for granted was still denied to African Americans. But since the passage of the Voting Rights Act of 1965, complacency has set in again and many of us who are white have assumed that everyone can vote and that all votes count equally. However, racism is deeply embedded in our electoral system and, not surprisingly, it is one area where people of color are most disenfranchised.

In this section I will deal primarily with the situation in the United States because of the widespread and well-documented practice of disenfranchising voters of color. However, all white-dominated countries have histories of denying the right to vote to people of color.

Voting is always influenced by racial factors, although we are not usually given information that breaks down votes by race. In the 2000 election in the United States, whites constituted almost 95 percent of George W. Bush's total vote. People of color accounted for almost 30 percent of Al Gore's total vote, although they were only 19 percent of the total voters.[1] But were people of color adequately represented? Did their votes count?

On election day, African-American and Haitian voters were harassed by police; their names were removed from the rolls; they were turned away from the polls even when they had valid I.D.; they were asked to show more I.D. than white voters had to show; they were threatened with deportation; they had the polls close early on them (some as early as 4:30); and they saw their ballots left uncounted by outdated machinery. These "irregularities" and illegalities affected the votes of tens of thousands of voters in Florida, which turned out to be the pivotal state in determining the final presidential election results. But Florida was not the only state to report voting irregularities, nor were African Americans and Haitians the only voters kept from voting. Reports indicate that there were incidents of voter intimidation, voter turn-backs, and other illegal practices in several other states, including Michigan, Georgia, Missouri, New York, Arkansas, and Illinois.[2] In Texas, and possibly in other states, Latinos were asked to show extra identification that whites weren't required to show, and they reported being intimidated by men hanging around the voting booths dressed in green, the color of the uniform of immigration officials. Older Mexicans who requested absentee ballots were visited by sheriffs and other law-enforcement officials in what appeared to be attempts at intimidation. There were also many cases where polls had an inadequate supply of bilingual ballots and poll watchers.[3]

Denying people of color the right to vote is a practice deeply embedded in our political system, and we need to understand that history so we don't consider the present practices as simple "irregularities." Our Founding Fathers, in a compromise with the South to ensure that the Southern states would participate in the union, agreed that slaves, although they could not vote, would count as three-fifths of a person for the purpose of calculating the representatives that a state was allotted. Then the number of representatives was used to calculate the number of electoral votes that each state would have. This gave the Southern states a political advantage so powerful that Virginia slave owners controlled the presidency in eight of the first nine U.S. elections.

African Americans received the right to vote with the passage of the 15th Amendment in 1870. But the two-party, winner-take-all Electoral College system continues to discriminate against and marginalize people of color. In the 2000 election, Bush won the electoral votes of every Southern state and every border state except Maryland, despite the fact that 53 percent of all blacks (over 90 percent of whom voted for the Democrats) live in the Southern states. There are more white Republicans than black votes in each of those states, so the votes of almost half of the people of color in the entire country were negated. Millions of Native-American and Latino voters who live in overwhelmingly white, Republican states like Arizona, Nevada, Oklahoma, Utah, Montana, and Texas were equally unrepresented.

A further dilution of the votes of people of color occurs because of the way electoral votes are unequally distributed between rural and urban states. For example, in Wyoming, one Electoral College vote corresponds to 71,000 voters, while in more populated states, with more voters of color, the ratio is one Electoral College vote to over 200,000 voters.

The Electoral College system is not the only way that people of color lose voting representation. After emancipation and the passage of the 14th and 15th amendments, the Southern states worked to exclude newly enfranchised black voters. The white ruling class of the South was very explicit about what it was doing.

For example, in Virginia, U.S. Senator Carter Glass worked to expand the disenfranchisement laws along with poll taxes and literacy tests. He described the state's 1901 convention this way:

> *Discrimination! Why that is precisely what we propose. That, exactly, is what this Convention was elected for — to discriminate to the very extremity of permissible action under the limits of the Federal Constitution, with a view to the elimination of every Negro voter who can be gotten rid of legally, without materially impairing the numerical strength of the white electorate.[4]*

In Alabama, the criminal code in the constitution of 1901 was, according to the chair of the convention, John Knox, designed to "ensure white supremacy," and crimes worthy of disenfranchisement were classified depending in large part by whether delegates thought blacks were likely to commit them.[5] The state was also focused on excluding poor whites. Delegates "wished to disfranchise most of the Negroes and the uneducated and propertyless whites in order to legally create a conservative electorate," wrote historian Malcolm McMillan.[6]

Historically, another way white people disenfranchised voters of color was by disenfranchising felons — but not just any felons.[7] Many states disenfranchised criminals even before the Civil War. But in the South, after the Civil War and Reconstruction, legal codes were created to limit the effects of the 14th and 15th amendments, which gave blacks equal protection under the law and gave black men the right to vote. In Mississippi, the convention of 1890 replaced laws disenfranchising all convicts with laws disenfranchising only people convicted of the crimes blacks were supposedly more likely to commit. For almost a century thereafter, you couldn't lose your right to vote in Mississippi if you committed murder or rape, but you could if you married someone of another race. In Florida, the constitution drafted in 1868 disenfranchised ex-felons as well as anyone convicted of larceny, again a crime that whites considered ex-slaves were most likely to commit.

The provisions that came out of those post-Reconstruction conventions, from poll taxes to grandfather clauses to literacy tests, were almost all struck down by the Civil Rights Act of 1965. The only one still standing is the felony provision, which means that 1.8 million black men (13 percent of all black men in America — approximately one out of seven) are currently denied the right to vote because of incarceration or past felony convictions. Although the rules vary state by state, the United States is the only industrialized country that denies former prisoners the vote. In Maine and Vermont, convicts can vote even when behind bars. In 34 states, felons are not allowed to vote until they leave parole. Maryland and Arizona permanently disqualify two-time felons, Washington bans felons convicted before 1984, and Tennessee bans felons convicted before 1986. And in 10 states, if you commit a single felony, you are essentially barred from voting until you die. The result is that about 1 million Americans of all races are disenfranchised for the rest of their lives, even though they have completed their sentences and are fully integrated into the community. In an extensive study of two poor and mostly black communities in Tallahassee, Florida, criminal justice professor Todd Clear was unable to find a single family without at least one disenfranchised man — he concluded that this made it unlikely the community would be able to band together when, for example, a state senator proposes locating a toxic waste dump nearby.

As journalist Nicholas Thompson of the Washington Monthly has noted, "Felons, of course, aren't just murderers and muggers. Three out of every five felony convictions don't lead to jail time, and there's no clear line you have to cross to earn one .... Stopping payment on a check of more than $150 with intent to defraud makes you a felon in Florida. Being caught with one-fifth of an ounce of crack earns you a federal felony, but being caught with one-fifth of an ounce of cocaine only earns a misdemeanor." (As I describe later, racist and discriminatory sentencing has led to disparate penalties for crack and cocaine possessors, thus disproportionately disenfranchising voters of color.)

Besides being arbitrary, racially biased, and a continuation of historic patterns of discrimination, Thompson notes, "Denying felons the right to vote after they have served their sentences and done their time runs against both the idea that people can redeem themselves and one of the nation's most important principles, the right to choose who governs you."[8] As prominent neoconservative social theorist James Q. Wilson says, "A perpetual loss of the right to vote serves no practical or philosophical purpose."

Finally, millions of mainly Latino and Asian immigrants cannot vote because, according to current law, they are not citizens.

Even when they can vote, however, people of color are marginalized due to our two-party political system. I think Bob Wing, editor of Colorlines magazine, has described this most clearly.

> *To win elections, both parties must take their most loyal voters for granted and focus their message and money to win over the so-called undecided voters who will actually decide which party wins each election. The most loyal Democrats are strong liberals and progressives, the largest bloc of whom are people of color. The most loyal Republicans are conservative whites, especially those in rural areas and small towns. The undecideds are mostly white, affluent suburbanites; and both parties try to position their politics, rhetoric and policies to woo them. The interests of people of color are ignored or even attacked by both parties as they pander to the "center."[9]*

There are, of course, other strategies white people use to keep people of color from voting or to keep their votes from counting: at-large elections, gerrymandering, failure to redistrict when called for, "packing" (drawing electoral districts so that the majority of a group is packed into one area, which therefore gives it only a single representative), and its opposite "cracking" (spreading out voters of color over several districts so that their votes are diluted). Finally, because the electoral vote distribution is tied to the census and we know that the census undercounts communities of color, those communities lose political representation through this mechanism as well. The Census Bureau has refused to adjust the 2000 census results to account for a known undercount that leaves 3.3 million people, all of whom are poor and many of whom are people of color, out of the count. This undercount furthers denies communities of color full allocation of electoral votes and representation at the local level. (It also has serious repercussions in the distribution of federal and state funds for social programs and community development grants.)

We like to think that we live in a democracy, and a hallmark of democracy is that all members have the right to vote and their vote counts equally, but that is not the reality. In reality the votes of most people of color in the United States, and to some extent in other white-dominated countries, count for very little, certainly much less than most white votes. White people often complain that people of color don't vote in large enough numbers. I've heard it said that "They must not care enough." But how many white people would vote if we were harassed on the way to the poll and, when we got there, told we weren't listed or that we needed to show extra identification? How many would vote if, when we tried to make a complaint, there was no one who spoke our language to help us, and all the complaint lines were busy and understaffed? How many would vote if we discovered later that many of our votes were thrown out because of voting "irregularities" in the ballots and voting machines? What if this had been going on for over a hundred years?

Our system of voting needs a drastic overhaul. There are some simple places to begin.

- Eliminate the electoral system
- Develop a system of proportional representation for elections (This type of system is already in place in many municipal and county elections, and various forms are used throughout the world)
- Institute federal monitoring of elections
- Allow for district voting in local elections
- Develop a multi-party system of government
- Redistrict by population, supervised by widely representative bodies of citizens from each community
- Remove restrictions on ex-felons' voting and set up programs to help them register, as Canada does
- Install modern, easy-to-use, voting machinery, keep the polls open 24 hours or more, and declare voting day a national holiday
- Institute election day registration

There are already community groups working on many of these issues. By becoming active on this issue you are strengthening democracy and making sure that all votes, including yours, count.

Affirmative Action

THERE ARE MANY WAYS TO ATTACK RACISM – affirmative action is one particular legal remedy. It is supposed to eliminate institutional discrimination, situations where decisions, policies, and procedures that may not be explicitly discriminatory have had a negative impact on a specific group of people. Affirmative action policies address and redress systematic economic and political discrimination against any group that is underrepresented or has a history of being discriminated against in particular institutions. Beneficiaries of these programs have included white men and women, people with disabilities, and poor and working-class people, but their primary emphasis has been on addressing racial discrimination.

Affirmative action has been one of the primary public policy controversies of the last 40 years. Even now debates about its effectiveness continue. The following overview of some affirmative action issues provides another example of how to think critically about public policy issues.

Affirmative action is more than a legal issue. Every section of this book describes steps you can take to eliminate racism. Everything you do in this area is an affirmative action. Affirmative action to end racism should be the challenge and responsibility of every single person in our society, as well as of the institutions and organizations that have such a large impact on our lives. Yet today we have a vocal minority saying we should stop affirmative action not only as a legal remedy, but also as a social commitment. These people are saying we have gone too far in correcting racial injustice, but of course they are not challenging traditional forms of preference and discrimination that favor the rich, the educated, white people, and men.

Affirmative action is practiced in many areas of our society. We have hiring and recruiting preferences for veterans, women, and the children of alumni of many universities; special economic incentives for purchase of U.S.-made products; import quotas against foreign goods; and agricultural and textile subsidies. These practices have led to a huge over-representation of white people, men, and people of middle-, upper-middle- and upper-class backgrounds in our universities, in well-paid jobs, and in the professions. One indication that attacks on affirmative action are part of a white backlash against equality is that affirmative action that primarily benefits white people is not being questioned.

Many forms of discrimination in our society are illegal. The federal government put in place affirmative action programs to redress racial inequality and injustice in a series of steps, beginning with an executive order issued by President John F. Kennedy in 1961. The Civil Rights Act of 1964 made discrimination illegal and established equal employment opportunity for all Americans regardless of race, cultural background, color, or religion. Subsequent executive orders, in particular Executive Order 11246 issued by President Lyndon B. Johnson in September 1965, made affirmative action goals mandatory for all federally funded programs and moved monitoring and enforcement of affirmative action programs out of the White House and into the Labor Department. These policies and the government action that followed were a response to the tremendous mobilization of African Americans and white supporters pushing for integration and racial justice during the late 1950s and early 1960s.

However, there is still pervasive racism in all areas of U.S. society. For example, in 1991, Diane Sawyer, with ABC-TV, filmed two men, one African American and one white, who were matched for age, appearance, education, and other qualities. A camera crew followed them for some weeks. The white man received service in stores while the African American was ignored or, in some cases, watched closely. The white man was offered a lower price and better financing at a car dealership, jobs where the African American was turned down, and apartments for rent after the African-American man was told they were no longer available. A police car passed the white man while he was walking down the street, but it slowed down and took note of the African American. At least once a day the African American experienced an incident of racism.[1] Many studies like this one demonstrate discrimination against people of color in different areas of everyday life.

Racism, rather than being self-correcting, is self-perpetuating. The disadvantages to people of color and the benefits to white people are passed on to each succeeding generation unless remedial action is taken. The disadvantages to people of color coalesce into institutional practices, such as those noted in the beginning of this section, that adversely affect people of color even though their intent may be race neutral. We have to take positive steps to eliminate and compensate for these institutional effects of racism, even when there is no discernible discriminatory intent.

For example, most people hear about job opportunities through informal networks of friends, family, and neighbors. Since the results of racism are segregated communities, schools, and workplaces, this pattern leaves people of color out of the loop for many jobs, advancement opportunities, scholarships, and training programs. Federal law requires widespread and public advertisement of such opportunities so that not only people of color, but also white women and men who are outside the circles of information have an equal opportunity to apply for these positions.

Affirmative action also addresses preferential hiring programs. Many times people of color have been excluded from hiring pools, overtly discriminated against, unfairly eliminated because of inappropriate qualification standards, or rendered unqualified because of discrimination in education and housing. Court decisions on affirmative action have made it illegal for employers to require qualifications that are not relevant to one's ability to do the job. They have also mandated hiring goals so that those employed begin to reflect the racial mix of the general population from which workers are drawn. There is no legal requirement to hire an unqualified person. There is a mandate, when choosing between qualified candidates, that the hiring preference should be for a person of color when past discrimination has resulted in white people receiving preferential treatment.

Sometimes people argue that affirmative action means the best-qualified person will not be hired. However, it has been demonstrated many times in hiring and academic recruitment that test and educational qualifications are not necessarily the best predictors of future success. This does not mean unqualified people should be hired. Rather, it means that qualified people who may not have the highest test scores or grades are still eminently ready to do the job. Employers have traditionally hired people not only for their test scores, but also based on personal appearance, family and personal connections, school ties, and race and gender preferences demonstrating that talent or desirability can be defined in many ways. These practices have all contributed to a segregated workforce in which whites hold the best jobs and people of color work in the least desirable and most poorly paid positions. Affirmative action policies serve as a corrective to such patterns of discrimination. They keep score on the progress toward proportional representation and place the burden of proof on organizations to show why it is not possible to achieve it.

Affirmative action programs have been remarkably effective in dampening discrimination and opening up work and educational opportunities for groups of people previously excluded. When these policies receive executive branch and judicial support, vast numbers of people of color, white women, and working-class men have gained access they would not otherwise have had.

It has been argued that affirmative action benefits people of color who are already well-off or have middle-class advantages, not the poor and working-class people of color who most need it. Affirmative action programs have benefited substantial numbers of poor and working-class people of color. Access to job-training programs, vocational schools, and semi-skilled and skilled blue-collar, craft, pink-collar, police, and firefighter jobs has increased substantially through affirmative action programs. Even in the professions, many people of color who have benefited from affirmative action have been from families of low income and job status.[2]

All people of color have experienced the effects of racial discrimination. Having more money may buffer the most extreme effects, but it doesn't protect people from everyday racial discrimination. The middle class in various communities of color is small and often fragile. Its members own less wealth and have less financial security than their white counterparts because of the past effects of racial discrimination. They also experience the full range of cultural racism and white prejudice that all people of color have to deal with. Affirmative action has benefited them.

Another argument raised against affirmative action is that individual white people, often white males, have to pay for past discrimination and may not get the jobs they deserve. It is true that specific white people may not get specific job opportunities because of affirmative action policies and may suffer as a result. This lack of opportunity is unfortunate and we need to address the reasons there are not enough jobs. We tend to forget that millions of specific people of color have also lost specific job opportunities as a result of racial discrimination. To be concerned only with the white applicants who don't get the job, while ignoring the people of color who don't get it, shows racial preference.

Is it true that white male candidates are being discriminated against or are losing out because of affirmative action programs? If we look at the composition of various professions such as law, medicine, architecture, academics, and journalism, or at corporate management or higher-level government positions — or if we look overall at the average income levels of white men — we see that people of color are significantly underrepresented and underpaid in every category. People of color don't even hold a proportion of these jobs equal to their percentage of the population. They don't earn wages comparable to white men. White men are tremendously over-represented in almost any category of work that is highly rewarded except for professional athletics. According to a 1995 government report, white males make up only 29 percent of the workforce, but they hold 95 percent of senior management positions.[3] Until there is both equal opportunity and fair distribution of education, training, and advancement to all Americans, we need affirmative action for people of color to counter the hundreds of years of affirmative action that have been directed at white males. We cannot reasonably argue that white males are discriminated against as a group if they are over-represented in most high-status categories.

We should note two other aspects of this dynamic. We have seen how all white people benefit from racism. White men receive more of the economic and other benefits of racism than white women of the same socio-economic status. White men have always been favored in families and schools and preferred for jobs, training, educational programs, athletic programs, military careers and job advancement, and promotion. Men still make more than women for comparable work, are given better educational opportunities, have more leisure time, and are accorded higher status than women.

The second and equally important part of this dynamic is that not all white men are equal. If you are a white male you may or may not have gained a lot from racism. If you are not well-off, well-educated, or well-rewarded in your life, you should look at white men who are and analyze how they accumulated such rewards. Why do many corporate executives make more in a week than their workers make in a year? Why does the average CEO "earn" as much as 475 factory workers?[4]

Business leaders are able to exploit male workers by appealing to common bonds and common fears among white men. They have played on white male fears of losing their jobs (and their manliness, which is defined differently, but no less exclusively, in the computer industry than in trucking or construction) to keep them working hard, claiming that only white men had the strength, skill, intelligence, independence, strength of character, and virility to do the job. White workers have often bought these arguments, feeling pride and increased self-esteem in their working abilities, and feeling personally threatened by the presence of people of color and white women in the workplace. Their ability to fight against low wages, unsafe working conditions, the restructuring of their jobs, and plant closures has been diminished even while they thought they were protecting their jobs by supporting race riots, anti-immigration laws, attacks on affirmative action, and workplace discrimination, harassment and exclusion.

It is not in the best interests of poor, working-, and middle-class men to collude with well-off white men against affirmative action. Yet many have bought the lie that who they are is based on the manliness of the work they do and on their ability to keep their workplaces as white male preserves.

Affirmative action programs have been effective in many areas of public life because they open up opportunities for people who would not otherwise have them, including white women and working-class white men. Attacks on affirmative action are part of a systematic attempt to roll back progress in ending discrimination and to curtail a broad social commitment to justice and equality. Attacking affirmative action is self-destructive for all of us except the rich.

Affirmative action helps mitigate the effects of institutional racism. It also counters the effects of current discrimination, intentional or not. We know that not all white people are well-intentioned. Others of us believe that everyone should have an equal chance but still hold deep-seated prejudices against people of color. For a substantial number of us, those prejudices lead us to practice discrimination. Studies show that without specific, numerical goals, many people and organizations continue to practice discrimination while professing agreement with affirmative action.

There are so many subtle and not-so-subtle ways to eliminate people of color from the job application process, it is not surprising that employers have found ways around affirmative action unless it is tied to visible hiring and promotion targets. In a society with such overwhelming evidence of racism, we must assume that individuals and organizations will resist efforts to end it. For instance, in 1993 the Equal Employment Opportunity Commission had a backlog of 70,000 discrimination cases, and the backlog has increased steadily since then.[5] We have to set goals and enforce and monitor standards because it is the only way we can measure compliance. These are the mechanisms we need to ensure that affirmative action is more than a facade.

Quotas have been used in the past to exclude particular groups of people from jobs or educational opportunities. They have been used to limit the number of Asian Americans or Jews in universities so white people would continue to have unequal access. Setting minimum goals for inclusion is the opposite of setting maximums. We need numerical goals to guarantee compliance with affirmative action policies. Numerical goals promote democratic access to education, jobs, and job training.

Some people have claimed that affirmative action programs lower self-esteem in those who are favored by them, and perhaps even in those who do not directly benefit from them. There is no systematic evidence for this effect. It seems to be something that white people worry about more than people of color.

Persistent denial of equal opportunity — and therefore inadequate access to good jobs, good education, and housing — leads to poor self-esteem. If we are truly worried about low self-esteem among people of color, then we need more effective affirmative action programs to counter discrimination. Discrimination seems to be the more important harm we should be trying to eliminate.

Affirmative action is not a cure-all. It will not eliminate racial discrimination, nor will it eliminate competition for scarce resources. Affirmative action programs can only ensure that everyone has a fair chance at what is available. They cannot direct us to the social policies we need to pursue so we do not have to compete for scarce resources in the first place. In the larger picture we must ask ourselves why there aren't enough well-paying, challenging, and safe jobs for everyone. Why aren't there enough seats in the universities for everyone who wants an education? Expanding opportunity for people of color means expanding not only their access to existing jobs, education, and housing (affirmative action), but removing the obstacles that cause these resources to be limited (social justice).

Affirmative action has been a symbol of white people's acknowledgement of and serious commitment to eradicating racial discrimination. It has been interpreted as such by most people of color. It is crucial that at this stage of backlash against the gains of the last three decades, we don't abandon one tool that we know works.

When whites attack affirmative action — if they are truly committed to American ideals of justice and equality — they should be proposing other remedies for racial inequality in our society. The hypocrisy is clear when white people who say they support equal opportunity attack affirmative action, yet want to leave intact the basic economic and racial injustices it is designed to correct. Ask people who oppose affirmative action how they propose to eliminate racial discrimination. You can learn a lot about their true beliefs from their answers.

QUESTIONS AND ACTIONS:
AFFIRMATIVE ACTION

1. List some of the obvious and subtle ways that people of color may be discriminated against in the hiring, promotion, and benefits processes at your workplace or other workplaces you encounter in your daily life.

2. Which of these areas do you have some control over or participation in?

3. What leverage do you have as a manager to make changes? What leverage as a worker? As a client or consumer?

4. What is the role of any labor organizations related to your workplace regarding affirmative action? Does the membership of the organization reflect the diversity of the community?

5. How are people recruited to the organizations you are involved in?

6. How might these recruitment practices discriminate against people of color?

7. Have there been charges, lawsuits, or public action against discrimination in any institution you use such as a bank, school, city government, retail store, or manufacturer? How was it resolved? Did you ignore or feel angry about the disruption? Did you support the action against discrimination by:

      a. Joining the action?

      b. Boycotting the store or product?

      c. Writing letters of support?

      d. Encouraging your friends, family, or co-workers to be supportive?

8. What would the composition of your workplace look like at all levels if it truly reflected the racial diversity of the community?

9. What effect do you think it would have on your metropolitan area if all people had access to good education and decent jobs? What would have to happen for this to become a reality?

10. Affirmative action is a tool for full inclusion and equal opportunity for all people, not only people of color. Go back through these questions and substitute women for people of color. Substitute lesbians and gay men for

people of color. Substitute people with disabilities. Substitute seniors and young people.

11. What fears, doubts, questions, or concerns do you have about affirmative action? Where do your fears come from? What could you do to answer your questions? Who could you talk with about your concerns?

12. Have you ever been chosen for a job, training program, college-level program, or housing opportunity for which you were less qualified than others? Have you ever been given preference because of family connections, economic background, age, race, or gender?

13. Think again about Question 12 and try to understand ways that family connections, economic background, race, age, or gender may have given you the benefit of the doubt compared to other applicants.

14. Do you think that veterans, sons of alumni, farmers, or other people who receive preferential treatment experience self-doubt, lowered self-esteem, or feelings of guilt because of it?

15. Besides numerical goals, what measures would you suggest be used to monitor racial and other forms of discrimination?

16. How are you going to respond to people who say that affirmative action unfairly discriminates against white males?

17. List three things you can do to defend or strengthen affirmative action programs in your workplace, community, or state.

18. Choose one that you will start doing.

Angry White Guys for Affirmative Action

I N 1996, CONFRONTED WITH PROPOSITION 209 (which would have eliminated affirmative action programs in California if it were passed), a group of white men in Oakland came together to discuss ways that we could add our efforts to those of people of color who were defending affirmative action. We were angry that racism continued, angry that affirmative action was being curtailed, and angry that white men were being portrayed as the victims of affirmative action programs. We named ourselves Angry White Guys for Affirmative Action and began a campaign to address white people on the issue. We chose the name to challenge the conventional thinking that all white men were racist, reactive, and resentful of affirmative action.

As a group, we felt that since we had benefited so directly from affirmative action programs it would be hypocritical to deny these benefits to people of color just when they had finally gained access to them. That, of course, would be further racism.

When we gathered for meetings of Angry White Guys for Affirmative Action, our goal was not to understand our privilege, but to use our status as white men to counter the racist attacks on communities of color. Working closely with organizations led by people of color, we mapped out a strategy to reach white people in the urban and suburban areas around us. We gave talks and conducted workshops, we wrote editorials, we stood on street corners with our banner, we conducted a walk of hope between urban and suburban churches and synagogues, we educated white people about the history of affirmative action and about the deceptive and manipulative tactics being used to attack it. And we talked about our own experiences as beneficiaries of affirmative action, challenging the myth of a level playing field. (See the section on white benefits in Part II of this book for my personal account.)

In this work we were following a long tradition of white people who have been allies to people of color in the struggle to end racism. Abolitionists, anti-imperialists, anti-lynching crusaders, Civil Rights movement activists — we have a proud history of white people, including white men, using their education, their experience, their money, their access, their voices, their hearts, and their minds to challenge racism.

Although institutional change seems difficult to tackle, we are already involved in several institutions in our daily lives. Our workplace, the schools we or our children attend, the stores we patronize, the places we socialize, the community with which we congregate for religious worship — we have some leverage at each of these institutions. We need to analyze the institutions we are a part of, evaluate the influence we have either alone or with others, and devise effective strategies for challenging racism. The next sections suggest some ways you might focus on institutions you are already involved with, including your workplace, your school system, the police, the criminal justice system, and your religious organization.

At Work

WHITENESS HAS LONG BEEN RELATED TO RACISM in the workplace and economy. As David Roediger explains in his book *The Wages of Whiteness*, part of the campaign to entice white male workers into industrial jobs during the 19th century was the rationalization that at least they were not slaves. They could keep their white masculinity intact, even while giving up their economic independence, because they were told that being a worker in a factory was not the same as being a slave working for a master.

Male industrial workers eventually borrowed the language of slavery to describe their "waged slavery." They played on similarities between their work situation and that of slaves, at the same time trying to keep the differences clear so they could preserve industrial jobs for whites. The relationship of racism to work issues is complex. In general, early white industrial workers were manipulated by racism, and in turn they used racism to gain economic benefits. Employers manipulated racism to create a false sense of pride and opportunity among white workers, which workers then used to separate themselves from male workers of color.

Work in the United States is still highly segregated by class, race, and gender. The overall economy, as well as most large organizations, is vertically segregated as well. Upper-middle- and upper-class white men have access to the jobs with the most money, power, and status. Women, working-class whites, and people of color are strung out on the economic hierarchy, but are found disproportionately at the bottom in the least secure, most unsafe, poorest paid jobs.

Racism has always been intimately tied to the economic hierarchy, and an early purpose of racism in the United States was to justify economic exploitation (see the section "African Americans" in Part IV). W.E.B. Du Bois was one of the first historians to note the impact racism had on both blacks and whites in the South. Because of slavery, there was no major labor movement to protect the region's 5 million poor whites, who owned no slaves, from being heavily exploited by the 8,000 largest slave owners. The availability of cheap slave labor undermined white workers' ability to bargain for higher wages and better working conditions. More recently, Michael Reich has demonstrated that where the gap between the wages of blacks and whites is the greatest, wages of whites are the lowest, and profit to the wealthy the highest. He describes how racism works in the workplace.

> *Wages of white labor are lessened by racism because the fear of a cheaper and underemployed Black labor supply in the area is invoked by employers when labor presents its wage demands.*

Racial antagonisms on the shop floor deflect attention from labor grievances related to working conditions, permitting employers to cut costs. Racial divisions among labor prevent the development of united worker organizations both within the workplace and in the labor movement as a whole. As a result union strength and union militancy will be less the greater the extent of racism.[1]

The immediate impact of racism on working people of color is economic. Profits from racism, or "super-exploitation" as economist Victor Perlo describes it, are the profits that employers make when they underpay workers of color. In other words, super-exploitation is the wage differential between white workers and workers of color, multiplied by the number of workers in private enterprises. Perlo notes that the profits from racism against all minorities grew from $56 billion in 1947 to $197 billion in 1992 (expressed in 1995 dollars). When the earnings of white workers are compared with those of specific other groups, we find that the profits from super-exploitation (the gap in earnings between the groups) more than doubled from African-American workers, and increased tenfold from Latino, Native-American, and Asian-American workers.

In addition, racism benefits employers and hurts white workers because the existence of a low-waged segment of the workforce exerts significant downward pressure on all wages. Perlo concludes his chapter on racism and work by stating that the extra profits employers gained from racism — either directly at the expense of minority workers, or indirectly at the expense of white workers — came to approximately $500 billion in 1995.[2]

Inequality and injustice exist at every level of our economic system, inside the country and abroad, and racism contributes to an international system of economic exploitation. The United Nations has reported that the income gap between the richest fifth of the world's nations and the poorest fifth increased from 30 to 1 in 1960 to 74 to 1 in 1997. The top fifth of nations possessed 86.1 percent of the world's gross domestic product. Between 1980 and 2000, the wealth of the United States alone grew from $7 trillion to $32 trillion.[3] Between 1994 and 1998 the world's 200 richest people doubled their wealth to $1 trillion when more than 1.3 billion people in the developing world scraped by on less than one dollar a day.[4] At the same time, the amount spent by industrialized countries on humanitarian aid has gone down by 30 percent.[5]

Winning the broader struggle for economic democracy is crucial for truly ending racism, and a key to achieving economic justice is solidarity between white workers and workers of color, between U.S. workers and workers from other countries. Racism undermines both levels of solidarity.

During the 1990s, problems in the Mexican, Japanese, and Southeast Asian monetary systems made the interdependence of the world economy evident. What may not be so clear to us in the United States are the brutal living conditions in non-Western countries that result from the economic policies imposed by the International Monetary Fund (IMF), the World Bank, and other U.S.-dominated institutions. The colonial practices of European countries, beginning in the late 15th century and later taken up by the United States, have concentrated international power and wealth in the hands of white people and have given us the ability to dictate the economic fortunes of the rest of the world.

One way to challenge these patterns is to organize against new attempts by U.S. financial interests to consolidate further their dominance through such trade agreements as North American Free Trade Agreement (NAFTA), General Agreement on Tariffs and Trade (GATT), Multilateral Agreement on Investment (MAI), and Free Trade Agreement of the Americas (FTAA). These agreements enhance the ability of multinational corporations to move jobs and factories from country to country, to pollute and destroy environments, and, in general, to wreak havoc on the lives of hundreds of millions of people, including ourselves. They encourage us to believe that our own (white) U.S. jobs will be protected at the expense of those of people of color in other countries. In reality, we get played off against foreign workers and are able to exert even less control over corporate policy.

The result of these policies is that jobs are moved overseas to countries where multinational companies and local elites buy up land that is then diverted from growing food for local consumption to growing cash crops for U.S. consumption. Foreign workers cannot grow their own food and are forced to move to the cities. If they are lucky, they find work on plantations or in multinational factories to earn enough cash to buy food that they could formerly grow. Treaties like NAFTA and GATT make it easy for companies to move to where wages are lowest and where there are the lowest labor standards and environmental regulation.

We have created an international racial hierarchy of wealth, power, and control that mirrors our internal one. This international hierarchy subjects us to economic and cultural exploitation camouflaged by racist justifications that blame workers of color and foreign capitalists of color for our declining standard of living and social problems instead of blaming the decision-makers in our corporate boardrooms.

We are not powerless against multinational corporations if we overcome our training in racism to work together with people from other countries. We can challenge the dumping of toxic waste and unsafe products in other countries; the exploitation of foreign workers by U.S. companies; the sexual exploitation of women of color overseas by U.S. tourists and corporate and military personnel; the economic policies of the IMF and the World Bank; the displacement of local agricultural production to grow export crops for the United States; the manipulation of unequal trade and other agreements; the scapegoating of foreign workers for U.S.-generated problems; and the scapegoating of foreign capitalists of color, such as the Japanese and Arabs, when (white) British and Canadian capitalists go unmentioned. (The British own as much U.S. property as the Japanese and are increasing their stake at a faster rate.)

Many of us work for these same corporations and can challenge their policies from within. We all have specific opportunities to confront racism where we work.

To identify where you have the most leverage related to your work, it is important to make an assessment of your workplace. Use the following questions. Talk with others, particularly people of color, to help you do the assessment.

ASSESSMENT:
AT WORK

1. What is the gender, race, and class composition in your workplace? Which groups hold which positions?

2. Who, by race, gender, and class, has the power to make decisions about hiring, firing, wages, and working conditions in your workplace? Who gets promoted and who doesn't? Are there upper levels (glass ceilings) beyond which some groups of people (i.e., people of color, white women) cannot go?

3. Is hiring non-discriminatory? Are job openings posted and distributed? Do they attract a wide variety of applicants? Are certain groups excluded? Does the diversity of your workplace reflect the diversity of the wider community?

4. Do layoffs, reassignments, workplace closures, or other cutbacks disproportionately affect people of color?

5. What are the salary differentials between the lowest- and highest-paid workers? Are salaries for comparable work equal?

6. Are there "invisible" workers — people who cook, clean, or do maintenance, for example — who are not generally noticed or paid well?

7. Do the board of directors and the top-level management of your employer include significant numbers of people of color?

8. What is the racial composition of the group of people that actually owns your workplace? Who makes money from the profits of your work?

9. Are there jokes, teasing, put-downs, or harassment of people based on race, gender, sexual orientation, age, religion, or other differences?

10. Has there been or is there any racial or sexual harassment or discrimination, or charges of such, or investigations by any outside agency about such things? Do people of color describe discrimination or harassment at your workplace?

11. Does your organization provide products or services to people of color? If it does, is the clientele treated with respect and dignity? Do staff members make racial comments about clients? Is there any discrimination in how people are served or treated?

12. Do the advertising and publicity images that your employer produces convey a multiracial image or do they reinforce racial or sexual stereotypes?

13. Are there any workplace groups such as unions or affirmative action committees that monitor or respond to racial discrimination? Are they effective? Are they supported or hindered by management? Do they challenge or do they support racism?

14. Is your employer part of a larger organization, with manufacturing or other facilities at other sites? Are those sites in communities of color? If they are, are workers paid the same as, and treated equally to, workers at your site?

15. Has your employer closed down or moved facilities to areas of the United States or to other countries in order to pay workers less or to avoid unionization, workplace safety regulations, or other oversight?

16. Does your company produce any kinds of toxic waste? If so, in which communities is the waste dumped?

As you can see from these questions, racism affects every level of our workplaces. Starting with an assessment, you can pinpoint just how racism operates. Then you can figure out where you and other workers can start to use your own knowledge to make changes. It is difficult to do alone, although individuals can make a big difference. You will be even more powerful, and less vulnerable to retaliation, working with others who are similarly committed to eliminating racism.

Look to the leadership of the people of color you work with, if there are any. They know where the racism lies in your organization. They may be quite clear about what kind of solidarity they need from white co-workers. Ask them how they see things and what their priorities are.

You will need to work with other white workers, building a core group dedicated to eliminating racism. Many of your white co-workers may not have questioned the racism in your workplace. They need information and support for making changes in workplace practices and environment. You may meet with solid resistance from others who feel they have something to lose from eliminating racism. Challenging them will require more strategic thinking.

Many workers have such pressing financial and emotional needs they may not understand at first why racial equality and economic justice need to be a priority. The information provided in this book can help you devise effective strategies to show them the costs of racism in their lives.

A good way to begin, once you have the information you need, is to ask questions. "Why is this person of color paid less than that white person who was hired more recently?" "Why aren't there any people of color at management level?" "Why don't people of color stay with this organization very long?" "What effect does that kind of comment (e.g., a racial put-down) have on other people around here?"

Asking questions raises issues for people to think about. Sometimes that alone will encourage other people to make some changes. Often you'll get excuses, justifications, or cynicism in response. Those responses will let you and others see how white people are thinking about racism and what level of awareness they have. It will also help you map out where you'll meet resistance to further actions.

It is generally not useful to label people as racist. This strategy produces defensiveness. You will do better to document racism within the organization, build allies, and propose concrete changes. If you attack people personally, they will probably counterattack. Everyone within the organization will feel unsafe. Instead, you want to focus on policies, practices, and procedures.

This is not to say you won't face resistance, innuendo, slander, isolation, and threats. But it is harder for people to present a reasonable defense of previous patterns when injustice and inequality are the focus, than it is if they are personally attacked.

Eliminating racism is not a question of economic cost but of injustice. However, when you organize against specific forms of racism, it can be a useful short-term strategy to point out the economic benefits of the changes desired or the economic costs of the old patterns. What does it cost an organization when there are high turnover rates for personnel who are people of color, when clients of color are not well served, or when the leadership talent of people of color is not used? What does it cost when there are discrimination lawsuits, strikes, boycotts, or government investigations because of racism within the organization? Organizations have different levels of vulnerability to such costs. What does it cost you and those you work with when injustice is allowed to continue without protest? (It may be difficult to make an effective cost-analysis when corporate investment in personnel and infrastructure is scandalously low and when many company policies are based on such short-term considerations that financial payoffs must be almost immediate, but your struggles against racist practices may end up raising consciousness about management policies and economics as well.)

There is no one formula for fighting racism in the workplace. Hiring more people of color or providing more culturally appropriate services are not necessarily steps forward. If your organization was established by and continues to be maintained by white people to provide services for people of color, then developing more culturally appropriate services perpetuates a deeper pattern of racism. On the other hand, hiring more people of color in key management positions and reevaluating the mission of the organization might lead to long-term change. Similarly, hiring more police officers of color doesn't address police harassment and control of communities of color, nor does it address the culture of white supremacy found in some police departments. But more diverse hiring coupled with a civilian review board, anti-racist training for management and line staff, and a reassessment of policy/community relations could provide opportunities for the police to become more responsive to the communities they serve.

It helps to start with an analysis of the organization, work, labor, and history of racism that can highlight the key contradictions in your workplace. As A. Sivanandan has accurately noted:

> *The challenge for such organizations, then, is to examine their particular roles, the context in which they work and the way in which racism has developed in their fields ... and has therefore to be fought specifically, in terms of specific policies, practices and procedures of a specific institution and its specific function in society.*[6]

What is the mission of the organization or business you are working for?

What is the relationship of the mission to communities of color?

What are the needs of those communities?

How do white people hold power in your organization?

The most important question to ask might be, what long-term changes will be made in who holds power and how decisions are made?

These are the kinds of questions that can guide us in formulating policies for planning, service provision, recruitment, hiring, retention, promotion, decision-making, organizational structure, and other aspects of organizational existence. Then we can work with people of color and other white allies to develop strategies for achieving specific policy changes that can possibly lead to organizational change.

Each particular fight against racism is part of the long-term struggle. Even when it is unsuccessful, it can educate and organize other workers. Our long-term goal is to create a broad movement of people committed to eliminating racism in all aspects of our lives.

I am not going to romanticize the power of workers; in most circumstances multinational companies can play off workers from many sites against each other. However, keeping the issue of race- and gender-based exploitation on the table in every workplace struggle will further the move toward economic justice. Doing so keeps people of color and white women in leadership positions, demonstrates the interconnected ways that people are exploited, and produces the informed solidarity that is essential to the success of any struggle for economic justice.

Education and Schools

MOST OF US spent a considerable amount of our childhood in school. Our children still do. Social activism is needed to create equal opportunity in the educational system, which is a major gatekeeper for the distribution of the social and economic benefits of this society. What's going on in this system in the new millennium?

Most students in the United States are still attending segregated schools. Within schools, students are segregated by race and tracked by class or by smaller divisions of economic difference. Segregation and tracking destine most students from an early age for a particular socio-economic role in their adult life.

White suburban schools have approximately twice as much money per student as urban schools, where students of color are congregated.[1] When this is multiplied by the number of students in a classroom or school, the impact is enormous. That money buys fewer students per teacher; classroom necessities like books, pencils, and paper, not to mention computers; art and music classes; recreational equipment; teacher's aides; special events and field trips; and in the long run, the best teachers. Students are given a direct measure of their social worth and future chances by the amount of money they see being spent on their education.

When we look at the differences in educational expenditures, we have to acknowledge that most white students have tremendous educational advantages over students of color. I am not saying that enough money is spent on their education, or that it is spent effectively, or that all white youth have the same opportunities. We need to school all our children better than we do. But money makes a difference. As parents, we know this is true. That is why, when we can afford it, and sometimes even when we can't, we move to school districts with better schools or send our children to private ones.

Given the economic and educational realities of this society, it makes sense for us to give our children the best education possible. We shouldn't feel guilty for doing so. But insofar as many children of color are abandoned to the disaster of inadequately funded public schooling, our individual actions do contribute to the overall gap between white children and children of color. Furthermore, it is hypocritical for us to contend that everyone has an equal chance to succeed when white children systematically have better educational opportunities than children of color.

It is a continuation of racism to spend different amounts of money on students according to race, class, or any other factor. Yes, there is waste in the school system. Yes, there is bad management, poor teachers, and poorer administrators. We need to attend to those problems. And we need to increase and equalize our spending so that every student has a chance.

Find out per student expenditures in your district and others.
What differences do you find? Where does the extra money come from?
How can you work with others to develop new school-funding strategies?
We urgently need to develop more equitable ways to finance
our educational system.

However, education is more than money. It includes teachers, curricula, school buildings, safety to learn, and many other factors. Racism affects the quality and quantity of each of these resources. Teachers in the United States are disproportionately white. Although students of color will soon make up 40 percent of the student population, the percentage of teachers who are white is increasing and presently approaches 90 percent. This means that few students of color have role models of their own ethnicity, and few white students have contact with people of color in positions of authority. In this environment, it is harder to organize challenges to the white-culture-based curricula because there aren't enough teachers of color to counter those traditional curricula. In addition, many white teachers carry with them some of the subtle and not-so-subtle biases against people of color that white people are exposed to in our culture. Researchers have found that white people display subtle discriminatory behavior in their reactions to people of color. This behavior might include: less assistance, greater aggression, overt friendliness coupled with covert rejection, and avoidance. People who supervised workers made assessments of people of color that were inconsistent with their actual work performance. The researchers also noted that whites were often unaware of their prejudice.[2]

White teachers, like all white people, also have racial assumptions and prejudices that they bring to the classroom. These assumptions affect what they teach, how they teach it, and how they interact with students. Teachers are part of the middle class that has traditionally had the function of supervising, training, and disciplining the poor and working people of this country and of acting as a buffer between them and the wealthy (see "Allies, Collaborators, and Agents" in Part III). Their livelihoods depend on their ability to instill particular values and attitudes in their students so that the economic system runs smoothly. When middle-class white teachers are preparing poor and working-class students of color for a future of mostly unskilled jobs, economic and racial prejudices work to the double disadvantage of the students.

Who is teaching in our schools? How are they trained? What do they do in the
classroom? How does racism in schools affect teachers of color?

The answers to these questions can guide us to action. For instance, knowing about changing teacher demographics leads us to work against changes in educational policy, such as the National Teacher's Exam and longer teacher education courses, that present unnecessary obstacles to teachers of color and contribute to their increasing exclusion from our classrooms.

We also need to eliminate racism in the curriculum. School curricula in the United States have a European/American historical focus that emphasizes the development of ideas and political processes from Greece through Rome and Europe to the United States. "Western" knowledge is actually a conglomeration of ideas and developments from every part of the world. Much of what we call the Greek or classical roots of our civilization was borrowed from Egypt and the Near East. The Greeks themselves acknowledged the source of their learning and made many references to their Egyptian mentors.[3]

In our classrooms we still deny or diminish the importance of other world civilizations. Textbooks often present them as if they were only significant when they were affected by Europeans or Americans. The dynamic interchange between the West and other cultures is glossed over. Cultures from other geographic regions are presented superficially, particularly in the lower grades, through their food, holidays, traditional clothes, and little else.

Our curricula also omit the history of white colonialism as colonialism, and they don't address racism and other forms of exploitation. People of color are marginally represented as token individuals who achieved great things rather than as members of communities of resistance. The enormous contributions that people of color have made to our society are simply not mentioned.[4]

For example, textbooks describe the influence of British and French philosophers on our founding fathers and completely ignore the equally important influence of Iroquois theory and political practice on the roots of our democratic traditions. This is despite the fact that key participants, including Franklin and Jefferson, explicitly describe the Iroquois models as influential in their thinking.[5]

Arab contributions to mathematics, astronomy, geology, mineralogy, botany, and natural history are similarly unmentioned. The Arabic numbering system, which replaced the cumbersome and limited Roman numeral system, and trigonometry and algebra, which serve as cornerstones of modern mathematics, were all contributions from Muslim society.[6]

As a result, children of color do not see themselves at the center of history and culture. They do not see themselves as active participants in creating this society. The roles played by their foreparents have simply been written out of history, giving white children and children of color distorted understandings of their own heritages.

We need to challenge all aspects of racism in educational curricula, including, but not limited to, the teaching of European-focused history; the use of literary texts in which only white authors are presented; the trivializing of other cultures by focusing on their food and holidays or by caricaturing their people; the exclusion of poor and working people from written histories of the struggles which shaped our country; the glossing over of European and U.S. colonialism; the exclusive use of white cultural examples for math problems; the teaching of science as a purely Western tradition; and the omission of racism as a pervasive and central component of lessons in history, social studies, and other subjects.

There are further questions we need to ask.

How are students treated? Are students of color systematically harassed, disciplined, or tracked by teachers or administrators? Does the school have anti-racist policies in place, and are these known and enforced?

How are students prepared to deal with racism?

Social scientists once thought that if white students and students of color just had contact with each other, prejudice would diminish. They have since found that contact by itself doesn't necessarily eliminate prejudice. White people often claim that the people of color they know are different. In any case, most white students don't go to school with students of color. Because of tracking, even those who do may not share the same classes.

Some schools took the next step and developed policies against racial teasing and targeting to help eliminate racism between students. These policies help but don't go far enough.

Students need support for taking an explicitly anti-racist stand. They need to be taught critical thinking skills so they can see where racism is operating and know how to intervene. We can challenge schools to provide these skills.

Many people are already involved in the struggle to make our schools more democratic, safer, and less racist. These efforts include two kinds of interventions.

The first approach is to help individual students of color succeed in spite of the limited opportunity provided by their family or community. Tutoring programs, scholarship funds, special training programs — these are effective in helping specific individuals acquire higher education or better jobs. Such programs do not address the systemic inequality between the educational opportunities of white students and students of color. On the contrary, the results of these programs, a few highly successful people of color, are often used by whites to put down the rest of the community and blame those who don't succeed.

The second approach is to attack the structural roots of inequality. People are organizing around the issues of school funding, curriculum development, resource allocation, teacher training, and the control and administration of educational programs. Such activity is probably already occurring in your community, and you can join. If it isn't happening, get together with concerned parents, teachers, and educational activists to get something going. The questions we must keep asking ourselves as we analyze the status quo or evaluate changes we want to make are:

What are the effects of these policies on students of color?
Who is going to benefit from the changes?
How can we achieve greater equality of opportunity?

Health Care

OUR HEALTH CARE SYSTEM is so riddled with racism that tens of thousands of people of color die needlessly every year because of its inadequacies. Others are permanently disabled, live with remediable conditions, or suffer seriously inferior quality of life. The impact of race is felt in every area from basic accessibility to health care, through adequacy of coverage, treatments prescribed, prenatal care, cultural sensitivity of care, availability of specialized treatments, and physical proximity to hospitals, to underprescription of routine diagnostic tests and painkillers and overprescription of amputations and sterilization. U.S. Surgeon General David Satcher has labeled these disparities "institutionalized racism."[1]

The cumulative impact is devastating to people of color. To give just a couple of figures for the African-American community, which is the best documented, it is estimated that blacks suffer over 91,000 "excess deaths" a year — that is 37 percent of all black deaths.[2] "Excess deaths" are unnecessary or avoidable deaths, so this means that, all other factors being equal, 91,000 black people die each year because of racism. And the situation has been getting worse. Since 1984, excess deaths in the black community have increased by half. Testimony before the United States Congress in 1994 stated that "health care for African Americans and the poor has not substantially changed since the 1960s and may be deteriorating."[3] Because of these excess deaths, African Americans have a life expectancy a full six years less than white Americans. For parts of the Latino/a and Southeast Asian communities, life expectancy and health care status are equally low, and in many Native-American communities they are even lower. Obviously not all the deaths of people of color are attributable to racism, but it is well documented that tens of thousands of them are.

I want to give just a few other examples of how racism operates in our health care system. In one recent study, medical residents viewed a video showing a white male and a black female patient (the students did not know they were actors), who described identical systems of chest pain indicative of heart disease. 74 percent of the students believed the white male had heart disease, but only 46 percent believed that the black female did.

Another study of Medicare patients found that only 64 percent of black patients receive potentially curative treatment for early stage lung cancer, while 77 percent of white patients receive it, leading to survival rates of 34 percent for whites and just 26 percent for blacks after five years. A UCLA study found that Hispanics in emergency rooms in Los Angeles are twice as likely as white people in comparable circumstances to end up with no pain medication — not even a Tylenol. Over 20 years' worth of studies show that people of color who arrive at a hospital while having a heart attack are significantly less likely to receive aspirin, beta-blocking drugs, clot-dissolving drugs, acute cardiac catheterization, angioplasty, or bypass surgery. Race and gender clearly make a difference in how patients are diagnosed and treated.

The situation will not get better on its own. For instance, the number of blacks, Native Americans, Mexican Americans, and mainland Puerto Ricans who were accepted to medical school in 2000 was smaller than in the previous three years. According to Marian Gornick at the Georgetown University Public Policy Institute, "The disparities [in health care] are growing, they are greater today than they were when Medicare started in the 1960s."

Racism in the health care system is also an international problem. The example of the drug development, pricing, and delivery system shows how people of color in economically exploited countries suffer needlessly from policies that ultimately benefit white people in developed countries, and financially benefit an even smaller number of the white Western elite.[4]

Pharmaceutical companies do not develop many treatments to cure diseases that primarily affect people in economically exploited countries (and kill millions of people annually). During the period from 1975 to 1997, multinational drug companies brought 1,233 new medications to the market, yet only 1 percent of those were specifically designed to treat tropical diseases. The main emphasis of drug company research programs is "lifestyle drugs" for conditions like obesity, baldness, face wrinkles, and impotence. Although the companies complain that doing otherwise would be unprofitable, the worth of the five largest pharmaceuticals is twice the combined GDP of all sub-Saharan Africa. We might ask "Profits at whose expense?"

Drug companies often defend these profits at the cost of millions of lives in Africa, South America, and Asia. Recently GlaxoWellcome threatened legal action against the Indian company Cipla for trying to provide Ghana and Uganda with a cheap version of Combivir, two drugs developed in the U.S. with public funding. Nearly 40 companies took the South African government to court to prevent its making low-cost generic equivalents of certain AIDS drugs available to people who could not otherwise afford to be treated for AIDS. This lawsuit was dropped only after there was a large international outcry in response to the fact that about 4 million South Africans are HIV-positive, and most will die much sooner without access to low-cost drug treatments.

Brazil is a country that shows the significant saving of life that is possible with more humane drug availability policies. In the early 1990s the country had the fourth-largest number of reported cases of HIV/AIDS in the world. The government began to import, produce, and distribute large quantities of anti-retroviral drugs, which lowered the price for a year's treatment to $600, compared with $10,000 for the drug company's version of the drugs. This policy has reduced the number of AIDS-related deaths by 38 percent. However, the United States government, at the urging of pharmaceutical companies, has threatened retaliatory measures if the policies are not discontinued and has already applied to the World Trade Organization for a hearing on the matter.

All people should have a basic right to adequate health care. Yet we live in a system that provides vastly superior medical and health benefits to white people compared to people of color in our own countries, and even greater benefits in comparison with people in economically exploited countries. Of course economic factors also play a role in who has access to health care, and we need to address the concerns of many white people who suffer from inadequate care. But we have seen that race is an independent variable and we need to develop race-specific remedies that address the systemic ways that people of color are denied, have limited access to, or experience inadequate medical care, leading to needless suffering and death for many.

The Police

JUST AS TEACHERS have the middle-class function of training young people for their future roles in the economic hierarchy, police officers, security guards, prison wardens, and immigration officials have the working-class function of disciplining those who don't follow the rules. Teachers are primarily women because women are trained to be caretakers of young people. Police officers and other security personnel are primarily men because men are trained to enforce class, gender, and racial roles. Both occupations are primarily white because their function is also to train people of color to accept their place in society and to punish them when they don't. They act as a buffer between people of color and the rest of the white community. They maintain and enforce the economic and racial hierarchies we have developed in the United States.

For these reasons we have a very different relationship to the police than do people of color. Our economic status also influences our experience with and trust of the police. We are more respectful and trusting if we are middle class because the police are protecting our property and upholding our values. If we are poor or working class we have more likely experienced harassment from the police and have less at stake in their role of maintaining the status quo.

As a middle-class white child I was raised to trust the police and to look upon them as a source of help. The ensuing decades have worn off much of that trust, but in general, I do not fear being stopped and searched arbitrarily by the police. People of color, particularly young African-American and Latino men, are very likely to be stopped and searched by the police for no apparent cause. This doesn't just happen to young men hanging out on the street. Groups of young people of color, men and women, are stopped, searched, or otherwise harassed in many situations where we would not even imagine fearing police interference. If the police think you look suspicious — and to some police any man of color looks suspicious — you may be stopped even if you are with your family, even if there is no apparent cause for suspicion, even if you are just driving by somewhere.[1]

Every year there are hundreds of reports of police brutality. In Los Angeles alone, the L.A. Police and Sheriff's departments have paid out tens of millions of dollars to victims of brutality and their surviving families.[2] The results of police brutality investigations in many cities are frequently not even released to the public. An early (May 1993) conference of gang leaders in Kansas City had as one of its demands that these cases be opened to the public and that the national travesty of police brutality be stopped. Young people, youth advocates, and citizens groups across the country continue to push for full police review and accountability as more incidents involving the questionable use of force by police continue to occur.

The riots in Harlem in 1935 were in response to police brutality, as were many of the riots in the 1960s, the riots in Miami in the 1980s, the uprising in Los Angeles in 1992, and the one in Cincinnati in 2001. Nothing makes more of a mockery of our legal system than police abuse of African Americans, Latino/as, and Native Americans. We have allowed them to criminalize an entire segment of our population under the pretense of protecting us.

At this time in our history, the police are seen as the representatives of white power in communities of color. When they trample people's rights, they are acting in our name. When they are protecting the lives and property of white people at the expense of those of people of color, they are a visible tool used by white people to enforce the racial and economic hierarchy in our country.

The racism behind much police brutality makes people of color unsafe in two ways. First, they are vulnerable to attack from the police. Most people of color know of someone who was stopped arbitrarily by the police; many know someone who was shot without justification. Everyone saw the footage of the Rodney King beating. To most people of color, particularly Native Americans, Latino/as, and African Americans, such occurrences, including the killing of unarmed and innocent people, are common.

This knowledge of police brutality prevents many people of color, particularly women, from seeking protection from non-racial crimes such as domestic violence. Many women of color are understandably hesitant about handing their men over to a racist and violent police force and a discriminatory criminal justice system, even though their refusal to do so might increase their own vulnerability to violence.

These dynamics also make it unsafe for white people. Police resources are directed at communities of color and not at the interpersonal and economic crimes that we are most likely to be victims of.

Many of us are afraid of being robbed, beaten, raped, or burglarized. Some of us have been already. Most of the crime we experience is committed by other white people, many of them people we know. When there are racist patterns to police practices, we are even more at risk because the police are looking in the wrong direction.

This is not to say that white people are never robbed by people of color. You may even know someone who was. You have certainly read about someone who was, because the racial bias of the news media presents us with a disproportionate number of these cases, giving them wide publicity, which in turn exacerbates our fears. We then allow the police to continue their practices, justifying their "excesses" by attributing them to rogue officers who, it is claimed, are the exception.

Police racism and brutality fuel the anger of communities of color, which in turn gets directed at us. But our vulnerability to that anger depends on who we are and where we live. Poor and working-class white people live closer to, and are less protected from, retaliatory racial violence than the wealthy are. Working-class white men are hired as police or security guards for the dangerous work of protecting white neighborhoods and businesses. The wealthy live in secluded, secure areas.

When we don't respond strongly and actively to police brutality in our communities, we increase polarization and justify the anger of people of color who say that the police represent the interests of white people. If we want to deal with racism we have to rein in, retrain, and redirect the police so they don't initiate acts of violence in our name while defending the lives and property of the wealthy.

I am discussing the police in general, as they actually manage relations between the white community and communities of color. Individual officers may be better or worse at carrying out this role. The answer is not simply more multicultural awareness for police, or more "community" policing. (Community policing refers to the practice of assigning police to specific neighborhoods so they can get to know the area and the people.) We need to make the police accountable to the entire community and, at the same time, challenge the racism of our society, which continues to use the police to enforce inequality and injustice.

How should we redirect the police? There are obvious areas upon which they could focus. Most acts of physical and sexual violence are between people who know each other. Police response to incidents of domestic violence, child sexual assault, and rape are crucial indicators of the safety of our communities. White-collar crime and high-level drug importation and distribution are more devastating to our lives and pocketbooks than petty thievery and small-scale drug dealing.

Where do the police devote their time and attention? How do they allocate resources? How well are they trained, including training in racism, domestic violence, community relations, and community building? These are the kinds of questions we need to ask. Here are some places to start.

ASSESSMENT:
The Police

1. Is there an independent police review board or commission in your city or county? How effective is it?

2. Are there allegations of police brutality or civil suits against the police or sheriff's department? What is their status, and how have law enforcement officials responded? What is the history of allegations, lawsuits, and police response in your local police and sheriff's departments?

3. Are the police and sheriff's departments fully integrated? Are members trained to deal with a multicultural population? How do they respond to different kinds of calls? Do they work well with community agencies and organizations?

4. Is the response to family violence racially biased? Is there a policy of mandatory arrest for incidents of domestic violence? Are reports of child sexual assault and rape investigated and prosecuted vigorously and without discrimination?

5. Is community policing used by the police department? How is the community involved? Are people of color from within the community represented and empowered?

6. White adults and adults of color can collude to blame and criminalize young people for high crime and drug abuse rates. This conveniently ignores the responsibility adults have for youth safety, education, family support, and

recreational opportunities. Do the police in your area respond without prejudice and undue force to the needs of young people in your community? (Ask young people.) How can young people be more involved in police-community relations?

When you see the police stop people of color, slow down and drive around the block. Let them know you're paying attention. Don't assume that because the detained are people of color they must have done something wrong. Don't assume that because you respect the police, they respect everyone in the community.

Get together with other concerned citizens to monitor police activities. The single biggest deterrent to police abuse is an alert community. Good community-based policing can help make all our lives safer. And we can each help ensure that police action does not further racial violence.

The Criminal Justice System

MOST OF US DON'T HAVE AN ACTIVE, everyday role in the criminal justice system, but we do have some influence on what happens within it. Our advocacy of crime legislation, the death penalty, and police practices, and our funding of prisons, jails, and wars on crime and drugs all play a part in how different people are treated on a daily basis by the legal system.

Wealthy white people have controlled the legal system since its inception in feudal England. Our country's founding legal documents were written by white men who owned property — about 10 percent of the population at that time — and they limited most rights to white men who owned property.[1]

The history of racism within the British and U.S. legal systems is well documented. Even today there is ample evidence of substantial racial bias in police arrest policies, charging practices, trail and sentencing procedures, judicial attitudes, and the use of the death penalty, not to mention manifest bias in the laws themselves.

Two reports released in spring 2000 pulled together the most comprehensive collection of data yet on race and crime in the United States, which showed that at every stage of the nation's criminal justice system — from arrest through plea bargaining to sentencing — African Americans and Latino/as get tougher treatment than whites.[2] This led to a tripling of Latino incarceration in the ten years between 1985 and 1995. There are now 1 million African Americans behind bars, out of a total prison population of over 2 million. In 1996, 54.6 percent of those arrested for a violent criminal act were white, but we would never know that from looking at the makeup of the prison population.[3]

I will briefly describe two examples of institutional racism in the criminal justice system. Whites and blacks use drugs at the same rate, yet nearly two-thirds of those convicted of drug offenses are black (about 14 times the rate for whites). Powder cocaine is purer than crack and worth more. Yet a person would have to possess 500 grams of powder (worth $40,000 in 1994) to receive the same five-year sentence that someone possessing 5 grams of crack (worth only $250 that same year) would receive. Whites are the main users of powder cocaine, and African Americans the primary users of crack.[4] This discrepancy has resulted in fewer arrests and lighter sentences for whites than for African Americans.

Whites do use and sell crack, and even here there are disparities in arrests, prosecution, and sentencing. The Los Angeles Times reported that police in southern California waged the war against crack almost exclusively in minority neighborhoods. When they are arrested, whites are prosecuted in state court, where sentences are lighter. Not a single white was convicted of a crack cocaine offense in federal courts serving Los Angeles and the surrounding areas between 1988 and 1994, at the height of the cocaine epidemic. This pattern creates a two-tier system in which African-American and Latino crack dealers get ten-year mandatory sentences in federal courts, while whites get a maximum of five years, often receiving no more than a year in jail, from state courts.[5] Human Rights Watch reported on an investigation in which it found that every single one of 37 states studied sent black men to prison at far higher rates than they sent white men, averaging between 27 and 57 times the rate of white men.[6]

The increased criminalization of communities of color through racial profiling, the war on drugs, mandatory minimum sentences, etc., has had a severe impact on African-American women and Latinas — they have become the fastest-growing group of people coming into prison. The number of women in prison increased tenfold within a decade, rising to 138,000 by 1999. Sixty percent of the women incarcerated are women of color, and up to 80 percent of these women are there for non-violent crimes, almost all of them are poor, and 80 to 90 percent of them have experienced male violence in the form of child sexual assault, rape, or domestic violence.

Racial disparities in the criminal justice system hit youth of color particularly hard, as documented in *And Justice for Some*, a report released by the U.S. Justice Department in the spring of 2000. Among young people who have not been sent to a juvenile prison before, blacks are more than six times more likely than whites to be sentenced by juvenile courts to prison rather than being given alternative sentences. Black teenagers who are charged with a violent crime and have not been in juvenile prison previously are nine times more likely to be sentenced to juvenile prison than whites in the same situation. For those charged with drug offenses, black youths are 48 times more likely than whites to be sentenced to juvenile prison. White youths charged with violent offenses are incarcerated for an average of 193 days after trial, blacks for 254 days, and Hispanics for 305 days.

Part of the problem is subtle racism rooted in the structure of the probation system itself. A study by University of Washington sociologists George Bridges and Sara Steen found a consistent bias in probation officers' written reports on young black and white offenders with the same backgrounds, offenses, and ages. The officers routinely described blacks as bad kids with character flaws, while they wrote about white offenders as victims of negative environmental factors such as exposure to family conflict or delinquent friends.[7]

The combination of racially biased perceptions and racism built into the structures of the criminal justice system contributes to the fact that blacks under the age of 18 make up 15 percent of their age group in the U.S., 26 percent of those young people arrested, 31 percent of those sent to juvenile court, 44 percent of those detained in juvenile jails, and 32 percent of those found guilty of being a delinquent. Black youths account for 46 percent of all juveniles tried in adult criminal courts, 40 percent of those sent to juvenile prisons, and 58 percent of juveniles confined in adult prisons.

This has harsh consequences for the youth themselves, and for the entire community. As Mark Soler, president of the Youth Law Center in Washington DC, remarks, "These disparities accumulate, and they make it hard for members of the minority community to complete their education, get jobs, and be good husbands and fathers. When you look at this data, it is undeniable that race is a factor."[8]

Racism also plays another role. Sentencing is different depending on the race of the victim. White victims are considered more valuable, and those who harm them are given harsher sentences. As Richard Morin, writing in the Washington Post, reports:

A black man is run over and killed by a drunken driver.
A typical sentence: two years in prison.

A white man is run over and killed by a drunken driver.
A typical sentence: four years in prison

A white woman is run over and killed by a drunken driver.
A typical sentence: seven years in prison.

In the same article Morin cites a report by Edward Glaeser and Bruce Sacerdote which leads him to conclude that, holding constant all other key factors about the crime, the killer, and the victim, "murderers who kill black victims receive 26.8 percent shorter sentences than they would have received if the victims had been white."[9] In fact, from 1976 to 2000 there were about 530 executions in this country, and in only 11 cases were whites executed for killing someone black.[10]

The death penalty gives a classic example of the effects of racism throughout the criminal justice system. As George Kendall, lawyer with the National Association for the Advancement of Colored People (NAACP) Legal Defense and Education Fund, has stated, "Is it conceivable in our country with these traditions and this history, that we can have a death penalty without race playing a role?" This question is being asked nationally with more and more urgency.

In January 2000, George Ryan, the Republican governor of Illinois, put a halt to executions in that state after Northwestern University journalism students discovered that several death row inmates were actually innocent. Since 1977, Illinois has exonerated 13 death row inmates and killed 12. The Chicago Tribune recently examined the almost 300 death penalty cases in Illinois since the death penalty was reinstated and found that half of the 260 cases that were appealed were ultimately reversed.[11] Currently 16 of the 38 states with death penalty laws have, or are reviewing, moratoriums on executions.

What we need is not a moratorium but a ban, such as the Supreme Court declared in 1972. Only five nations — China, Congo, Iran, Saudi Arabia, and the U.S. — account for 85 percent of the world's executions. Some states and most countries have long abandoned the need to kill people. The death penalty has been proven ineffective as a deterrent, racially and economically biased, cruel punishment, and a diversion from the pressing issues of racial and economic justice. But the death penalty is just the peak of the criminal justice system. Or should we call it the prison-industrial complex?

There has been a huge increase in the criminalization not only of communities of color, but of American society in general. The surge in crime rates occurred between 1965 and 1973. Since that time, with 1989 and 1991 being the exceptions, crime has either remained stable or declined. In spite of those numbers, about 4 to 5 million Americans receive criminal records every year. Roughly one in five U.S. citizens has a criminal record. This affects those who are poor and people of color most harshly. A third of all prisoners were unemployed at the time of their arrest, with the others earning average annual incomes of less than $15,000 in the year prior to their arrest.[12]

We have become a policed society. The fastest-growing male occupations are security guards, police, immigration officials, and prison wardens. There are over 600,000 police officers, and another 1.5 million private security guards in the U.S. More than 30,000 of the police are members of heavily armed, military-trained SWAT teams, deployed primarily in communities of color.[13] We now routinely find metal detectors and security in airports, government buildings, schools, and other public facilities. Incarceration costs run over $30 billion a year and have shifted expenditures away from education. The state of California, which used to be second in education spending per student and now is 41st, has built 21 prisons in the last 20 years and only one university. It costs $30,000 a year to incarcerate a prisoner and much less to send him or her to a university.

Between the police brutality we have witnessed over and over again, the racial and class biases in the criminal justice system, the increasing surveillance of our daily lives, the encroachment of large corporations into the prison-industrial complex, and recent anti-terrorism legislation, we are seeing our civil rights being eroded. By not standing up against the attacks on, and the criminalization of, communities of color, we are sliding down a slope of more white fear but less safety for all of us.

Unequal enforcement of the law undermines respect for and compliance with it. White criminals, especially those who are well off, have less fear of being caught or prosecuted. People of color have less respect for the legal system because of the arbitrary and racist patterns of abuse within it.

As noted earlier, Americans are afraid. We have turned our fear into the unconstitutional criminalization, incarceration, and surveillance of communities of color. These practices are particularly aimed at Latino, Native-American, and African-American male youth. Such policies are shortsighted and ineffective. Our fears are used to promote the building of more prisons, the mandatory sentencing of juveniles, and the continuing surveillance and control of communities of color by the police. Funding appropriations support a huge prison construction industry and an army of professionals, guards, and other staff, but do little to reduce crime. When we are spending more to lock up youth of color than to educate them, we know something is wrong.

Would you want white youth to be treated as harshly as youth of color are now? What about your own children, grandchildren, nieces, nephews, or the children of friends? Should 13- and 15-year-olds be treated as adults and imprisoned for life? What responsibility does our society have for their behavior?

We need to look within the criminal justice system to understand and eliminate the ways that racism blames and then punishes youth of color. Young people of color don't grow, make, import, or transport drugs; adults do, primarily white adults. Young people of color don't manufacture and sell guns; white adults do. Young people of color don't move jobs and stores out of neighborhoods; white adults do. Young people of color don't keep information about birth control, sexually transmitted diseases, drugs, and violence away from young people; white adults do. Young people of color don't decrease funds for education while increasing spending on defense and prisons; white adults do.

Young people of color are the focus of our attention and our wrath when it comes to behavior we don't approve of. As white adults, we need to take responsibility for the policies and decisions that set them up to fail and then punish them for their lack of success.

We also need to look at the broader social context to understand the root causes of violence and criminal behavior. We know what the answers are for crime prevention — well-paid and safe jobs, challenging and supportive educational opportunities, recreational activities, adequate health care, and adequate economic and psychological family support services. We must measure every dollar we spend on prisons and jails, which can never be a long-term solution, against the other ways we know we can make a dent in the violence we all fear. As an individual, you can become involved with efforts to end the death penalty, fund rehabilitation, shift funding from prisons to schools, and stop the building of new prisons.

Religion

SPIRITUALITY REFERS TO OUR EXPERIENCE of being connected to a reality greater than ourselves. Religions are the organized social structures in which some of us put our spirituality into practice. We are all spiritual beings. Many of us are also connected to a particular religious institution through our upbringing or through current affiliation.

Most white people who are part of an organized religion in the United States are Christian, so I am going to focus this discussion on Christianity. If you are a white person who is Muslim, Jewish, Buddhist, or pagan, or who belongs to a new age spiritual community much of this section will be relevant to you as well, with some adaptations.

The major denominations of the Christian church have contributed to racism and anti-Semitism in both Europe and the United States for many centuries. At the same time, many individual Christians and church leaders have been inspired by Christian teachings to work for social justice and for an end to racism and anti-Semitism. In other words, the Christian church and its teachings have been used by Christians both to support and resist racism.

In U.S. society, many white people have assumed a correlation between whiteness and Christianity. As I discussed in Part I, some of the attributes of whiteness have been based on Christian values. Defending whiteness has sometimes been seen as defending Christianity against unbelievers, sinners, witches, pagans, and infidels. Various sectors of the Christian church have contributed to this confusion as a result of specific teachings about Jesus, evangelism, salvation, and sin.

This is not the place for a detailed discussion of Christian history or theology. Nor can the important role that faith plays in white Christian resistance to racism be addressed. It is important that we build on the inspiration our religious faith gives us to work for social justice, while resisting racism in our religious institutions. Use the following questions to guide you in these tasks.

ASSESSMENT:
RELIGION

1. What is your religious upbringing?
2. What did you learn about people of color in Sunday school or sermons? About Jewish people?
3. Was your religious community all white? Was the leadership of your religious organization all white?
4. What attitudes were expressed about people of color during discussion of missionary work, charity, or social problems?

5. What is the history of your church's practice of establishing missions in, or sending missionaries to, areas of this country or to other parts of the world such as Africa and Asia?

6. What connections, if any, were made in your church between sin, evil, and the lives or situations of people of color or Jewish people? What Christian virtues were used for making negative judgments about people of color (e.g., "We are hardworking, industrious, thrifty, chaste, patient, … ; they are not")?

6. What religious or historical role do the Jewish people have in your denomination's teachings? How may that role have contributed to anti-Semitism?

7. What do you know about the history of resistance to racism in your religion or denomination (e.g., abolitionist or civil rights struggles or the resistance to Nazism during World War II)?

8. What Christian values did you learn that have directed or might direct you to work against social injustice? What values specifically inspire or support anti-racism work?

9. Where does racism appear in your current religious organization, if you participate in one?
   a. In the leadership?
   b. In the theology?
   c. In the membership?
   d. In the educational curriculum?
   e. In the practice of the church as a community institution that owns land, employs people, develops projects, and allocates resources?

10. Is your religious group actively addressing racism?
   a. Is addressing racism seen as a priority by the membership and by the leadership of the church?
   b. Is racism defined as a problem in the community and/or within the church?
   c. Does your church have an active committee or program to address racism?
   d. Is it equipped and authorized to make real changes?
   e. What has it accomplished?
   f. Where has there been resistance?
   g. How can you be more involved?

You probably participate in other institutions besides work, school, and church, such as social service agencies, recreational clubs, youth service organizations, or volunteer agencies. Think about each in turn and ask yourself some of the questions from the previous sections. What do you notice? Where are you going to become involved?

The final section of this book looks at how we might create democratic, anti-racist, multicultural organizations and institutions. Many of these ideas can be applied to our efforts at work, in school, and with the police, the criminal justice system, and religion.

PART VI

Democratic, Anti-Racist Multiculturalism

Introduction

A<small>NY FOURTH-GRADE HISTORY TEXTBOOK</small> will tell you that living in a western democracy commits one to a common set of legal rights and responsibilities that are supposed to apply equally to all people. All people means all people regardless of gender, race, class, physical condition, sexual orientation, religion, place of residence, length of time here, level of education, and English-speaking ability.

Beyond that, our differences are infinite. In fact, our diversity is what makes us a strong, dynamic, energetic, and creative nation.

We are not all the same. Other people do not look like you, think like you, cook like you, eat like you, or act like you. For many of us this is hard to accept. We are used to having things done in ways that are familiar and comfortable. Most of us have experienced tremendous upheaval and change in our lifetimes. We may not be anxious to invite more by embracing diversity.

Being a multicultural nation does not mean that we all fit together easily, or that our differences complement each other. We should expect conflict and get good at it! As a nation and individually we need to develop tools for dealing with conflict without resorting to violence. The word "multicultural" describes a process in which we all participate in making the decisions that affect our lives. It is a strategy toward full inclusion, participation, and justice for all people.

When any principle is turned into practice, it can fuel greater inequality or it can fuel further progress toward ending racism. Multiculturalism can be used to deflect attention away from racism or to dilute attempts at racial inclusion. It can be used to address broader issues of inclusion and social equity, issues of gender, sexual orientation, class, religion, and disability. We have to examine how multiculturalism is conceived and put into practice. We need to look at who has power, who retains power, who benefits, and who doesn't. Let's look at this matter more closely.

Democratic, Anti-Racist Multiculturalism

W E LIVE IN A MULTICULTURAL SOCIETY. This is not something we're striving for; it already is our reality. However, our multicultural society is neither democratic nor anti-racist. We have much to do to achieve those goals. In our daily lives, most of the organizations we are involved with are not even multicultural; they are segregated. One way to achieve racial justice is to build democratic, anti-racist, multicultural organizations.

What does it mean for an organization to be democratic, anti-racist, and multicultural? At a minimum the membership, staff, administration, and board of directors would all have to reflect the ethnic, gender, economic, religious, and other diversity of the larger community. The organization would have to be serving the needs of a broad-based section of the community. What the organization does, how decisions are made, and who is served would have to reflect an inclusive process.

That is not enough, though. We need to look more closely at the internal process, structure, and context of the organization to see if it meets our criteria. Before we do that we have to develop a basic framework for understanding what multicultural, democratic, and anti-racist mean.

As we have seen, our dominant Western tradition is based on an either/or logic. Even complex racial matters get reduced to black-white contrasts, win-lose situations. We have also seen how this simplified perspective distorts our perception of reality and can make our actions ineffective.

When people come together to make decisions affecting their lives, their differing perspectives, needs, and desires will probably not reduce to an either/or choice. If we expect differences to lead to conflict, then we come in defensively, ready to protect our own interests. We won't be striving for common solutions that take into account everyone's needs.

How would it make a difference in your interactions with other people

if you always assumed there was a cooperative solution possible

that would benefit all parties?

The assumption of competition built into Western modes of thinking strongly influences our interactions with each other. Boys are particularly well trained by academic competition, sports, and the military not to find cooperative solutions to problems. One reason they get into fights with other guys so often is the expectation that there can be only one winner. One reason they hit young women is they feel they cannot afford to lose to anyone, much less a "girl." This binary opposition, with one person on top, is expressed in many ways. We talk of winners and losers, champs and chumps, bullies and wimps. We don't teach people to negotiate, compromise, or work out creative solutions. Instead, particularly for men, aggression becomes the best defense. Action precedes discussion.[1]

We need innovative ways of thinking about reality that embrace diversity and cooperation. Otherwise we are stuck in a competitive framework with all parties feeling that if they don't win, they will lose — that they can only win if others lose. We need a different framework for thinking about the world and for making decisions.

Some people have suggested that we adopt a "both/and" way of thinking. In this framework we assume that the needs and perspectives of different parties are not necessarily in conflict. Using this approach allows us to embrace the perspectives of both sides and draw up a solution that includes elements of each. This kind of thinking shifts the emphasis from fighting to negotiating.

People who employ both/and thinking understand that truth is not absolute. Truth comes from the understanding, traditions, and experience of the people whose lives are involved. Different people have different experiences, and what is true for one person or culture may not be true for another. Although there may be simple truths in science (and even those are hotly debated), our social reality is much more complex. One mark of a mature person is the ability to accept differing opinions and ideas respectfully and without attack.

Both/and thinking is an improvement over either/or thinking because it helps people reduce conflict and develop cooperative solutions. Yet even both/and thinking assumes there are two sides that are mutually exclusive. There may be as many "truths" as there are people or groups involved in the process. How do we deal with three, four, or eight different sides?

None of our truths are mutually exclusive. We share a lot as human beings, even though we come from different cultures, families, and personal experiences. There is usually common ground on which we can build our decisions. Finding that common ground needs to be a process in which everyone is included.

Beyond either/or and both/and thinking is inclusiveness. In a democratic, multicultural process, everyone is included. Each person's opinions are respected, and each person's needs are taken into account. Even more importantly, each person participates in making the decisions that affect her or his life.

Democratic, anti-racist multiculturalism requires time, inclusion, and more complex decision-making processes than most of us are used to participating in. Such processes necessarily take time because each person has to have the opportunity to be heard. We need more versatile decision-making tools than simple majority rule or majority take all. We need to refine consensus models, systems of proportional representation, and other group processes that are more inclusive than those we have relied on so far.

Full inclusion can only occur if we don't throw anyone away. Our society tends to discard people whenever there is trouble. One common way we deal with conflict is to label some people as the problem and then try to make them disappear by locking them up, isolating them, or segregating their communities. Often those thrown away are people of color, lesbians, gays, bisexuals, women, people from different religions and cultures than ours, people with disabilities, transgendered people, and young people. We cannot throw some of the participants away and then claim that we are being inclusive just because we have included everyone who is left.

For example, labeling students troublemakers and kicking them out of school, which consigns them to a future with little prospect for success, is a way of throwing them out rather than working to include them. Locking up teenagers for long prison terms is a way of throwing them out.

A cardinal rule of conflict resolution is to attack the problem, not the person. More often we attack the people and leave the problem unattended. We talk about the poor rather than about poverty, the unemployed rather than the lack of jobs, the homeless rather than homelessness, women who are abused rather than male violence, and violent youth rather than violence against young people. The people who are suffering the effects of discrimination or violence become the objects of our discussion but are not themselves participants in that discussion. Most of the solutions we come up with are based on blaming and then punishing the victims.

I don't think we can solve problems if we exclude the people who are experiencing those problems from the discussion of solutions. Their active participation in problem solving is essential to its success. If we exclude them, we guarantee that they will remain part of the problem. Multiculturalism has to be based on inclusion.

Multicultural Competence

IN ORDER TO MAKE SURE that everyone is not only present, but can also participate fully, we need to be what many people call "culturally competent." Cultural competency is the ability to understand another culture well enough to be able to communicate and work with people from that culture.

We are all culturally competent in our own culture. We know the language, the nuances, and the assumptions about how the world is defined and organized. We know where there are disagreements and differences and generally what the rules are for solving problems. Most of us know how to get around in our cultural neighborhood. Multicultural competence is fluency in more than one culture, in whichever cultures are part of your surroundings.

"Culture" is a vague, shorthand word to name the complex ways that people who form a "community" (another vague, shorthand word) interact with each other. There are usually cultural norms within a community, but cultural practices can change, can be contradictory, and usually overlap with practices of other cultures. Cultures form around specific identities, geographies, beliefs, and daily practices. Besides our ethnicity and race, our gender, class, religion, sexual orientation, physical ability, work, and family history influence the cultures we are a part of and our roles and experiences within them. Multiculturalism means more than racial balance and inclusion. All members of the community must be competent to communicate with each other for an effective multicultural process.

Learning to be sensitive to the cultural expressions of another group is not difficult, but does require time and energy. We must learn to observe, empathize, and appreciate other people's ways of doing things to become culturally competent. Even beginning levels of such competency open doors to understanding different perspectives. People who are culturally competent in even one culture besides their own have a broader, richer, and more accurate view of the world. They are able to work with others as full and equal partners.

It is difficult for white people to become multiculturally competent because we are the mainstream culture — we are in the culture of power. Wherever we look we see ourselves, our language, our values, our images, and our history. We are given little sense of the importance of cultural competency and an overinflated sense of the importance and centrality of our culture. We have learned how great European-based American culture is. Most of the heroes we studied were white men like Shakespeare, Washington, Jefferson, and Lincoln. We were taught that our values, form of government, literature, science, and athletic accomplishments are not only the best of all, but also an entire level above any others. We have been trained to think that other cultures are less literate, less civilized, less efficient, less practical, less worldly, and not sanctioned by God. It is impossible to make a good-faith effort to respect and learn about other cultures when we hold a core assumption that they are inferior to ours. Operating from that assumption, we naturally believe, even if at a very subtle level, that we, white people, are the ones who should be in control, who should make the important decisions.

The difficulty of valuing multicultural competency is increased for white people who are Christian. Christianity places such importance on the individual's relationship with Jesus that culture has often been seen as a distraction to faith. (This is less true for Christians of color.) Since people who don't believe in Jesus are consigned to damnation, many denominations focus exclusively on saving the souls of non-Christians. The primary value in understanding another group's language is to translate the New Testament and win them over to God. This perspective makes it difficult for Christians to respect and value the beliefs and cultural expressions of non-Christians. Sometimes non-Christians come to think they are only of interest to Christians as potential converts. Multicultural understanding can only be achieved when there is no ulterior agenda, when other people's cultures are treated as already complete, not needing improvement by white people or Christians.

Many white people — women, people with disabilities, people who are poor or working class, Jews, lesbians, gays, and bisexuals — are already competent in two or more cultures. They understand mainstream American culture and are fluent in their own. Sometimes this understanding gives them the impetus to challenge the cultural assumptions of whiteness. It can give them insight into how the dominance of one culture oppresses and exploits people outside the mainstream.

However, white cultural dominance puts pressure even on alternative cultures to be white. Women's cultures, lesbian, gay, bisexual, disability, Jewish, and working-class cultures often accept white norms and fail to be inclusive.

Furthermore, the more economically privileged we are, the more racially isolated we tend to be. We have less opportunity to learn from different cultures. The people of color we do come in contact with are in less powerful roles or are in jobs that provide services for white people. We are trained to value them less highly and to devalue the contributions of their cultures. Without a good understanding of how white racism has set up this hierarchy of status and sense of entitlement, we don't have much incentive to value or understand other cultures.

Our culture has drawn from many different cultural traditions. We have valued them enough to appropriate their strengths and achievements. It is time explicitly, sincerely, and publicly to acknowledge these contributions. It is not a question of valuing diversity, but of acknowledging rather than exploiting the contributions of all people to our society.

Cultural competence is not something we have or don't have. It is a process of learning about and becoming allies with people from other cultures, thereby broadening our own understanding and ability to participate in a multicultural process. The key element to becoming more culturally competent is respect for the ways that others live in and organize the world and an openness to learn from them.

One way we retain our assumptions of white superiority while increasing our cultural competency is to split off the culture from the people who live it. White people have appropriated music, art, spiritual practices, stories, and beliefs from other cultures while killing or excluding the people who created them.

For example, it is not difficult for a white person to become a connoisseur of jazz — learning to appreciate, collect, and even perform the music — while remaining opposed to the full participation of African-American people in society. It is possible for a white person to become an expert on the Dine or the Cherokee or the Pomo while supporting the federal government's exploitation of their culture and land. One of the ways that white people have traditionally become experts in other people's cultures is by participating in exploitation.

There is also the danger that we will use our knowledge of another culture to feel superior to the people whose culture it is. Even if we know a lot about the holidays, practices, cooking, music, or beliefs of another culture, we still have a lot to learn from the people who live it.

We need to use what we learn to be stronger allies for people of color. An ally is an advocate, a person who supports other people's right to speak for themselves, who resists the temptation to speak as an expert on their behalf. Other white people will ask us to speak for, translate for, or have an expert opinion about people of color we know, have studied, or lived with. We will be pressured to use our knowledge and professional expertise against those whose lives it is based on. If we do not defer to the leadership of people of color and defend their ability to speak for themselves, we will end up using our expertise to promote ourselves. Only if we are clear that we do not want to reinforce white dominance can we resist the temptation to profit from the accomplishments of people of color.

If we are not careful, cultural competency can also become a substitute for full inclusion. I previously mentioned that the teaching profession is overwhelmingly (about 90 percent) white. It is crucial that every white teacher becomes multiculturally competent, but white teachers and administrators who are anti-racist must not rest on their competency laurels. Schools will remain fundamentally racist until people of color are full participants at all levels of the educational system. White educators who are anti-racist activists should be fighting for the training, hiring, and retention of teachers, counselors, and administrators of color because they know that in the long run, nothing can replace the understanding and experience that they bring to the classroom. Part of being multiculturally competent is realizing the limits of your understanding. It should make you less arrogant and more humble. It should provide you with skills for promoting the leadership of those from the cultures in which you are competent. As we become more multiculturally competent, we increase our effectiveness in working with diverse populations, but we cannot substitute for people who are experts in their own culture.

Making multicultural processes work is essential to our success as a 21st-century society. Our nation faces complex social, political, economic, and interpersonal challenges. Diverse experience, complex approaches, and critical thinking are tremendous assets to us. We must learn how to value the experience and understanding that people of color possess. Diversity is essential to the vitality, strength, and maintenance of our society. Valuing diversity is not just a personal preference. Nor is it something we can choose not to do. We have no choice but to draw on the rich and multifaceted experience of all peoples in this country if we are to survive and thrive.

The goals of multicultural competency are increased understanding, respectful communication, and full inclusion of all people, not cultural competence by itself. We are striving for a democratic, anti-racist multiculturalism in which all people are part of the decision-making process. To participate effectively, we need at least a minimum level of understanding, cultural competency, and openness to learning from other people's cultures.

Anti-Racism

WHY DOES ANTI-RACISM, including anti-Semitism, have to be one of the components in a multicultural process? Isn't it enough that we are inclusive and democratic, that we value diversity and are culturally competent?

If we were starting out today, without 500 years of history, we might be able to ignore racism and anti-Semitism. However, when we come together in a multicultural environment, it is in a context of white, Christian-based racism. Even if we are all included, even if we listen, value, and respect each other, and even if we focus on the challenges we face, we still need to address this ongoing legacy.

Anti-racism is the process of actively and consistently confronting racism and anti-Semitism wherever they occur. The only way to build a democratic multicultural society from a society dominated by white, Christian-based racism is through a commitment to use anti-racist analysis and action.

We have seen how white people hold power in ordinary interactions and in institutional settings and receive unequal and unjust benefits from the social system. We bring this history of inequality and injustice and our training in racist assumptions of power and privilege with us wherever we go. All too often, people who are proponents of multiculturalism refuse to acknowledge or address the persistent effects of racism on our ability to create an inclusive process.

Other dynamics of racism make it difficult to achieve our goals unless we focus on eliminating them. For instance, people of color and Jews carry with them varying levels of distrust, unease, and internalized racism and anti-Semitism from their prior experience. In addition there are the many levels of institutional racism that influence particular situations. Unless we pay explicit attention to the specific, ongoing dynamics of racism, it will inevitably sabotage our efforts to build an inclusive, diverse, and respectful society.

The first efforts to create a multicultural event, program, or staff may be greeted with great anticipation and fear by all parties. Whether it's a new employee of color, a new policy, inclusion of new material in a program, or even one new song or book in a curriculum, pent-up feelings hoping for and fearful of change can interfere with the normal process of interaction and evaluation. That person, policy, program, or item becomes the test of whether multiculturalism will work. The high stakes may well jeopardize the long-range prospects for successful change, as white people quickly judge something or someone as less than perfect and therefore as a failure. If we pay attention to the way that racism undermines the considered responses of both white people and people of color, we are better able to counteract its effects.

A clear anti-racist agenda can also help prevent multiculturalism from being watered down. It is possible to use our emphasis on inclusiveness to divert attention from racial issues. Concerns of gender equality, sexual orientation, physical access, or even anti-Semitism can become dominant issues while the struggle against racism is ignored. This dynamic occurs in part because we tend to treat any other inclusion issue as a white issue. This is another manifestation of racism.

Even if we disagree with, or are violently opposed to, homosexuality, for example, it is often more comfortable to talk about lesbian and gay rights if we have created a white context. We define issues of disability, gender, class, and sexual orientation as white issues, not having to do with race. (Most of us would actually say these issues are racially neutral, but in a racist society "neutral" means not taking into account the reality of racism and therefore is a code for "white.") In trying to be so broadly inclusive, we end up excluding people of color with disabilities, women and lesbians of color, gay men and bisexuals of color. Without a strong and continuous focus on racism we can end up with a group of heterosexual white men and women, white lesbians, white gay men, white people with disabilities, white Jews, and some people of color who "represent" their racial groupings. This setup perpetuates racism under the guise of multiculturalism. We do need to focus on complete inclusion, but we cannot let that become a substitute for dealing with racism.

The effects of racism will linger with us for a long time, even if we immediately institute massive changes to create a democratic multicultural nation. Unchallenged, racism makes a mockery of our democratic multicultural values. It turns multiculturalism into the same kind of false promise that integration has been, camouflaging the continued dominance of white people in our society. A commitment to anti-racism encourages us to pay attention to the effects that racism and anti-Semitism continue to have so that we can take action against them.

Unequal distribution of wealth is a keystone of racism. We haven't achieved much if we produce a multicultural ruling class. Our government, large corporations, and other institutions are capable of becoming multicultural while continuing to exploit the majority of us.

The word "democracy" implies more than a cultural democracy where every culture is represented. We also need to make sure it includes the concept of economic democracy, that this multicultural agenda includes the goal of ending economic injustice. We have already noted how sections of the African-American, Latino/a, Asian-American, and Jewish communities have been given economic opportunities in exchange for supporting the status quo. Without an economic analysis we can continue to support injustice while appearing multicultural.

There are many ways that inattention to the distribution of wealth can subvert our efforts at democracy. For instance, we might bring only middle- or upper-class people of color into the organizations we are involved with, and this will do little to redress the unequal participation of broad groups of poor and working-class people of color. We can become professionals, specializing in multicultural or diversity trainings, and not change the segregation in our schools, neighborhoods, and workplaces. Diversity training now supports an industry generating millions of dollars a year for professional trainers. Multiculturalism without attention to issues of wealth and power can become a form of collusion among professionals, both white and of color, to maintain control of the movement to end racism and to benefit themselves.

Multiculturalism supports each person or group's articulation of their economic, political, and cultural needs and concerns. It also demands that people work toward solutions that are inclusive and for the good of everyone. We each must learn to address the entire agenda, not just our own particular concerns. There are many complex issues before us, and only full inclusion and cooperation will lead to lasting democratic solutions.

This collaboration is inherently difficult because our society is large and complex, and no one can represent the interests of very many others. People of color have come together around racial identities in response to political and economic exclusion. People can act as if these racial boundaries are well drawn and clear, even though we know that they are not. We may find ourselves negotiating for the participation of people from particular racial groups in an organization, even though we know such homogeneous groups with clearly defined agendas do not exist. We must begin by focusing on the racial configurations that have developed under racism while understanding they are temporary, artificial, and dictated by history.

This means that people cannot represent "their" group. A Korean American cannot speak for all Korean Americans, much less for Asian Americans or people of color. People speak as individuals, perhaps sharing interests with others. When we bring a group of diverse individuals together, each person must be allowed to speak from his or her own understanding, experience, and integrity, not as a representative of some group or constituency. We don't want multiculturalism to degenerate into a collection of individuals jockeying for power by claiming to represent different constituencies. We don't want to become complacent and believe that we understand the needs of a community of people after hearing from a few "representatives." We must avoid the tendency to think of multiculturalism as a device for representing the interests of different constituencies, while holding onto the necessity for our organizations to be diverse enough to reflect the diversity of the larger society.

We also need to be looking out for the interests of whoever is not included in the process. We can't represent them. But we can push to have the broadest possible inclusion. We should be thinking seriously about how the needs and interests of anyone not already involved can be taken into account, how their voices can be heard. In this sense, multiculturalism is a strategy toward full inclusion, i.e., democracy. If any policy, practice, or program labeled multicultural increases exclusion, tokenism, false representation, or the unequal distribution of resources, then it is not an effective strategy for ending racial injustice.

You can become an advocate for democratic, anti-racist multiculturalism in every setting you participate in. Many of the exercises in this book have probably started you thinking about how you can be effective at work, at home, in school, and in community settings. Pick a group that you are a part of, formal or informal, and use the following questions to sharpen your strategic thinking.

QUESTIONS AND ACTIONS:
Anti-Racism

1. Describe the group you are thinking about in terms of composition, purpose, and decision-making process.

> a. Is it multicultural? Who is involved and who is excluded?
>
> b. Is it democratic? Who holds power and how are decisions made?
>
> c. Is it anti-racist? Is racism talked about and dealt with effectively within the group?

2. What needs to change?

> a. Who needs to be brought into the group?
>
> b. How would the group need to change to be truly open to their participation?
>
> c. How could the group be more democratic?
>
> d. How would this change affect how the group operates?
>
> e. What forms of racism need to be dealt with?
>
> f. Who can you talk with about these challenges?
>
> g. Who might be allies in changing the dynamics of the group?
>
> h. What is one thing you will do to begin this process?
>
> i. What fears or concerns do you have about raising these issues?
>
> j. What will you and the group lose if you don't raise them?

Integration and Tokenism

MANY PEOPLE OF COLOR have expressed concern that multiculturalism will become (or already is) a new form of integration and tokenism. Unless we are vigilant it certainly can become so.

Integration is based on the belief that people of color have been segregated from the mainstream of U.S. society and need to be incorporated into it for full participation. Even before the Brown vs. Board of Education decision in 1954, the discussion about racial equality in the United States revolved around integration. I want to look at these issues more closely because they influence our efforts to build a democratic, anti-racist multiculturalism.

Our belief in the importance of integration is based on the assumption that there is one mainstream, normal set of (white) values, practices, and procedures that other people can learn and adapt to. We assume that people of color want to be included in the mainstream but have previously been excluded because of prejudice and discrimination — racism.

There is real cause for concern about the exclusion of people of color from mainstream institutions in the United States. To a great extent people of color and white people live separately, pray separately, go to different schools, do different jobs, and socialize separately. Insofar as people of color are not only separate but unequal, this is a tragedy of injustice, as the Supreme Court ruled in 1954.

Integration is not necessarily the solution to racism. Integration assumes that people of color will adapt to a white, mainstream way of doing things and that the institutions they integrate into will accept them as equal participants. There is certainly some question whether present U.S. institutions will ever welcome people of color as full and equal participants because of the deep levels of white culture and racism embedded in them. Many people of color also feel that having to give up cultural, traditional, and ethnic ways of thinking, acting, and relating to others in order to "integrate" simply maintains white power. Integration fails to address the problem of white racism. It's a form of tokenism — small or insignificant change in lieu of fundamental transformation.

The question is: "Integration into what, on whose terms?" When we assume that the terms and the institutions are fixed, we are advocating not integration, but assimilation — continued control by those who have traditionally held it. For example, under pressure from African Americans, many traditionally white colleges and universities integrated their classrooms in the 1960s and 1970s. When students of color started to demand participation in decisions about the curriculum and policies, these same institutions reacted by calling the students ungrateful and irresponsible. When students demanded that the faculty and administration include people of color, with the power to make decisions, school officials dismissed such demands as impossible.

Today, over 30 years after integration of those schools, most public and private school administrators, deans, and professors are white. Obviously most college and university student bodies are integrated to varying degrees. Just as obviously, white people remain at the center of power and decision-making. This "you can join us, but we're going to keep control" form of integration does not deal with the fundamental inequalities of racism.

Not everyone wants to be integrated, and few people want to be assimilated. Some people of color are cynical about the ability of white people to fully accept them as equals. Others are skeptical about most white people's willingness to seriously question their own privilege. Many people of color have rich cultures, practices, and identities they don't want to give up. There are some Native Americans and Black Nationalists who want cultural and political sovereignty. Still others are only willing to integrate into democratic, multicultural, and explicitly anti-racist institutions because only these will protect them from further white racism.

We need to develop a much more sophisticated view of racial progress in which we don't make assumptions about what people of color want or don't want. In some cases, for some people, integration is an appropriate strategy. In other cases it may be a step backwards. In still others it may be a way to sidestep demands for justice. Integration can only be a strategy for justice and equality, not a goal. As a goal, it too often leads to various forms of tokenism and isolation.

Tokenism plays out in our society in many ways. When people of color demand greater power and participation, they meet with white resistance at each stage. White people seldom voluntarily give up control or willingly look at our role in resisting change. If people of color push hard enough, we slowly and reluctantly accept their participation. We meet each stage with cries of "We've already done so much, what more do they want?" or "They're so unappreciative of what we've done; they'll never be satisfied until they control everything" or "We're moving as fast as we can." All the tactics of denial, minimization, blame, and counterattack discussed in Part I are marshaled to justify the slow pace toward equal participation.

The first and simplest stage of tokenism occurs when a small and insignificant number of people of color are allowed to integrate a school or workplace. Or we add a few names and pictures of people of color to a textbook or a wall. We treat people of color and their contributions as the exception. People of color are extremely isolated in these situations and acutely vulnerable to personal abuse. They do not have much support and usually succeed only if they assimilate by thoroughly internalizing the values of the institution.

Another early stage of token integration occurs when white people include only those people of color who fit a certain mold or support the traditional values of the institution. Any who might challenge traditional patterns are screened out, isolated, fired, or otherwise neutralized. People of color are accepted for their decorative role and to deflect concerns about discrimination or diversity, not to be full participants.

This is also the stage where we quote or point to particular people of color, such as well-off people in academia or politics like Shelby Steele, Ana Chavez, Clarence Thomas, Elaine Chao, or Thomas Sowell, to give a seal of approval to our policies and statements.

These tactics may not work to derail integration. There may be significant numbers of people of color who are demanding equality. We will then seek input from people of color. We allow them to speak out or testify, we study the situation, we do research, and we remain in control. This process creates the illusion of participation, but there is still no sharing of power.

This stage might be coupled with another form of tokenism that involves paying attention to racism only when people of color are in the room, outside the door, or in the streets. When they are not visibly present, it is business as usual. Racism is viewed as a problem for people of color and only of incidental concern to the main business of the organization.

If these tactics don't succeed in quelling protest, white people will give up some control, but only in special areas that are deemed culturally appropriate to people of color. We may allow them to teach in ethnic studies departments but not in the sciences, or to write about news in their community but not about mainstream events.

These are just some of the ways that white people control the participation of people of color and prevent a democratic multiculturalism from developing. Each involves a token form of integration in which white people retain ultimate power and control.

Many organizations can look multicultural from the outside — they are often intended to. Multiculturalism can become token integration, hiding our failure to redistribute power and resources. To break these patterns of white control we must see through these tactics and understand why the democratic and anti-racist components of multiculturalism are crucial. Most importantly, we must be willing to share power.

We should be actively organizing to create a democratic, anti-racist, multicultural process in our workplaces, schools, police and fire departments, religious organizations, athletic clubs, unions, and city, state, and national governments. The assessments we did in the last section can be guidelines for proceeding. The four key questions are:

1. *Is this organization multicultural?*

2. *Is it democratic?*

3. *Is it anti-racist (and anti-sexist, etc.)?*

4. *What are you going to do about it?*

Up to this point we have been talking about institutions that may have more effect on us than we have on them. There is much that we can do to change them, particularly if we work in concert with others. But they can present formidable challenges to our ability to organize and sustain social action.

There is one institution over which we have a lot of control. It is a place where we can work to make changes with the people who are closest to us. This is a place where we can practice the skills we want to develop and model the kind of society we want to build. This is a place that can nurture and sustain our struggles against social injustice "out there." This place is at home with our family.

Home and Family

VERY OFTEN WE THINK OF RACISM as an issue out there, in the community. We don't think of social action as including how we live with other family members. The walls separating us from the community are permeable, and racism doesn't stop at the door. This section will give you ideas for eliminating racism in the ways you live with others and raise your children.

Although your family members may all be white and your neighbors appear so, there may well be people of other cultures, people in interracial families, people of mixed heritage, or people who are passing as white among your friends. People of color may also be providing services for you, your children, your apartment, house, or yard. Our environment is seldom as white as we assume it to be because we generally don't notice people of color when their presence doesn't challenge our sense of their proper role.

Our homes are less separable from the greater community than they have ever been. They are connected to the outside world via TV (including cable channels), computer games, the internet, toys, music from CDs and cassettes, radio, books, magazines, the daily newspaper, and direct market catalogs. Each of these provides a vehicle by which racism can enter your home, but they also give you opportunities to respond to it.

Do you talk about racism where you live?

When you and other family members watch a movie, discuss the news,

or talk about daily events, do you notice and discuss racism?

Talking about racism is not easy for most of us to do. Few of us grew up in homes where racism or other difficult and emotional issues were mentioned at all. We come from backgrounds of silence, ignorance, or a false belief that to talk about racism is to further it. When talk about race did occur, some of us experienced conflict with family members because we disagreed over racial issues. We can acknowledge and overcome these past experiences and create an atmosphere in our own homes where we can openly and respectfully talk about issues of race, gender, or class.

It is challenging to raise white children in the highly racist society we live in. When babies are born they are unaware of racial difference and attach no intrinsic value to skin color. We know that they begin to notice racial differences and their effects between the ages of two and five. Throughout their childhood they are bombarded with stereotypes, misinformation, and lies about race. Without our intervention they will become the racist shock troops of the next generation. They may not (or they may) become members of extremists groups or commit hate crimes, but they may well become white people who accept the injustice, racial discrimination, and violence in our society and perpetuate racism through their collusion. That is why we must begin teaching them at an early age to embrace differences and to become anti-racist activists. We can start this process by assessing our home and family environment for evidence of racism.

We have an impact on family, friends, and neighbors by the physical environment we create in our home. Do the calendars, pictures, and posters on your walls reflect the diverse society we live in? Are there books by women and men, lesbian, straight, and gay people from many different cultures? Are there magazines from communities of color? We don't get extra points if there are. Nor are we trying to create an ethnic museum. But paying attention to our environment broadens our perspective and counters the stream of negative racial stereotypes that otherwise enter our home through the media.

It is even more important to discuss racism and to pay attention to our home if we have children. As responsible parents we need to think about the toys, games, computer games, dolls, books, and pictures that our young ones are exposed to. It is not just children of color who need Latino/a, Asian-American, Native-American, and African-American dolls. It is not just children of color who are hurt by computer games that portray people of color as evil, dangerous, and expendable.

I am not recommending that you purge your house of favorite games and toys or become fanatical about the racism you find in your child's life. Children don't need to be protected from racism. They see it all the time. They need to be given critical thinking tools for recognizing, analyzing, and responding to the different forms that racism takes. Discussing the racism (or sexism) in a children's book or movie, helping them think about the injustices of racism, and providing alternative, anti-racist materials — all these contribute to your children's awareness and their ability to respond to injustice.

Our children need to listen to the experiences of people of color.[1] Placing our children in multicultural childcare settings, encouraging multiracial friendships, reaching out to co-workers and colleagues who are of diverse backgrounds, and choosing professionals like doctors and dentists who are people of color are all ways to broaden our children's experience. Our society is so highly segregated that any of these efforts may turn out to be more complex than we imagined. But that complexity also can become material for understanding how racism operates and for introducing our children to the issues.

If our neighborhood or school is segregated, we can still introduce our children to a multicultural world experience that breaks down stereotypes. The best and often most accurate way is to read what people of color write about their lives. Many new children's books realistically portray the lives of adults and children who are African American. There are a substantial number of books about the lives of Latino/as. Books by Native-American, Arab-American, and Asian-American writers for young people are still few and hard to find, but there are some good ones available. Many of us, especially if we live or visit large cities, have access to photo exhibits, live musical performances, museums, and cultural centers where we can take our children. Hearing and seeing examples of other people's diverse experiences is extremely valuable for our children.

If we understand that we live in a multicultural society, we will begin to question any situation where people of color are not present. For example, if our children are in a Scout troop, sports team, Math Olympics team, or a religious school class that is all white, we will ask ourselves, "Why is this group all white? Are there any barriers that keep children of color out?" Then we might question the curriculum or program. Is it multicultural? Does it reflect the diversity of the larger community? What values are being taught? Are issues of racism being addressed? Are other groups excluded, such as girls or gay youth?

Children notice differences in people and how they are treated. We probably want to teach children not to judge people in biased and unkind ways, and therefore we may downplay the significance of differences. But this can sometimes lead children to conclude that avoiding discrimination means avoiding differences. On the contrary, we want children to notice differences and similarities in people and to notice when differences lead to people being treated unfairly because of them. As early childhood teachers Ann Pelo and Fran Davidson have discovered, "Children who notice differences and who are comfortable with them can identify discrimination more clearly and can explore the unfairness that arises from biased understandings of difference. This is the beginning of activism."[2]

When we notice and remark on the ways that people are separated and treated differently, it validates our children's own perceptions and lets them build a sharper awareness of how racism works. When my son was caught shoplifting a couple of years ago, the store manager called me and released him to my care without calling the police and having him arrested. Of course my son was scared when he was caught and was relieved that he was not taken to jail. He was fined and banned from the store but did not get an arrest on his record. Afterwards, when we talked about this incident I asked him how Charles, an African-American friend of his, might have been treated if he had been the one caught shoplifting. I didn't tell him he would have been treated differently. I asked him what difference he thought it might make. We had a thoughtful discussion of what might have happened if the store had called the police, how his friend might have been treated, what it would have meant if he had an arrest record. I brought this up not to make him feel guilty or lucky, but to give him practice in noticing that race makes a constant difference in how people are treated.

It is hard to know at what age we should begin talking about institutionalized racism and the history of racial injustice, because we don't want to overwhelm our children. I think that certainly by age six to eight, young people are capable of understanding patterns of discrimination such as slavery, the Holocaust, or the genocide of Native Americans when the information is presented to them in age-appropriate ways. They can begin to see the difference between individual white responses to people of color, and government or corporate policies.

I think it is crucial that we be honest with our children about racial inequality in the larger society. When we are answering their questions about poverty, homelessness, or AIDS, we can discuss the ways that racism makes people of color more vulnerable to these problems. We can point out how people of color are blamed for having these problems while the large number of white people in the same situation are not blamed as much or are not even discussed. For instance, there are more white people than African Americans on welfare in the United States, but the media often present images of welfare mothers who are black, not white.

Because people of color are disproportionately presented as problems in our society, with their positive contributions correspondingly minimized, our children need to understand these messages for what they are — part of the reinforcement of white dominance — and need to realize that the anger of people of color is legitimate and arises from the discrimination and abuse they experience.

Another effect of these biased representations of people of color is to reinforce the unstated belief that white people are superior. In almost every interpersonal and institutional setting the assumption is that white is better because white people are in charge, white images are taken for granted, white history is taught in our schools, and white people receive more respect. This instills in white children a sense that they are entitled to respect, power, and inclusion, and justifies disrespect for, violence towards, and exclusion of people of color. Our children need to hear from us that white is not superior and that white people are not smarter, nor do they work harder than people of color. They will only understand this if they have a grasp of how racism works as a system, a set of interlocking institutions that deny equal opportunity to people of color in education, housing, and jobs.

When we talk about poverty, for example, we can discuss job discrimination and unequal funding for education. This will help our children understand the social roots of individual problems. Whether the issue is race, gender, economics, or disability, nothing is more important than to give our children insight into the systemic nature of power, violence, and blame at a level at which they can absorb it. We do this not to excuse abusive or destructive behavior, but to put it into a context and to help our children move beyond blaming individuals for social problems.

It empowers white children when they see that they have a role to play in ending racism and all forms of social injustice. Historically there have always been white people who have been strong allies to people of color in the fight against racism. White people took stands against slavery and lynching, worked in the civil rights movement, and some risked and lost their lives for their efforts. White people continue to fight against hate crimes, police brutality, housing and job discrimination, and other forms of racism. There are probably local people, possibly members of your extended family or community, who are also models of white people who have been allies with people of color in the fight for racial justice. We can give our children models of white people (including young white people) who have resisted racism so that they know it is racism as a system, not every white person, that is the problem.

At the same time, we can help our white children recognize that white people in general have been resistant to acknowledging and ending racism. We need to be honest about our own role and the roles of our foreparents. Many of us have relatives who did not support the civil rights movement or the struggles for racial justice by Latino/a and Native Americans. Adult whites, either actively or passively, are the biggest supporters of racism in this country. Some of us have family members who are today speaking out against or acting against equal opportunity, school and residential integration, immigrant rights, and affirmative action. These stories need to be told as well.

Young white people need to see that they can choose to support racist policies or they can choose to become anti-racist activists. We can present all sides — the complex dimensions of white responses to racism — so that our children will see that they have moral choices to make. When they understand how racism is institutionalized, they will know that they are not responsible for it, but they are responsible for how they respond to it. Will they stand for racial justice and equal opportunity? Will they stand with people of color? Their answers to these questions will depend on how we raise them.

You might want to initiate family discussions about racism by talking about this book and how you don't want your home to support racism. You can describe what racism is and how it affects white people and people of color in terms appropriate for the ages of your children. You can solicit their help in doing an assessment of your home and thinking about how different games, books, videos, or posters might be racist.

Let your children help decide what to do to make your home different. It is one thing to create an anti-racist, multicultural environment by yourself. It is an entirely different level of education, empowerment, and activism to include your children as valued participants in the process. Again, the goal is not to create an ethnic museum but to acknowledge and celebrate the diversity of people and cultures represented in our society.

Obviously, this kind of assessment and interactive process should address issues of gender, class, disability, sexual orientation, and religious and cultural difference as well as race. We don't want to foster stereotypes that people of color are not also women, poor or working class, people with disabilities, lesbian, gay, or bisexual, and/or Muslim, Buddhist, or Jewish. These issues are inseparable. When dealt with in a context of social justice, young people are quick to develop principles of fair treatment and equality, eager to become co-participants in creating a healthier environment and challenging injustice. They may well end up inspiring and leading us with their readiness to challenge authority, take risks, and stand up for fairness.

QUESTIONS AND ACTIONS:
HOME AND FAMILY

1. Were people of color and racism talked about in your childhood home? Think about particular incidents when they were. Who initiated discussions and who resisted them? Was there tension around it? What was the general tone?

2. Were Jews, the Holocaust, or anti-Semitism talked about? Think about particular incidents. What was the general tone? Who initiated discussions, and how was tension handled if there was any?

3. Was there silence in your home on issues of racism or anti-Semitism? What did you learn from the silence?

4. Was there conflict within your family because of racism or anti-Semitism (over integration, interracial or interfaith dating, music, busing)? Think of particular incidents. How was the conflict dealt with?

5. Were there people of color who cared for you, your parents, house or yard? If so, how were they treated? How did their presence and your family's attitudes toward them influence you?

6. As a child, what stories, TV shows, or books influenced you the most in your attitudes about people of color? About Jews? What do you carry with you from that exposure?

7. Talk with your partner, housemates, and friends about these issues. Notice the whiteness of your surroundings out loud to family and friends. This needn't be done aggressively or with great anger. You don't need to attack other people. Ask questions, notice things out loud, express your concerns, and give other people room to think about and respond to what you say.

8. If you did a room-by-room assessment of your home today, would you find a diversity of images and items?

9. If the answer to Question 8 is no, what do you and other family members lose because of that lack? How might it contribute to racial prejudice and discrimination?

10. Bring up feelings or thoughts about reading this book at dinner or other family time. What is difficult or awkward about doing this? What is the response?

11. Do an assessment of your home including the following items:

a. Books	f. Magazines	k. Toys
b. Posters	g. Newspapers	l. Art materials
c. Cookbooks	h. Videos	m. Religious articles
d. Calendars	i. Games	n. Sports paraphernalia
e. Paintings	j. Computer games	o. Music

12. What would you like to remove?

13. What would you like to add to what you have? Try to go beyond the tokenism of putting up pictures of Martin Luther King, Jr. or Michael Jordan, or adding a book or two to your children's collection. Explore the roles and contributions of people of color in areas where you and other family members share an interest, such as sports, science, music, books, or movies.

14. Are women well represented in the items in your home? Are poor and working-class people? Are people with disabilities? Are Muslims, Jews, and Buddhists? Are lesbians and gay men? Are children? Are the creations of children themselves included?

15. Do you employ people of color? How well are they paid? How well are they treated? How do your children respond and relate to them? How will you talk with your children about these relationships? How will you balance these relationships with friends and neighbors from different cultures who are not employees? Are your children exposed to professionals such as teachers, doctors, and dentists who are people of color? How could you increase such exposure?

These are small, personal steps, but they have two important consequences. The more contact we have with people of color and with images and information about them, the more we are motivated and equipped to challenge racism. We are able to see more clearly the tremendous gap between average white perceptions about people of color and the lives and communities of people of color themselves. This awareness can guide our action and enrich our lives.

Second, we prepare our children to notice how racism operates and to become champions for racial justice. There are resources in the bibliography for enhancing your parenting skills and continuing this process.

For the Long Haul

RACISM IS NOT GOING TO END tomorrow or next year. Every delay and setback saps our strength and strains our hope. It is easy to despair, easy to give up. How do we nurture and sustain ourselves for what may well be a lifetime struggle? How do we keep alive the vision of racial justice and multicultural democracy that guides our action?

The first step is to stop and think about how we are taking care of ourselves for the long term. Our guilt, desperation, anger, fear, the immediate pressure of events, or even our enthusiasm may make it difficult for us to think about how to keep going after this next action, campaign, or crisis.

If we are not thinking about how to nurture ourselves in the coming years, we are probably also not thinking strategically about the future. We may have become bogged down reacting to everyday events. We may have lost sight of our goals, not noticed how the world is changing, and forgotten that we are going to have to renew ourselves to remain effective.

We need to create time in our overworked, overcommitted lives to reflect on the future. Some of us do this best alone, others with friends and family. In either case, we must start with time for reflection.

Take a moment to think about how you center your energy or calm yourself amidst the pressures and stress of your daily routines? How could you strengthen this part of your life?

Reflection is a spiritual practice for some of us. Any spiritual practice that connects us to a reality greater than our individual lives — that connects us to other people, to animal and plant life, and/or to a larger energy in the world — can increase our respect for life and our valuing of difference. It can renew and guide our pursuit for a better world. We each have, or can find, our own unique way to reflect and connect.

What activities help you connect to a greater reality?

How could these activities support your work for social justice?

How might you create more time for reflection in your life?

We also need to take care of ourselves physically and emotionally. We need to live as if we wanted to be alive when our visions are realized. It goes without saying that we need to eat, exercise, relax, have fun, play, enjoy, and smile. Yet how many of us don't take these parts of our lives seriously until we can't continue our work because of exhaustion or poor health? How do we expect to continue in the struggle? What are we modeling for the young people around us?

For people from a white Christian background there may be a big divide between work and leisure. Taking care of oneself, goofing off, and having fun may seem self-indulgent, even sinful. Some people can turn exercise and other forms of recreation into work, canceling out some of their value to us. These attitudes can also make it difficult to exult in the singing, dance, drama, and other celebratory rituals that can be so renewing to our lives.

Reclaiming or developing cultural rituals can heal and reinvigorate us. Rituals build community, connect people, and inspire new visions and strategies. Singing or going to hear music; writing, reading or listening to a poem; participating in a holiday ritual; sharing a meal with friends — we need to allow ourselves the cultural activities that nurture our souls.

Mainstream male, white, and Christian traditions also push people to be rugged individuals. The message is "Go it alone." This assumes there is an individual path to salvation and that people shouldn't make mistakes or ask for help. We become isolated, scared, confused, and lost. We don't know where to turn for support. Many of us find it easier to support others than to ask for help. We have to overcome our pride and fear to admit that we can't do it all by ourselves.

We can't fight racism alone. We can't create social justice by ourselves. Cultural activities and broad-based community support and action networks are essential to sustain us in this work. Friends, family members, and community networks keep us connected, supported, and inspired. They help us maintain perspective on who we are and what we can do. Working with others aids us in evaluating what we can or cannot take on, what our share is. Taking care of ourselves through healthy lifestyles, rituals, cultural activities, and support networks builds and sustains a community of people dedicated to the struggle for social justice.

Finally, we need to celebrate our successes, no matter how small; our victories, no matter how tenuous. We need to see how far we've come as well as how far there is to go. Although racism is still a central constituent of our society, we have made progress, things have changed. They have changed because multitudes of courageous people of color and white people have fought, resisted, and refused to be overwhelmed by racism. They have changed because the human spirit is indomitable and we each share that spirit. We can only sustain our efforts by building on and celebrating the achievements of the people who have contributed to getting us as far as we are today.

ASSESSMENT:
FOR THE LONG HAUL

1. Who are family and friends you could talk with about doing racial justice work? Who will you talk with first?
2. Who are co-workers who might help you form a racial justice action/support network? Who will you talk with first?
3. Do you know or know of people of color who you want to talk with about fighting racism? List the one you will talk with first. Ask if he or she has time and is willing to do this with you.
4. Name one network, action committee, or support group that you are going to join.

5. What kind of cultural events, rituals, or celebrations have inspired you to fight racism? What kind of cultural activity brings you together with others? Which ones renew your spirit?

6. How can you make your work to end racism an honoring and a celebration of the efforts of those who have preceded you?

Conclusion

A FEW YEARS AGO my colleagues at the Oakland Men's Project and I did a five-day workshop in Ohio in which we focused extensively on racism. Six months later we were back for a two-day follow-up with the same participants. To start the workshop we asked them to talk about how the previous workshop had affected them.

I sat listening to several people describe how the workshop had changed their understanding of racism, how it had affected their relationships with co-workers, and how it had sensitized them to racial injustice in their community. I was pleased that our work had a positive impact, but was a little uneasy without knowing why. Finally a white man, Mark, who works at a large social service agency, began to speak.

> *That workshop has influenced me in more ways than I can say.*
> *But I think it made the biggest difference at work. This fall we*
> *needed to hire five new staff and I made sure that three of those*
> *five people were people of color because our staff has been*
> *mostly white until now.*

"That's it," I said to myself, realizing what had been missing from the others' accounts.

It is important for us to unlearn prejudice, broaden our understanding of racism, and learn to recognize racist acts when we see them. But unless we are actively involved in the fight against racism, we haven't taken it far enough. Mark understood that he needed to take his awareness and turn it into concrete action. He changed his workplace. He didn't just try to get one person of color into the organization, because he knew that one person would probably not last long. He wanted to make a significant impact, so he focused on the difficult but reachable goal of making three of the five new hires people of color.

Mark was not a high-level manager or director. When I talked with him later he described in more detail what he had done. It had taken him many discussions, both one-on-one and with the full staff, to convince his peers and supervisors how important it was to hire qualified people of color. He had prepared a staff presentation about racism, looking at the agency, its staff, policies, and clientele. He had lobbied long and hard, at some personal risk, to convince people that they needed to address racism concretely in their hiring practices. He had helped with the job search and interviewing so that qualified candidates would be found. Now he was supporting the new staff as they came on-line.

We don't always have the visible impact Mark had in fighting racism. Even if he had not been able to diversify the staff, he would have made a difference. By raising the issue of racism within the organization, he was questioning established patterns and expectations. He challenged everyone to rethink how hiring was done and what the implications were for the organization and for the community.

Sometimes change doesn't come in the first round, but in the second, third, or fourth. Change starts with one person questioning, challenging, speaking up, and doing something to make a difference. We can each make a difference.

We can make a difference because each of us is already part of the community where racism exists and thrives. We are connected to neighborhoods, workplaces, schools, and religious organizations. Our connections, our relationships, our positions in these organizations give us some leverage to make a difference.

Notes

Introduction

1. Ron Romanovsky and Paul Phillips, "Burning Angels" on *Let's Flaunt It!*. (Santa Fe, NM: Fresh Fruit Records, 1995).

2. Unlearning racism refers to workshops where participants can "unlearn" the lies, myths, and stereotypes about people of color and white people that foster racial prejudice.

PART I WHAT COLOR IS WHITE?

"I'm Not White"

1. See Kathleen McGinnis and Barbara Oehlberg, *Starting Out Right: Nurturing Young Children as Peacemakers* (New York: Crossroad Publishing, 1988) and Louise Derman-Sparks and the A.B.C. Task Force, *Anti-Bias Curriculum: Tools for Empowering Young Children* (Washington, D.C.: National Association for the Education of Young Children, 1989).

2. Annie S. Barnes, *Everyday Racism: A Book for All Americans* (Naperville, IL: Sourcebooks, Inc., 2000), p. 38.

What is Whiteness?

1. In some northern and western European countries there are still strong and abusive patterns of racism against southern and eastern Europeans.

2. Quoted in Ronald Takaki, *Strangers From a Different Shore: A History of Asian Americans* (New York: Penguin, 1989), p. 47.

3. This separation of white from Christian occurred officially in Virginia in 1667 when legislators passed a law which stipulated that "The conferring of baptisme doth not alter the condition of the person as to his bondage or freedom." Quoted in Bill Bigelow and Bob Peterson, eds., *Rethinking Columbus: The Next 500 Years* (Milwaukee, WI: Rethinking Schools, 1998), p. 26.

4. Thandeka. *Learning to be White* (New York: Continuum, 1999), p. 43.

5. Stephen J. Gould, *The Mismeasure of Man* (New York: W.W. Norton, 1981).

6. Ian F.H. Lopez, *White by Law: The Legal Construction of Race* (New York: New York University Press, 1999).

7. Tomas Almaguer, *Racial Fault Lines: The Historical Origins of White Supremacy in California* (Berkeley: University of California Press, 1994), pp. 9–10, 54.

8. Sandra Harding, ed., "Science Constructs Race," section 2 of *The "Racial" Economy of Science: Toward a Democratic Future* (Bloomington, IN: Indiana University Press, 1993).

9. For cogent refutations see Stephen J. Gould, *Ever Since Darwin: Reflections in Natural History* (New York: W.W. Norton and Company, 1977) and *The Mismeasure of Man*; David Theo Goldberg, ed., *Anatomy of Racism* (Minneapolis: Univ. of Minnesota, 1990); and R. Lewontin, et al., *Not in Our Genes: Biology, Ideology and Human Nature* (New York: Pantheon, 1984).

10. See Steven Fraser, ed., *The Bell Curve Wars: Race, Intelligence and the Future of America* (New York: Basic Books, 1995); Lewontin, et al., *Not in Our Genes*; and Gould, *Ever Since Darwin* and *The Mismeasure of Man*.

11. Bernard Glassman, *Anti-Semitic Stereotypes Without Jews: Images of the Jews in England 1290–1700* (Detroit: Wayne State University Press, 1975).

White Benefits, Middle-Class Privilege

1. See the important work on privilege done by Peggy McIntosh, *White Privilege and Male Privilege: A Personal Account of Coming to See Correspondences Through Work in Women's Studies* (Wellesley, MA: Wellesley College, Center for Research on Women, 1988), as well as material from Allan Creighton with Paul Kivel, *Helping Teens Stop Violence* (Alameda, CA: Hunter House, 1992), and George Lipsitz, *The Possessive Investment in Whiteness: How White People Profit from Identity Politics* (Philadelphia: Temple University Press, 1998).

White Benefits? A Personal Assessment

1. Bristow Hardin, "Race, Poverty and the Militarized Welfare State," Poverty & Race Research Action Council (January/February 1999), available on the internet at <http://www.prrac.org/topics/jan99/hardin.htm>.

2. Of course there were few women of any color who were eligible for veterans' benefits, although women served in many capacities vital to the war effort. Many white women and men and women of color were, in fact, displaced from manufacturing and sales jobs after the war in favor of affirmative action for white men.

3. According to West's *Encyclopedia of American Law* at <http://www.wld.com/conbus/weal/wgibill.htm>.

4. Eric Foner, "Hiring Quotas for White Males Only," *The Nation*, June 26, 1995, p. 24.

5. Dalton Conley, *Being Black, Living in the Red: Race, Wealth, and Social Policy in America* (Berkeley: University of California Press, 1999), p. 36.

6. Melvin L. Oliver and Thomas M. Shapiro, *Black Wealth/White Wealth: A New Perspective on Racial Inequality* (New York: Routledge, 1997), p. 39.

7. George Lipsitz, *The Possessive Investment in Whiteness: How White People Profit from Identity Politics* (Philadelphia: Temple University Press, 1998), p. 6.

8. Oliver and Shapiro, *Black Wealth/White Wealth*, p. 151.

9. Legacy admissions were started in the 1920s by elite eastern schools to give the children of old monied white families an edge, a clear preference over the children of Jewish and other recent immigrants who were outscoring them on entrance exams. As recently as the late 1980s, legacies were three times more likely to be accepted to Harvard than non-legacies, and on average, 20 percent of Harvard's freshmen class were legacy admissions. At Yale the ratio was 2 times more likely to be accepted, and Dartmouth admitted 57 percent of its legacy applicants, compared to 27 percent of non-legacies. The University of Pennsylvania even has a special office of alumni admissions that actively lobbies

for alumni children. Legacy admissions are clearly preferences for less-qualified students. The Office of Civil Rights found that the average admitted legacy at Harvard between 1981 and 1988 was significantly less qualified than the average admitted non-legacy. This information is from John Larew, "Who's the Real Affirmative Action Profiteer?" *The Washington Monthly*, June 1991, reprinted in Nicolaus Mills, *Debating Affirmative Action: Race, Gender, Ethnicity, and the Politics of Inclusion* (New York: Delta, 1994), pp. 247–258.

10. This phrase and the statistics on the draft are presented in Michael Eric Dyson, *I May Not Get There With You: The True Martin Luther King Jr.* (New York: The Free Press, 2000), pp. 60–61.

11. This generational advantage of affirmative action is quite common. The Los Angeles Survey of Urban Inequality, for instance, indicates that white home buyers are twice as likely to receive family assistance in purchasing a home as blacks (Oliver and Shapiro, *Black Wealth/White Wealth*, p. 145).

12. Home ownership among whites overall is 63.8 percent. It is 41.6 percent for blacks, a 22 percent gap. In other words, blacks are about 65 percent as likely as whites to own their own homes (Oliver and Shapiro, *Black Wealth/White Wealth*, p. 109).

13. This checklist works well as an exercise in a workshop or other group situation. As each item is read by a facilitator, all the people in the group to whom the item applies stand up or raise their hands silently for a moment, then sit down (or lower their hands) before the next item is read. Discussion in pairs or as a whole group follows.

14. These statistics on wealth are cited in Edward N. Wolff, "Recent Trends in Wealth Ownership, 1983-1998," Jerome Levy Economics Institute Working Paper #300 (April 2000), available on the internet at <www.levy.org/docs/wrkpap/papers/300.html>.

The Economic Pyramid
1. Percentages are from 1998 and drawn from Edward N. Wolff, "Recent Trends in Wealth Ownership, 1983-1998," Jerome Levy Economics Institute Working Paper #300 (April 2000), available at <www.levy.org/docs/wrkpap/papers/300.html>.

2. Michael Goldfield, *The Color of Politics: Race and the Mainsprings of American Politics* (New York: New Press, 1997).

The Costs of Racism to People of Color
1. See Ellis Cose, *The Rage of a Privileged Class* (New York: HarperCollins, 1993); Joe R. Feagin and Vera Hernan, *White Racism: The Basics* (New York: Routledge, 1995); Annie S. Barnes, *Everyday Racism: A Book for All Americans* (Naperville, IL: Sourcebooks, Inc., 2000); and Philomena Essed, *Everyday Racism* (Alameda, CA: Hunter House, 1991) and *Understanding Everyday Racism: An Interdisciplinary Theory* (Newbury Park, CA.: Sage Publications, 1991).

The Costs of Racism to White People
1. Copyright the Oakland Men's Project, 1990. Adapted from Allan Creighton with Paul Kivel, *Helping Teens Stop Violence* (Alameda, CA: Hunter House, 1992). Reprinted with permission.

2. I borrow this word from Margo Adair and Sharon Howell, *The Subjective Side of Politics* (San Francisco: Tools for

Change, 1988).

Retaining Benefits, Avoiding Responsibility
1. Ward Churchill, *Indians Are Us? Culture and Genocide in Native North America* (Monroe, ME: Common Courage Press, 1994), p. 35.

2. Women's Action Coalition, *Stats: The Facts About Women* (New York: New Press, 1993), pp. 55–57.

3. Ibid.

It's Good to Talk About Racism
1. farai chideya, *Don't Believe the Hype: Fighting Cultural Misinformation about African Americans* (New York: Plume, 1995), p. 18.

2. Ibid., pp. 37–45.

3. Ibid.

Who Is a Victim?
1. *Oakland Tribune*, March 31, 1995, p. A–9.

PART II THE DYNAMICS OF RACISM

Fear and Danger
1. This number is from U.S. Census 2000 figures. Racially motivated government policies exclude Hispanics and African Americans with Native-American ancestry from current estimates, so all current demographic figures are highly contested.

2. "Sexual Violence Facts and Statistics," brochure from the Illinois Coalition Against Sexual Assault, 1993.

3. Quoted in Julian Bond, "Civil Rights, Now & Then," a May 27, 1998, speech before the National Press Club; reprinted in *Poverty & Race* 7, no. 4 (July/August 1998), p. 3.

Exotic and Erotic
1. See Allan Creighton with Paul Kivel, *Helping Teens Stop Violence: A Practical Guide for Counselors, Educators, and Parents* (Alameda, CA: Hunter House, 1992); Allan Creighton and Paul Kivel, *Young Men's Work: Stopping Violence & Building Community* (Center City, MN: Hazelden, 1995 and 1998); and Paul Kivel, *Boys Will Be Men: Raising Our Sons for Courage, Caring, and Community* (Gabriola Island, BC: New Society, 1999).

2. Angela Y. Davis, *Women, Race & Class* (New York: Random House, 1981), pp. 184–187, and Elizabeth Pleck, "Rape and the Politics of Race, 1865–1910," Working Paper No. 213 (Wellesley, MA: Wellesley College, Center for Research on Women, 1990).

3. Davis, *Women, Race & Class*, pp. 110–126.

4. Ibid., p. 172.

5. Ibid., and bell hooks, *Ain't I a Women: Black Women and Feminism* (Boston: South End Press, 1981).

6. Davis, *Women, Race & Class*, p. 195.

7. See "Disloyal to Civilization: Feminism, Racism, Gynephobia" in Adrienne Rich, *On Lies, Secrets and Silence: Selected Prose, 1966–1978* (New York: W.W. Norton, 1979), and Ann Braden, "A Second Open Letter to Southern White Women" in *Southern Exposure* 4, no. 4, (Winter 1977).

8. Davis, *Women, Race & Class*, p. 83.

Part III Being Allies

Getting Involved

1. Adapted from Paul Kivel, *Men's Work: How to Stop the Violence that Tears Our Lives Apart* (Hazelden/Ballantine, 1992, revised 1998).

2. Gertrude Ezorsky, *Racism and Justice: The Case for Affirmative Action* (Ithaca, NY: Cornell University Press, 1991), p. 13.

Allies, Collaborators, and Agents

1. Taiaiake Alfred, *Peace, Power, Righteousness: An Indigenous Manifesto* (Toronto: Oxford University Press, 1999), p. 73.

Part IV The Effects of History

People of Mixed Heritage

1. Maria P. Root, ed., *Racially Mixed People in America* (Newbury Park, CA: Sage Publications, 1992), p. 9.

2. Ibid., pp. 217 and 251.

Native Americans

1. M. Annette Jaimes, ed., *The State of Native America: Genocide, Colonization, and Resistance* (Boston: South End Press, 1992), pp. 23–53.

2. Ward Churchill, *Indians Are Us? Culture and Genocide in Native North America* (Monroe, ME: Common Courage Press, 1994), pp. 28–38.

3. John Krist, "The mission way of death," *Oakland Tribune* January 29, 1998.

4. Churchill, *Indians Are Us?* pp. 309-316. Used by permission.

5. Bill Bigelow and Bob Peterson, eds., *Rethinking Columbus: The Next 500 Years* (Milwaukee, WI: Rethinking Schools, 1998), p. 56.

6. Churchill, *Indians Are Us?* pp. 309–316..

7. Churchill, *Indians Are Us?* p. 343; also in Jaimes, *The State of Native America,* pp. 31–34.

8. See Jack Weatherford's *Indian Givers: How the Indians of the Americas Transformed the World* (New York: Fawcett/Columbine, 1988) pp. 133-150.

9. Sally Wagner, *The Untold Story of the Iroquois Influence on Early Feminists* (Aberdeen, SD: Sky Carrier Press, 1996).

10. Jaimes, *The State of Native America.*

African Americans

1. Ronald Takaki, *A Different Mirror: A History of Multicultural America* (Boston: Little, Brown and Company, 1993), p. 54.

2. Ibid., p. 67.

3. Howard Zinn, *A People's History of the United States* (New York: Harper Colophon, 1980), p. 29.

4. The devastating effects on African societies have been well documented in such books as Walter Rodney's *How Europe Underdeveloped Africa* (Washington, DC: Howard University Press, 1982).

5. Zinn, *A People's History*, p. 186.

6. See Angela Y. Davis, *Women, Race & Class* (New York:

Random House, 1981), and Paula Giddings, *When and Where I Enter: The Impact of Black Women on Race and Sex in America* (New York: Bantam Books, 1985).

Asian Americans

1. Gary Y. Okihiro, *Margins and Mainstreams: Asians in American History and Culture* (Seattle: University of Washington Press, 1994), p. 53.

2. Ibid., pp. 8–9.

3. Ibid., pp. 28–29.

4. Ibid., Chapter 2, and Ronald Takaki, *A Different Mirror: A History of Multicultural America* (Boston: Little, Brown and Company, 1993), pp. 202–204.

5. Yen Le Espiritu, *Asian American Panethnicity: Bridging Institutions and Identities* (Philadelphia: Temple University Press, 1992), p. 135.

6. Ibid., pp. 141–143.

7. Robert Gooding-Williams, ed., *Reading Rodney King, Reading Urban Uprising* (New York: Routledge, 1993), p. 201.

8. Ibid., pp. 196–211.

Latino/as

1. Howard Zinn, *A People's History of the United States* (New York: Harper Colophon, 1980), pp. 305–306.

2. Ronald Takaki, *A Different Mirror: A History of Multicultural America* (Boston: Little, Brown and Company, 1993), p. 176.

3. Zinn, *A People's History,* pp. 306–310.

4. Denis Lynn Daly Heyck, *Barrios and Borderlands: Cultures of Latinos and Latinas in the United States* (New York: Routledge, 1994), p. 6.

5. Tomas Almaguer, *Racial Fault Lines: The Historical Origins of White Supremacy in California* (Berkeley, CA: University of California Press, 1994), pp. 54–56.

6. Ibid., pp. 7–9.

Arab Americans

1. Joseph, Saud, "Against the Grain of the Nation—The Arab" in Michael W. Suleiman, ed., *Arabs in America: Building a New Future* (Philadelphia: Temple University Press, 1999), p.260.

2. Suleiman, *Arabs in America*, p. 7.

3. Southern Poverty Law Center, *"Intelligence Report* Summer 2001," Issue 102, p. 39.

Jewish People

1. Paul Lawrence Rose, *German Question/Jewish Question: Revolutionary Antisemitism from Kant to Wagner* (Princeton, NJ: Princeton University Press, 1990), p. 3.

2. Rosemary Radford Ruether, *Faith and Fratricide: The Theological Roots of Anti-Semitism* (New York: Seabury Press, 1974), pp. 184–204.

3. See Evyatar Friesel, *Atlas of Modern Jewish History* (Oxford: Oxford University Press, 1990), and Martin Gilbert, *Atlas of Jewish History* (New York: William Morrow and Company, 1992).

4. Rose, *German Question/Jewish Question,* p. 7.

5. David G. Singer, "From St. Paul's Abrogation of the Old Covenant to Hitler's War Against the Jews: The Response of American Catholic Thinkers to the Holocaust, 1945-76" in David A. Gerber, ed., *Anti-Semitism in American History* (Urbana, IL: University of Illinois Press, 1987), p. 386.

6. Elly Bulkin, Minnie Bruce Pratt, and Barbara Smith, *Yours in Struggle: Three Feminist Perspectives on Anti-Semitism and Racism* (Ithaca, NY: Firebrand, 1988), p. 104.

Recent Immigrants

1. Grace Chang, *Disposable Domestics: Immigrant Women Workers in the Global Economy* (Cambridge, MA: South End Press, 2000), p. 2.

2. Ibid., pp. 3–4.

3. Southern Poverty Law Center, "Intelligence Report: The Immigrants: Myths and Reality," Issue 101 (Spring, 2001), p. 12.

4. Quoted in Chang, *Disposable Domestics*, p. 29.

5. Julian Simon, *The Economic Consequences of Immigration* (Cambridge, MA: Blackwell, 1989).

6. Quoted in "A Fiscal Portrait of the Newest Americans," available on the internet at <www.immigrationforum.org /CurrentIssues/Legal%20Imigration/Tax_study.html>.

PART V
FIGHTING INSTITUTIONAL RACISM

Institutional Racism
1. Jonathan Kozol, *Savage Inequalities: Children in America's Schools* (New York: HarperCollins, 1991), pp. 236–237.

Public Policy
1. Some of this information comes from Salim Muwakkil, "Why American Blacks Deserve Reparations," *Chicago Tribune*, February 5, 2001 (available on the internet at http://chicagotribune/news/opinion/commentary/ article/0,2669,SAV0102050176,FF.h).

2. These statistics on wealth are cited in Edward N. Wolff, "Recent Trends in Wealth Ownership, 1983-1998," Jerome Levy Economics Institute Working Paper #300 (April 2000), available on the internet at <www.levy.org/docs/wrkpap/papers/300.html>.

3. *Third Force*, March/April 1995, p. 7.

4. Donald L. Barlett and James B. Steele, *America: Who Really Pays the Taxes?* (New York: Simon & Schuster, 1994), pp. 338–341.

Critical Analysis of Immigration Policy
1. "Newsletter of the Coalition for Immigrant and Refugee Rights and Services" (Spring 1995).

Voting
1. Gore received the votes of 90 percent of the African Americans who voted, 63 percent of Latinos, 55 percent of Asians, and 81 percent of Jews. (No data is available for Native Americans.) These voting statistics are from Voter News Service and were quoted in Bob Wing, "White Power in Election 2000," *Colorlines* magazine (Spring 2001), p. 6.

2. Testimony of Hilary Shelton, director, Washington bureau of the NAACP before the Senate governmental affairs committee, May 9, 2001.

3. Elizabeth Martinez, "The Next Four Years: Ally or Die," *Shades of Power* (Winter 2000-01), pp. 1, 20.

4. Quoted in Nicholas Thompson, "Locking Up The Vote: Disenfranchisement of former felons was the real crime in Florida," available on the internet at <http://www.washingtonmonthly.com/features/2001/ 0101.thompson.html>.

5. Quoted in Laura Conaway and James Ridgeway "Democracy in Chains," *Village Voice*, November 29-December 5, 2000 (available on the internet at http://www.villagevoice.com/issues/0048/ridgeway.shtml).

6. Quoted in Thompson, "Locking up the Vote." It is important to note that states where people of color are disenfranchised or where they receive the lowest wages are often the same states in which poor and working-class whites are disenfranchised and paid the lowest wages as well.

7. The following information is adapted from Manning Marable, "Stealing the Election: The Compromises of 1876 and 2000" (December 2000), available on the internet at

8. Thompson, "Locking Up The Vote." The quote from James Q. Wilson is also from this article.

9. Bob Wing, "The Structure of White Power and the Color of Election 2000," available on the internet at <http://www.colorlines.com>.

Affirmative Action
1. "True Colors" ABC Prime Time 1991, distributed by Coronet/MTI film and video.

2. Gertrude Ezorsky, *Racism and Justice: The Case for Affirmative Action* (Ithaca, NY: Cornell University Press, 1991), p. 64.

3. Holly Sklar, *Chaos or Community? Seeking Solutions, Not Scapegoats for Bad Economics* (Boston: South End Press, 1995), p. 115.

4. Holly Sklar, "CEO Gravy Train Keeps on Rolling," *Z Magazine* 13, no. 6 (June 2000), p. 7.

5. farai chideya, *Don't Believe the Hype: Fighting Cultural Misinformation about African Americans* (New York: Plume, 1995), p. 110.

At Work
1. Michael Reich, *Racial Inequality* (Princeton, NJ: Princeton University Press, 1981), quoted in Victor Perlo, *Economics of Racism II* (New York: International Publishers, 1996), p.159.

2. Perlo, *Economics of Racism II*, p.171.

3. Hal Hixson, "Seeds of Poverty and Forests of Wealth," *Clamor Magazine* (February/March 2001), p. 10.

4. Paul Street, "Free to Be Poor," *Z Magazine* (June 2001), pp. 25-26.

5. Hixson, "Seeds of Poverty," p. 11..

6. A. Sivanandan, "UK: Reclaiming the struggle," *Race & Class*, 42, no. 2 (2000), p. 73.

Education and Schools
1. Jonathan Kozol, *Savage Inequalities: Children in America's Schools* (New York: HarperCollins, 1991), pp. 236–237.

2. F. Crosby, S. Bromley, and L. Saxe, "Recent Unobtrusive Studies of Black and White Discrimination and Prejudice: A Literature Review," *Psychological Bulletin* 87 (1980), quoted in Lisa Delpit, *Other People's Children: Cultural Conflict in the Classroom* (New York: New Press, 1995), p. 115.

3. Martin Bernal, *Black Athena: The Afroasiatic Roots of Classical Civilization* (New Brunswick, NJ: Rutgers University Press, 1987).

4. See Bernal, *Black Athena*; Jack Weatherford, *Indian Givers: How the Indians of the Americas Transformed the World* (New York: Fawcett/Columbine, 1988); and Ivan Van Sertima, ed., *Blacks in Science: Ancient and Modern* (New Brunswick, NJ: Transaction Books, 1986).

5. John Mohawk, *Exiled in the Land of the Free: Democracy, the Indian Nations, and the U.S. Constitution* (Santa Fe, NM: Clear Light Publishers, 1992).

6. Seyyed Hossein Nasr, *Islamic Science: An Illustrated Study* (London: World of Islam Festival Publishing, 1976), pp. 75–88.

Health Care
1. Much of the following information is summarized in an article by Neil Rosenberg, "Separate and Unequal: U.S. Practices a System of Medicine that Shortchanges Minorities and Women," *Milwaukee Journal Sentinel*, April 16, 2001.

2. W. Michael Byrd and Linda A. Clayton, *An American Health Dilemma: A Medical History of African Americans and the Problem of Race, Beginnings to 1900* (New York: Routledge, 2000), p. 29.

3. Ibid., pp. 27–28.

4. The examples in this section are taken from Jordi Martorell, "Drug Companies Putting Profits Before Millions of People's Lives," April 9, 2001 (available on the internet at <www.mail-archive.com/brc-news@lists.tao.ca/msg00377.html>.

The Police
1. See "Anatomy of a Party Gone Wrong: When Police Brutality Hits Home," a chilling account of a police attack on a private party by Mandisa-Maia Jones and Valerie Willson Wesley in *Essence*, December 1991.

2. farai chideya, *Don't Believe the Hype: Fighting Cultural Misinformation about African Americans* (New York: Plume, 1995), p. 204.

The Criminal Justice System
1. Joe R. Feagin and Vera Hernan, *White Racism: The Basics* (New York: Routledge, 1995), p. 189.

2. The two reports are *Justice on Trial: Racial Disparities in the American Criminal Justice System* by the Leadership Conference on Civil Rights (available at <http://www.civilrights.org/publications/cj/>) and *The Juvenile Justice System in Black and White* by Vince Schiraldi and Building Blocks for Youth (available at <www.buildingblocksforyouth.org/issues/dmc/schiraldi.html>).

3. Monique Williams and Isis Sapp-Grant, "From Punishment to Rehabilitation: Empowering African-American Youths," *Souls*, 2, no. 1 (Winter 2000), p. 55.

4. farai chideya, *Don't Believe the Hype: Fighting Cultural Misinformation about African Americans* (New York: Plume, 1995), p. 195.

5. "Crack penalties appear to hit minorities harder," *Oakland Tribune*, May 21, 1995, p. A-5.

6. Human Rights Watch, "Punishment and Prejudice: Racial Disparities in the War on Drugs," May 2000.

7. George S. Bridges and Sara Steen, "Racial Disparities in Official Assessments of Criminal Offenders: Attributional Stereotypes as Mediating Mechanisms," *American Sociological Review*, August 1998.

8. Quoted in Fox Butterfield, "Racial Disparities Are Pervasive in Justice System, Report Says," *New York Times*, April 26, 2000 (available on the internet).

9. Richard Morin, "Justice Isn't Blind," *Washington Post*, September 3, 2000, p. B05 (available on the internet at <http://www.washingtonpost.com/wpdyn/articles/A16952000Sep2.html>).

10. Remarks by Tonya McClary recorded in "Race and the Death Penalty," an article recording a panel discussion that was part of the symposium, "Race-ing Justice: The Prison Industrial Complex vs. Black America," in *Souls*, Vol. 2, 1 (Winter 2000), p. 62.

11. Manning Marable, "Halt the Machinery of Death," *Colorlines* (February 2000).

12. Manning Marable "Race-ing Justice: The Political Cultures of Incarceration" *Souls*, Winter 2000. Vol. 2, no.1 p. 10.

13. Ibid.

PART VI
DEMOCRATIC, ANTI-RACIST MULTICULTURALISM

Democratic, Anti-Racist Multiculturalism
1. For a discussion of male training, see Paul Kivel, *Men's Work: How to Stop the Violence that Tears Our Lives Apart* (New York: Hazelden/Ballantine, 1992/1998).

Home and Family
1. The following sections are adapted from my book *Boys Will Be Men: Raising Our Sons for Courage, Caring and Community* (Gabriola Island, BC: New Society, 1999).

2. Ann Pelo and Fran Davidson, *That's Not Fair! A Teacher's Guide to Activism with Young Children* (St. Paul, MN: Red Leaf Press, 2000), p. 31.

Bibliography

Acuna, Rodolfo. *Occupied America: A History of Chicanos.* 2nd ed. New York: Harper and Row, 1981.

Adair, Margo, and Sharon Howell. *The Subjective Side of Politics and Breaking Old Patterns, Weaving New Ties: Alliance Building, and Democracy at Work.* San Francisco: Tools for Change (P.O. Box 14141, San Francisco, CA, 94114), 1988, 1990, 1995.

Adams, Maurienne, et al. *Readings for Diversity and Social Justice.* New York: Routledge, 2000.

——, et al. *Teaching for Diversity and Social Justice.* New York: Routledge, 1997.

Adamson, Madeline. *This Mighty Dream: Social Protest Movements in the United States.* Boston: Routledge, 1984.

Adleman, Jeanne, and Gloria Enguidanos, eds. *Racism in the Lives of Women: Testimony, Theory and Guides to Antiracism Practice.* New York: Harrington Park Press, 1995.

Aguilar-San Juan, Karin, ed. *The State of Asian America: Activism and Resistance in the 1990s.* Boston: South End Press, 1994.

Alaniz, Yolanda, and Nellie Wong, eds. *Voices of Color.* Seattle: Red Letter Press, 1999.

Albrecht, Lisa, and Rose M. Brewer, eds. *Bridges of Power: Women's Multicultural Alliances.* Philadelphia and Gabriola Island, BC: New Society Publishers, 1990.

Alfred, Taiaiake. *Peace, Power, Righteousness: An Indigenous Manifesto.* Don Mills, ON: Oxford University Press, 1999.

Allen, Paula Gunn. *The Sacred Hoop: Recovering the Feminine in American Indian Traditions.* Boston: Beacon Press, 1986.

Allen, Robert. *Black Awakening in Capitalist America: An Analytic History.* Cambridge, MA.: MIT Press, 1970.

Allen, Theodore W. *The Invention of the White Race.* London: Verso, 1994.

Allport, Gordon. *The Nature of Prejudice.* New York: Doubleday, 1954.

Almaguer, Tomas. *Racial Fault Lines: The Historical Origins of White Supremacy in California.* Berkeley, CA: University of California Press, 1994.

Amott, Teresa, and Julie Matthaei. *Race, Gender, and Work: A Multicultural Economic History of Women in the United States.* Boston: South End Press, 1991.

Anthias, Floya, and Nira Yuval-Davis with Harriet Cain. *Racialized Boundaries: Race, Nation, Gender, Colour and Class and the Anti-Racist Struggle.* New York: Routledge, 1992.

Anzaldua, Gloria, ed. *Making Faces, Making Soul,*

Hacienda Caras: Creative and Critical Perspectives by Women of Color. San Francisco: Aunt Lute Foundation Books, 1990.

Aptheker, Herbert. *Anti-Racism in U.S. History.* Westport, CT: Praeger, 1993.

——, ed. *A Documentary History of the Negro People in the United States.* New York: Citadel Press, 1964.

Arendt, Hannah. *Antisemitism: Part One of The Origins of Totalitarianism.* New York: Harcourt, Brace and World, 1968.

Armstrong, Louise. *Of 'Sluts' and 'Bastards': A Feminist Decodes the Child Welfare Debate.* Monroe, ME: Common Courage Press, 1995.

——. *Rocking the Cradle of Sexual Politics: What Happened When Women Said Incest.* Reading, MA : Addison-Wesley, 1994.

Asian Women United of California, eds. *Making Waves: An Anthology of Writings by and About Asian American Women.* Boston: Beacon Press, 1989.

Augenbraum, Harold, and Ilan Stavans. *Growing Up Latino: Memoirs and Stories.* Boston: Houghton Mifflin, 1993.

Ausdale, D.V. and J.R. Feagin. *The First R. How Children Learn Race and Racism.* New York: Rowman and Littlefield, 2001.

Ball, Edward. *Slaves in the Family.* New York: Ballantine Books, 1998.

Barkan, Elazar. *The Retreat of Scientific Racism: Changing Concepts of Race in Britain and the United States Between the World Wars.* New York: Cambridge University Press, 1992.

Barlett, Donald L., and James B. Steele. *America: Who Really Pays the Taxes?* New York: Simon & Schuster, 1994.

Barndt, Deborah. *Women Working in the NAFTA Food Chain: Women, Food & Globalization.* Toronto: Second Story Press, 1999.

Barndt, Joseph. *Dismantling Racism: The Continuing Challenge to White America.* Minneapolis: Augsburg, 1991

Barnes, Annie S. *Everyday Racism: A Book for All Americans.* Naperville, IL: Sourcebooks, Inc., 2000.

Barrera, Mario. *Race and Class in the Southwest.* North Bend, IN: University of Notre Dame Press, 1979.

Barry, Kathleen. *Female Sexual Slavery.* Englewood Cliffs, NJ: Prentice-Hall, 1979.

Beam, Joseph, ed. *In the Life: A Black Gay Anthology.* Boston: Alyson Publications, 1986.

Beck, Evelyn Torton, ed. *Nice Jewish Girls: A Lesbian Anthology.* Watertown, MA: Persephone Press, 1982.

Bell, Derrick. *Faces at the Bottom of the Well: The Permanence of Racism*. New York: HarperCollins, 1992.

Bell, Linda, and David Blumenfeld. *Overcoming Racism and Sexism*. Lanham, MD: Rowman & Littlefield, 1995.

Bennett, Lerone Jr. *Before the Mayflower: A History of Black America*. Chicago: Johnson Publishing, 1986.

Berger, Maurice. *White Lies: Race and the Myths of Whiteness*. New York: Farrar, Strauss, Giroux, 1999.

Bernal, Martin. *Black Athena: The Afroasiatic Roots of Classical Civilization*. New Brunswick, NJ: Rutgers University Press, 1987.

Berzon, Betty. *Setting Them Straight: You Can Do Something About Bigotry and Homophobia in Your Life*. New York: Plume, 1996.

Biale, David. *Power and Powerlessness in Jewish History*. New York: Schocken Books, 1987.

Bigelow, Bill. *Rethinking Our Classrooms: Teaching for Equity and Justice*. Milwaukee, WI: Rethinking Schools, 1995.

Bigelow, Bill and Bob Peterson, eds. *Rethinking Columbus: The Next 500 Years*. Milwaukee, WI: Rethinking Schools, 1998.

Black Scholar, ed. *Court of Appeal: The Black Community Speaks Out on the Racial and Sexual Politics of Thomas vs. Hill*. New York: Ballantine, 1992.

Blauner, Bob. *Black Lives, White Lives: Three Decades of Race Relations in America*. Berkeley, CA: University of California Press, 1989.

Blauner, Bob. *Still the Big News: Racial Oppression in America*. Philadelphia: Temple University Press, revised 2001.

Blaut, J.M. *The Colonizer's Model of the World: Geographical Diffusionism and Eurocentric History*. New York: Guilford Press, 1993.

Blee, Kathleen. *Women of the Klan: Racism and Gender in the 1920s*. Berkeley, CA: University of California Press, 1991.

Bonilla-Silva, Eduardo. *White Supremacy and Racism in Post-Civil Rights Era*. Boulder, CO: Lynne Rienner Publishers, 2001.

Booker, Janice L. *The Jewish American Princess and Other Myths: The Many Faces of Self-Hatred*. New York: Shapolsky Publishers, 1991.

Boxill, Bernard R. *Blacks and Social Justice*. Lanham, MD: Rowman and Littlefield, 1984.

Boyarin, Jonathan, and Daniel Boyarin. *Jews and Other Differences: The New Jewish Cultural Studies*. Minneapolis, MN: University of Minnesota Press, 1997.

Boyd, Herb, and Robert Allen. *Brotherman: The Odyssey of Black Men in America*. New York: One World, 1995.

Brackman, Harold. *Ministry of Lies: The Truth Behind the Nation of Islam's "The Secret Relationship Between Blacks and Jews."* New York: Four Walls Eight Windows, 1994.

Bradley, David. *The Chaneysville Incident*. New York: Harper & Row, 1981.

Brant, Beth, ed. *A Gathering of Spirit: Writing and Art by North American Indian Women*. Rockland, ME: Sinister Wisdom Books, 1984.

Brod, Harry, ed. *A Mensch Among Men: Explorations in Jewish Masculinity*. Freedom, CA: Crossing Press, 1988.

Brodkin, Karen. *How Jews Became White Folks & What That Says About Race in America*. New Brunswick, NJ: Rutgers University Press, 1998.

Brown, Dee. *Bury My Heart at Wounded Knee: An Indian History of the American West*. New York: Bantam, 1970.

Bulkin, Elly, Minnie Bruce Pratt, and Barbara Smith. *Yours in Struggle: Three Feminist Perspectives on Anti-Semitism and Racism*. Ithaca, NY: Firebrand, 1988.

Butler, Judith. *Gender Trouble: Feminism and the Subversion of Identity*. New York: Routledge, 1990.

Camper, Carol, ed. *Miscegenation Blues: Voices of Mixed Race Women*. Toronto: Sister Vision, 1994.

Caraway, Nancie. *Segregated Sisterhood: Racism and the Politics of American Feminism*. Knoxville, TN: University of Tennessee Press, 1991.

Carbado, Devon W. *Black Men on Race, Gender, and Sexuality: A Critical Reader*. New York: New York University Press, 1999.

Carlsson Paige, Nancy and Diane E. Levin. *Helping Young Children Understand Peace, War, and the Nuclear Threat*. Washington, DC: National Association for the Education of Young Children, 1985.

Carroll, Rebecca. *Sugar in the Raw: Voices of Young Black Girls in America*. New York: Crown. 1997.

Center for Contemporary Cultural Studies, ed. *The Empire Strikes Back: Race and Racism in 1970s Britain*. London: Hutchinson, 1982.

Chan, Suchen. *Asian Americans: An Interpretive History*. New York: Twayne Publishers, 1991.

Chang, Grace. *Disposable Domestics: Immigrant Women Workers in the Global Economy*. Cambridge, MA: South End Press, 2000.

Chang, Robert S. *Disoriented: Asian Americans, Law, and the Nation-State*. New York: New York University Press, 1999.

Chesler, Phyllis. *Patriarchy: Notes of An Expert Witness*. Monroe, ME: Common Courage Press, 1994.

chideya, farai. *Don't Believe the Hype: Fighting Cultural Misinformation about African Americans*. New York: Plume, 1995.

Churchill, Ward. *Fantasies of the Master Race: Literature, Cinema and the Colonization of American Indians*. Monroe, Maine: Common Couarge Press, 1992.

———. *Indians Are Us? Culture and Genocide in Native North America*. Monroe, ME: Common Courage Press, 1994.

———, ed. *Marxism and Native Americans*. Boston: South End Press, 1983.

Chutzpah Collective. *Chutzpah: A Jewish Liberation Anthology*. San Francisco: New Glide Publications, 1977.

Clark, Christine, and James O'Donnell, eds. *Becoming and Unbecoming White*. Westport, CN: Bergin & Garvey, 1999.

Cleage, Pearl. *Deals with the Devil and Other Reasons to Riot*. New York: Ballantine, 1993.

Cockburn, Cynthia. *In the Way of Women: Men's Resistance to Sex Equality in Organizations*. Ithaca, NY: ILR Press, 1991.

Collins, Chuck, and Felice Yeskel. *Apartheid in America: A Primer on Economic Inequality & Insecurity*. New York: New Press, 2000.

Collins, Patricia Hill. *Black Feminist Thought: Knowledge, Consciousness, and the Politics of Empowerment*. Boston: Unwin Hyman, 1990.

Conley, Dalton. *Being Black, Living in the Red: Race, Wealth, and Social Policy in America*. Berkeley: University of California Press, 1999.

Connell, R.W. *Gender and Power*. Stanford, CA: Stanford University Press, 1987.

Cooney, Robert, and Helen Michalowski. *The Power of the People: Active Non-Violence in the United States*. Philadelphia: New Society, 1987.

Coontz, Stephanie. *The Way We Really Are: Coming to Terms with America's Changing Families*. New York: Basic Books, 1997.

Cortés, Carlos E. *The Children Are Watching: How the Media Teach About Diversity*. New York: Teachers College Press, 2000.

Cose, Ellis. *The Rage of a Privileged Class*. New York: HarperCollins, 1993.

Cottle, Thomas J. *Black Children, White Dreams*. New York: Delta Book, Dell Publishing, 1974.

Council on Interracial Books for Children. *Guidelines for Selecting Bias Free Textbooks and Storybooks*. New York: Council on Interracial Books for Children, n.d.

Council on Interracial Books for Children Bulletin. *Children, Race and Racism: How Race Awareness Develops*. Vol. 11, nos. 3–4. New York: Council on Interracial Books for Children, 1980.

Creighton, Allan, with Paul Kivel. *Helping Teens Stop Violence: A Practical Guide for Counselors, Educators, and Parents*. Alameda, CA: Hunter House, 1992.

Creighton, Allan, and Paul Kivel. *Young Men's Work: Stopping Violence & Building Community*. Center City, MN: Hazelden, 1995, 1998.

Currie, Elliott. *Crime and Punishment in America: Why the Solutions to America's Most Stubborn Social Crisis Have Not Worked—and What Will*. New York: Henry Holt and Co., 1998.

Daniels, Jessie. *White Lies: Race, Class, Gender, and Sexuality in White Supremacist Discourse*. New York: Routledge, 1997.

Davis, Angela Y. *Blues Legacies and Black Feminism. Gertrude "Ma" Rainey, Bessie Smith, and Billie Holiday*. New York: Pantheon Books, 1998.

———. *Women, Culture, Politics*. New York: Vintage Books, 1989.

———. *Women, Race & Class*. New York: Random House, 1981.

Day, Kathleen. *Savings and Loan Hell: The People and the Politics Behind the $1 Trillion Savings and Loan Scandal*. New York: W.W. Norton and Company, 1993.

Deloria, Philip J. *Playing Indian*. New Haven: Yale University Press, 1998.

Delpit, Lisa. *Other People's Children: Cultural Conflict in the Classroom*. New York: New Press, 1995.

Derman-Sparks, Louise, and the A.B.C. Task Force. *Anti-Bias Curriculum: Tools for Empowering Young Children*. Washington, DC: National Association for the Education of Young Children, 1989.

Derman-Sparks, Louise, and Carol Brunson Phillips. *Teaching/Learning Anti-Racism: A Developmental Approach*. New York: Teachers College Press, 1997.

Dines, Gail, et al. *Pornography: The Production and Consumption of Inequality*. New York: Routledge, 1998.

Dinnerstein, Leonard. *Natives and Strangers: Blacks, Indians, and Immigrants in America*. New York: Oxford University Press, 1979.

Dobash, R. Emerson, and Russell Dobash. W*omen, Violence and Social Change*. New York: Routledge, 1992.

Domhoff, G. William. *Who Rules America? Power and Politics in the Year 2000*. Mountain View, CA: Mayfield Publishing, 1998.

Drinnon, Richard. *The Metaphysics of Indian-Hating and Empire-Building*. Minneapolis: University of Minnesota Press, 1980.

Du Bois, W.E.B. *Black Reconstruction in America: An Essay Toward a History of the Part Which Black Folk Played in the Attempt to Reconstruct Democracy in America, 1860–1880*. New York: Atheneum, 1977.

Dumas, Lynne S. *Talking with Your Child about a Troubled World*. New York: Fawcett Columbine, 1992.

Duneier, Mitchell. *Slim's Table: Race, Respectability, and Masculinity*. Chicago: University of Chicago Press, 1992.

Durning, Alan Thein. *How Much is Enough: The Consumer Society and the Future of the Earth*. New York: W.W. Norton, 1992.

Duvall, Lynn. *Respecting Our Differences: A Guide to Getting Along in a Changing World*. Minneapolis: Free Spirit Publishing, 1994.

Dworkin, Andrea. *Life and Death: Unapologetic Writings on the Continuing War Against Women*. New York: The Free Press, 1997.

Dyer, Richard. *White*. New York: Routledge, 1997.

Dyson, Michael Eric. *I May Not Get There with You: The True Martin Luther King, Jr.* New York: Touchstone, 2000.

——. *Reflecting Black: African American Cultural Criticism*. Minneapolis: University of Minnesota, 1993.

Edsall, Thomas Byrne, with Mary Edsall. *Chain Reaction: The Impact of Race, Rights and Taxes on American Politics*. New York: Norton, 1992.

Ehrenreich, Barbara. *Fear of Falling: The Inner Life of the Middle Class*. New York: HarperCollins, 1990.

Enloe, Cynthia. *Bananas, Beaches and Bases: Making Feminist Sense of International Politics*. Berkeley, CA: University of California Press, 1990.

——. *Maneuvers: The International Politics of Militarizing Women's Lives*. Berkeley, CA: University of California Press, 2000.

Espiritu, Yen Le. *Asian American Panethnicity: Bridging Institutions and Identities*. Philadelphia: Temple University Press, 1992.

Essed, Philomena. *Everyday Racism*. Alameda, CA: Hunter House, 1991.

——. *Understanding Everyday Racism: An Interdisciplinary Theory*. Newbury Park, CA: Sage Publications, 1991.

Evans, Sara. *Personal Politics: The Origins of the Women's Liberation Movement in the Civil Rights Movement and the New Left*. New York: Vintage, 1980.

Ezorsky, Gertrude. *Racism and Justice: The Case for Affirmative Action*. Ithaca, NY: Cornell University Press, 1991.

Fanon, Frantz. *Black Skin, White Masks*. Translated by Charles Markmann. New York: Grove, 1967.

——. *The Wretched of the Earth*. Translated by Constance Farrington. New York: Grove, 1963.

Fausto-Sterling, Augusta. *Myths of Gender: Biological Theories about Women and Men*. New York: Basic Books, 1985.

Feagin, Joe R. *Racist America: Roots, Current Realities, & Future Reparations*. New York: Routledge, 2001.

Feagin, Joe R., and Vera Hernan. *White Racism: The Basics*. New York: Routledge, 1995.

Feagin, Joe R., and Melvin P. Sikes. *Living With Racism: The Black Middle-Class Experience*. Boston: Beacon Press, 1994.

Featherston, Elena, ed. *Skin Deep: Women Writing on Color, Culture and Identity*. Freedom, CA: Crossing Press, 1994.

Feelings, Tom. *The Middle Passage: White Ships/Black Cargo*. New York: Dial Books, 1995.

Feinberg, Leslie. *Trans Gender Warriors: Making History from Joan of Arc to Dennis Rodman*. Boston: Beacon Press, 1996.

Fine, Michelle, et al., eds. *Off-White: Readings on Race, Power, and Society*. New York: Routledge, 1997.

Ford, Clyde W. *We Can All Get Along: 50 Steps You Can Take to Help End Racism*. New York: Dell, 1994.

Frankenberg, Ruth, ed. *Displacing Whiteness: Essays in Social and Cultural Criticism*. Durham: Duke University Press, 1997.

——. *The Social Construction of Whiteness: White Women, Race Matters*. Minneapolis: University of Minnesota Press, 1993.

Franklin, Raymond S. *Shadows of Race and Class*. Minneapolis: University of Minnesota Press, 1991.

Fraser, Steven, ed. *The Bell Curve Wars: Race, Intelligence and the Future of America*. New York: Basic Books, 1995.

Freire, Paulo. *Pedagogy of the Oppressed*. New York: Continuum, 1970.

Friesel, Evyatar. *Atlas of Modern Jewish History*. Oxford: Oxford University Press, 1990.

Frosch, Mary. *Coming of Age in America: A Multicultural Anthology*. New York: New Press, 1994.

Frye, Marilyn. *The Politics of Reality: Essays in Feminist Theory*. Freedom, CA: Crossing Press, 1983.

——. *Willful Virgin: Essays in Feminism*. Freedom, CA: Crossing Press, 1992.

Fulani, Lenora, ed. *The Psychopathology of Everyday Racism and Sexism*. New York: Harrington Park Press, 1988.

Funderberg, Lisa. *Black, White, Other: Bi-racial Americans Talk About Race and Identity*. New York: William Morrow, 1994.

Fussell, Paul. *Class: A Guide Through the American Status System*. New York: Summit Books, 1983.

Gandhi, Mohandas K. *Autobiography* New York: Dover, 1983.

Garcia, Richard A., ed. *The Chicanos in America, 1540–1974*. Dobbs Ferry, NY: Oceana Press, 1977.

Gates, Henry Louis Jr., ed. *"Race," Writing, and Difference*. Chicago: University of Chicago Press, 1986.

Gatto, John Taylor. *Dumbing Us Down: The Hidden Curriculum of Compulsory Schooling*. Gabriola Island, BC: New Society, 1992.

Gerber, David A., ed. *Anti-Semitism in American History*. Urbana, IL.: Univ. of Illinois Press, 1987.

Gibbs, Jewelle Taylor, ed. *Young, Black and Male in America: An Endangered Species*. New York: Auburn House, 1988.

Giddings, Paula. *When and Where I Enter: The Impact of Black Women on Race and Sex in America*. New York: Bantam Books, 1985.

Gilbert, Martin. *Atlas of Jewish History*. New York: William Morrow and Company, 1992.

Gill, Dawn, et al. *Racism and Education. Structure and Strategies*. Newbury Park, CA: Sage Publications, 1992.

Gilman, Sander. *Difference and Pathology: Stereotypes of Sexuality, Race, and Madness*. Ithaca, NY: Cornell University Press, 1985.

———. *Jewish Self-Hatred: Anti-Semitism and the Hidden Language of the Jews*. Baltimore: Johns Hopkins University Press, 1986.

Gilroy, Paul. *There Ain't No Black in the Union Jack: The Cultural Politics of Race and Nation*. Chicago: University of Chicago Press, 1987.

Giovanni, Nikki. *Racism 101*. New York: William Morrow and Company, 1994.

Glassman, Bernard. *Anti-Semitic Stereotypes Without Jews: Images of the Jews in England 1290–1700*. Detroit: Wayne State University Press, 1975.

Goldberg, David Theo, ed. *Anatomy of Racism*. Minneapolis: University of Minnesota, 1990.

Goldberg, David Theo and Michael Krausz, eds. *Jewish Identity*. Philadelphia: Temple University Press, 1993.

Goldfield, Michael. *The Color of Politics: Race and the Mainsprings of American Politics*. New York: New Press, 1997.

Gonzalez, Ray, ed. *Muy Macho: Latino Men Confront Their Manhood*. New York: Doubleday, 1996.

Gooding-Williams, Robert, ed. *Reading Rodney King, Reading Urban Uprising*. New York: Routledge, 1993.

Goodman, Mary Ellen. *Race Awareness in Young Children*. New York: Collier Books, 1964.

Goonatilake, Susantha. *Aborted Discovery: Science and Creativity in the Third World*. London: Zed Books, 1984.

Gordon, Linda. *Heroes of Their Own Lives: The Politics and History of Family Violence*. New York: Penguin Books, 1988.

Gould, Carol C., ed. *Beyond Domination: New Perspectives on Women and Philosophy*. Totowa, N.J.: Littlefield, Adams, 1983.

Gould, Stephen J. *Ever Since Darwin: Reflections in Natural History*. New York: W.W. Norton and Company, 1977.

———. *The Mismeasure of Man*. New York: W.W. Norton, 1981.

Grahn, Judy. *Another Mother Tongue: Gay Words, Gay Worlds*. Boston: Beacon Press, 1984.

Gramsci, Antonio. *Selections from the Prison Notebooks*. New York: International Publishers, 1971.

Gross, Beatrice and Ronald Gross, eds. *The Children's Rights Movement: Overcoming the Oppression of Young People*. Garden City, NY: Doubleday, 1977.

Guha, Ranajit, and Gayatri Chakravorty Spivak, eds. *Selected Subaltern Studies*. New York: Oxford University Press, 1988.

Guinier, Lani. *The Tyranny of the Majority: Fundamental Fairness and Representative Democracy*. New York: Free Press, 1994.

Guthrie, Robert V. *Even the Rat Was White: A Historical View of Psychology*. New York: Harper & Row, 1976.

Gwaltney, John Langston. *Drylongso: A Self-Portrait of Black America*. New York: Vintage Book, 1980.

Hacker, Andrew. *Money: Who Has How Much and Why*. New York: Touchstone, 1997.

———. *Two Nations: Black and White, Separate, Hostile, Unequal*. New York: Ballantine, 1992.

Hansen, Karen V. and Ilene J. Philipson, eds. *Women, Class, and the Feminist Imagination: A Socialist-Feminist Reader*. Philadelphia: Temple University Press, 1990.

Haraway, Donna. *Primate Visions: Gender, Race and Nature in the World of Modern Science*. New York: Routledge, 1989.

Harding, Sandra, ed. *The "Racial" Economy of Science: Toward a Democratic Future*. Bloomington, IN: Indiana University Press, 1993.

Harding, Sandra, and Merrill Hintikka, eds. *Discovering Reality: Feminist Perspectives on Epistemology, Metaphysics, Methodology, and Philosophy of Science*. Dordrecht, Holland: Reidel, 1983.

Harding, Vincent. *There is a River: The Black Struggle for Freedom in America*. New York: Vintage, 1981.

Hay, Malcolm. *The Roots of Christian Anti-Semitism*. New York: Freedom Library Press, 1981.

Heath, Shirley Brice and Milbrey W. McLaughlin. *Identity and Inner-City Youth: Beyond Ethnicity and Gender*. New York: Teachers College Press, 1993.

Heintz, James, et al. *The Ultimate Field Guide to the U.S. Economy*. New York: The New Press, 2000.

Hennessy, Rosemary. *Profit and Pleasure: Sexual Identities in Late Capitalism*. New York: Routledge, 2000.

Heyck, Denis Lynn Daly. *Barrios and Borderlands: Cultures of Latinos and Latinas in the United States*. New York: Routledge, 1994.

Hitchcock, Jeff. *Unraveling the White Cocoon*. Dubuque, IA: Kendall/Hunt Publishing, 2001.

Holt, John. *Freedom and Beyond*. New York: Dell Publishing, 1972.

hooks, bell. *Ain't I a Women: Black Women and Feminism*. Boston: South End Press, 1981.

———. *Black Looks: Race and Representation*. Boston: South End Press, 1992.

———. *Feminist Theory from Margin to Center*. Boston: South End Press, 1984.

———. *Talking Back: Thinking Feminism, Thinking Black*. Boston: South End Press, 1989.

———. *Yearning: Race, Gender, and Cultural Politics*. Boston: South End Press, 1990.

Hopson, Darlene Powell, and Derek S. Hopson. *Different and Wonderful. Raising Black Children in a Race-Conscious Society*. New York: Fireside Books, 1990.

Horne, Gerald. *Reversing Discrimination: The Case for Affirmative Action*. New York: International Publishers, 1992.

Horton, Robin. *Patterns of Thought in Africa and the West: Essays on Magic, Religion and Science*. Cambridge: Cambridge University Press, 1997.

Hountondji, Paulin. *African Philosophy: Myth and Reality*. Bloomington, IN: Indiana University Press, 1983.

Howard, Gary R. *We Can't Teach What We Don't Know: White Teachers, Multiracial Schools*. New York: Teachers College Press, 1999.

Hoxie, Frederick E., ed. *Indians in American History*. Arlington Heights, IL.: Harlan Davidson, 1988.

Hughes, Langston. *The Ways of White Folks*. New York: Vintage Books, 1990.

Hull, Gloria, et al. *All the Women Are White, All the Blacks Are Men, But Some of Us Are Brave: Black Women's Studies*. New York: Feminist Press, 1982.

Hurtado, Aida. *The Color of Privilege: Three Blasphemies on Race and Feminism*. Ann Arbor, MI: The University of Michigan Press, 1996.

Jacob, Margaret. *The Cultural Meanings of the Scientific Revolution*. New York: Knopf, 1988.

Jacobson, David, ed. *The Immigration Reader: American in a Multidisciplinary Perspective*. Malden, MA: Blackwell, 1998.

Jaimes, M. Annette, ed. *The State of Native America: Genocide, Colonization, and Resistance*. Boston: South End Press, 1992.

Jelloun, Tahar ben. *Racism Explained to My Daughter*. New York: New Press, 1999.

Jennings, Francis. *The Invasion of America: Indians, Colonialism, and the Cant of Conquest*. New York: Norton, 1975.

Jewell, K. Sue. *From Mammy to Miss America and Beyond: Cultural Images and the Shaping of U.S. Social Policy*. New York: Routledge, 1993.

Johnson, Allan G. *Privilege, Power, and Difference*. Toronto: Mayfield Publishing, 2001.

Johnson, Charles. *Soulcatcher and other stories: Twelve Powerful Tales about Slavery*. San Diego: Harvest/Harcourt, 1998.

Jordan, June. *Technical Difficulties*. New York: Vintage Books, 1992.

Jordan, Winthrop. *White Over Black: American Attitudes Toward the Negro, 1550–1912*. Chapel Hill, NC: University of North Carolina Press, 1968.

Kadi, Joanna. *Thinking Class: Sketches from a Cultural Worker*. Boston: South End, 1996.

Kaeser, Gig, and Peggy Gillespie. *Of Many Colors: Portraits of Multiracial Families*. Amherst, MA: University of Massachusetts Press, 1994.

Katz, Judith H. *White Awareness: Handbook for Anti-Racism Training*. Norman, OK: University of Oklahoma Press, 1978.

Katz, Phyllis A., and Dalmas A. Taylor, eds. *Eliminating Racism*. New York: Plenum, 1988.

Kaye/Kantrowitz, Melanie. *The Issue is Power: Essays on Women, Jews, Violence and Resistance*. San Francisco: Aunt Lute Books, 1992.

Kaye/Kantrowitz, Melanie, and Irena Klepfisz, eds. *The Tribe of Dina: A Jewish Women's Anthology*. Montpelier, VT: Sinister Wisdom Books, 1986.

Keister, Lisa A. *Wealth in America: Trends in Wealth Inequality*. Cambridge, England: Cambridge University Press, 2000.

Kendall, Frances E. *Diversity in the Classroom*. New York: Teachers College Press, 1983/1998.

Kim, Elaine H., Lila V. Villanueva and Asian Women United of California. *Making More Waves: New Writing by Asian American Women*. Boston: Beacon Press, 1997.

Kimmel, Michael. *Manhood in America: A Cultural History*. New York: The Free Press, 1996.

Kimmel, Michael S. and Thomas E. Mosmiller. *Against the Tide: Profeminist Men in the United States 1776-1990*. Boston: Beacon Press, 1992.

Kincheloe, Joe L., et al. *White Reign: Deploying Whiteness in America*. New York: St. Martin's Griffin, 1998.

Kitzinger, Sheila, and Celia Kitzinger. *Tough Questions: Talking Straight with Your Kids about the Real World*. Boston: Harvard Common Press, 1991.

Kivel, Paul. *Boys Will Be Men: Raising Our Sons for Courage, Caring, and Community*. Gabriola Island, BC: New Society, 1999.

———. *Men's Work: How to Stop the Violence that Tears Our Lives Apart*. New York: Hazelden/Ballantine, 1992/1998.

Kivel, Paul, and Allan Creighton. *Making the Peace: A 15-Session Violence Prevention Curriculum for Young People*. Alameda, CA: Hunter House, 1997.

Kohl, Herbert. *Should We Burn Babar? Essays on Children's Literature and the Power of Stories*. New York: The New Press, 1995.

Kohn, Alfie. *No Contest: The Case Against Competition*. Boston: Houghton Mifflin Company, 1986.

Kozol, Jonathan. *Savage Inequalities: Children in America's Schools*. New York: HarperCollins, 1991.

Ladner, Joyce, ed. *The Death of White Sociology*. New York: Random House, 1973.

Lapham, Lewis. *Money and Class in America*. New York: Weidenfeld and Nicolson, 1988.

Lazarre, Jane. *Beyond the Whiteness of Whiteness: Memoir of a White Mother of Black Sons*. Durham, NC: University of North Carolina Press, 1996.

Leadbeater, Bonnie J. Ross, and Niobe Way. *Urban Girls: Resisting Stereotypes, Creating Identities*. New York: New York University Press, 1996.

Lee, Enid, et al. *Beyond Heroes and Holidays: A Practical Guide to K-12 Anti-racist, Multicultural Education and*

Staff Development. Washington, DC: Network of Educators on the Americas, 1998.

Lerner, Gerda, ed. *Black Women in White America*. New York: Pantheon Books, 1972.

Lerner, Michael. *The Socialism of Fools: Anti-Semitism on the Left*. Oakland, CA: Tikkun Books, 1992.

———. *Surplus Powerlessness: The Psychodynamics of Everyday Life*. Oakland, CA: Institute for Labor and Mental Health, 1986.

Lerner, Michael and Cornel West. *Jews and Blacks: Let the Healing Begin*. New York.: G.P. Putnam's Sons, 1995.

Lester, Joan Steinau. *The Future of White Men & other Diversity Dilemmas*. Berkeley, CA: Conari Press, 1994.

Levins, Richard, and Richard Lewontin. *The Dialectical Biologist*. Cambridge, MA: Harvard University Press, 1987.

Lewontin, R., Leon Kamin, and Stephen Rose. *Not in Our Genes: Biology, Ideology and Human Nature*. New York: Pantheon, 1984.

Lipsitz, George. *The Possessive Investment in Whiteness: How White People Profit From Identity Politics*. Philadelphia: Temple University Press, 1998.

Lopez, Ian F.H. *White by Law: The Legal Construction of Race*. New York: New York University Press, 1999.

Lorde, Audre. *Sister Outsider: Essays and Speeches*. Freedom, CA: Crossing Press, 1984.

Louis, Debbie. *And We Are Not Saved: A History of the Movement as People*. Columbia, MD: The Press at Water's Edge, 1970.

Lowance, Mason. *Against Slavery: An Abolitionist Reader*. New York: Penguin Books, 2000.

Lowe, Marian, and Ruth Hubbard, eds. *Woman's Nature: Rationalizations of Inequality*. New York: Pergamon Press, 1983.

Lowen, James W. *Lies My Teacher Told Me: Everything Your American History Textbook Got Wrong*. New York: New Press, 1995.

Lubiano, Wahneema. *The House That Race Built: Black American, U.S. Terrain*. New York: Pantheon Books, 1997.

Madhubuti, Haki R. *Black Men, Obsolete, Single, Dangerous? The African American Family in Transition*. Chicago: Third World Press, 1990.

Majors, Richard and Janet Mancini Billson. *Cool Pose: The Dilemmas of Black Manhood in America*. New York: Touchstone, 1992.

Mallon, Gerald L., ed. *Resisting Racism: An Action Guide*. San Francisco: National Association of Black and White Men Together, 1991.

Manmer, Jalna, and Mary Maynard, eds. *Women, Violence and Social Control*. Atlantic Highlands, NJ: Humanities Press International, 1987.

Marable, Manning. *The Crisis of Color and Democracy: Essays on Race, Class and Power*. Monroe, ME: Common Courage Press, 1992.

Martinez, Elizabeth. *De Colores Means All of Us: Latina Views for a Multi-Colored Century*. Cambridge, MA: South End Press, 1998.

Mazer, Anne. *Going Where I'm Coming From: Memoirs of American Youth: A Multicultural Anthology*. New York: Persea Books, 1995.

McCarthy, Cameron, and Warren Crichlow, eds. *Race Identity and Representation in Education*. New York: Routledge, 1993.

McGinnis, Kathleen, and Barbara Oehlberg. *Starting Out Right: Nurturing Young Children as Peacemakers*. New York: Crossroad Publishing, 1988.

McIntosh, Peggy. *White Privilege and Male Privilege: A Personal Account of Coming to See Correspondences Through Work in Women's Studies*. Wellesley, MA: Wellesley College, Center for Research on Women, 1988.

McLaurin, Melton A. *Separate Pasts: Growing Up White in the Segregated South*. Athens, GA: University of Georgia Press, 1987.

Meier, Matt, and Feliciano Rivera. *The Chicanos: A History of Mexican Americans*. New York: Hill and Wang, 1972.

Memmi, Albert. *The Colonizer and the Colonized*. Translated by Howard Greenfield. Boston: Beacon Press, 1965.

———. *Racism*. Minneapolis, MN: University of Minnesota Press, 2000.

Mies, Maria. *Patriarchy and Accumulation on a World Scale: Women in the International Division of Labour*. London: Zed Books, 1986.

Mies, Maria, Veronika Bennholdt Thomsen, and Claudia von Werlhof. *Women: The Last Colony*. London: Zed Books, 1988.

Mills, Nicolaus. *Debating Affirmative Action: Race, Gender, Ethnicity, and the Politics of Inclusion*. New York: Delta, 1994.

Mishel, Lawrence, et al. *The State of Working America: 2000/2001*. Ithaca, NY: Cornell University Press, 2001.

Mohawk, John. *Exiled in the Land of the Free: Democracy, the Indian Nations, and the U.S. Constitution*. Santa Fe, NM: Clear Light Publishers, 1992.

Moraga, Cherrie, and Gloria Anzaldua, eds. *This Bridge Called My Back: Writings by Radical Women of Color*. New York: Kitchen Table — Women of Color Press, 1981.

Morales, Aurora Levins. *Medicine Stories: History, Culture, and the Politics of Intergrity*. Cambridge, MA: South End Press, 1998.

Morris, Jenny. *Pride Against Prejudice: Transforming Attitudes to Disability*. Gabriola Island, BC: New Society Publishers, 1991.

Morrison, Toni. *Playing in the Dark: Whiteness and the Literary Imagination*. Cambridge, MA: Harvard University Press, 1992.

——, ed. *Racing Justice, En-gendering Power: Essays on Anita Hill, Clarence Thomas, and the Construction of Social Reality.* New York: Pantheon, 1992.

Mosse, George L. *Toward the Final Solution: A History of European Racism.* New York: Howard Fertig, 1978.

Mudimbe, V.Y. *The Invention of Africa: Gnosis, Philosophy, and the Order of Knowledge.* Bloomington, IN: Indiana University Press, 1988.

Mura, David. *When the Body Meets Memory: An Odyssey of Race, Sexuality, and Identity.* New York: Anchor, 1995.

Muse, Daphne. *The New Press Guide to Multicultural Resources for Young Readers.* New York: The New Press, 1997.

Nasr, Seyyed Hossein. *Islamic Science: An Illustrated Study.* London: World of Islam Festival Publishing, 1976.

Newman, Louise Michele. *White Women's Rights: The Racial Origins of Feminism in the United States.* New York: Oxford University Press, 1999.

Nieto, Sonia. *Affirming Diversity: The Sociopolitical Context of Multicultural Education.* New York: Longman, 1996.

Novick, Michael. *White Lies White Power: The Fight Against White Supremacy and Reactionary Violence.* Monroe, ME: Common Courage Press, 1995.

O'Hearn, Claudine Chiawei, ed. *Half + Half: Writers on Growing Up Biracial + Bicultural.* New York: Pantheon, 1998.

Okihiro, Gary Y. *Margins and Mainstreams: Asians in American History and Culture.* Seattle: University of Washington Press, 1994.

Oliver, Melvin L., and Thomas M. Shapiro. *Black Wealth/White Wealth: A New Perspective on Racial Inequality.* New York: Routledge, 1997.

Omi, Michael, and Howard Winant. *Racial Formation in the United States: From the 1960s to the 1990s.* New York: Routledge, 1986.

Orfalea, Gregory. *Before the Flames: A Quest for the History of Arab Americans.* Austin, TX: University of Texas Press, 1988.

Owen, David. *None of the Above: Behind the Myth of Scholastic Aptitude.* Boston: Houghton Mifflin, 1985.

Parenti, Michael. *History As Mystery.* San Francisco: City Lights Books, 1999.

Pelo, Ann, and Fran Davidson. *That's Not Fair! A Teacher's Guide to Activism with Young Children.* St. Paul, MN: Red Leaf Press, 2000.

Penelope, Julia. *Out of the Class Closet: Lesbians Speak.* Freedom, CA: The Crossing Press, 1994.

Perlo, Victor. *Economics of Racism, I and II.* New York: International Publishers, 1996.

Perry, Theresa, and James W. Fraser. *Freedom's Plow: Teaching in the Multicultural Classroom.* New York: Routledge, 1993.

Pfeil, Fred. *White Guys: Studies in Postmodern Domination & Difference.* London: Verso, 1995.

Pharr, Suzanne. *In the Time of the Right: Reflections on Liberation.* Berkeley, CA: Chardon Press, 1996.

Pinderhughes, Howard. *Race in the Hood: Conflict & Violence Among Urban Youth.* Minneapolis, MN: University of Minnesota, 1997.

Piven, Frances Fox, and Richard A. Cloward. *Poor People's Movements: How They Succeed, Why They Fail.* New York: Vintage, 1979.

——. *Regulating the Poor: The Functions of Public Welfare.* New York: Vintage Books, 1971.

Platt, Tony, and Suzie Dod Thomas, eds. "Rethinking Race." *Social Justice*, 20, nos. 1–2 (1993).

Pleck, Elizabeth. *Rape and the Politics of Race, 1865–1910.* Working Paper No. 213. Wellesley, MA: Wellesley College, Center for Research on Women, 1990.

Pratt, Minnie Bruce. *Rebellion: Essays 1980–1991.* Ithaca, NY: Firebrand Books, 1991.

Price, Frederick K.C. *Race, Religion & Racism Vol. I: A Bold Encounter with Division in the Church.* Los Angeles: Faith One Publishing, 1999.

Reddy, Maureen T. *Everyday Acts Against Racism: Raising Children in a Multiracial World.* Seattle: Seal Press, 1996.

Reich, Michael. *Racial Inequality.* Princeton, NJ: Princeton University Press, 1981.

Rich, Adrienne. *On Lies, Secrets and Silence: Selected Prose, 1966–1978.* New York: W.W. Norton, 1979.

Richie, Beth E. *Compelled to Crime: The Gender Entrapment of Battered Black Women.* New York: Routledge, 1996.

Ridgeway, James. *Blood in the Face: The Ku Klux Klan, Aryan Nations, Nazi Skinheads, and the Rise of a New White Culture.* New York: Thunder's Mouth Press, 1990.

Robinson, Randall. *The Debt: What America Owes to Blacks.* New York: Plume, 2000.

Robinson, Sally. *Marked Men: White Masculinity in Crisis.* New York: Columbia University Press, 2000.

Rodney, Walter. *How Europe Underdeveloped Africa.* Washington, DC: Howard University Press, 1982.

Rodriguez, Nelson, and Leila Villaverde, eds. *Dismantling White Privilege: Pedagogy, Politics, and Whiteness.* New York: Peter Lang Publishing, 2000.

Roediger, David R. *Towards the Abolition of Whiteness.* London: Verso, 1994.

——. *The Wages of Whiteness: Race and the Making of the American Working Class.* London: Verso, 1991.

——, ed. *Black on White: Black Writers on What It Means to Be White.* New York: Schocken Books, 1998.

Root, Maria P., ed. *The Multiracial Experience: Racial*

Borders as the New Frontier. Thousand Oaks, CA: Sage, 1996.

——, ed. *Racially Mixed People in America*. Newbury Park, CA: Sage Publications, 1992.

Rose, Paul Lawrence. *German Question/Jewish Question: Revolutionary Antisemitism from Kant to Wagner.* Princeton, NJ: Princeton University Press, 1990.

Rossides, Daniel. *The American Class System*. Boston: Houghton Mifflin, 1976.

Rothenberg, Paula S. *Racism and Sexism: An Integrated Study.* New York: St. Martin's Press, 1988.

——. *White Privilege: Essential Readings on the Other Side of Racism*. New York: Worth Publishers, 2002.

Rubin, Lillian B. *Families on the Fault Line*. New York: HarperCollins, 1994.

——. *Worlds of Pain: Life in the Working Class.* New York: Basic Books, 1976.

Ruether, Rosemary Radford. *Faith and Fratricide: The Theological Roots of Anti-Semitism*. New York: Seabury Press, 1974.

Runnymede Trust. *The Parekh Report: The Future of Multi-ethnic Britain*. London: Profile Books, 2000.

Ryan, William. *Blaming the Victim*. New York: Pantheon Books, 1971.

Said, Edward. *Covering Islam: How the Media and the Experts Determine How We See the Rest of the World*. New York: Vintage, 1981, 1997.

——. *Orientalism*. New York: Random House, 1978.

Salomon, Larry R. *Roots of Justice: Stories of Organizing in Communities of Color*. Berkeley, CA: Chardon Press, 1998.

San Francisco WritersCorp. *Same Difference: Young Writers on Race*. San Francisco: WritersCorps Books, 1998.

Santoli, Al. *New Americans: An Oral History*. New York: Ballantine, 1988.

Saracho, Olivia N., and Bernard Spodek, eds. *Understanding the Multicultural Experience in Early Childhood Education*. Washington, DC: National Association for the Education of Young Children, 1983.

Schniedewind, Nancy, and Ellen Davidson. *Open Minds to Equality: A Sourcebook of Learning Activities to Promote Race, Sex, Class and Age Equity*. Englewood Cliffs, NJ: Prentice Hall, 1983.

Schoem, David, ed. *Inside Separate Worlds: Life Stories of Young Blacks, Jews and Latinos*. Ann Arbor, MI: University of Michigan, 1991.

Segrest, Mab. *Memoirs of a Race Traitor.* Boston: South End Press, 1994.

——. *My Mama's Dead Squirrel: Lesbian Essays on Southern Culture*. Ithaca, NY: Firebrand Books, 1985.

Sennett, Richard, and Jonathan Cobb. *The Hidden Injuries of Class*. New York: Vintage Books, 1972.

Shapiro, Joseph P. *No Pity: People with Disabilities Forging a New Civil Rights Movement*. New York: Random House, 1993.

Sivanandan A. *Communities of Resistance: Writing on Black Struggles for Socialism*. London: Verso, 1990.

Sklar, Holly. *Chaos or Community? Seeking Solutions, Not Scapegoats for Bad Economics.* Boston: South End Press, 1995.

Slapin, Beverly, and Doris Seale. *Through Indian Eyes: The Native Experience in Books for Children.* Gabriola Island, BC: New Society, 1992.

Sleeter, Christine E. *Multicultural Education as Social Activism*. Albany, NY: State University of New York Press, 1996.

Smith, Barbara. *The Truth That Never Hurts: Writings on Race, Gender, and Freedom*. New Brunswick, NJ: Rutgers University Press, 1998.

——, ed. *Home Girls: A Black Feminist Anthology.* New York: Kitchen Table—Women of Color Press, 1983.

Smith, Lillian. *Killers of the Dream.* New York: W.W. Norton, 1961.

Sojourners. America's Original Sin: A Study Guide on White Racism. Washington, DC: Sojourners, 1992.

Spelman, Elizabeth V. *Inessential Woman: Problems of Exclusion in Feminist Thought*. Boston: Beacon Press, 1988.

Spivak, Gayatri Chakravorty. *In Other Worlds: Essays in Cultural Politics.* New York: Methuen, 1987.

Stalvey, Lois. *The Education of a Wasp*. New York: Bantam Books, 1971.

Stanko, Elizabeth A. *Everyday Violence: How Women and Men Experience Sexual and Physical Danger.* London: Pandora Press, 1990.

Staples, Robert. *Black Masculinity: The Black Male's Role in American Society*. San Francisco: Black Scholar Press, 1982.

Starhawk. *Truth or Dare: Encounters with Power, Authority, and Mystery.* San Francisco: Harper & Row, 1987.

Steiner, Stan. *The New Indians.* San Francisco: Harper Colophon, 1968.

Stepan, Nancy. "Race and Gender: The Role of Analogy in Science." *Isis* 77 (1986).

Stoltenberg, John. *The End of Manhood: A Book for Men of Conscience*. New York: Dutton, 1993.

Stout, Linda. *Bridging the Class Divide and Other Lessons for Grassroots Organizing*. Boston: Beacon Press, 1996.

Suhl, Yuri. *They Fought Back: The Story of the Jewish Resistance in Nazi Europe*. New York: Schocken Books, 1967.

Suleiman, Michael W., ed. *Arabs in America: Building a New Future*. Philadelphia: Temple University Press, 1999.

Sway, Marlene. *Familiar Strangers: Gypsy Life in America*. Urbana, IL: University of Illinois, 1988.

Swerdlow, Amy, and Hanna Lessingler, eds. *Class, Race, and Sex*. Boston: G.K. Hall, 1983.

Takagi, Dana Y. *The Retreat from Race: Asian Admissions and Racial Politics*. New Brunswick, NJ: Rutgers University Press, 1993.

Takaki, Ronald. *A Different Mirror: A History of Multicultural America*. Boston: Little, Brown and Company, 1993.

——. *Strangers From a Different Shore: A History of Asian Americans*. New York: Penguin, 1989.

——, ed. *From Different Shores: Perspectives on Race and Ethnicity in America*. New York: Oxford University Press, 1987.

Tatum, Beverly. *"Why Are All the Black Kids Sitting Together in the Cafeteria?" and Other Conversations about Race*. New York: Basic Books, 1997.

Taylor, Jill McLean, et al. *Between Voice and Silence: Women and Girls, Race and Relationship*. Cambridge, MA: Harvard University Press, 1995.

Terkel, Studs. *Race: How Blacks and Whites Think and Feel About the American Obsession*. New York: New Press, 1992.

Terry, Robert W. *For Whites Only*. Grand Rapids, MI: William B. Eerdmans, 1970.

Thandeka. *Learning to be White*. New York: Continuum, 1999.

Thompson, Becky. *A Promise and A Way of Life: White Antiracist Activism*. Minneapolis: University of Minnesota Press, 2001.

Tolley, Howard Jr. *Children and War: Political Socialization to International Conflict*. New York: Teachers College Press, 1973.

Torres, Rodolfo D., et al. *Race, Identity, and Citizenship: A Reader*. Malden, MA: Blackwell, 1999.

Troyna, Barry, and Richard Hatcher. *Racism in Children's Lives: A Study of Mainly-white Primary Schools*. London: Routledge, 1992.

Tuan, Mia. *Forever Foreigners or Honorary Whites?: The Asian Ethnic Experience Today*. New Brunswick, NJ: Rutgers University Press, 1998.

Turner, Margery Austin, Michael Fix, and Raymond J. Struyk. *Opportunities Denied: Discrimination in Hiring*. Washington, DC: Urban Institute, 1991.

van Dijk, Teun A. *Elite Discourse and Racism*. Newbury Park, CA: Sage Publications, 1993.

Van Sertima, Ivan. *They Came Before Columbus*. New York: Random House, 1976.

——, ed. *Blacks in Science: Ancient and Modern*. New Brunswick, NJ: Transaction Books, 1986.

Vanneman, Reeve, and Lynn Weber Cannon. *The American Perception of Class*. Philadelphia: Temple University Press, 1987.

Vasquez, Hugh, and Isoke Femi. *No Boundaries: A Manual for Unlearning Oppression and Building Multicultural Alliances*. Oakland, CA: TODOS Institute, 1993.

Wagner, Sally Roesch. *The Untold Story of the Iroquois Influence on Early Feminists*. Aberdeen, SD: Sky Carrier Press, 1996.

Walkowitz, Daniel J. *Working With Class: Social Workers and the Politics of Middle-Class Identity*. Chapel Hill, NC: University of North Carolina Press, 1998.

Ware, Vron. *Beyond the Pale: White Women, Racism and History*. London: Verso, 1992.

Waring, Marilyn. *Counting for Nothing: What Men Value and What Women Are Worth*. Toronto: University of Toronto Press, 1999.

——. *If Women Counted: A New Feminist Economics*. San Francisco: HarperCollins, 1988.

Waters, Mary. *Ethnic Options*. Berkeley, CA: University of California Press, 1990.

Weatherford, Jack. *Indian Givers: How the Indians of the Americas Transformed the World*. New York: Fawcett/Columbine, 1988.

——. *Native Roots: How the Indians Enriched America*. New York: Crown Books, 1991.

Weis, Lois, and Michelle Fine. *Beyond Silenced Voices: Class, Race, and Gender in United States Schools*. Albany, NY: State University of New York Press, 1993.

Wellman, David, ed. *Portraits of White Racism*. New York: Cambridge University Press, 1977.

West, Cornel. *Prophetic Reflections: Notes on Race and Power in America*. Monroe, ME: Common Courage Press, 1993.

——. *Race Matters*. New York: Vintage, 1993.

Wijeyesinghe, Charmaine, and Bailey W. Jackson III. *New Perspectives on Racial Identity Development: A Theoretical and Practical Anthology*. New York: New York University Press, 2001.

Wilkinson, Doris Y., and Ronald L. Taylor, eds. *The Black Male in America*. Chicago: NelsonHall, 1977.

Williams, Patricia J. *The Alchemy of Race and Rights*. London: Virago Press, 1993.

Winant, Howard. *Racial Conditions: Politics Theory Comparisons*. Minneapolis: University of Minnesota Press, 1994.

Wise, Tim J. *Little White Lies: The Truth about Affirmative Action and Reverse Discrimination*. New Orleans: Twomey Center for Peace Through Justice, 1995.

Wolff, Edward N. *Top Heavy: The Increasing Inequality of Wealth in American and What Can Be Done About It.* New York: The New Press, 1995.

Women's Action Coalition. *Stats: The Facts About Women.* New York: New Press, 1993.

Wray, Matt, and Annalee Newitz. *White Trash: Race and Class in America.* New York: Routledge, 1997.

Wright, Richard. *12 Million Black Voices.* New York: Thunder's Mouth Press, 1988.

Wright, Richard A., ed. *African Philosophy: An Introduction.* Washington, DC: University Press of America, 1979.

X, Malcolm. *The Autobiography of Malcolm X as told to Alex Haley.* New York: Ballantine, 1964.

Zia, Helen. *Asian American Dreams: The Emergence of an American People.* New York: Farrar, Strauss and Giroux, 2000.

Zinn, Howard. *A People's History of the United States.* New York: Harper Colophon, 1980.

Zweigenhaft, Richard L., and William G. Domhoff. *Blacks in the White Establishment? A Study of Race and Class in America.* New Haven, CN: Yale University Press, 1991.

Index

D

Davis, Angela, 76

Democracy, 83, 176, 185, 197, 222, 231

Discrimination, 2, 6, 20, 37, 39, 44, 47, 50, 51, 53, 59, 68, 100, 109, 116, 177, 193, 201, 225, 234, 239, 242

and affirmative action, 187, 189, 191, 193

allies against, 99

of Arabs, 156

of Asian Americans, 140, 143-5

based on age, 20, 109, 193

based on gender, 2, 37, 109, 177

based on physical ability, 37, 177

based on sexual orientation, 2, 37, 177

based on skin color, 37

of black people, 27, 138, 175

of immigrants, 167, 168

and institutional racism, 172-3

of interracial couples, 122

of Jewish people, 161

of Latino/as, 148

of people of color, 36, 46, 66, 91, 101, 188

in voting, 183, 185

Discrimination, reverse, 61

Domination, 24, 89, 133, 145, 151-2, 158

Dow, George, 155

Du Bois, W.E.B., 196

Dworkin, Andrea, 76

E

Economic benefits, 27

Economic development, 1, 132

Economic justice, 65, 163, 202

Economic pyramid, 35, 64, 115-7, 167

buffer zone of, 115-8

Entitlement, 42-5, 88

Equal Employment Opportunity Commission, 191

Ethnicity, 2, 9, 17

Exploitation, 2, 18, 24, 27, 35, 43, 46, 53, 126, 136, 138, 145, 176

as form of racism, 44, 65, 69, 133, 168, 205

Exploitation, corporate, 166

Exploitation, cultural, 36, 132, 161, 164, 198, 228

Exploitation, economic, 9, 133, 144, 164, 170, 197

Exploitation, gender-based, 202

Exploitation, sexual, 73

F

Family, happy

myth of, 78-80, 101

Fanaticism, religious, 87

Farrakhan, Louis, 162

Fear, racial, 70, 122, 133-4, 143, 151

Federal Housing Authority (FHA), 29

Franklin, Benjamin, 127, 205

Free Trade Agreement of the Americas (FTAA), 198

G

Gage, Matilda Joslyn, 127

Gay people, 10, 20, 30, 34, 72-4, 77, 83, 158, 224, 227, 231, 238, 241-2

Gender, 9, 11, 20, 22, 50, 76, 89, 94, 97, 130, 140, 142, 144, 193, 196, 210, 222, 237, 240

discrimination based on, 109, 199

and fear, 72

and race, 134, 241

General Agreement on Tariffs and Trade (GATT), 150, 198

Genocide, 53-4, 120, 124-6, 129, 131, 175, 239

Giddings, Paula, 76

Gore, Al, 182

Gulf War, 155

H

Harassment, 2, 36, 46-7, 50, 56, 109, 134, 156-7, 161, 181, 190, 199, 210

Harper, Frances E.W., 76

Hate crimes, 83, 157, 168, 237

Holocaust, 160, 239, 241

hooks, bell, 76

I

Illegal aliens, 60, 67, 149, 180

Illegal Immigration Reform, 156

Immigrant Responsibility Act, 156

Immigrants, 1, 27, 64, 83, 85, 87, 130-2, 140, 143, 145, 148, 150, 152, 154-6, 180, 185

with refugee status, 169, 181

See also Exploitation

Racial groups, 166, 170

Racial hierarchy, 16, 20, 23, 25, 39, 42, 116, 123, 150, 161, 162, 173, 198, 210-11

Racial identity, 36, 89

Racial injustice, 163, 174, 176-7, 187, 192, 232, 239, 246

See also Injustices ·

Racial justice, 1, 27, 61, 92, 98, 105, 110-11, 174, 178, 180, 188, 223, 240-2

Racial profiling, 156-7

Racial putdown (joke), 107-9, 161, 199-200

Racial relations, 79, 174

Racial scapegoating, 14

Racial solidarity, 35

Racial stereotypes, 12, 107-8, 180

See also Stereotypes

Racial violence, 21, 67, 87, 112

See also Violence

Racism, 6ñ9, 14-7, 21, 25, 52-5, 62, 66, 69, 76-84, 95, 97-100, 110, 113, 126, 150, 222, 230-2, 234, 237-8, 240-3, 245-7

and affirmative action, 188-9

and African Americans, 135-9

and anger, 56-7

and Asian Americans, 140, 144-6

benefits to white people, 27, 41, 190

built on superiority, 44-5

challenging it, 20, 68, 83, 109, 111-2, 115, 117, 134, 202, 239, 244

costs of, 36, 46-7, 49, 61, 115, 200

and the criminal justice system, 214, 216

and eroticism, 73-4

effects of, 35, 46-7, 58, 64, 145

effects on people of color, 37, 197, 207

eliminating it, 11, 51, 88, 92, 94, 123, 175, 198, 200

in health care system, 207-9

intertwined with anti-Semiticism, 2, 13

and Jewish People, 158-9, 161-5

justification of, 105, 108, 122

and people of color, 90-1, 116

and police, 210-3

and public policy, 174-8, 187

in religion, 219-20

resisting it, 4, 85, 89, 92, 103, 114, 117, 120, 123, 152, 187

in schools, 203-6

in workplace, 196, 200-1

Racism, institutional, 36, 109, 111, 123, 170, 172-3, 191, 207, 214, 239-40

Racism, white, See White racism

Racist society, 12, 41, 237

Racists, 8, 13-4, 56, 92, 113, 115, 148, 194, 200, 228

Rape, 20, 50, 67, 74, 76-9, 126, 132, 134, 160, 184, 211-2, 215

Reagan, Ronald, 155

Reich, Michael, 196

Religion, 2, 17, 219-20, 222

Reparations, 174

Richie, Beth, 76

Roediger, David, 196

Roma (Gypsies), 21, 158

Ruffin, Josephine St. Pierre, 76

S

Santana, Carlos, 151

Satcher, David, 207

Schools, See Racism, in schools

Schwarzkopf, General Norman, 155

Segregation, 21, 75, 81, 85, 91, 122, 132-3, 138, 152, 172-3, 188, 196, 234

Selena, 151

Sexism, 3, 75-6, 97, 100, 113, 134, 173, 238

Sexual orientation, 9, 20, 50, 85, 89, 109, 130, 199, 222, 241

Simpson, O.J., 134

Sister Souljah, 162

Sivanandan, A., 201

Skin color, 2, 12, 20, 39, 41, 68, 97, 122, 140, 162, 237

Slavery, 16, 22, 53-4, 67, 103, 120, 126, 130-3, 136, 138, 141, 149, 174-5, 180, 196, 239

Social activism, 203, 237

Social change, 110

Social Darwinism, 16

Social inequity, 64

Social injustice, 2-3, 103, 220, 240

See also Injustices

See also Racial injustice

Social justice, 3, 191, 219, 244

Social Security, 29, 31, 59, 168, 177

Sowell, Thomas, 236

Spanish-speaking communities, 60, 81-2, 147-52

Stanton, Elizabeth Cady, 127

Steele, Shelby, 235

Stereotypes, 68, 108-9, 121, 125, 128, 138-9, 141, 143-4, 146, 155, 159-61, 163, 167, 172, 199, 237-8

    See also Racial, stereotypes

T

Takaki, Ronald, 131

Talbert, Mary, 76

Terrell, Mary Church, 76

Terrorists, 60, 154, 156

Thomas, Clarence, 134, 235

Thompson, Nicholas, 184-5

Tokenism, 232, 234-6, 242

Trask, Huanani-Kay, 76

Truth, Sojourner, 76

U

V

Veteran Administration Health care system, 28

Veteran Administration Housing Authority, 28

Veterans Administration (VA), 29

Victimization, 51, 54, 61

Villa-Lobos, 151

Violence, 3, 36, 46, 51, 53, 67-8, 87, 100, 126, 132, 143, 145, 148, 155, 157-8, 167, 218, 237

    enforced by racism, 6, 15, 22, 52, 65, 77, 97, 161-2, 168, 213, 240

    and fear, 72, 74, 76

    towards Jewish people, 2, 163-4

    victims of, 61, 70

    See also Racial violence

Violence, domestic, 75, 78-9, 211-2

Violence, economic, 101, 144

Violence, physical, 20, 37, 134, 144

Violence, sexual, 20, 127, 181

Vote, right to, 182-6

Voting Rights Act (1965), 182

W

Washington, George, 125, 131, 226

Welfare mothers, 59, 64, 239

Wells, Ida B., 76

White benefits, 26, 28, 31-2, 34-6, 38, 42, 50, 90, 115, 188

White culture, 44, 90, 146

White dominance, 87, 228, 240

White fear, 67

White hegemony, 94, 148

White men (males), 28-31, 39, 43, 54, 124, 126, 134, 189-90, 193-4, 211

White people,

    as agents of ruling class, 115-6, 118

    as allies to people of color, 94-8, 100-6, 106-7, 109-5, 118, 200-1, 228, 240

    history of racial relationships, 120-1

    and institutional racism, 172-3, 176, 178, 180, 182, 187-8, 191, 201, 208

    in multicultural nation, 228, 230, 235

    and people of mixed heritage, 122

    and racism, 65-6, 70, 72, 74-5, 77-80, 82-3, 85-6, 89-92

    relating to other racial groups, 121, 126-7, 130-4, 137-9, 141-5, 148, 151, 158, 162-4, 170

    state of being white, 1, 4, 6, 8, 12-4, 20-1, 27-8, 35-8, 40-1, 43-5, 59, 54, 57-8

    and voting rights, 184-6

White power, 95, 112, 123, 137, 180, 211, 234

White privilege, 23, 90, 95, 117, 123, 137, 150

    See also Privileges

White racism, 2-3, 22, 49, 61, 72, 86-9, 120-2, 130, 133, 137, 141, 144-5, 147, 151-2, 172, 179, 235

White society, 57, 91, 133-4, 136, 145

White superiority, 21, 44, 201, 227

White women, 20, 22-3, 29, 31, 39, 72, 75, 103, 124, 126, 131, 134-5, 172

Whiteness, 9-11, 13, 15, 17-8, 20, 22-4, 26, 34, 62, 77, 84, 88, 91, 95, 118, 134, 137, 158, 160, 196, 219, 227, 242

Wilson, James Q., 185

Wing, Bob, 185

Women of color, 29, 72-3, 76, 135

World Trade Organization, 208

About the Author

PAUL KIVEL is the co-founder of the internationally recognized Oakland's Men's Project and has conducted hundreds of workshops on racism and anti-violence for teens and men all over the country. The author of *Men's Work* and *Boys Will Be Men*, he also co-authored the *Making the Peace Curriculum* and *Young Men's Work Curriculum*. He lives with his partner and their daughter and two sons in Oakland, California.

If you have enjoyed *Uprooting Racism,*
you might also enjoy other

BOOKS TO BUILD A NEW SOCIETY

Our books provide positive solutions for people who want to
make a difference. We specialize in:

Sustainable Living • Ecological Design and Planning

Natural Building & Appropriate Technology • New Forestry

Environment and Justice • Conscientious Commerce

Progressive Leadership • Resistance and Community • Nonviolence

Educational and Parenting Resources

New Society Publishers

ENVIRONMENTAL BENEFITS STATEMENT

New Society Publishers has chosen to produce this book on New Leaf EcoBook
100, recycled paper made with 100% post consumer waste, processed chlorine
free, and old growth free.

For every 5,000 books printed, New Society saves the following resources:[1]

33	Trees
2,989	Pounds of Solid Waste
3,289	Gallons of Water
4,290	Kilowatt Hours of Electricity
5,434	Pounds of Greenhouse Gases
23	Pounds of HAPs, VOCs, and AOX Combined
8	Cubic Yards of Landfill Space

[1]Environmental benefits are calculated based on research done by the Environmental Defense Fund
and other members of the Paper Task Force who study the environmental impacts of the paper
industry. For more information on this environmental benefits statement, or to inquire about
environmentally friendly papers, please contact New Leaf Paper – info@newleafpaper.com
Tel: 888 • 989 • 5323.

For a full list of NSP's titles, please call 1-800-567-6772 or check out our web site at:

www.newsociety.com

NEW SOCIETY PUBLISHERS